Managerial Accounting

Bassim Hamadeh, CEO and Publisher
Angela Schultz, Senior Field Acquisitions Editor
Michelle Piehl, Senior Project Editor
Alia Bales, Production Editor
Emely Villavicencio, Senior Graphic Designer
Stephanie Kohl, Licensing Coordinator
Natalie Piccotti, Director of Marketing
Kassie Graves, Vice President of Editorial
Jamie Giganti, Director of Academic Publishing

Printed in the United States of America.

ISBN:978-1-5165-3568-2 (pbk) / 978-1-5165-3569-9 (br)

cognella | ACADEMIC PUBLISHING

Managerial Accounting

A Competency-Based Approach

First
Edition

Mary Cline
Rock Valley College

cognella® | ACADEMIC PUBLISHING

BRIEF CONTENTS

DETAILED CONTENTS

ACKNOWLEDGMENTS

I would like to thank the many students for their role in helping me test the effectiveness of the preliminary edition text during the spring semester of 2017. Every student from the day and evening sections of the 2017 spring classes appears in this edition or will appear in future editions in some form. Andy's Excel was the inspiration of student who suggested that I include Excel examples of the quantitative problems. Thank you to my students for helping to improve this textbook. Your feedback was greatly appreciated!

SECTION I

THE THEORETICAL FOUNDATION OF MANAGERIAL ACCOUNTING

The theoretical foundation of managerial accounting addresses the competency to:

Demonstrate an understanding of the history and theory that drives the field of managerial accounting into being a field that helps management be competitive.

The following topics have been introduced in Section One as topics imperative to learning the theoretical foundation.

- Introduction to Managerial Accounting
- History and Rationale for Managerial Accounting
- Skills and Tools Needed for the Management Accountant

The purpose of Competency 1 is to help students make the connection between managerial accounting and its role in modern business. Theory is at the heart of the process of planning, performing, and evaluating. The topics noted above expand to involve the purpose of the managerial accountant in businesses, the connection the managerial accountant has with both management and accounting, the role of the managerial accountant, and key basic terms and concepts of understanding for the managerial accountant.

FIGURE I.1 Theory: Planning, Evaluating, Performing

TOPIC 1 What Is Managerial Accounting?

LEARNING GOALS

1. Discuss the phases of managerial accounting as they relate to the functions of management.
2. Outline the differences between managerial accounting and financial accounting.
3. Identify ethical considerations and the role of the Institute of Management Accountants (IMA) in managerial accounting.
4. Investigate sustainability and how sustainability influences the role of managerial accounting in a corporation.

INTRODUCTION

As a field still in its infancy, managerial accounting is becoming progressively more refined over time. As business itself has become more refined over time, today's managerial accountants understand the basics of financial accounting but use the basics of financial accounting in such a way that management can use accounting information for internal purposes and benefits. Managerial accountants provide support to management in a variety of ways that help managers become more informed and better equipped to handle the competitive market in which businesses operate.

In this chapter, I first define managerial accounting by reviewing the three phases that exist in support of the functions of management. Secondly, I will address the basic question of what makes managerial accounting different from financial accounting. Both financial accounting and managerial accounting use the same set of financial data, but each discipline uses the data differently in the distinct field. In the third learning goal, I focus on the role that ethics plays within the managerial accounting discipline. As managerial accountants seek to provide support to their managers, ethical behavior ensures that the data reported by managerial accountants and the behavior of the managerial accountants fall within the ethical standards set by the Institute of Managerial Accountants (IMA). I will also take time in this chapter to investigate how sustainability influences the role of managerial accountants within a corporation. Finally, I will discuss learning competencies as such competencies relate to managerial accounting and form the framework for this textbook.

LEARNING GOAL 1: Discuss the Phases of Managerial Accounting as They Relate to the Functions of Management

As managerial accountants seek to support management, they must be keenly aware of the functions of management. The functions of management ensure that organizations run efficiently and effectively. The job of a managerial accountant is to support such functions. If managerial accountants are responsible to provide management with the accounting tools management needs to carry out the functions they are charged to fulfill, managerial accountants must understand how to support management within management's designated functions. Functions of management ensure that organizations will continue into the future and typically revolve around the concepts of making goals for the organization, carrying out such goals, and evaluating the goals. In this textbook, I will refer to the managerial accountant's role in supporting such functions as phases. The three phases that reflect support for management functions include planning, performing, and evaluating (PPE).

In Figure 1.1., note that managerial accounting is in the center of the phases, serving as a "hub" which continually provides feedback for all areas of management. The outer circle of planning, performing, and evaluating is cyclical. Once the managerial accountant reaches the evaluating phase, the process begins again.

FIGURE 1.1 Phases of Managerial Accounting.

Managerial accounting is a discipline of accounting for which the functions are fully integrated with management for the good of an organization. Additionally, the functions of managerial accounting are fully integrated with accounting. Thus, the information provided by managerial accountants allows management to fully understand all aspects of their organization. As the "hub," the managerial accounting profession is an integral part of an organization, holding a wide variety of skills necessary for the progression of an organization. Management relies on the managerial accountant for the success of the organization. The three phases of managerial accounting represented in Figure 1.1 are defined below.

Planning Phase

Planning is the phase that sets the foundation for all other phases. If management is to successfully carry out performing and evaluating, it must first plan. The "whole" of planning involves building a guide for where the organization wants to go. The planning phase is not a phase that should be viewed independently but a phase that will lay the groundwork from which every other phase will draw. The managerial accountant's role within the planning phase is to provide accounting data that supports management's need to plan. Thus, the managerial accountant will provide data that assists management in forming the foundation and laying the groundwork. Tools of the managerial accountant within the planning phase include 1) evaluating strategy, 2) understanding cost behavior, 3) performing Cost Volume Profit (CVP) analysis, 4) calculating standard costs, 5) capital budgeting, and 6) master budgeting (Figure 1.2).

Strategy. Strategy is directly tied to organizational structure and is the way a company matches its own capabilities with the needs of the marketplace. Strategy must be developed very early in a company's existence. If a company does not take time to develop a strategy, it becomes like a ship with no rudder. In the planning phase, strategy serves to provide direction for the future activities of the organization and is the footing for other functions of management and other phases of managerial accounting. The managerial accountant's role in providing feedback for strategy supports the

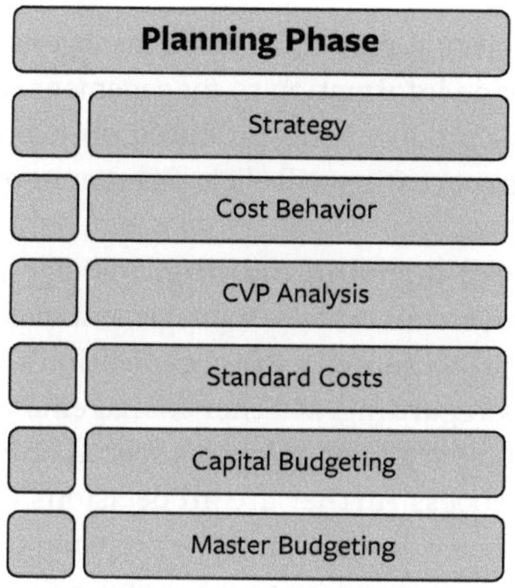

FIGURE 1.2 Managerial Tools for the Planning Phase.

strategic direction a company will take. Managerial accountants must incorporate strategy into every phase. As a profession charged with the task of helping management achieve strategic goals, managerial accountants must be heavily involved in understanding and implementing strategy.

Cost behavior. Understanding how costs behave is an essential element of managerial accounting within the planning phase. Understanding cost behavior helps the managerial accountant better predict management's desired outcomes, thereby guiding management in the competitive process. Costs have unique behaviors that managerial accountants must understand as they provide reports for management support.

CVP (Cost Volume Profit) analysis. CVP analysis is a tool used by the managerial accountant and involves using cost behavior to perform sensitivity analysis. By using CVP, managerial accountants are able to answer "what if" questions posed by management. Management may wonder, "What if I change the sales staff to part commission?" or "What if my cost of goods sold increases 10%?" CVP analysis provides managerial accountants with tools that enable management to make informed decisions. The use of CVP also allows the managerial accountant to perform break-even and risk analyses.

Standard costs. An organization's budget is built with the use of a number of different inputs. Standard costs are used in the process of budgeting for their simplicity in the budgeting process. Managerial accountants investigate and interpret standards for use in various areas of the organization. Standards provide benchmarks for costs, rates, and the quantity of inputs.

Capital budgeting. Capital expenses are large outflows of cash which must be accounted for within the planning phase. Failing to account for such costs could be detrimental to an organization. Managerial accountants must be aware of the evaluation tools for accepting or rejecting capital purchases, as well as the impact of such purchases to the budget.

Master budgeting. Budgeting analyzes the goals of an organization and reduces them to a quantitative expression. Budgeting is at the heart of the planning phase and consists of the operating and financial budgets. This combination of operating and financial budgets is known as the master budget. The master budget serves many roles within an organization, ranging from providing a quantitative expression of goals for the organization to providing a tool for communication of strategy. The master budget is an organization-wide document that requires the input of many different areas and levels of management. The managerial accountant is responsible for collecting data needed for the master budget and then preparing the master budget.

Performing

The performing phase is supported by the managerial accountant in a variety of ways. As management seeks to carry out that which was planned, managerial accountants provide feedback as to the proper accounting treatment of transactions as well as how specific types of performance will impact the financial statements. Additionally, a managerial accountant provides management with timely performance reports, indicating the current performance of the organization. The performing tools center on calculating the cost of selling or producing a product. The tools include 1) job-costing, 2) process costing, 3) activity-based costing, 4) absorption costing, 5) direct costing, and 6) short-term decision making (Figure 1.3).

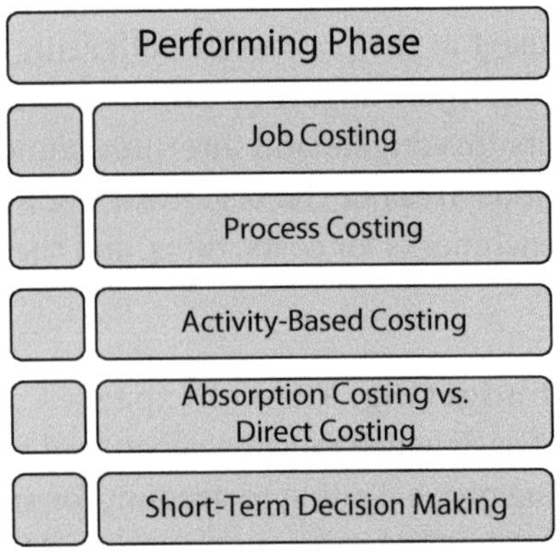

FIGURE 1.3 Managerial Tools for the Performing Phase.

Job costing. Managerial accountants are familiar with the variety of ways in which management determines the cost of producing the product they sell. Job costing is a method in which costs are tracked and calculated based on a given job. Managerial accountants serve a vital role in keeping management informed as to the costs of a given job. Such information ensures that management properly prices the job and fully understands the cost of the job.

Process costing. As another costing method, process costing is used in a number of types of organizations where costs must be tracked by department. In process costing, costs are not driven by jobs as they are in job costing but are driven by the processes and the departments in which products flow. Managers seek costing data for the departments in order to maintain a profitable production process. Managerial accountants track such data and report to management in a timely manner. Such information ensures that management property prices the products and understands the cost of each individual unit.

Activity-based costing (ABC). As a supplementary costing tool, activity-based costing is used in combination with activity-based management. Managerial accountants use ABC when an organization's production process merits a more refined system than either job costing or process costing provide.

Absorption costing vs. direct costing. Absorption costing and direct costing are tools assigning costs to the production process, specifically deciding which costs to include as product costs. As managerial accountants provide information to management regarding costs of the product being produced, absorption costing and direct costing will elicit different information.

Short-term decision making. Managers rely on managerial accountants as management makes a host of decisions to support the organization's strategy. Decisions regarding whether management should add or drop a segment, take on a special order, or sell as-is or process further are all decisions for which managerial accountants must be prepared to support management in providing accounting data. Additionally, managers look to managerial accountants to provide data that supports pricing decisions.

Evaluating

Evaluating is the final phase and is a process of relating everything accomplished during the performing phase back to the planning phase. In short, did the organization perform as expected? A managerial accountant's role in the evaluating phase is to provide the quantitative data that allows management to evaluate that which occurred during the performing phase. Evaluating tools include 1) creating flexible budgets, 2) performing variance analysis, 3) implementing and evaluating performance based on Balanced Scorecard performance indicators, and 4) providing data for performance evaluations (Figure 1.4).

Flexible budgets and variance analysis. Flexible budgets are a modification on the master budget and allow for an "apples-to-apples" comparison of performance to the planned budget. Managerial accountants provide valuable feedback to management regarding

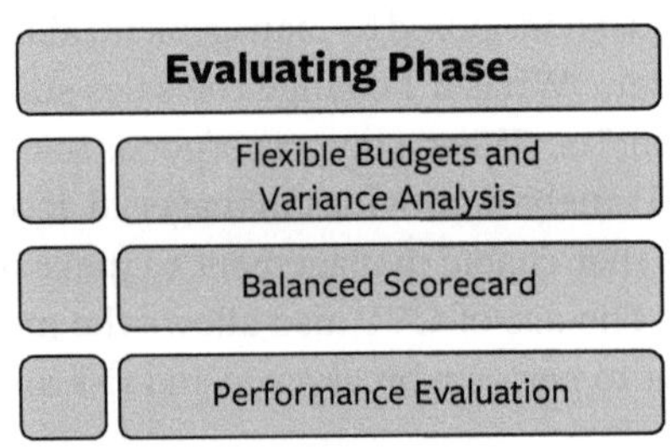

FIGURE 1.4 Managerial Tools for the Evaluating Phase.

MAKE IT REAL 1-1

In a message from the Chair of the Institute of Managerial Accountants (IMA), William F. Knese (2013) indicated that in order to assure the highest level of quality in the profession of managerial accounting, managerial accountants should seek to:

Become part of the Certified Managerial Accountants (CMA) program.
Obtain CMA certification.
Sharpen skills through continuing education.
Associate with like-minded individuals.
Become involved in IMA chapters and councils.

Knese (2013) noted in several parts of his message the importance of managerial accounting to any business.

Reference

Knese, W.F. "Management Accounting Is Important." *Strategic Finance, 95* (1), p. 60–61. (2013).

the planned performance as compared to the actual performance.

Balanced Scorecard. The Balanced Scorecard is an alternative way of measuring the success of an organization and helps to expand the role that managerial accountants play inside an organization. Driven by mostly non-quantitative data, the implementation of the Balanced Scorecard is becoming a key role in the managerial accountant's areas of responsibility. Managerial accountants should be able to implement and interpret the results of a Balanced Scorecard.

Performance evaluation. Traditional ways of measuring performance allow management to hone in on problem areas, including the performance of certain segments or divisions. Managerial accountants use methods that help break the company down into such reporting segments, providing managers with the tools they need to make tough decisions.

LEARNING GOAL 2: Outline the Differences Between Managerial Accounting and Financial Accounting

As stated in Learning Goal 1 of this chapter, managerial accounting is a discipline that is still in its infancy. As a distinct discipline from financial accounting, the field of managerial accounting came into existence because of management need in the early 1900s. Financial accounting did not provide the accounting support needed for management to be competitive. Thus, the field of managerial accounting became a new twist on an old discipline. The history of managerial accounting will be discussed in detail in Chapter 2.

Key Differences Between Financial Accounting and Managerial Accounting

One of the largest roadblocks to management success in a competitive environment is not having timely information. Because financial reports are prepared after the close of a given period, the information provided from financial accounting does not provide accounting data in a timely manner.

Additionally, the information provided in the financial reports is prepared in accordance with Generally Accepted Accounting Principles (GAAP) and must follow a specific format. In order to be competitive, management may need data, other than what is listed in the financial reports.

Thus, although financial reports prepared in accordance with GAAP provide outside investors with that which they need to make decisions regarding investments in a company, such reports do not necessarily provide the internal users (management) with what they need to run their organization effectively and competitively.

Managerial accounting and financial accounting must work together, however, to accomplish the goals of accounting within an organization. Each discipline must understand the other discipline's strengths and limitations as well as their distinctions. Both managerial accounting and financial accounting use the same set of data, but the way in which they use the data is distinct to each discipline's goals and obligations to the organization. Figure 1.5 outlines the distinctions between managerial accounting and financial accounting.

As you can see in Figure 1.5, the purpose and motivation for providing accounting data is different under each of the two disciplines of financial accounting and managerial accounting. Managerial accounting is internally driven to be "custom" performed to the needs of management, whereas financial accounting must strive for consistency across industries, being sure to follow the guidelines of GAAP.

Because the users of the financial data are different, the ways in which the financial data is presented are also inherently different. Figure 1.6 provides a graphic representation of how the disciplines of financial accounting and managerial accounting coexist inside an organization.

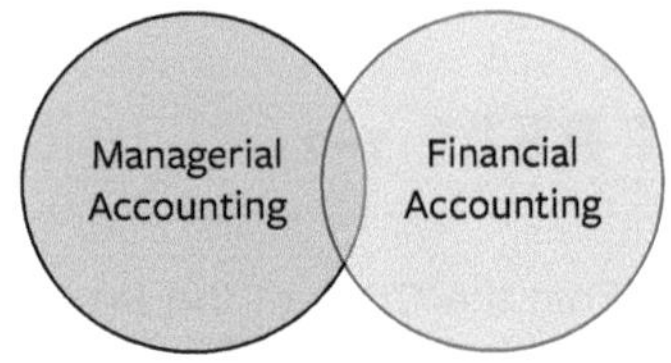

FIGURE 1.6 The Coexistence of Managerial Accounting and Financial Accounting.

Note that each discipline exists within its own circle. However, the area where the two circles overlap represents the shared data, used by both disciplines.

Roles Within the Organization

The role of a financial accountant within a traditionally structured organization is fairly clear. A financial accountant will be part of the line of employees that exist under the Chief Financial Officer (CFO), contributing to the accounting area of the organization.

Managerial accounting, on the other hand, does not have such a distinct role. The role of managerial accountants may have started within the accounting department, but over time, the role of a managerial accountant has changed to include a much broader scope of duties. The complexities of the business environment and the global competition that exists have caused the roles and responsibilities of a managerial accountant to change and, thus, their position on the organizational chart. Managerial accountants can be found in various areas of an organization, often outside the accounting department, becoming engaged in operational aspects of a business so that the operational side of business can better manage costs.

As organizations become global, however, and as competition becomes more prevalent, the traditional organizational chart is falling into a distant past. The traditional "command and control" type of organizational

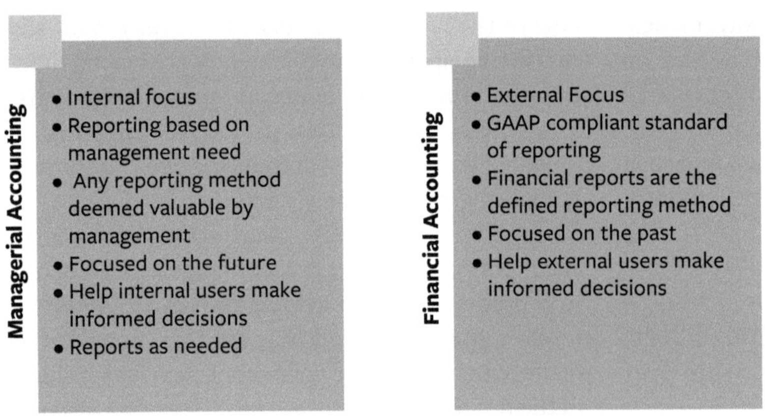

FIGURE 1.5 Difference between Managerial Accounting and Financial Accounting.

GIVE IT A WHIRL 1-1

1. Each of the following statements describes the role of a managerial accountant. Indicate the function of management for the statement. Functions of management are Planning (P), Performing (PF), and Evaluating (E).

Statement

1. Providing data to managers that helps them know if they should add or drop a segment. ___________
2. Keeping management informed as to the costs of a given job.___________
3. Helping managers answer questions as to if they should pay sales staff a salary or a commission.___________
4. Providing feedback to management regarding planned performance as compared to actual performance. ___________
5. Preparing flexible budgets and variance analysis. ___________
6. Implementing and interpreting the results of a Balanced Scorecard. ___________
7. Determining standards to be used in building the master budget. ___________

(Answers: PF, PF, P, E, E, E, P)

2. Do the following statements describe managerial accounting (MA) or financial accounting (FA)?
   1. Prepare financial reports. ___________
   2. Create reports per management request. ___________
   3. Adhere to GAAP standards of reporting. ___________
   4. Focus on future goals of the organization. ___________
   5. Focus on supporting management. ___________
   6. Concerned with past performance. ___________
   7. Prepare reports at the end of an accounting period. ___________

(Answers: FA, MA, FA, MA, MA, FA, FA)

structure (Figure 1.7) is being replaced by structures that report by process, function, and division. Thus, instead of vertical lines that control work through authority, such alternatives function in lateral lines that promote effectiveness instead of efficiency. Whatever the organizational structure, however, the central issue, when it comes to organizational design, is how to allocate work and how to coordinate efforts.

For the managerial accountant, the organizational structure serves as a link to strategy. Strategy is derived directly from a company's organizational structure. The relationship between the structure and strategy will be discussed in greater depth in the "Strategy" chapter.

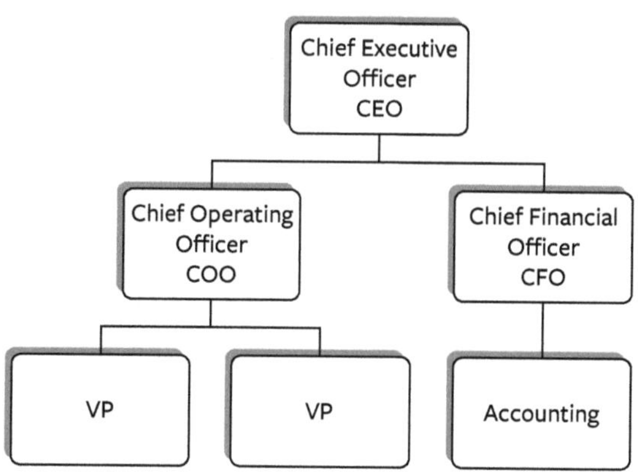

FIGURE 1.7 Traditional Organization Chart.

LEARNING GOAL 3: Identify Ethical Considerations and the Role of the IMA in Managerial Accounting

Ethical dilemmas are a part of every walk of life, including business functions. Managerial accountants can be faced with a variety of ethical challenges as they seek to support management decisions. Management accountants work in an environment where managers operate competitively, and sometimes the ethical choice is not always clear. Concepts such as Agency Theory may enter the picture, blurring the role of the managerial accountant.

Agency Theory

Agency Theory is an organizational theory that focuses on the principal-agent relationship. In a principal-agent relationship, one party acts in the interest of another party. In modern organizations, the principal and the agent are typically not the same individual. The principal is the owner, whereas the agent is the manager. The agent has the fiduciary duty to act in the best interest of the principal. Ethical problems exist in such a relationship, however.

To understand the ethical problems that exist within the principal-agent relationship, one must understand each perspective. Each perspective seeks to achieve an agenda to maximize economic wealth (Ogunyemi, 2014). Principals want to grow profits and stock prices, while agents are interested in growing in salary and position within the organization. Thus, the self-interests of each party are in conflict. This conflict can lead to questionable ethical behavior.

If the managerial accountant's role is to support management (the agent), and management's role is to act in the best interest of the owner (the principal), the ethical dilemma becomes clear when management's self-interest is not in congruence with the organizational goals. The role of managerial accounting is to support management for the overall good of the company. If supporting management does not lend to the overall good of the company, the role of the managerial accountant comes into deep ethical dilemma.

Managerial accountants are not left to figure out the "right" ethical choice on their own. Managerial accountants are held to the standards set by the Institute of Managerial Accountants (IMA). In the following paragraphs, I will discuss the IMA's role in helping to achieve ethical business conduct, specifically as it relates to the managerial accountant.

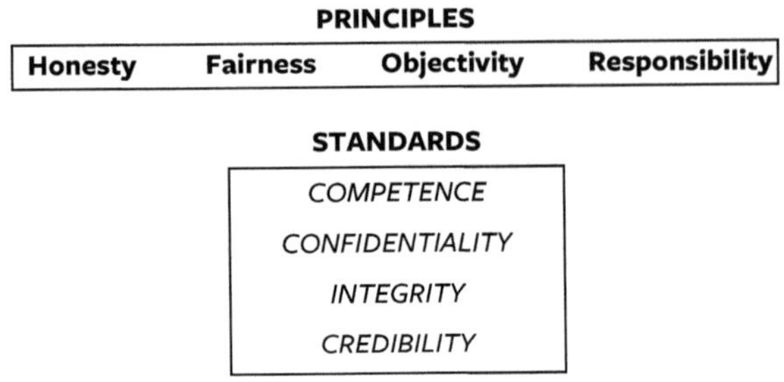

FIGURE 1.8 IMA's Statement of Ethical Professional Practice.

IMA

The IMA's mission is to provide forums that lend to supporting research, practice development, education, knowledge sharing, and ethical practices in management accounting. In its commitment to ethical business practices, the IMA has provided four standards which are described in the *IMA Statement of Ethical Professional Practice*. The standards include 1) competence, 2) confidentiality, 3) integrity, and 4) credibility. Additionally, the IMA provides guidance on the solution of ethical conflict by providing confidential guidance to ethical issues through the use of a free service known as the Ethics Helpline. See the following *IMA Statement of Ethical Professional Practice* (Figure 1.8).

Principles. The IMA principles outline the topics of honesty, fairness, objectivity, and responsibility that serve as an umbrella to the standards of conduct.

Standards. The standards of conduct are guided by:

> *Competence:* The IMA holds each member responsible for professional competence, which involves professionalism in the area of expertise, conduct, recommendation, and potential limitations.

Confidentiality: The IMA holds each member responsible for confidentiality, which involves keeping confident all required information, except in cases where the managerial accountant is authorized to share information to those parties that maintain appropriate use of such information.

Integrity: The IMA holds each member responsible for maintaining professional integrity by mitigating conflicts and abstaining from engaging in or supporting information that discredits the profession.

Credibility: The IMA holds each member responsible for ensuring that communications are objective and disclosed in a time-relevant manner.

Resolution of ethical conflict. The IMA addresses the resolution of ethical conflict by providing the principles and standards noted above. If, however, the ethical standards and principles do not work in resolving the conflict, the IMA recommends three alternative solutions:

Discuss the conflict with appropriate managers or levels higher in authority, or
Initiate confidential discussion with an IMA counselor, or
Consult one's own attorney.

LEARNING GOAL 4: Investigate Sustainability and How Sustainability Influences the Role of Managerial Accounting in a Corporation

Sustainability is defined as the endurance of systems and processes. Specifically, sustainability focuses on practices that refer to a system's viability to continue indefinitely without depleting or permanently damaging resources. Such resources may fall into categories of economic, ecological, political, or cultural.

As society becomes aware of the damaging actions that can take place within production processes, organizations have a variety of reasons for wanting to take on sustainability initiatives. Such reasons may revolve around an organization's ability to be competitive in the marketplace. Society's focus on becoming "green" filters down to individual purchases made by members of society. If an individual has a choice between purchasing from one of two companies, an environmentally conscious consumer will purchase from the organization that touts concepts of sustainability rather than the organization that does nothing toward the effort of sustainability. Therefore, managerial accountants find that sustainability becomes something that needs to be considered in the decision-making processes regarding the success of the organization.

Sustainability does not only refer to the competitive component of an organization, however. Sustainability may also refer to the employees an organization attracts. Environmentally conscious organizations will attract environmentally conscious employees, who support sustainability efforts. Pictured below in Figure 1.9 are the Circles of Sustainability.[1]

The Circles of Sustainability provide a way to understand the sustainability effort by distinguishing the four social domains of sustainability as economic, ecological, political, and cultural. By using the circles of sustainability, organizations are able to manage and improve processes directed towards socially sustainable outcomes. As one considers practices that refer to a system's viability to continue indefinitely into the future, the following four social domains become evident:

Economic Domain: The economic perspective is concerned with improving the quality of life by decreasing resource consumption. Such resource consumption may take place within the production process. Thus, managerial accountants consider economic perspectives relating to the use of resources. Considerations within the economic domain include activities such as production and resourcing, accounting and regulation, and consumption and use.

---

1 http://www.circlesofsustainability.org/circles-overview/profile-circles/

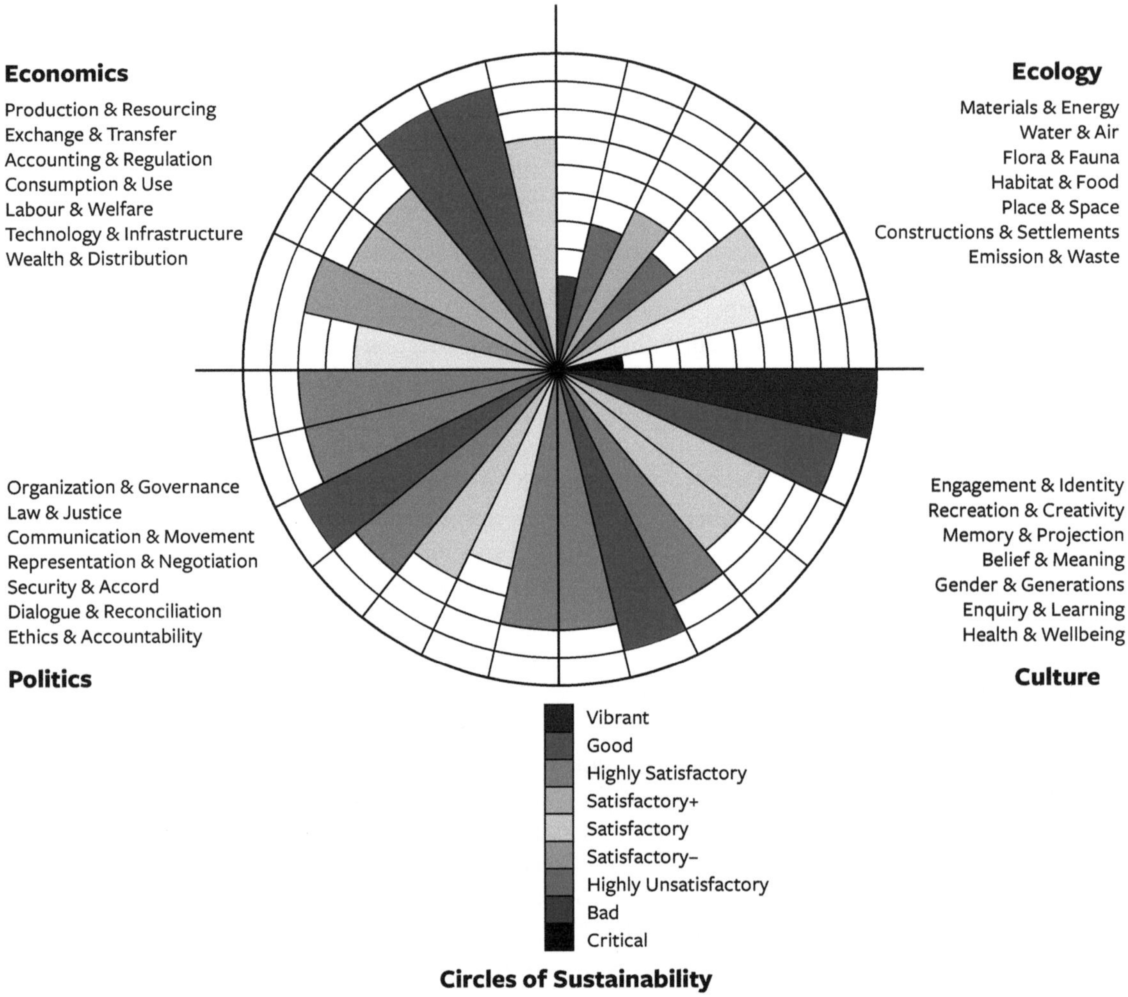

FIGURE 1.9 Circles of Sustainability Categories and Subcategories.

Ecological Domain: The ecological perspective is concerned with the relationship between humans and nature. As humans need air, water, food, and shelter, the ecological domain works to support sustainable development that ensures such necessities are available in the future. Organizations that maintain a sustainable focus are concerned not just with the economic domain referring to resource consumption but also with the preservation of the resources that are necessary for human survival. Considerations within the ecological domain are water and air, materials and energy, and emission and waste.

Political Domain: The political perspective is concerned with the political policy framework which may pertain to sustainability efforts of an organization. In considering the managerial accountant's role in sustainability initiatives, political factors may surface in the form of organizational governance, ethics and accountability, and law and justice.

Cultural Domain: The cultural domain emphasizes social meaning and is concerned with things such as beliefs and ideas as well as well-being and health. The current culture within the United States is one of movement toward

MAKE IT REAL 1-2

Auto Alliance is an organization headquartered in Washington, D.C. that is an advocacy group for the auto industry. The group is represented by well known auto manufacturers such as Ford Motor Company, General Motors Company, Toyota, and nine others. The group's vision is to be a united industry committed to enriching society through sustainable mobility efforts.

Review the Ford Motor Sustainability Report at the following link:
http://corporate.ford.com/microsites/sustainability-report-2013-14/blueprint-strategy.html

Reference

"About the Alliance." Auto Alliance (n.d.). Retrieved from http://www.autoalliance.org/about-the-alliance/overview

sustainability. The U.S. Sustainability Alliance (USSA) is a group committed to continuous improvement in the management of resources. Items of evaluation that fall under the cultural domain include enquiry and learning, health and wellbeing, and recreation and creativity.

The above referenced social domains represent social life as understood in the broadest possible sense.

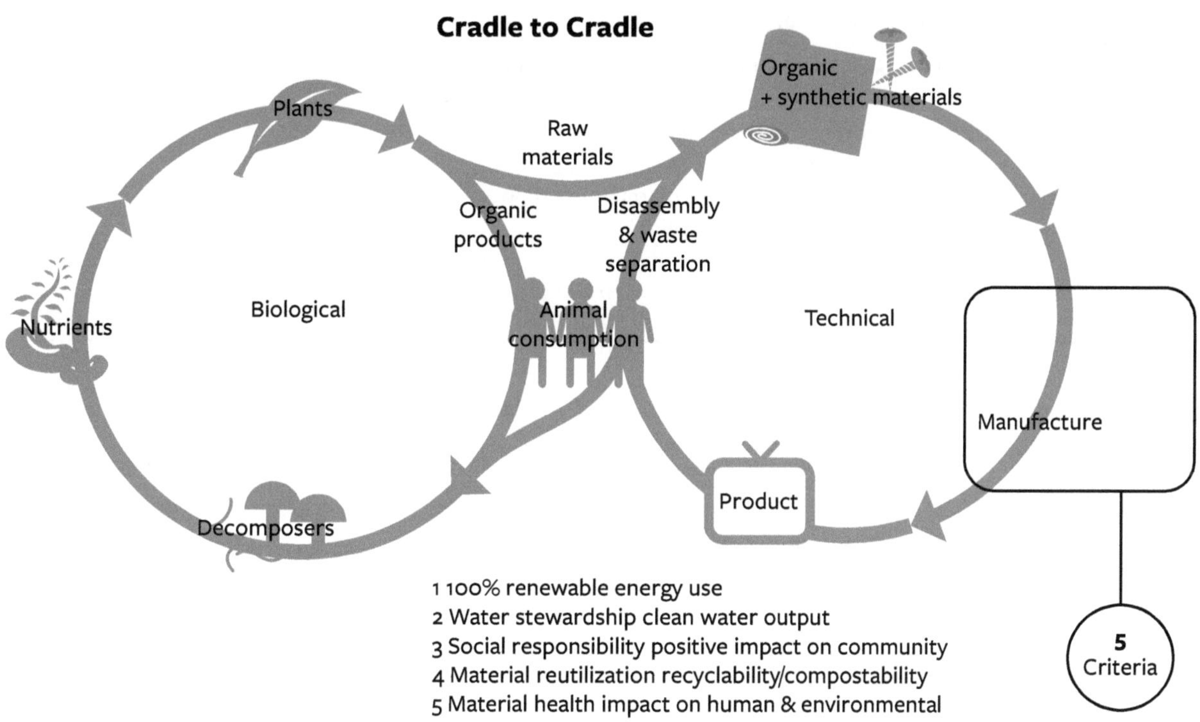

FIGURE 1.10 Cradle to Cradle.

GIVE IT A WHIRL 1-2

1. The following ethical scenarios have presented themselves to you. Recommend the action you should take.
   a. Amanda is a managerial accountant at ABC Industries. In Amanda's position, she is responsible for preparing management variance-analysis reports to inform management of their performance as it relates to the budget. Amanda is dating Tom who works for the competition. During the time that Amanda and Tom have been dating, they talk about their work, without discussing specifics. After preparing the performance this time, Amanda notes that ABC Industries has been well under the budgeted revenue amount in her last several reports. During dinner, Amanda tells Tom that she is concerned about her job because of the variances and seeks his advice.

Has Amanda acted in a way that would fall outside of the ethical professional practices established by the IMA? If so, explain.

Answer: Yes, Amanda has violated the confidentiality standard in sharing confidential company information with the competition.

   b. Bob works for XYZ Corp. where he has been employed for two years. Bob was new to the field of managerial accounting but feels like he enjoys the job and would like to learn more. Bob's boss announced that he is retiring and is concerned for who will replace him. Bob's boss does not feel that Bob is a qualified candidate for the position. However, Bob applies for the job, indicating that he knows things that he does not. Bob gets the job. Has he acted in a way that would fall outside of the ethical professional practices established by the IMA? If so, explain.

Answer: There is nothing wrong with Bob wanting to learn more about his boss's job. However, by claiming to know how to do things he does not know, he has violated the standard of competence.

2. Match the following perspectives to the appropriate domain: Economical (E), Ecological (L), Political (P), or Cultural (C).
   a. May surface in the form of regulation. ________
   b. Addresses social meaning and beliefs. ________
   c. Perspective that understands that humans need air, water, food, and shelter. ________
   d. Concerned with decreasing consumption. ________

Answer: P, C, L, E

The circles of sustainability consider the human condition across time from a number of perspectives that impact an organization's motivation and ability to maintain efforts towards sustainability. Managerial accounting incorporates the domains into productivity measures of an organization. By using the Circles of Sustainability, companies are able to indicate whether the contributions of an organization are critical, satisfactory, or vibrant as such contributions relate to the various concerns within each of the four domains.

Cradle-to-Cradle Approach

Sustainability is about practices that strive to operate in such a way to encourage indefinite life of resources. The "cradle-to-cradle" approach focuses specifically on material use. The "cradle-to-death" approach considers that resources final resting ground ends in a landfill, whereas the "cradle-to-cradle" approach encourages designing products in such a way that they can be recycled for their technical or biological nutrients (Figure 1.10). German chemist Michael Braungart and American architect William

McDonough championed the cause of cradle to cradle in their book "Cradle to Cradle: Remaking the Way We Make Things."[2]

Sustainability and Managerial Accounting

As the field of managerial accounting continues to grow and expand, sustainability becomes part of the typical business effort in which the managerial accountant is expected to engage. Managerial accountants help management succeed by minimizing the human impact of manufacturing and other processes by economically, ecologically, politically, and culturally considering sustainability efforts.

The modern company seeks to make positive social contributions. Consequently, sustainability has become a focus. Practices such as recycling, waste management, and using alternative energy sources are some of the top initiatives used in organizations. By engaging in sustainable and socially responsible practices, organizations can be granted a competitive advantage over companies who do not engage in sustainability measures.

TOPIC 1 REFERENCES

"About the Alliance" [Webpage]. Auto Alliance (n.d.). Retrieved from http://www.autoalliance.org/about-the-alliance/overview

Braun, K.W. and Tietz, W.M. *Managerial Accounting* (4th ed.). Upper Saddle River, NJ: Prentice Hall, 2014.

"Profile Circles." Circles of Sustainability (n.d.). Retrieved from http://www.circlesofsustainability.org/circles-overview/profile-circles/

Generally Accepted Accounting Principles (GAAP). http://www.fasb.org

"Statement of Ethical Professional Practice." Institute of Managerial Accountants. (2017). Retrieved from https://www.imanet.org/-/media/b6fbeeb74d964e6c9fe654c48456e61f.ashx

Knese, W.F. "Management Accounting Is Important." *Strategic Finance, 95*(1), p. 60-61. (2013).

Kranendijk, S. "A Cradle-to-Cradle Approach to Environmental Protection." Business Ethics. (2011). Retrieved from http://business-ethics.com/2011/03/11/1414-opinion-the-cradle-to-cradle-approach-to-environmental-protection/

McDonough, W. and Braungart, M. *Cradle to Cradle: Remaking the Way We Make Things.* New York, NY: North Point Press, 2002.

SaintGeorgeIV. "Circles of Sustainability" [jpeg]. (2012). Retrieved from https://commons.wikimedia.org/wiki/File:Circles_of_Sustainability_image_%28assessment_-_Melbourne_2011%29.jpg

Schramm, J. "Promoting Sustainability." *HR Magazine, 56*(3), (2011). p. 88–88.

Ogunyemi, K. "Teaching Ethics Across the Management Curriculum: A Handbook for International Faculty." *Business Expert Press.* (2014).

Zhiying, L. "Biological and Technical Nutrients (C2C)" [jpeg]. (2012). Retrieved from https://commons.wikimedia.org/wiki/File:Biological_and_technical_nutrients_%28C2C%29.jpg

TOPIC 1 FIGURE CREDITS

Fig. 1.8: Adapted from http://www.imanet.org/docs/default-source/default-document-library/statement-of-ethical-professional-practice_2-2-12.pdf?sfvrsn=0.

Fig. 1.9: Copyright © SaintGeorgeIV (CC BY-SA 3.0) at https://commons.wikimedia.org/wiki/File:Circles_of_Sustainability_image_%28assessment_-_Melbourne_2011%29.jpg.

Fig. 1.10: Copyright © Zhiying.lim (CC BY-SA 3.0) at https://commons.wikimedia.org/wiki/File:Biological_and_technical_nutrients_(C2C).jpg

2 McDonough, W. and Braungart, M. *Cradle to Cradle: Remaking the Way We Make Things.* New York, NY: North Point Press, 2002.

TOPIC 2 History and Rationale for Managerial Accounting

LEARNING GOALS

1. Discuss the origins of managerial accounting.
2. Outline theories of accounting.
3. Outline theories of management.
4. Investigate theories of managerial accounting.
5. Understand the whole picture of managerial accounting.

INTRODUCTION

The purpose of Topic 2 is to establish a theoretical foundation for learning the topics of managerial accounting. In Learning Goal 1, we will explore the practice of managerial accounting by delving into the origins and concepts and objectives. Exploring theories of accounting will be the object of Learning Goal 2. By learning the theories of accounting, one can more easily understand how the elements of accounting imbed themselves in managerial accounting. Learning Goal 3 will explore theories of management. As managerial accounting seeks to supply management with that which is needed to be competitive, theories of management must be explored. Learning Goal 4 will explore managerial accounting theories that have a basis in functionalism, sociology, and psychology. Such theories will be compared and contrasted to allow for an understanding of the differences in the perspectives and how the differences play a role in evaluating the efficiency and effectiveness of managerial accounting in the workplace. Finally, Learning Goal 5 will examine the big picture of managerial accounting.

LEARNING GOAL 1: Discuss the Origins of Managerial Accounting

Managerial accounting is a branch of accounting that lends itself to planning, performing, and evaluating future internal activities of an organization. Financial accounting, on the other hand, is a branch of accounting that lends itself to objectively reporting the financial consequences of past activities. Therefore, unlike financial accounting, which has an external focus of reporting to owners, creditors, tax authorities, and regulators, managerial accounting maintains an internal reporting focus, presenting accounting data to management and other internal decision makers. The discipline of managerial accounting has not been applied within organizations for as long as financial accounting has been applied within organizations. However, the origins of managerial accounting are grounded in practical need.

Origins

Glimpses of managerial accounting concepts can be found as early as the mid- to late 1800s. Then, with the development of U.S. corporations, the demand for information that provided for internal planning and control took the early managerial accounting concepts of the mid 1800s and expanded upon them. Consequently, the early concepts of managerial accounting could be found in the late 1800s in firms such as textile mills and railroads (Kaplan, 1984). In an undeveloped form, the concepts of managerial accounting began to take wings as companies sought to understand the costs of materials and labor used in production. Management found that by putting the accounting data for materials and labor into monthly or daily reports, they could make pricing and improvement decisions. Since the early formation of managerial accounting, the concept of materials and labor ultimately developed into terms like prime and direct costs (Kaplan, 1984). Prime costs are costs that include direct materials and direct labor. Such costs are considered to be directly associated with a product and are primary to the making of a product, thus, the terms "prime" and "direct." Hence, the raw form of managerial accounting that developed in the mid-1800s is the source of many of the concepts and terminologies used today. Out of necessity, management began to find answers to questions they had regarding costs.

Although undeveloped, the beginnings of managerial accounting provided management with information needed to become more efficient and effective in the marketplace. The scientific management movement of the early 1900s began as a direct response to the concepts of the 1800s and drove the managerial accounting field into an area where more competitive information was needed. Thus, managerial accountants began to learn how to allocate overhead costs to products (Kaplan, 1984). Allocating overhead costs to products was much more difficult than the process of determining prime costs. Allocating overhead required gathering costs that were not considered prime costs and lumping them together to allow for their application to the product. By including overhead costs in the calculation of total product costs, managers had a clearer understanding for how much their product costs to make, all costs considered.

With the new information for calculating the costs of a product, management could be more competitive in the marketplace. The task for managerial accountants, however, was to develop ways in which to allocate the overhead. In order for overhead costs to be allocated to products, managerial accountants were required to understand the multiple ways in which overhead could be applied to products. From that point forward, the concepts of managerial accounting began to snowball, with the use of standard costs, break-even calculations, the use of statistical methods to estimate cost behavior, decentralization, and local profit measures such as ROI (Return on Investment) (Kaplan, 1984). Thus, the innovation that began to take hold opened the door to more innovation that became part of a system of planning, performing, and evaluating within an organization.

The beginnings of managerial accounting that developed in the 1800s paved the way for a more refined system in the 1900s. From early 1900s to current day, managerial accounting has not experienced any major innovations but has seen a refinement of concepts (Kaplan, 1984). As with any new system, the process of refining the system helps to highlight problems and improve upon those problems. The direction of improvement is where managerial accounting is headed today.

Concepts and Objectives

The origins of managerial accounting, noted above, provided the groundwork for the concepts and

MAKE IT REAL 2-1

In the IMA 2015 salary survey, the base salary for a managerial accountant is $42,660. Increases in salary can be seen for level of management, number of years in the field, and advanced degrees.

AVERAGE U.S. SALARY CALCULATOR

This calculator provides an estimated average salary for U.S. management accounting professionals based on broad demographic data.

YOUR CALCULATION

Base Figure	$42,660
Management Level	
Top-Level Management	Add $59,595
Senior-Level Management	Add $39,191
Middle-Level Management	Add $22,089
Number of Years in Field: ____	Times $979 -
Advanced Degree? Yes	Add $20,102
CMA Designation? Yes	Add $21,919
CPA Designation? Yes	Add $5,907
Estimated Salary Level:	

FIGURE 2.1 Average U.S. Salary Calculator.

Reference

Krumwied, K.R. "IMA's 2015 Global Salary Survey." *Strategic Finance.* (2016). Retrieved from http://sfmagazine.com/post-entry/march-2016-imas-2015-global-salary-survey/

objectives of the managerial discipline of accounting. As the manufacturing industry developed, management needs rose above a mere desire for establishing prices and understanding costs into a need to better compete in the marketplace. The ability to compete in the marketplace is dependent upon an organization's ability to provide quality products in a timely manner, ensuring high performance and attractive prices (Ciuhureanu, 2012). Thus, the concepts of managerial accounting focus on such abilities. The objectives of managerial accounting are, then, to provide managers with the information needed to make decisions about production, consumption, product costs, revenues, expenditures, and a host of other decisions. Managerial accounting meets the needs of management by collecting, processing, and presenting accounting data (Ciuhureanu, 2012). Managerial accounting has a designated role in an organization to perform the above-mentioned functions. However, the actual benefits of a managerial accountant far outweigh the intended purpose.

In carrying out the roles and responsibilities of a managerial accountant, the field of managerial accounting experiences expanded benefits, including coordination of individuals within the company, forecasting abilities, controlling functions, and performance evaluation (Ciuhureanu, 2012). With all the benefits managerial accounting provides to an organization, the role of a managerial accountant is an indispensable role that should be coordinated with financial accounting.

LEARNING GOAL 2: Outline Theories of Accounting

The theories of accounting are derived from understanding the conceptual framework of accounting (Figure 2.2). Although managerial accounting is not bound by the same governing bodies as financial accounting, the history of managerial accounting experienced its beginnings in financial accounting, and, therefore, understanding financial accounting is at the heart of understanding managerial accounting.

The conceptual framework of GAAP is an explicit, yet broad scope of concepts that provides stability and consistency for the discipline of financial accounting. Having a conceptual framework accomplishes two things: 1) it eliminates the need to continually reestablish concepts each time the standard setters update standards, and 2) it encourages consistency of standards (Pounder, 2010).

In 2004, the International Accounting Standards Board (IASB) and Financial Accounting Standards Board (FASB) began work on a project that would converge the conceptual frameworks of both governing bodies so that future standards would be based on one conceptual framework instead of individual frameworks (Pounder, 2010). The history of the GAAP conceptual framework, however, is grounded in concepts that relate to

- objectives of financial reporting,
- characteristics of financial reporting,
- principles of recognition and measurement,
- assumptions made in financial reporting, and
- constraints associated with financial reporting.

Objectives of Financial Reporting

Providing useful information is of great importance in the reporting of financial information. When existing and potential investors and creditors review financial reports, they must be able to understand the information provided in order to make decisions. Investors and creditors are interested in the potential cash flows that the company will experience as well as the economic resources and the claims to those resources (Weiss, 1994). Therefore, the primary objective of the financial-reporting process is to provide useful information.

Characteristics of Financial Reporting

The characteristics of financial reporting help to ensure that the objectives of financial reporting are correctly carried out and that the financial statements are, in fact, useful. Characteristics include 1) relevance, 2) reliability, 3) verifiability, 4) comparability, and 5) consistency.

Relevance. Financial statements are relevant when they are capable of making a difference in decisions users are making in the *present*, confirm forecasts made in the *past*, and predict *future* outcomes.

Reliability. Financial statements are reliable when the information is complete, free from error, free from bias, and faithfully represents the economic event of the entity.

Verifiability. Financial statements are verifiable when independent users arrive at the same consensus regarding the economic events reported.

Comparability. Financial statements are comparable when users are able to locate similarities and differences among several different entities.

Consistency. Financial statements are consistent when such statements can be compared across time.

Principles of Recognition and Measurement

Principles of recognition and measurement provide directions for reporting under accrual basis of accounting. The principles include 1) historical cost,

2) revenue and expense recognition, 3) matching, and 4) full disclosure.

Historical cost. Historical cost is a principle that relates to the bases of measurement. The general policy is that an entity records assets and liabilities at historical cost or the price that was agreed upon at acquisition. Although other methods of measuring costs are available, they are beyond the scope of this text.

Revenue and expense recognition. Under accrual-based reporting, revenue is recognized when it is realized or realizable and when it is earned. An item is realized or realizable when the exchange of goods or services for cash or promises of cash has taken place. In the accrual bases of accounting, revenue is earned when the seller is entitled to the revenue, meaning the seller has provided the service or the good.

Expenses follow a similar pattern to revenue in that expenses are recognized when the future benefits that would otherwise be derived from the asset have been reduced, and the benefits are consumed.

Matching. The matching principle requires that expenses are matched with related revenues.

Full disclosure. Full disclosure ensures that any deviations from the above principles are adequately and fully disclosed.

Assumptions Made in Financial Reporting

The assumptions made in the financial-reporting process exist so that the users of the financial statements do not have to continually reestablish such assumptions. The assumptions include 1) economic entity, 2) going concern, 3) monetary unit, and 4) periodicity.

Economic Entity. The economic-entity assumption ensures that the users of the financial statements recognize that the events reported on the financial statements are that of the business entity and do not include personal transaction of the owners, related businesses, or any other party involved in the affairs of the organization.

Going concern. The going-concern assumption gives the users of the financial statements the assurance that unless otherwise stated, the entity will be in existence in the near and distant future.

Monetary unit. The monetary-unit assumption indicates that the financial reports are reported according to monetary units that do not factor in inflation.

Periodicity. Periodicity is a concept that divides an entity's economic activities into artificial periods of time. If entities are to accurately report the financial condition of their organizations, they would report all transactions from beginning to end. However, users of financial information need more frequent reports. Thus, the reporting process must be broken down into annual, quarterly, semiannual, or some other reporting period.

Constraints Associated With Financial Reporting

As organizations attempt to meet all of the principles and assumptions highlighted above, they experience certain constraints that limit the accuracy of reporting. Constraints include 1) cost benefit, 2) materiality, 3) industry practices, and 4) conservatism.

Cost benefit. The cost-benefit constraint recognizes that to provide users with financial reports that meet all of the above conditions, there is a significant cost involved. Therefore, the benefits of reporting in the level of detail required should outweigh the costs.

Materiality. Materiality is not a static number but refers to a level of significance within the reporting process. Materiality emphasizes the level at which a reasonable user would make a different decision. For example, the user of a company with $1 million in sales would be unaffected by a $10 error on the income statement. However, an error of $10,000 on the

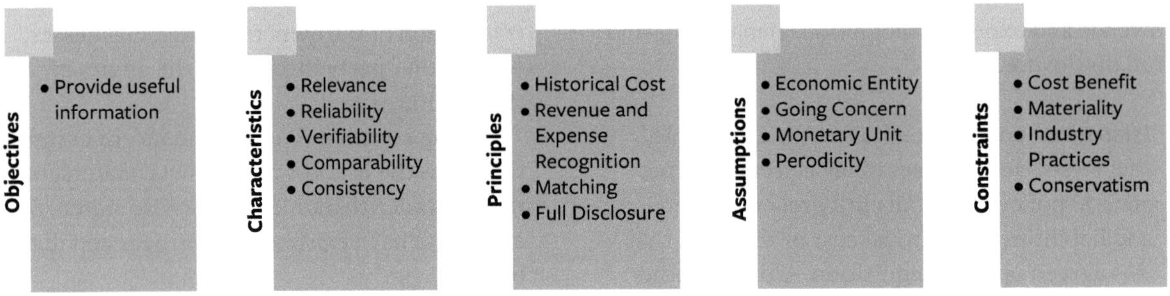

FIGURE 2.2 Conceptual Framework of Financial Accounting.

GIVE IT A WHIRL 2-1

1. Managerial Accounting is a field derived out of management need. It began with management's need to obtain costs of their products and expanded into a field that would help management to be more competitive. Fill in the blanks in the following sentences as the sentences relate to the origins of managerial accounting.
   1. The early concepts of managerial accounting could be found in the__________ in firms such as textile mills and railroads.
   2. ______ ______ are costs that include direct materials and direct labor.
   3. The beginnings of managerial accounting provided management with information companies needed to become more ______ and ______ in the marketplace.
   4. ____________ to products was much more difficult than the process of determining prime costs.
   5. From early 1900s to current day, managerial accounting has not experienced any major innovations but has seen a ______ of concepts.
   6. The direction of ______ is where managerial accounting is headed today.

(Answers: late 1800s, Prime costs, efficient, effective, allocating overhead costs, refinement, improvement)

2. Financial accounting is based upon a conceptual framework that includes objectives, characteristics, principles, assumptions, and constraints. Label each of the following as either an objective (O), a characteristic (C), a principle (P), an assumption (A), or a constraint (CT).
   1. Verifiability__________
   2. Economic entity__________
   3. Usefulness__________
   4. Comparability__________
   5. Full disclosure__________
   6. Materiality__________
   7. Going concern __________

(Answers: C, A, O, C, P, CT, A)

income statement could potentially cause the user to make a different decision.

Industry practices. Certain industries divert from GAAP. Entities within the given industries will be constrained in using GAAP because reporting like others in the industry is of greater use.

Conservatism. Conservatism in financial reporting means that it is better to err on the conservative side.

LEARNING GOAL 3: Outline Theories of Management

Peter F. Drucker is a name that is synonymous with management. Having authored nearly thirty-five books on management that have been translated into twenty different languages, most management principles can be attributable to Drucker (Prasadunder, 2004). As managerial accountants whose role is to understand and support the tasks of management, we need to draw from such authority to fully understand how to best support management. The managerial accountant is halfway between accounting and management, bridging the gap that must be bridged to enable a successful outcome of a given organization (Figure 2.3).

According to Drucker, two key components of a business include 1) customers and 2) innovation. It becomes management's job to transfer the organization's objectives into work. In doing so, management must use financial resources in a way to attract the best human resources. The work of a manager can be boiled down into five functions:

- Set objectives and determines goals
- Organize and analyze activities
- Motivate and communicate
- Establish measurement yardsticks
- Develop people (Prasadunder, 2004)

This text uses the five functions of management as defined by Drucker and applies the functions to the phases of planning, performing, and evaluating so that the managerial accountant can use the appropriate tools to meet the needs of each function of management. The planning phase of managerial accounting incorporates the functions of setting objectives and determining goals as well as the function of organizing and analyzing activities. The performing phase involves motivating and communicating. The evaluating phase involves establishing measurement yardsticks and developing people.

Drucker indicates that management has evolved over time and that the evolution that has taken place in management can be broken down into six distinct schools of thought (Figure 2.4). The schools of thought consist of:

- Classical
- Human Relations
- Management Science
- Systems Approach
- Neoclassical (Behavioral)
- Situational (Contingency)

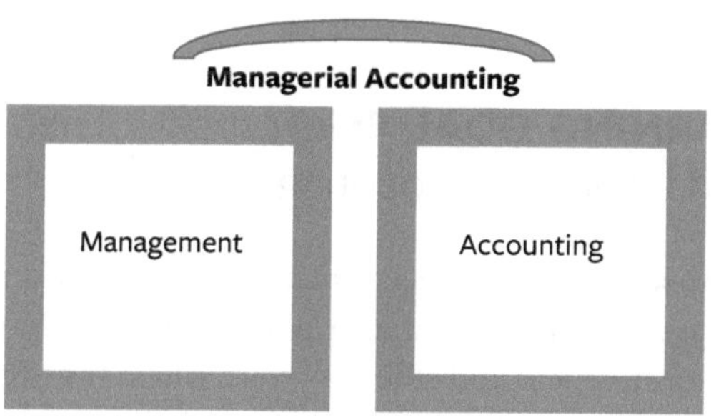

FIGURE 2.3 Bridging the Gap.

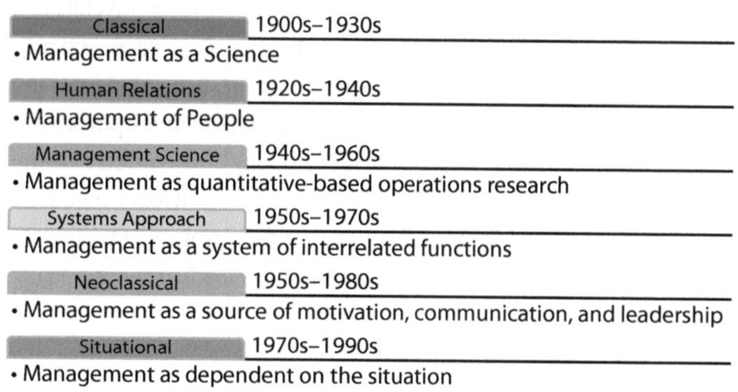

FIGURE 2.4 Drucker's Management Schools of Thought.

Classical

The classical theories formed from the 1900s to the 1930s in a period referred to as "scientific management." These theories brought management to a scientific level. Among the contributors were Frank and Lillian Gilbreth, who are attributed with work in time-motion studies; Max Weber, who developed the Theory of Social and Economic Organization—Bureaucratic Organization; and Henry Foyal, who is known as the father of modern management. Henry Foyal introduced the first "functions of management" in which he indicated the functions included planning, organizing, commanding, coordinating, and controlling (Prasadunder, 2004).

Human Relations

According to Drucker, management theories within the human relations school of thought focused on the management of people and were developed from the 1920s to the 1940s. Among the contributors to the human-relations theories were Abraham Maslow, who developed the hierarchy of needs; McGregor Douglas, who developed Theory X and Theory Y; and William Ouchi, who developed Theory Z. The theories centered on motivational factors and how to motivate employees (Prasadunder, 2004).

Management Science

Management science was a school of thought that formed from the 1940s to the 1960s. Drucker indicated that this school of thought is not the same as the classical school of thought but stressed operations research and quantitative-based decision making. Emphasis during this period was on managing production and operations. Contributors to this school of thought included Russell Ackoff, known as the founder of operations research (OR), and Patrick Blacket, who combined statistical theories with microeconomics (Prasadunder, 2004).

Systems Approach

Systems approach made its entrance half way through the management-science era and developed from the 1950s to the 1970s. Systems approach to management saw organizations as a group of interrelated functions contributing to the overall outcome. Contributors to the systems approach included Von Bertalanffy, who is viewed as the founder of Systems Theory, and Peter Senge, who developed the concept of learning organizations (Prasadunder, 2004).

Neoclassical (Behavioral Approach)

The neoclassical approach developed at the same time as systems approach but lasted longer, from the 1950s to the 1980s. This approach emphasized the human element once again as it reviewed the interrelationships of individuals by addressing motivation, communication, and leadership. Contributors to this school of thought included Kevin Lewin, who developed Field Theory, which proposed that human behavior is a function of the person and the environment, and Rensis Likert, who identified four main management styles to include 1) exploitative-authoritative, 2) benevolent-authoritative, 3) consultative, and 4) participative-group system (Prasadunder, 2004).

Situational (Contingency)

The situation school of thought began in the 1970s and ran through the 1990s. During the situational time period, the school of thought stressed dependence of the situation. Contributors during this time period included Fielder, who developed Contingency Theory; Hershey and Blanchard, who developed Situational Theory; and Vroom and Yetton, who developed the Normative Decision Theory (Prasadunder, 2004).

LEARNING GOAL 4: Investigate Theories of Managerial Accounting

Because managerial accounting came about due to management need, managerial accounting enhances the effectiveness and efficiency with which the organization operates. Additionally, managerial accounting is unlike any other branch of accounting in that organizational behavior and social factors may influence

MAKE IT REAL 2-2

As professionals in the field of managerial accounting, it is important to continue to educate oneself on the advancements in the field. Attending conferences is a wonderful way to stay up-to-date with such advancements. The IMA hosts an annual conference held in various geographical locations. Speakers discuss various topics and exhibitors provide resources for further learning.

Reference

"IMA's Annual Conference and Expo." IMA. (2016). Retrieved from https://www.imaconference.org/index.cfm

managerial accounting (Gong and Tse, 2009). To understand the role of managerial accounting within an organization, we will look at theories of functionalism, sociology, and psychology.

> The *functionalist* perspective argues that every organization can function optimally (Gong and Tse, 2009). Such a perspective is concerned with systematic influences on individuals. Functionalism focuses on restoring social order by looking from the external environment inward. Thus, functionalism theories look to various structures and systems as a way of maintaining order.
>
> Managerial accounting crosses the boundaries of accounting and *sociology* because of the benefits managerial accounting provides to an organization. Managerial accounting provides social benefits such as staff coordination and performance evaluation. Additionally, managerial accounting potentially becomes a social practice more than simply an accounting practice. An entirely different perspective can be gained as managerial accounting steps outside the role of accounting and takes on sociological meaning.
>
> *Psychological* theories are concerned with individual behavior. Thus, psychological theories attempt to understand implications of individual behavior within organizations (Gong and Tse, 2009). The human element of an organization is an important element for efficient functioning. Organizations must understand what types of things motivate individuals to make various decisions.

The three perspectives noted above form the groundwork for the following theory. Each perspective lends itself to a different understanding of managerial accounting practices. Thus, each theory noted below will provide for a further examination of a given perspective. Comparing and contrasting these theories will provide an understanding of the differences the perspectives play in the role of evaluating the effectiveness of managerial accounting within a given organization.

Functionalism Theories

Agency Theory

As noted in Topic 1, Agency Theory has to do with the problems that exist between agents and principals, or owners and employees. The key idea is that the principal-agent relationship should create an efficient relationship but is plagued by issues of information and risk. A problem exists, however, between principals and agents because individuals have different goals and expectations they bring to an organization (Ogunyemi, 2014). Thus, with individuals bringing different goals to an organization, problems arise between the principal and the agent. Agency Theory assumes that individuals will act in their own self-interest (Gong and Tse, 2009).

Origins. Relatively speaking, Agency Theory is a new theory, emerging in the early 1970s. The theory came about as a result of research in risk-sharing problems. Agency Theory was intended to broaden the scope of research to include an agency problem (Eisenhardt, 1989) and address how and why the problem exists.

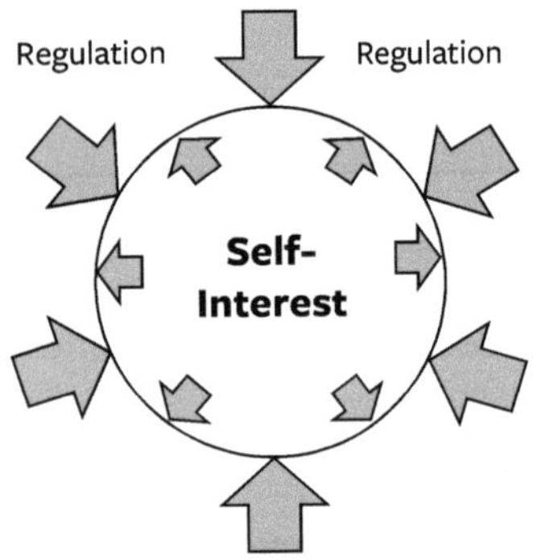

FIGURE 2.5 Levels of Analysis of Agency Theory.

In the early 1970s, researchers saw a gap in research and addressed the gap by way of Agency Theory.

In addressing how and why agency problems exist, Agency Theory was divided to address two major problems. The first problem had to do with the desires and goals of each principal and agent and the way in which the principal verifies the job that the agent is doing (Eisenhardt, 1989). The second problem had to do with the shared level of risk and the perspective of each principal and agent regarding risk (Eisenhardt, 1989). From its origins, Agency Theory was intended to understand the principal-agent relationship.

Problems that exist regarding agents and principles are both micro- and macro-level problems (Figure 2.5). The macro level of analysis says that regulation explains why the agent acts in his or her own self-interest. The micro-level analysis says that individual acts of blame, such as lies, explain why an agent acts in his or her own self-interest (Eisenhardt, 1989).

Application to Managerial Accounting. Agency Theory has had many influences from the accounting and economic disciplines. Because of the influences from the financial realm, its application to managerial accounting is a somewhat seamless application. The principal-agent relationship depends on the principal's reliance on the agent. Issues regarding performance, including compensation and budgeting, are all relevant to managerial accounting effectiveness. The principal (owner) depends upon the agent (management) to provide a profit. Managerial accounting needs to accurately convey feedback to the agent and ultimately to the principal. By viewing Agency Theory from a macro level, managerial accounting is viewed as part of the regulation process. However, managerial accountants must not be part of the pressure that comes from regulation to act in one's own self-interest. Instead, compensation measures and budgeting, as they relate to performance, must all be presented in a way that discourages agents from acting in their own self-interest.

Contingency Theory

Contingency Theory is another theory of functionalism and is concerned with the continual process of fitting the performance of an organization within the organizational structure and other contextual variables (Gong and Tse, 2009).

Origins. The origins of Contingency Theory were derived from an unsettled management discipline. Thus, the contingency model recognizes the complexity of the management system and merges management with a scientific focus. The idea of the contingency model attempts to unify the discipline of management with one general theory that replaces the disconnect of the various other theories that came before it. Contingency Theory takes into account the dissimilarities that exist in management theories to bring the dissimilarities together under one theory. Contingency Theory focuses on the concept that everything depends upon something else and that there is no consistency as all variables are contingent upon other variables (Figure 2.6).

Application to Managerial Accounting. As a theory that attempts to understand managerial practices and evaluate different techniques of managerial accounting, Contingency Theory uses managerial practices as components of an organizational structure (Gong and Tse, 2009). In seeing managerial accounting practices as components of an organization, one can investigate a fit between managerial practices and the contextual variables associated with the organization. Thus, managerial accounting exists as one of the contingencies within an organization. Any number of variables could be added to Figure 2.6; one must just consider the variables

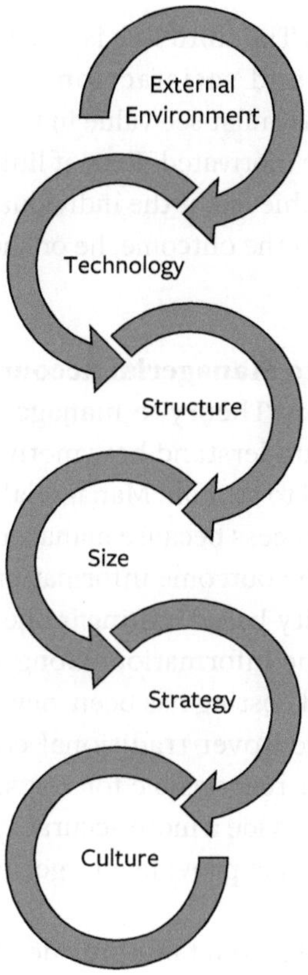

FIGURE 2.6 Analysis of Contingency Theory Relationships.

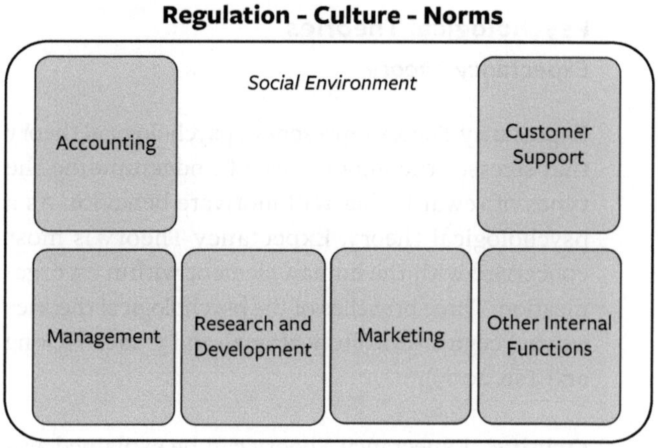

FIGURE 2.7 Institutional Theory Interaction of the Social Environment within an Institution.

chosen in the process of reviewing the effectiveness of management.

Sociological Theories

Institutional Theory

Institutional Theory is a sociological theory concerned with organizational dynamics (Cohen, Krishnamoorthy, and Wright, 2008). According to Institutional Theory, institutional logic provides rules that become guidelines for social behavior (Gong and Tse, 2009).

Origins. Old institutional theories saw humans as creatures of habit and the only key actors of society. Over time, however, the theory changed to recognize that humans were not the only key actors. Individuals, national states, and other organizations could all be considered "actors" in a larger society (Meyer, 2008).

The current version of Institutional Theory is a fairly new theory to modern society in that it has only been in existence since 1991. Since 1991, however, it has experienced several changes and revisions. The Theory, as it is known today, emphasizes the importance of institutions (Burns and Baldvinsdottir, 2005). As a sociological theory attempting to explain social reality, the institutionalist method looks to the process of change and changing relationships. Thus, the social aspect of an organization is dictated by the regulative, normative, and culturally appropriate systems in place (Figure 2.7).

Application to Managerial Accounting. In turning the focus to managerial accounting, Institutional Theory plays a role in understanding and explaining why certain managerial accounting practices are adopted by organizations and why some practices survive (Gong and Tse, 2009). With the institution at the center of the theory, the institution brings stability and continuity to management accounting (Burns and Baldvinsdottir, 2005) and defines the behavioral dynamics within the organization. Because management accounting is an internally used accounting tool, the rules that govern the institution will be the rules by which management accounting also abides.

Psychological Theories

Expectancy Theory

Expectancy Theory represents a psychological theory that stresses the importance of understanding the types of rewards that will motivate behavior. As a psychological theory, Expectancy Theory is most concerned with the human element within an organization. Three branches of the psychological theories exist: 1) cognitive, 2) motivational, and 3) social (Gong and Tse, 2009).

Origins. Expectancy Theory can be explained as a motivational theory attributed to Victor Vroom, an organization and management school professor who became well known for his work in the field of motivation. There are four basic elements to Vroom's theory: 1) effort, 2) performance, 3) outcomes, and 4) satisfaction (Figure 2.8).

> *Expectancy:* The first link between the four basic elements is that of expectancy. Expectancy is an individual's belief that great effort will produce great accomplishment (Kermally, 2005). Therefore, the link connects effort with performance. Thus, there is a perceived correlation between effort and performance. Motivation, then, is surrounded by one's ability to imagine that his or her effort can lead to some desired performance (Hamington, 2010).
>
> *Instrumentality.* The second link is between performance and outcomes. For instrumentality to hold true, an individual must believe that achieving a certain performance will trigger a certain outcome (Hamington, 2010). Thus, if he or she performs a task well, desired outcomes will be granted. The desire for the outcome motivates the behavior.

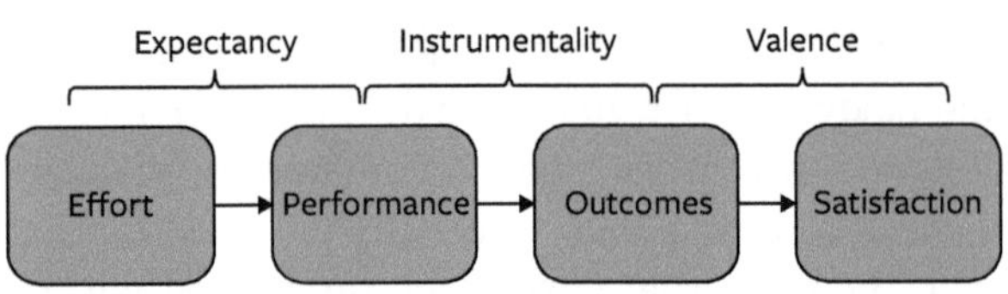

FIGURE 2.8 Expectancy Theory Analysis.

> *Valence.* The third link is the link between outcome and satisfaction. In short, an individual must see value in the outcome in order to be motivated. Even if link one and two are both achieved, if the individual does not see value in the outcome, he or she will not be motivated.

Application to Managerial Accounting. In applying Expectancy Theory to managerial accounting, one needs to understand how motivation levels are directly linked to stimuli. Managerial accounting has a role in the process because managerial accountants can provide the outcome information for individual actions. Activity-based costing is one method of providing outcome information (Gong and Tse, 2009). Activity-based costing has been viewed as a superior costing method over traditional costing systems. For a manager responsible for costs, activity-based costing may provide a more accurate picture of profit margins and thus provide a larger incentive to the manager.

Managerial accountants provide a host of outcome measures. The outcome measures will be evaluated by employees as to their level of satisfaction. Therefore, managerial accountants must be fully engaged in the managerial process in order to understand how and what motivates employees.

Similarities and Differences

Although the theories noted above come from different theoretical perspectives, similarities can still be found among the theories. Contingency Theory, Agency Theory, and Institutional Theory all approach managerial accounting from a macro-level perspective. In the macro-level perspective, each theory looks to the institution for explanation and effectiveness of managerial accounting. Contingency Theory relies on variables within the organization that may have an impact on the effectiveness of managerial accounting. Agency Theory stresses the principal-agent relationship as a function of an organization and looks to the contract to define the relationship within the organization. Finally, Institutional Theory relies upon the institution to govern the effectiveness of managerial accounting. All three theories have different theoretical bases but come together in the understanding of how managerial accounting fits into organizations.

Likewise, Expectancy Theory and Agency Theory focus on the importance of the individual within the organization. Expectancy Theory focuses upon the human element to understand motivating factors of individuals within organizations, and Agency Theory focuses on the relationship between the principal and the agent within an organizational setting. Both theories bring light to the vulnerability of individual will and motivations.

In managerial accounting, with awareness of the various theories that interplay within organizations, consideration should be given to that which enables efficient and effective application of managerial accounting within an organization. Each theory in Learning Goal 4 addresses the organization at a different level, encompassing different interactions.

LEARNING GOAL 5: Understand the Whole Picture of Managerial Accounting

Gaining a theoretical perspective of Contingency Theory, Agency Theory, Institutional Theory, and Expectancy Theory provides a foundation of information on which to draw in an effort to understand the "whole" of managerial accounting. Managerial accounting, from the perspective of each of the theories, takes on a new dimension.

Figure 2.9 encompasses the relationship of the four theories of managerial accounting with one another. Institutional Theory is represented by the purple band in the outer circle. Institutional Theory looks purely at the institutional relationship. From the Institutional Theory perspective, the outermost concept aids in the understanding of managerial accounting effectiveness. Thus, the social environment surrounding the organization can help to either lead to an organization's success or failure in its implementation of managerial accounting. At the institutional level, managerial accounting is viewed as an overall process, rather than as individual components.

Contingency Theory is represented by the yellow band in Figure 2.9. Although still in the outermost area

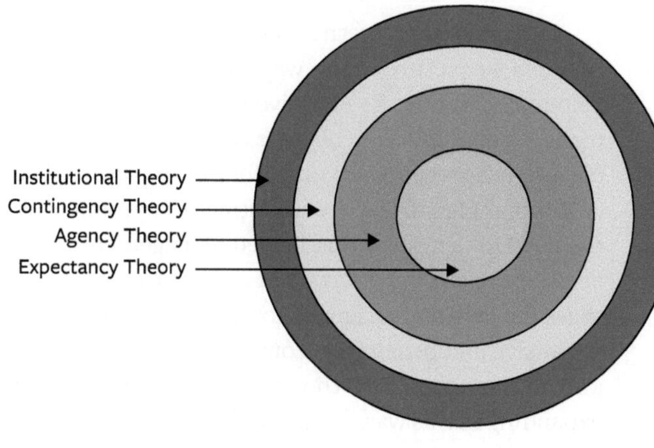

FIGURE 2.9 Theories of Managerial Accounting.

of the circle, Contingency Theory looks more closely at the detail of managerial accounting practices and at the detail of the organization in which the managerial system is integrated. Contingency Theory is widely adapted as a theoretical foundation of managerial accounting because the theory allows a researcher to break apart both the components of the organization and of the accounting system.

The blue band in Figure 2.9 represents Agency Theory. Agency Theory takes a closer look at the relationships of the individuals within an organization in an effort to understand the success of a managerial accounting system. The role of a managerial accounting system is purely an internal role in that the goal is to provide information to management for decision making. If management's role is to act as an agent and make decisions that are in the best interest of the principal, managerial accounting will need to provide information that will best align the two individuals. Thus, managerial accountants are successful if they can provide information that gives the whole picture to the principal and the agent, aligning the goals of both parties. Agency Theory hones in on the relational component of the people involved in the processes.

Finally, the green inner circle of Figure 2.9 represents Expectancy Theory. Expectancy Theory, as a psychological theory, focuses entirely on the individuals at work within the managerial accounting system. According to the perspective of Expectancy Theory, individuals are at the crux of whether a managerial accounting system is successful or not successful.

When putting together the entirety of the theories, a clear picture of the ways in which theory can help to determine the effectiveness and efficiency of managerial accounting becomes evident. All theories need all other theories in order for a clear picture. The beginnings of managerial accounting were grounded in the need for a system that helped management make decisions regarding pricing and cost. As the discipline grew, the field of managerial accounting became more expansive and began to encompass areas of financial and non-financial growth within an organization. In expanding in this way, managerial accounting met the needs of management by collecting, processing, and presenting accounting data. In meeting the financial needs of management, managerial accounting also provided non-financial benefits that outweighed the intended purpose (Ciuhureanu, 2012). Over time, managerial accounting expanded even further to provide a more refined and higher level of understanding for management decision making.

In order to truly understand the effectiveness and efficiency of managerial accounting, multiple theories that cover the broad spectrum of managerial accounting must be applied. For example, understanding managerial accounting involves an understanding of the dynamics in which managerial accounting exists within an organization, which exists inside the dynamics of an economy. Once the large-scale success has been achieved, it becomes important to look at the specifics of the organization in relation to the specific practices of managerial accounting. If large-scale success is not present, it will not matter if there is a "fit" or not between the organization and the managerial accounting practices because those successes will not be present either. However, once a "fit" has been achieved, and the managerial accounting practices are successfully implemented within an organization, the next level of success will involve the alignment between the individuals known as the principals and the agent. Once the principals and agents are seen to have alignment, individual motivators must be in existence. The success of managerial accounting filters downward, starting with institutional dynamics (many times the economy or a larger-scale organization) all the way to the individuals within the organization. All level of success must be present for a successful managerial accounting system (Figure 2.10).

FIGURE 2.10 Flow of Efficiency and Effectiveness.

The above figure conveys the concepts of the theories discussed in this topic in a functional representation of how efficiency and effectiveness needs to be accomplished. The interrelationship of the theories exemplifies a framework for how to accomplish an effective managerial accounting system.

In cooperation with Institutional Theory, the first level of efficiency and effectiveness happens within the outermost influences. The economy or the corporate culture would need to first experience efficiency and effectiveness. The outer environment must want and need managerial accounting. If the first level is satisfied, the second level of efficiency and effectiveness is the organization. Certain organizations may have characteristics that require specific features of managerial accounting to be needed. Contingency Theory addresses the idea of the variations that could take place from organization to organization within the field of managerial accounting. Once the first two levels have achieved efficiency and effectiveness, the third level can be addressed. The third level involves the

GIVE IT A WHIRL 2-2

1. The theories of management are important to the managerial accountant in order to help understand one's role within an organization. Indicate the managerial accounting function that matches the work of a manager as expressed by Peter Drucker. The functions of management are Planning (P), Performing (PF), and Evaluating (E).

   Organize______
   Develop people______
   Determine goals______
   Communicate______
   Analyze activities______
   Set objectives ______
   Motivate______
   Establish measurement yardstick______

(Answers: P, E, P, PF, PF, P, PF, E)

2. The theories of managerial accounting fit into the areas of functionalism, sociology, and psychology. Describe how managerial accounting fits into an organization from a functionalist perspective, a sociological perspective, and a psychological perspective.

(Answers:

Functionalism: Managerial accounting helps to restore and maintain social order in an organization within the framework of the organization.

Sociology: Managerial accounting helps to educate staff and keep individuals within the organization informed.

Psychology: Managerial accounting provides various individual levels of motivation to encourage optimal performance by way of meeting individual need. Managerial accounting helps to motivate staff by maintaining feedback and information.)

relationships between management and the principals. Effective and efficient managerial accounting systems adequately address this relationship by aligning the goals of both the principal and the agent. Without an alignment of goals, managerial accounting cannot be efficient or effective. Lastly, at the individual level, an effective managerial accounting system must understand what motivates individuals, thus coinciding with the Expectancy Theory.

The interdependence of efficiency and effectiveness trickles down from a macro level to the micro level. If efficiency and effectiveness are not attained at any prior level, all other levels that follow will not attain efficiency and effectiveness, either. However, a managerial accounting system implemented in an economy that calls for it, in an organization that needs it as defined by the organization, for the benefits of the principal-agency relationship, in the best interest of individual motivational factors will be a success.

TOPIC 2 REFERENCES

Burns J., and Baldvinsdottir, G. "An Institutional Perspective of Accountants' New Roles—The Interplay of Contradictions and Praxis." *European Accounting Review,* 14(4), 725–757. Doi: 10-1080/09638180500194171. (2005).

Ciuhureanu, A. "The Dualism of the Accounting Activity of the Company. Characteristics of the Managerial Accounting and Implications in the Management of a

Company." *Annals Of The University Of Petrosani Economics*, 12(2), 93–104. (2012).

Cohen, J. R., Krishnamoorthy, G., and Wright, A. M. "Form Versus Substance: The Implications for Auditing Practice and Research of Alternative Perspectives on Corporate Governance." *Auditing*, 27(2), 181-198. (2008).

Eisenhardt, M, K. "Agency Theory: An Assessment and Review." *The Academy of Management Review*, 14(1), 57. (1989).

Gordon E.A., Raedy, J.S., and Sannella, A.J. *Intermediate Accounting*. Boston, MA. Pearson Education, Inc., 2016.

Gong, M.Z., and Tse, M.C. "Pick, Mix or Match? A Discussion of Theories for Management Accounting Research." *Journal of Accounting, Business & Management*, 16(2), 54-66. (2009).

Hamington, M. "The Will to Care: Performance, Expectation, and Imagination." *Hypatia*, 25(3), 675-695. doi:10.1111/j.1527-2001.2010.01110.x. (2010).

IMA conference (1997-2016). *The Association of Accountants and Financial Professionals in Business*. Retrieved from https://www.imaconference.org/index.cfm

Kaplan, R.S. "The Evolution of Management Accounting." *Accounting Review*, 59(3), 390. (1984).

Kermally, S. *Gurus on People Management*. London: Torogood Publishing, LTD., 2005. Retrieved from http://eds.b.ebscohost.com.ezp.waldenulibrary.org/eds/detail?vid=13&sid=c380967d-be38-4118-a9c5-e47c08e8e90a%40sessionmgr198&hid=102&bdata=JnNpdGU9ZWRzLWxpdmUmc2NvcGU9c2l0ZQ%3d%3d#.

Meyer, J.W. "Reflections on Institutional Theories of Organizations." In R. Greenwood, C. Oliver, K. Sahlin, and R. Suddaby (Eds.), *The Sage Handbook of Organizational Institutionism* (pp. 790-811). Thousand Oaks, California: Sage Publications, Inc. (2008).

Ogunyemi, . *Teaching Ethics Across the Management Curriculum: A Handbook for International Faculty*. Business Expert Press, 2014.

Pounder, B. "A Common Framework for Accounting Standards." *Strategic Finance* 92(5), p. 20, 22, and 61. (2010).

Prasadunder, C.A. *Peter F. Drucker—Business Management and Beyond*. IBSCDC, 2004

Schiffel, L., Schroeder, D.L., and Smith, K.A. "IMA 2012 Salary Survey." *Strategic Finance*. Retrieved from http://www.imanet.org/docs/default-source/sf/06_2013_salary_survey-pdf.pdf?sfvrsn=0. (2013).

Weiss, L.A. *An Introduction to Financial Accounting*. Fontainebleau, France: Insead, 1994.

TOPIC 2 FIGURE CREDIT

Fig. 2.1: Adapted from http://sfmagazine.com/wp-content/uploads/2016/02/SBcalculator.jpg.

TOPIC 3 Skills and Tools Needed for the Managerial Accountant

LEARNING GOALS

1. Define the differences between service, merchandising, and manufacturing companies.
2. Describe the value chain and the supply chain.
3. Discuss the various ways in which managerial accounting defines costs.
4. Understand the differences in how a managerial accountant uses an income statement.

INTRODUCTION

In order to function effectively within an organization, a managerial accountant uses a different set of accounting tools than a financial accountant. The main tools used by a financial accountant are the financial statements and the guidance from GAAP. Because managerial accounting is not subject to external regulation, the authoritative body that governs how financial data is presented is not GAAP but management. Likewise, the tools required consist of performance reports and other management driven reports, not the traditional financial statements.

Learning Goal 1 reviews the types of companies in which managerial accounting can exist. Although typically associated with manufacturing industries, managerial accounting is gaining a larger presence in the service and merchandising industries. Learning Goal 1 will discuss the role of the managerial accountant in each type of industry. Learning Goal 2 incorporates the value chain and the supply chain as tools to which the managerial accountant refers frequently. The value chain helps the managerial accountant ensure that non-value activities are minimized throughout the organization, and the supply chain helps to refine the processes involved in the production and distribution of the organization's service or product. Learning Goal 3 provides definitional information regarding the ways in which managerial accountants view and analyze costs. Such definitions are important because of the multiple ways in which costs are used in managerial accounting. Finally, Learning Goal 4 delves into the ways in which managerial accountants use the income statement. The income statement used for financial reporting purposes serves its intended purpose of external reporting. However, for internal reporting the same information must be organized in a different way to provide management with a refined perspective of the income statement elements.

LEARNING GOAL 1: Define the Differences Between Service, Merchandising, and Manufacturing Companies.

In the business environment, a managerial accountant could become employed in any type of business. Although the history of managerial accounting was grounded in the manufacturing industry, service organizations and merchandising organizations have taken note of the benefits that internal accounting data can provide for managers and have, thus, led to expanded fields in which managerial accounting operates.

Service Companies

The product that a service-based company sells is a service (an intangible item). Although goods are sometimes sold with the service, the primary item that a consumer is purchasing involves a specific service. In most cases, a service-based company, generally, does not mass produce its service. Instead, each service is customized to the individual need of the consumer. For example, a tax accountant provides a service of tax preparation. Although, the delivery of the completed tax return (a tangible item) is part of the service, the accountant isn't selling tax returns; he or she is selling a service of preparing the tax returns. Such a service is individualized to each client. However, there are instances when purchasing a service is not individualized to the consumer needs. An example of a mass-produced service includes services in the transportation industry. Consider airlines. Individuals buy airfare to fly from point A to point B. In the process of the flight, the individuals may receive a meal. The meal is not what the consumer is purchasing. The consumer is purchasing the flight from point A to point B. In the case of the flight, the transportation from point A to point B is not specialized but depends on the level of ticket purchased. Other types of services may include attorneys, dentists, doctors, package delivery companies, etc.

Merchandising Companies

Merchandising companies are primarily concerned with selling a product but may include a service as part of selling the product. In a merchandising company, the product is not altered in any way. For example, in the typical retail clothing store, companies buy product from their suppliers at wholesale and resell to consumers by marking up the prices. When consumers shop at the stores, they may expect sales staff to serve them, but the price paid is for a tangible item that leaves the store. The markup may be larger or smaller, depending on the level of service provided. The purchased item, however, is a tangible piece of merchandise. Examples of merchandising companies include Walmart, Target, Marshall Fields, etc.

Service/Merchandising

Certain companies exist in both service and merchandising industries. Take, for example, the movie industry. When consumers go to the movies, they are purchasing the service of entertainment. However, if they decide to have some popcorn and a soda while enjoying the moving, they are also purchasing a product. Likewise, individuals purchase both the cell phone and the service through companies such as Verizon or T-Mobile.

Manufacturing Companies

A manufacturing company differs from either a service-based company or a merchandising company in that consumers purchase the completed manufactured product. Many times the consumers of manufactured products may be merchandising companies, who turn around and resell to the end user. An example of a manufacturing company would be General Motors or Dell Computers. Such companies do not sell the individual parts of the computer or of the car for you to assemble. Instead, they sell a completed and assembled product. The restaurant industry would also be considered a manufacturing industry. The purchased product is not a basket full of raw ingredients but is a completed product ready for consumption.

The Role of Managerial Accounting

Understanding the types of businesses that exist is important to the managerial accountant in that the type of business will determine the types of inventory that flows through to the balance sheet and the character of that inventory (Figure 3.1). The type of business will also determine the way in which the income statement is arranged and how the items flow through the income statements as cost of goods sold.

FIGURE 3.1 Types of Businesses.

LEARNING GOAL 2: Describe the Value Chain and the Supply Chain

Value Chain

The value chain is a concept that links a variety of business functions together into a series of steps that are required to carry out business processes. The value chain spans departmental boundaries. For the managerial accountant, the value chain signifies areas of the organization for which value must be added for the consumer. Managerial accountants track costs within each of the functions, attempting to eliminate nonvalue-added costs. The value chain consists of six business functions (Figure 3.3):

- Research and Development
- Product Design
- Manufacturing or Purchasing
- Marketing
- Distributing
- Customer Service

Research and Development

Research and development is generally the start of the business process. As companies decide on the product and the service they will be selling, time must be given to the research of the product. Such research can involve the creating of new products and services or upgraded products or services. In either case, the process of research and development is a necessary process. The managerial accountant is concerned with the value-added costs of research and development. Research and development, in total, is seen as a process that creates significant value for companies because it helps them to maintain a competitive edge.

Take, for example, the telephone. At one point in time, telephones existed as part of a party-line. When individuals wanted to make a phone call, they would ring the operator, who would then patch them through to the desired party. As the telephone industry conducted research and development, research told them that people didn't like party lines because others could listen in. Eventually, the party line was replaced by individual lines. Currently, the vast majority of individuals carry cell phones with them that can do everything from surfing the internet to paying at the cash register. Research and development is at the heart of how the telephone industry progressed from party lines to current cell phone usage.

Product Design

Product design is the business process that puts into action that which was learned from research and development. Product design involves engineering the product or the service so that it can fulfill its intended purpose. Managerial accountants look for value to be

MAKE IT REAL 3-1

Spending patterns have progressively been changing over time. As managerial accountants seeks to remain up to date on the needs of management, they should note that from 2009-2015, the rise and fall of the Gross Domestic Product (GDP) has been met by increases in services, specifically, professional and business services. Therefore, the need for managerial accountants to learn about how to work in service-based industries is increasing.

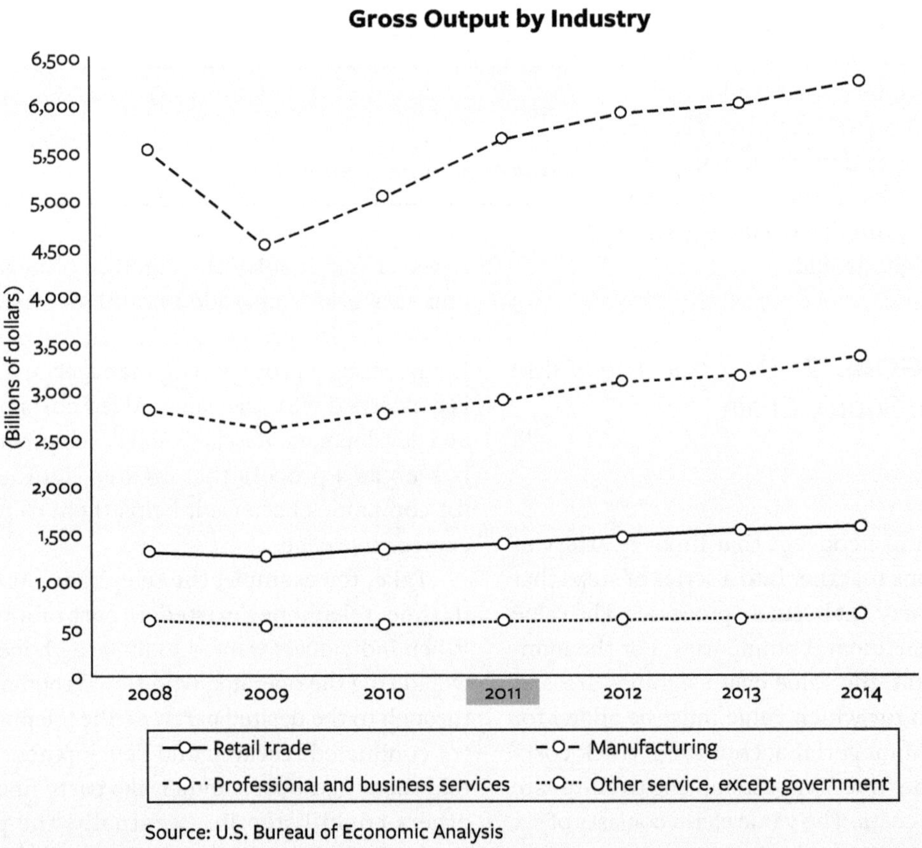

FIGURE 3.2 Gross Output by Industry.

Reference

"Industry Data." Bureau of Economic Analysis. (n.d.). Retrieved from http://www.bea.gov/iTable/iTable.cfm?ReqID=51&step=1#reqid=51&step=51&isuri=1&5114=a&5102=15

added in the product design function by eliminating activities that do not add value for the consumer. Such nonvalue items may involve design errors that would cause problems when the product moves onto the next process.

Manufacturing or Purchasing

Once the product or the service has been designed, the ideas and thoughts move into action with either the start of the manufacturing process or the purchasing of a merchandising product. If there have been design errors in product design, the manufacturing process will be halted until such design errors are fixed. Let's say, for example, that someone in the design department has designed a chair with only three legs. Once the product gets to the manufacturing stage and the first chair is tested, the company will learn of the design error and return the product back to the design process for redesign. Such a faux pas does not add value for the consumer. Thus, design errors should be eliminated as much as possible.

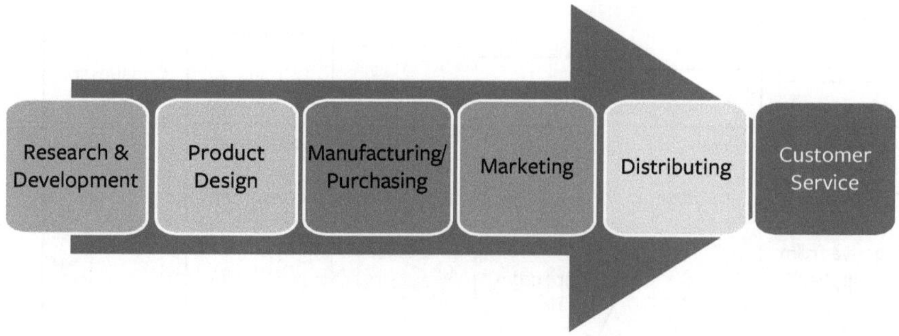

FIGURE 3.3 The Value Chain Functions.

Additionally, during the manufacturing process, the managerial accountant seeks to eliminate production errors in an effort to create an efficient working environment. Such errors may be cause for rework, which does not add value for the consumer. Therefore, the managerial accountant works to incorporate lean production and Kaizen manufacturing. Lean production is an approach to manufacturing that reorganizes the production environment to encourage a flow of the production process. Kaizen manufacturing is a tool of lean production that seeks constant improvement in the production process. Additionally, the managerial accountant may enlist the help of industrial engineers who specialize in time/motion studies to ensure the workforce is as efficient as possible.

Marketing

Marketing and advertising is the way in which an organization is able to "get the word out" about a product. The value-added component for the consumer is in learning about a product that may save the person time or money. The product will never be sold if it is not marketed effectively. Managerial accounting would seek marketing strategies directed towards the target market and advertising that directly supports the corporate strategy. As managerial accountants seek to help management be competitive in the marketplace, effective marketing should be of concern.

Distributing

Distribution involves the delivery method an organization will use to get the product into the hands of the consumer. A manufacturing organization may market directly to the consumer or may sell through a retail organization which will get the product into the hands of the consumers. However the company chooses to distribute, the distribution process must add value for the customer. Things that do not add value include breakage during delivery and slow or inefficient deliveries. The managerial accountant seeks to eliminate costs that do not add value for the consumer as such costs relate to distribution.

Customer Service

Customer service includes the after-sale service provided by the company. Most companies realize the need to provide continued service, not just service up until the point of sale. Repeat business depends on providing after-sale service. The value-added component for the consumer is that the service exists and is accessible to handle post-purchase issues in an appropriate and responsive way.

Supply Chain

The supply chain is different from the value chain in that the supply chain tracks the movement of supplies, not the value of the functional departments as in the value chain. In a manufacturing company, the supply chain is concerned with the movement of materials from the point of raw materials until such materials make it into the hands of the consumers as a completed

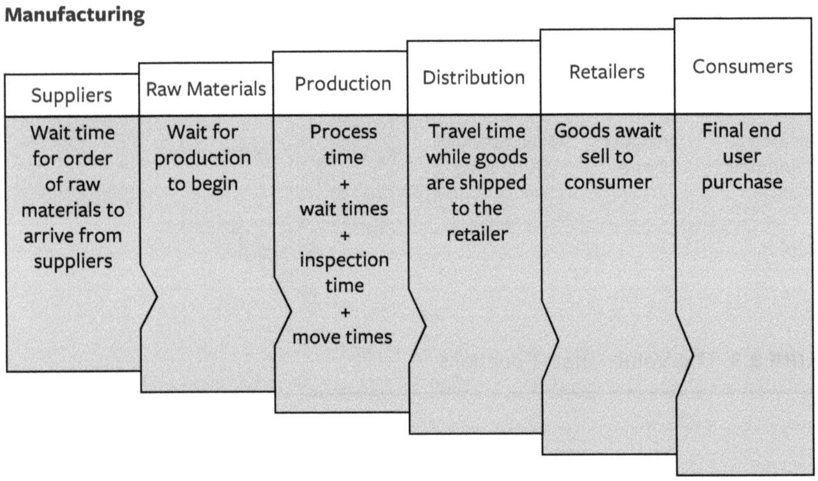

FIGURE 3.4 The Supply Chain.

product. In a service-based industry, the supply chain begins when the consumer requests a service until the point when the service is completed. In a merchandising company, the supply chain begins when the merchandiser orders the product and completes when the consumer receives the product.

In analyzing the supply chain, a managerial accountant would look at the time it takes from the start of the supply chain to the time the product or service is in the hands of the consumer. Such times are broken down and analyzed to ensure maximum efficiency. See the below examples for manufacturing, merchandising, and service-based business supply chains.

In looking at the manufacturing supply chain (Figure 3.4), the traditional supply chain begins by ordering the raw materials from the suppliers. In most situations, there will be a period of time between the time the order is placed and the time the order is shipped. Once the raw materials are received, the manufacturer waits for the production process to begin, at which stage the materials will move into the production process. During the production process, the materials may move through a series of production steps that may include processing, waiting, inspecting, and movement from step to step. Once the produced product becomes a finished good, the finished goods are distributed to the retailers, where they await sale to the consumer.

Note that the merchandising supply chain is much shorter than the manufacturing supply chain. The merchandising chain begins by purchasing the wholesale goods. Such goods are generally stored at the retailer until the consumer purchases the goods. Distribution may become a part of the merchandising supply chain when the retailer is not a physical brick and mortar store or if they sell via methods other than the physical location sales.

The final supply chain is for the service-based company. Such a company would start tracking supply-chain management when the customer places the order. Once a customer places the order, there may be wait times involved before the service can actually begin. For example, you may walk into a hair salon to get your hair cut, but you have to wait ten minutes before it becomes your turn. Consumers may be able to reduce their own wait times by calling in advance to set up an appointment. However, once the service begins, the time the service takes to complete is considered the service time. Services may occur in stages with wait times in between the various stages or may occur in one stage. In the example of the hair salon, the service may begin with a shampoo and then move to a cut. The time between the shampoo and the cut may be minimal, but the service is still occurring in more than one stage. Finally, some services would require that the service be returned to the customer. In the example of an accountant who prepares taxes for customers, the accountant may finish the tax return and need to set up an additional appointment to review and return the tax return to the customer.

In each of the types of businesses noted above, managers are concerned with the time it takes to provide the service or the product to the consumer. Imagine having to wait thirty minutes from the time your hair is shampooed to the time it is cut. Such a wait time would be unacceptable to customers purchasing a haircut. Therefore, suppliers of such a service need to

GIVE IT A WHIRL 3-1

1. Service, merchandising, and manufacturing companies have different behaviors as such behaviors related to internal business functions. Such differences begin with the ways in which the organization provides its goods or services. The following is a list of different types of organizations. Identify the organization as a manufacturer (M), a retailer (R), or a Service-based organization (S). You may have some organizations that are more than one.
   Starbucks_____
   Iowa State University_____
   Mayo Clinic_____
   Nestlé_____
   Marshall Fields_____
   Subway _____
   Whirlpool_____
   AMC Theaters_____
   Walgreens _____

(Answers: M & R, S, S, M, R, M & R, M, S & R, R)

2. The value chain and the supply chain are two frameworks in which managerial accounting can track data and provide feedback to managers. Fill in the elements for each of the figures below.

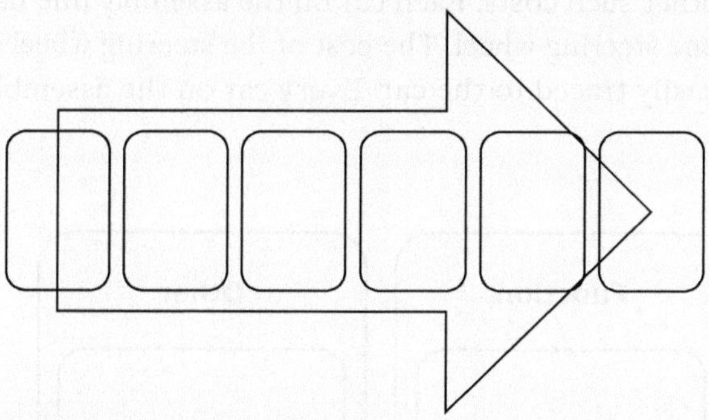

FIGURE 3.5 Value Chain.

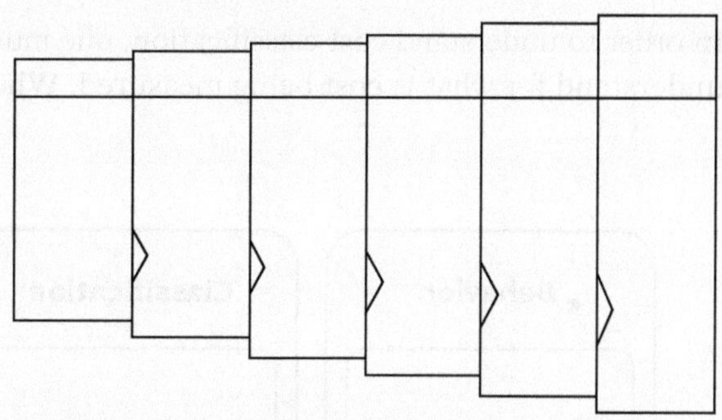

FIGURE 3.6 Supply Chain—Manufacturing.

be aware of time factors. Likewise, in a manufacturing organization, managers are concerned with the processes and the movement of the raw materials during the production of the product.

LEARNING GOAL 3: Discuss the Various Ways in Which Managerial Accounting Defines Costs

To the managerial accountant, the word "cost" conjures up a myriad of different ideas regarding the definition. Costs can be defined in terms of behavior, classification, and function.

Cost Behavior

One method of measuring costs involves defining how costs behave. Costs behave in two ways: 1) variable with the level of activity and 2) fixed with the level of activity. A cost that is variable with the level of activity means that as more units are produced, the cost increases. A cost that is fixed with the level of activity means that as the level of activity changes, the cost

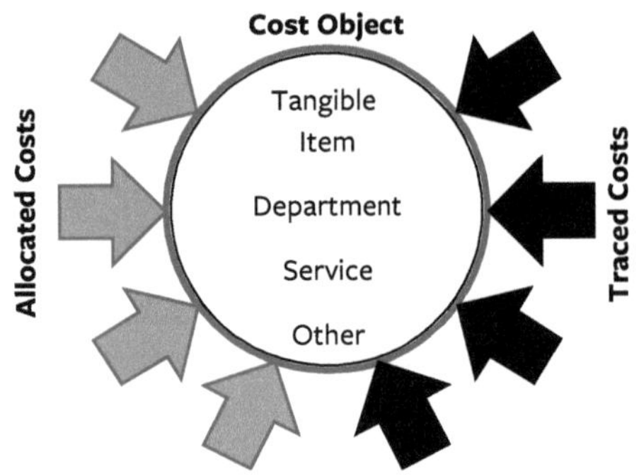

FIGURE 3.7 Cost Object.

is unaffected by the change in the level of activity. Understanding how a cost behaves allows managers to predict future costs, which is ultimately why the managerial accountant wants to understand costs. When a cost contains both elements of variable and fixed, the cost is referred to as mixed. Cost behavior will be discussed in greater detail in Topic 5.

Classification

In order to understand cost classification, one must understand for what is cost being measured. What is the cost object? When the managerial accountant wants to calculate the cost, he or she must know for what he or she is calculating the cost. The cost object is anything for which costs need to be calculated. The cost object can be a tangible item, a department, a service, or any other item for which cost data is needed (Figure 3.7).

Once the cost object has been defined, cost classifications can be established (Figure 3.8). Costs are typically classified as direct and indirect as they relate to a given cost object. When interpreting cost classification, the cost object is important to know. A cost that may be classified as indirect for one cost object could be direct for another cost object.

Direct Costs

A direct cost is a cost that can be quickly and easily traced to the cost object. For example: direct material costs for the body of an automobile (cost object) would include the steering wheel, the tires, the doors, and other such costs. Each car on the assembly line has one steering wheel. The cost of the steering wheel is easily traced to the car. Every car on the assembly

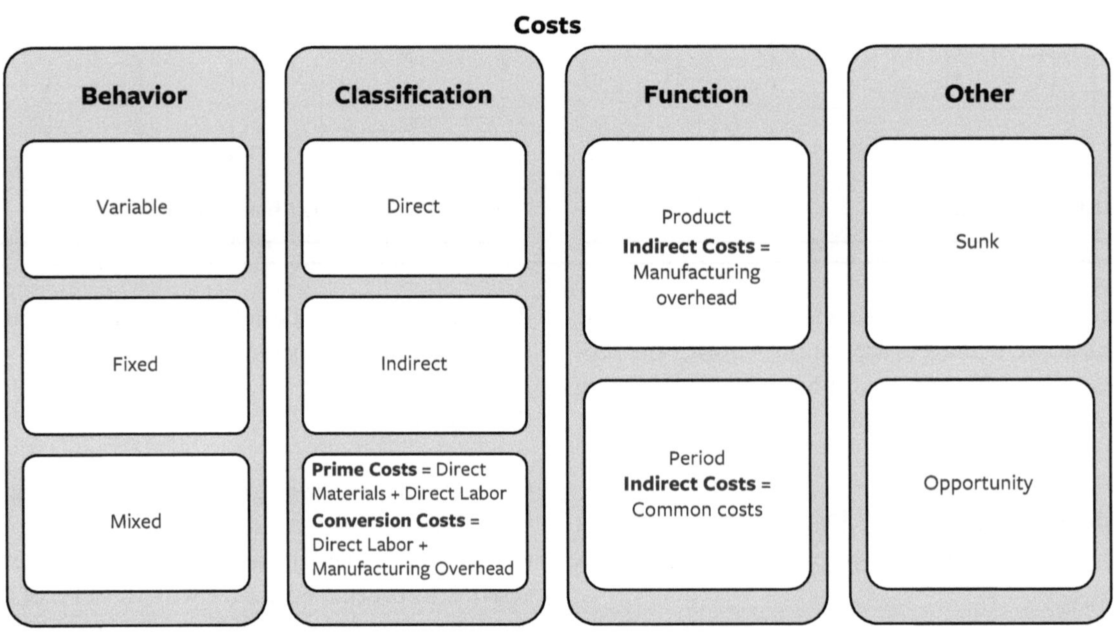

FIGURE 3.8 Cost Summary.

line has four tires. The cost of the tires is easily traced to the car. Labor costs can also be categorized as direct. Direct labor costs occur when the assembly line worker works on the car. The time the worker spends on a particular car can be measured via a timecard.

Cost objects can also be divisions of a company. If the cost object is a division of the company instead of an individual car, direct costs may be expanded to include the salaries of the management and any materials used specifically in that division.

Indirect Costs

Indirect costs cannot be economically traced to the cost object but must be allocated. For example, costs of small amounts of material used in building the body of the car would not be able to be quickly and easily traced to the automobile (cost object). Materials including glues and lubricants could not be economically traced to each individual car body because of the feasibility in tracing such a small amount. Instead, such costs would be allocated based on a calculated rate that would combine all indirect costs. Additionally, certain labor costs could also not be directly traced to an individual car. Salaries of factory management and maintenance staff could not be quickly and easily traced to the cost object if the cost object were the body of an automobile. If the cost object changed to the division of the company, such costs that may have been considered indirect for the automobile may be direct for the division.

Prime Costs and Conversion Costs

For ease of use, managerial accountants group costs as prime costs and conversion costs. Prime costs are the sum of direct material costs and direct labor costs. Conversion costs are the sum of direct labor costs and manufacturing overhead costs. Conversion costs represent the costs needed to convert raw materials into finished goods.

Function

Costs may also be described by the managerial accountant in terms of the function of the cost. Certain costs are related to the product being produced or the service being provided. Such costs are known as product costs. Period costs, on the other hand, are costs that are unrelated to the production of the product or the service being provided.

Product Costs

Product costs include all costs encompassed in the manufacturing process that can be associated with the product. Such costs include direct and indirect material and labor costs used in production. Product costs become part of the balance sheet in the form of work in process inventory. Thus, the costs are considered to be inventoriable.

Manufacturing Overhead. Manufacturing overhead is a product cost and is inventoriable. In the manufacturing environment, indirect costs are referred to as manufacturing overhead. Manufacturing overhead is how the managerial accountant classifies costs that are neither direct labor nor direct materials but still relate to the manufacturing process. All manufacturing processes will include direct materials, direct labor, and manufacturing overhead (indirect manufacturing costs).

Period Costs

Period costs are costs that do not become part of the balance sheet but instead run directly through the income statement. Period costs are costs that are not part of the production process and are not inventoriable. Examples of period costs include administrative costs that are incurred to keep the business running but are not part of production.

Common costs. Many times period costs are not used exclusively by one division or one cost object but are used by a number of different divisions. Thus, the cost is shared. Such a cost is referred to as a common cost. Common costs are shared between or among a variety of costs objects but cannot be directly traced to any one of them. Common costs must be allocated based on a reasonable system for allocating. The term common costs usually refers to non-manufacturing shared costs.

MAKE IT REAL 3-2

The Aproveche family owns a small independent winery located in Napa Valley, California. As part of the wine-making process, the company must determine cost data including the pounds of grapes to be harvested and the purchase price for the grapes. Additionally, costs such as the price of the oak barrels needed for the fermentation process must be included (the oak barrels have a useful life of four years). The winery traces direct materials such as the bottles, labels, and the corks for each bottle of wine. A total of $2.50 is traced for such costs. Direct labor is calculated by multiplying the average rate per hour times the total number of hours for laborers who harvest the grapes and those who crush the grapes. Overhead expenses are allocated and include building rent, depreciation of equipment used in the wine-making process, indirect material such as yeast and additives, lab expenses, liquor taxes, waste treatment, various salaries, and other miscellaneous expenses associated with the production of the wine.

Reference

Wisner, P.S. "A Votre Sante: Product Costing and Decision Analysis in the Wine Industry." *IMA Educational Case Journal, 4*(2). P. 1-4. (2011).

Other Costs

In addition to the various cost categories noted above, the managerial accountant works with two other basic types of costs, opportunity costs and sunk costs.

Opportunity Costs

An opportunity cost is a cost that will never appear on any balance sheet or income statement. However, opportunity costs are factored into various decisions managers make. Opportunity costs are defined as costs that represent the potential benefit that is given up by choosing one alternative over another alternative. For example, when a company decides to make a component of a product in-house, it gives up the opportunity to rent out that portion of the factory. The rent the company could have received had it not made the product in-house is an opportunity cost.

Sunk Costs

Costs that have already been incurred are considered sunk. Such costs cannot be changed by any future decision. For example, when a manager makes a decision as to whether he or she should purchase a new piece of equipment, the price paid for the old piece of equipment is sunk. Whether the manager purchases the new piece or not, he or she cannot change the price paid for the old piece of equipment.

LEARNING GOAL 4: Understand the Differences in How a Managerial Accountant Uses an Income Statement

The income statement is an essential tool for accountants (Figure 3.9). The managerial accountant, however, uses the income statement differently than a financial accountant. For the managerial accountant, the income statement is a reflection of how costs behave, and it serves the purpose of helping to understand the impact of costs on income. The income statement is more than a reporting statement to the managerial accountant; it is a tool for predicting future performance. Developing skills of interpretation and an understanding of how the income statement and the balance sheet work together is fundamental for the managerial accountant.

The financial accountant uses a traditional income statement to report past performance to outside parties. The format of the statement is governed by GAAP. Conversely, the managerial accountant uses the contribution format income statement to predict future performance for management. The format of

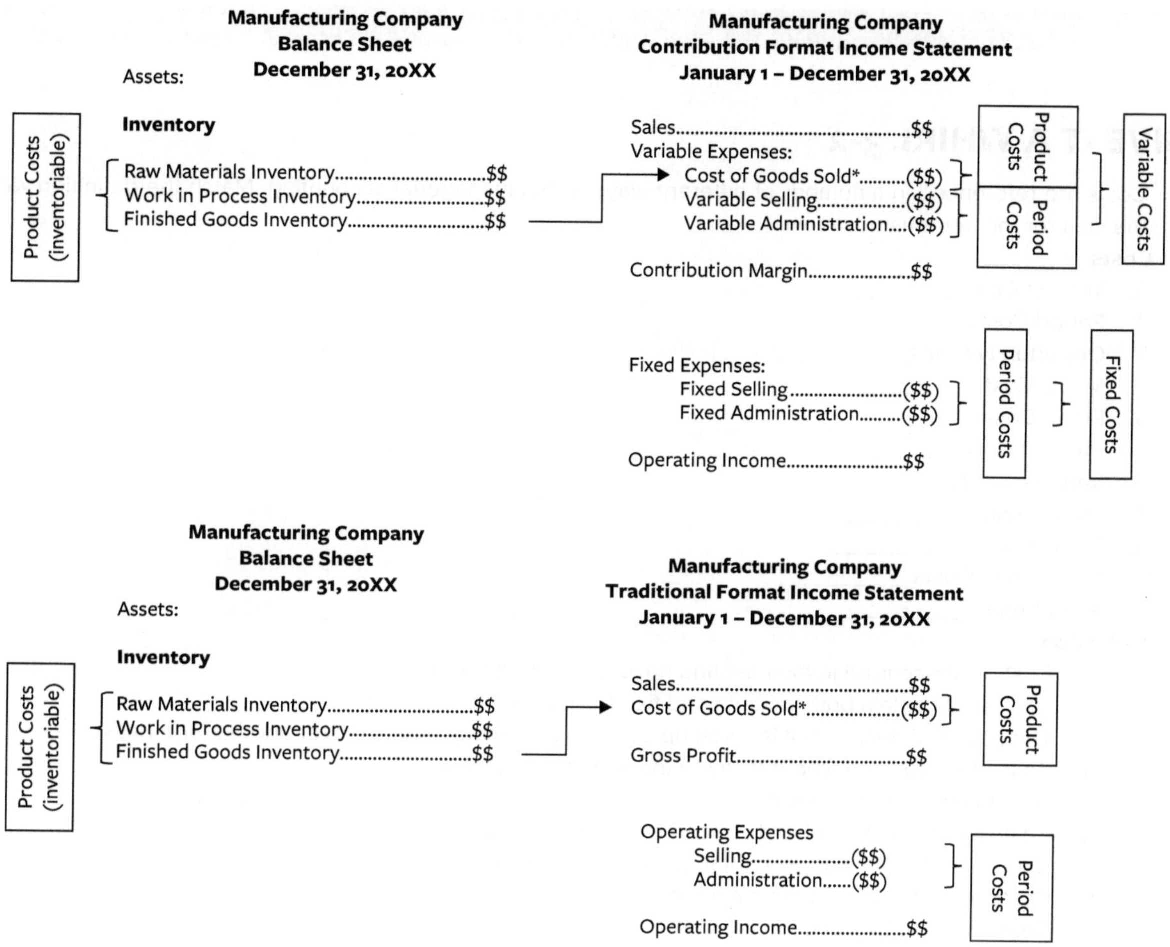

FIGURE 3.9 Manufacturing Company Balance Sheet and Income Statement.

the contribution format income statement is not governed by GAAP.

Traditional Format Income Statement

To arrive at operating income under the traditional format income statement, the accountant lists sales and subtracts cost of goods sold. Cost of goods sold is calculated differently, depending on whether the reporting organization is a manufacturing organization or a merchandising organization. However, the format of the income statement reports the subtraction of cost of goods sold from sales as gross margin. Selling and administrative expenses are then subtracted from gross margin so that operating income is the end result. In a traditional format income statement, costs are arranged by function as either product costs or period costs. Costs that flow from the balance sheet to the income statement via cost of goods sold are listed first (product costs), followed by period costs.

Contribution Margin Format Income Statement

To arrive at operating income under the contribution format income statement, the managerial accountant starts with sales and subtracts all variable expenses, including, but not limited to, cost of goods sold.

GIVE IT A WHIRL 3-2

1. Costs are referenced in a number of different ways within managerial accounting. Match the definition with the cost for the items listed below.

Costs

1. Indirect Costs__________
2. Period Costs__________
3. Opportunity Costs__________
4. Mixed Costs__________
5. Prime Costs__________
6. Product Costs__________
7. Variable Costs__________
8. Fixed Costs__________
9. Direct Costs __________
10. Conversion Costs__________
11. Sunk Costs__________

Definition

a. Costs that occurred in the past and have no future benefit.
b. Costs that contain both variable and fixed components.
c. The potential benefit that is given up by choosing one alternative over another alternative.
d. Costs that are expensed directly to the income statement.
e. Direct labor plus overhead costs.
f. Costs that cannot be directly traced to the cost object.
g. Costs that do not change in total regardless of the level of activity.
h. Costs encompassed in the manufacturing process.
i. Costs that can be traced to the cost object.
j. Costs that have a direct relationship with the level of activity in total but remain unchanged per unit regardless of the level of activity.
k. Direct costs plus direct labor.

(Answers: F, D, C, B, K, H, J, G, I, E, A)

2. Arrange the income statements for the traditional format and the contribution format. (Chart on next page.)

a. __________
b. __________
c. __________
d. __________
e. __________
f. __________
g. __________

Variable expenses can be either product or period costs. Once variable expenses have been subtracted from sales, the resulting amount is the contribution margin. Fixed expenses are then subtracted from the contribution margin to arrive at operating income. See Figure 3.9 for an example of a traditional income statement as compared with a contribution format income statement.

Note that the contribution format income statement responds better to the needs of management by arranging costs by behavior instead of function. Variable costs are listed first, followed by fixed costs.

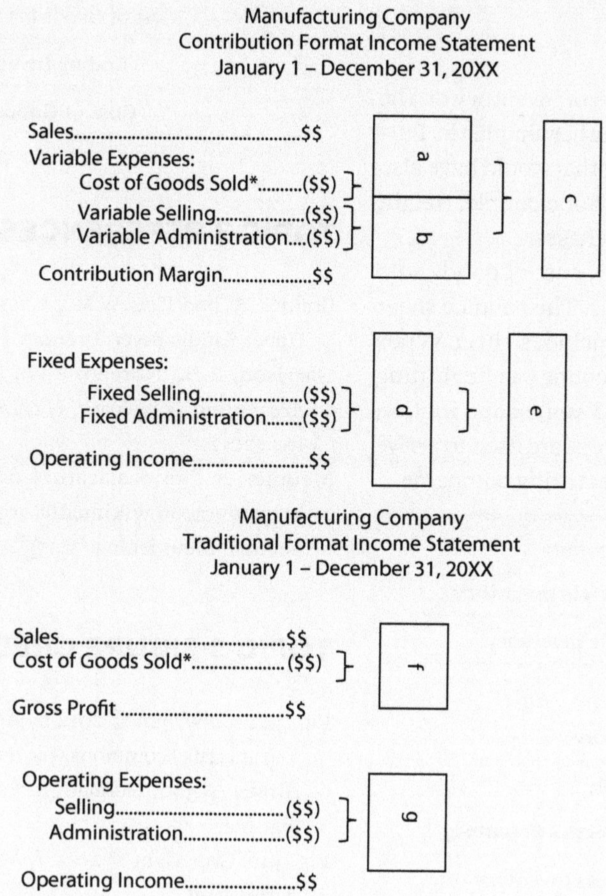

FIGURE 3.10 Manufacturing Company—Contribution and Traditional Format Income Statements.

Answers: a. product cost, b. period cost, c. variable cost, d. period costs, e. fixed costs, f. product costs, g. period costs

3. The traditional income statement is arranged by cost ___________. The contribution format income statement is arranged by cost ___________. (function, behavior)

Cost of Goods Sold

Cost of goods sold is found on both the traditional format income statement as well as on the contribution format income statement. The calculation of cost of goods sold is dependent on whether the company is a merchandising company or a manufacturing company. In a merchandising company, cost of goods sold is calculated in the following way:

Beginning Inventory + Purchases
– Ending Inventory
= Cost of Good Sold

Because there is only one class of inventory on the balance sheet, the calculation is rather simplistic. Purchases generally include anything that would have also been paid to make the purchase. For example, freight would be included as part of purchases.

In a manufacturing company, cost of goods sold is a result of multiple calculations. The balance sheet of a manufacturing company includes three types of inventory. Each inventory account has beginning inventory, ending inventory, and some contribution into the account. The following steps are used to arrive at cost of goods sold in a manufacturing company:

TABLE 3.1 Calculation for Raw Materials

Calculation for Raw Materials Inventory
Beginning Raw Materials Inventory
Purchases
(Ending Inventory)
Raw Materials Available for Use
Calculation for Work in Process Inventory
Beginning Work in Process Inventory
Raw Materials Available for Use
Labor
Overhead
(Ending Inventory)
Cost of Goods Manufactured
Calculation for Finished Goods Inventory
Beginning Finished Goods Inventory
Cost of Goods Manufactured
(Ending Inventory)
Cost of Goods Sold

TOPIC 3 REFERENCES

Braun K.W. and Tietz W.M. *Managerial Accounting* (4th ed.). Upper Saddle River: Prentice Hall, 2014.

Garrison, R.H., Noreen, E.W., Brewer, P.C. *Managerial Accounting.* New York, NY: McGraw-Hill Companies, Inc., 2012.

Meunier, A. "Autocaricatura de Adri." Retrieved from: https://upload.wikimedia.org/wikipedia/commons/b/be/Adri_Meunier.jpg (2015).

TOPIC 3 FIGURE CREDITS

Fig. 3.1a: Copyright © 2012 by Aeroprints.com (CC BY-SA 3.0) at https://commons.wikimedia.org/wiki/File:B-2348_Airbus_A.320_Sichuan_Airlines_%287182849745%29.jpg#file.

Fig. 3.1b: Copyright © 2013 by Vanity, Inc. Reprinted with permission.

Fig. 3.1c: Copyright © 2004 by Richard Smith (CC BY 2.0) at https://commons.wikimedia.org/wiki/File:1928_Model_A_Ford.jpg.

Fig. 3.2: Source: http://www.bea.gov/iTable/iTable.cfm?ReqID=51&step=1#reqid=51&step=51&isuri=1&5114=a&5102=15

SECTION II

THE PLANNING PHASE

The Planning Phase addresses the following competency:

Demonstrate an understanding of how organizations plan for effective and efficient operations.

The topics introduced in Section Two are imperative to learning the tasks involved in the Planning Phase.

- Strategy
- Cost Behavior
- CVP Analysis
- Master Budgeting
- Standard Costs
- Capital Budgeting

The purpose of Competency 2 is to help students understand that effective and efficient operations are the result of proper planning. Students will learn how strategy becomes an overarching concept that reaches through the organization, beginning with the planning phase. Planning is reflected by the building and implementation of budgets. Therefore, numerous budgets are covered to include the operating budgets, the financial budgets, and the capital budget.

FIGURE II.1 Theory: Planning, Evaluating, Performing.

TOPIC 4 Strategy

LEARNING GOALS

1. Identify various strategies.
2. Discuss the forces that shape strategy.
3. Understand management's use of strategy.
4. Discuss how responsibility accounting is a function of strategy.

INTRODUCTION

As managerial accountants begin to talk about the functions that exist inside the planning phase, they should begin the conversation with a discussion of strategy. Strategy initiates the planning phase by grounding the organization in its own vision and mission. As learned in Topic 2 of this text, the purpose of the managerial accountant began with management's desire for accounting to meet the internal needs of an organization. Eventually, the discipline progressed to help organizations be competitive in the marketplace. As a matter of alignment, it makes sense that for managerial accountants to help organizations be competitive in the marketplace, they would need to learn about and become familiar with corporate competitive strategy. This topic will focus on concepts with which the managerial accountant should become familiar regarding corporate competitive strategy.

Learning Goal 1 will identify various strategies. Strategy is not consistently applied to organizations in a one-size-fits-all manner. Various strategic models exist and each organization incorporates strategy in various stages. Strategy is pervasive, however, reaching throughout an organization from upper management to laborers to customer service employees. To accommodate for the pervasive nature, strategy goes through stages of development, implementation, and evaluation. This topic will provide an overall discussion of the stages of strategy. As this text moves from the planning phase to the performing phase, it will be assumed that the concepts of strategy discussed in this topic will be implemented within the performing phase. Evaluation of strategy takes place in many forms. In the evaluating phase of managerial accounting, evaluation of strategy will be discussed in Topic 16.

Learning Goal 2 discusses the forces that shape strategy. Michael Porter is well-known for addressing the five forces of the competitive environment. Among other models, this text will draw on Michael Porter's knowledge regarding the five forces.

Learning Goal 3 will discuss management's need for the use of strategy as well as how the managerial accountant becomes an integral part of strategy implementation and evaluation. Developing strategy must come from the top down as upper management establishes a long-term focus for their organization. As strategy moves into the executing phase, however, implementation can take on many forms. Managerial accounting is at the heart of ensuring upper management's strategic goals are being established in the day-to-day activities that take place. Additionally, managerial accounting helps to provide feedback on all levels relating to strategy.

Learning Goal 4 will discuss the concept of responsibility accounting. Before one can implement strategy or even evaluate strategy, lines of responsibility should be drawn, clarifying areas that will ultimately be evaluated.

As we enter the planning phase, it's important to note that the planning phase is very closely tied with the evaluation phase by way of performing. Once the managerial accountant gets to the evaluation phase, the goal is to match actual performance that occurred in the performing phase with what was originally planned. Strategy sets the stage as the opening act for the planning phase.

LEARNING GOAL 1: Identify Various Strategies

Strategy begins with the mission and the vision of an organization and identifies a firm's position and distinction within a competitive environment. Several models of strategy exist as a way to explain how business incorporates strategy into the organization. Whichever model is used, however, organizations need a strategy to gain competitive advantage in the marketplace.

Strategy is implemented within organizations in stages that include development, execution, and measurement.

Strategy Stages

Before a business can ever open its doors to its first customer, the business must develop an understanding for why it is in business, who the business serves, and what encompasses the future plans for the business. In short, the business must understand its mission and vision for the organization. Strategy, then, is built upon the mission and vision of the organization. Because the mission of an organization defines its purpose, mission statements provide strategic direction. When an organization has a clear mission statement that is communicated to its employees, performance levels increase because employees understand the purpose and meaning of their job. Thus, strategy provides competitive advantage in the marketplace but is also a way in which firms communicate and carry out their mission and vision. Strategy development is the first stage of the process.

Development

In the development of strategy, upper management clarifies the mission and vision statements of an organization as managers analyze plans for the advancement of the organization's goals. In developing strategy, managers think beyond processes and seek overall alignment of the activities and goals that occur inside the organization. Thus, the development of strategy is one of long-term thinking. Without long-term thinking, an organization could make short-term decisions that don't align with the long-term. Unaligned short-term decisions could disrupt the mission and vision for the organization.

Execution

Once strategy has been developed, it is executed. Executing the strategy means aligning the tasks and actions required with the skills of the individuals in the organization. In short, executing connects operations to the strategic goals. The execution of strategy takes place throughout the performing phase as management seeks to ensure operations fall in line with strategy goals.

Evaluation

Developing and executing the strategy should, then, be coupled with evaluation of the strategy to determine if the mission and the vision of an organization were carried out by way of operations. Hence, evaluation of the strategy serves as a way to measure and understand performance as it relates to the strategic goals. The Balanced Scorecard is one way of evaluating performance and strategic goals. The Balanced Scorecard will be discussed in Topic 16 as a method of evaluation.

Strategy Models

Because the main purpose of managerial accounting is to help organizations compete in the marketplace, its role in understanding the competitive strategy is imperative. Multiple models exist for developing a competitive strategy. This text will focus on two models: Porter's Generic Strategies and Ansari's QCT Triangle. Such models of strategy exist to provide a framework for strategy development and implementation.

Porter's Generic Strategies

Porter's Generic Strategies is a two-dimensional approach to strategy. The model started in the 1980s with the original three generic strategies that existed along two dimensions of narrow and broad. The three original strategies were cost leadership (broad), product differentiation (broad), and focus (narrow). Since its inception, Porter's Generic Strategies have expanded into five strategies that separate differentiation into three distinct categories of broad, focused, and focused low cost. Figure 4.1 shows the Porter model for the original three strategies.

Cost leadership strategy. The cost leadership strategy is a strategy in which an organization seeks a competitive advantage by way of delivering the lowest cost. Organizations hope to attract a broad spectrum of buyers by using the cost leadership strategy. Examples of organizations that exist under cost leadership heading include McDonald's, Walmart, and various other manufacturers, merchandisers, and service companies that focus on maintaining a competitive advantage through cost leadership.

Even when competitive forces are strong within an industry, the cost leadership strategy can prevail by gaining competitive advantage through low cost. In order to use a cost leadership strategy, however, managerial accountants spend a great deal of time controlling costs. Controlling costs depends on various influences and is easier for large companies to accomplish. For example, a large company may have a large market share, which would give the organization the ability to tap into economies of scale, purchasing large quantities of supplies in bulk for less cost.

Managerial accountants also focus on the supply chain as they seek to eliminate waste in the production process and minimize unwanted costs. Overall, the managerial accountant attempts to increase margin by decreasing the cost of producing or selling a product.

Product differentiation strategy. The differentiation strategy is a strategy in which an organization seeks a competitive advantage by way of delivering a distinctly different product. In the differentiation strategy, cost is no longer the attraction, but the uniqueness of the product is the attraction. Companies

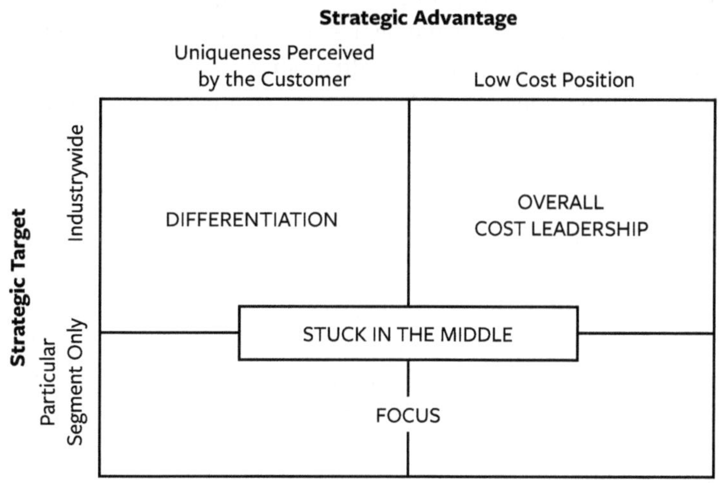

FIGURE 4.1 Porter's Generic Strategies.

like Starbucks, Lexus, Nike, and various other manufactures, merchandisers, and service companies fall into this category in which they provide a high-priced item that is unique in some way.

Porter noted that differentiation can take place in several ways such as design or brand image, technology, features, customer service, or various other dimensions. Companies that select the differentiation strategy establish brand loyalty with their consumers not because of low cost but because of a differentiated product. Because organizations that select this strategy do not focus on lowering cost, the managerial accountant must be able to balance costs effectively, understanding costs that will add value for the consumer. Margins can be increased by increasing prices rather than lowering costs.

Focus strategy. The focus strategy reaches a narrow spectrum of individuals who are seeking the specifics of what the merchandiser, the manufacturing, or the service company have to offer. Instead of being driven by low cost or differentiation, organizations that use the focus strategy deliver a product aimed at servicing a target market effectively and efficiently. Within the focus strategy, an organization may still deliver low cost or differentiation to the spectrum which falls into the focused group.

Stuck in the Middle. Organizations that find themselves stuck in the middle have no competitive advantage. Stuck in the middle means that the organization must take steps in one direction or another, laying claim in one of the three specific strategies in order to gain any type of competitive advantage. An organization that finds itself stuck in the middle may find that it takes time and considerable amount of effort to become "unstuck."

A managerial accountant inside an organization that is stuck in the middle will have conflicting goals and unclear objectives as to his or her role as it relates to controlling costs. Should increased margins be achieved through higher prices or lower costs?

QCT Triangle

The Strategic QCT Triangle is another model for implementing strategy. Different from Porter's model, the QCT Triangle model states that corporate competition includes three dimensions instead of two dimensions. The three dimensions of QCT are quality, cost, and time (Figure 4.2). Porter's dimensions were narrow and broad. The key to the QCT Triangle is that all three dimensions are occurring simultaneously for an organization's individual clients. Competition relies on meeting customer needs in all three areas. Customers want different levels of quality, cost, and time, so distinctions are made in competition based on the interactions of the three components.

Quality. Quality refers to the total experience of the customer with the product, including features found on the product and the performance of those features. According to the model, quality may also include after-sale support and service. Different customers have different expectations about the quality of the products or services they purchase, and, thus, distinctions between competitors can be found relating to quality.

Managerial accounting helps management achieve quality goals by the way in which the managerial accountant measures and reports information to management. Such information includes tracking reworking, costs associated with warranty, reports of losses from selling poor quality, and other similar information.

Cost. Costs for an organization refer to the resources used by the organization and may include various costs as presented in the value chain. Organizations incur costs from research and development, from suppliers, from production, from disposition, and from various other areas of the value chain. Costs may also include costs expended by the customer. There may be costs associated with maintaining and disposing of the product the customer purchases. As with quality, the costs a buyer is willing to pay will vary from buyer to buyer.

The managerial accountant's role as it relates to cost includes reporting on various resources used by products produced in order to determine profitability and analyze cost structures.

Time. Time refers to the supply chain data as well as the innovation of new technologies. As noted

MAKE IT REAL 4-1

McDonald's is a great example for what not to do when you have a strategy that is working. McDonald's is known for providing fast burgers to a family-friendly target market. However, in 1996, McDonald's attempted to come out with an adult line of sandwiches, which was completely contradictory to the current strategy of low-cost burgers with a target market of children and families. McDonalds spent $100 million on advertising the "Arch Deluxe," which was more than they had spent on advertising for any other sandwich. Lesson learned for McDonald's: "If it isn't broken, don't fix it."

Reference

McGrath, J. "Five Failed McDonald's Menu Items." Retrieved from http://money.howstuffworks.com/5-failed-mcdonalds-menu-items3.htm (2008).

in Topic 3, the supply chain is focused on various wait times, move times, production times, and other time constraints that occur within the supply chain. Time can also refer to the ability for a product to come out with new features and technologies.

Managerial accounting measures and reports on such time issues by noting lost sales and profits from late product introductions as well as late deliveries to clients caused by supplier delays or production process delays.

LEARNING GOAL 2: Discuss the Forces That Shape Strategy

When an organization uses a specific strategy to further its goals, the strategy is a direct result of the organization's mission and vision. However, selection of strategy is also driven by various forces that occur in the competitive environment. Such forces evaluate an organization's competitive behavior and shape the direction that an organization will take when deciding on a strategy that fits in line with its mission and vision. The competitive environment is an environment with its own set of rules. Understanding such rules helps to determine if an organization will succeed and be profitable. As managerial accountants, charged with providing accounting feedback in a competitive environment, an understanding for the competitive environment is vital.

Competition is a large part of conducting business in today's world. Several approaches have addressed the competitive environment, offering various explanations for how and why organizations maintain a competitive advantage. Strategy is intended to provide competitive advantage, but an organization must understand the competitive environment within the industry. Such approaches to understanding industry competition include 1) the Structure-Conduct-Performance (SCP) approach, 2) Porter's Five-Forces Model, 3) New Industrial Organization Approach, and 4) Resource-Based Perspective. In light of the competitive environment, organizations build strategy that will help them to be profitable.

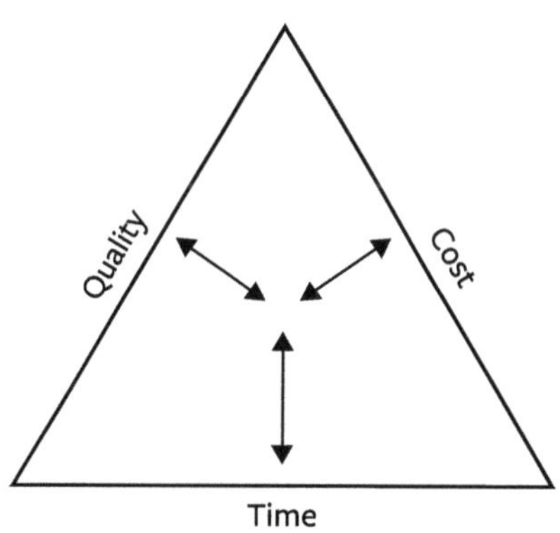

FIGURE 4.2 QCT Triangle.

Structure-Conduct-Performance (SCP) Approach

The SCP approach to the competitive environment is a classical approach and has served as the starting point for many other approaches (Figure 4.3). The SCP approach was the main approach used in the mid-1900s and consisted of three main elements: 1) *structure* of industries, degree of concentration; 2) *conduct* of firms, pricing advertising and spending, and 3) *performance* of industries, profitability and market power. Within the three main elements are causal relationships between structure and conduct, structure and performance, and conduct and performance. In the SCP approach, the strongest relationship is seen as that between structure and performance.

As structure relates to performance, the most important consideration relating to structure is barriers to entry. Simply put, barriers to entry refers to the difficulty new organizations have entering into an industry. In terms of performance, the more market power an organization has, the greater the profitability. Thus, the connection between structure and performance implies that the more difficult it is to enter the market, the greater market power an organization can have and, thus, a greater level of profitability. Conversely, the easier it is for organizations to enter the market, the less market power each organization has and, thus, a lesser level of profitability.

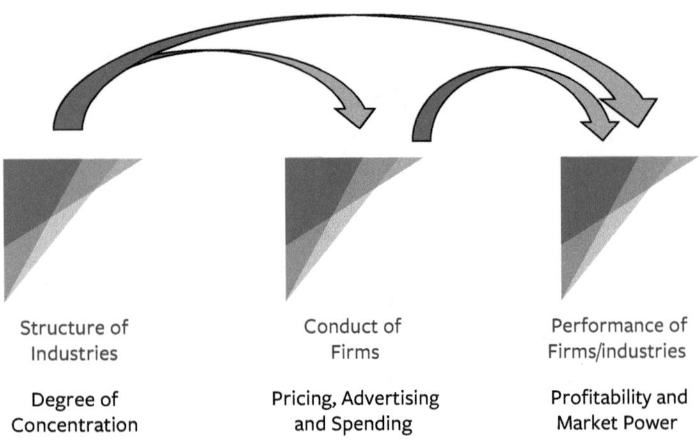

FIGURE 4.3 SCP Elements and Relationships.

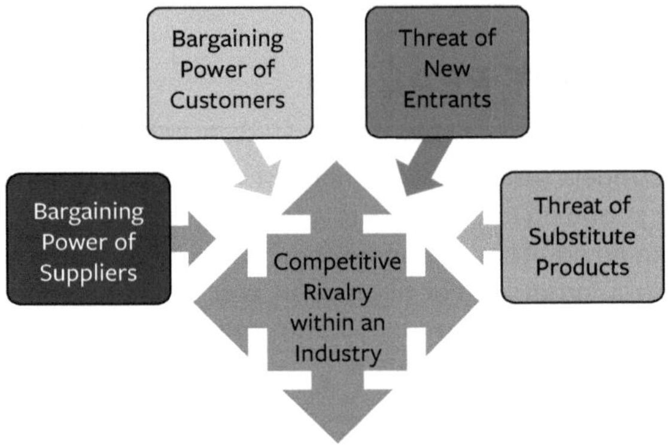

FIGURE 4.4 Porter's Five Forces.

Porter's Five-Forces Model

Porter's model was born from the SCP approach and emerged in 1980. Porter's model broke down the competitive environment into industries, which Porter referred to as "arenas" (Figure 4.4). The arenas, according to Porter, are where the competitive forces exist. Porter distinguished five competitive forces: 1) threat of entry, 2) intensity of rivalry among existing competitors, 3) pressure from substitute products, 4) bargaining power of buyers, and 5) bargaining power of suppliers. (Horngren, Datar, and Rajan, 2015).

Porter noted that a joint influence of the five forces determines the intensity of competition in each industry. The greater the strength of the five forces, the lower profitability will be in a given industry (Horngren, Datar, & Rajan, 2015).

Intensity of rivalry among existing firms. The intensity of the existing rivalry will impact the competitive environment. Growth rates, cost structures, and concentration of leading players may impact the attractiveness of an industry. The more intense the rivalry among existing firms, the less attractive the industry.

Threat of new entry. Threat of new entrants refers to the ability for competition to enter the market. For example, certain industries are easier to enter. Merchandising industries that are easy to enter include selling makeup or candles or just general merchandise sales. In the manufacturing industry, it may be relatively easy to open a restaurant or a company that manufactures coffee. In a service industry, it is relatively easy to enter the tax accounting profession, as there are no entrance exams or minimum qualifications. Industries that are easy to enter become flooded with competitors.

Threat of new entrants goes beyond simple ease of entry and considers various other factors such as economies of scales, brand identity, capital needed, government policy, and various other barriers that can be faced. Higher regulation also makes it difficult to enter an industry, as does existing successful organizations, or capital-intensive types of businesses. Higher barriers to entry means that less competition will exist while lower barriers to entry means that more competition exists.

Pressure from substitute products. Pressure from substitute products refers to customers' ability to look outside a given industry for their needs to be met. For example, if an organization enters into the car sales industry, the risk of substitute products would look different for a dealership located in a small town with no public transportation than it would look for a dealership in a large town with substitute opportunities. In New York City, individuals can take a taxi, ride the train, take the subway, walk from location to location, or ride a bike. In a small rural community, individuals may only have the substitute transportation opportunity of walking, riding a bike, or catching a ride from a friend. Thus, there are fewer substitutions. More opportunities for substitute products result in a less attractive industry. Substitute products are any products that can provide the same functional use as the product being sold in a given industry. If many substitute products exist, the rivalry within the competitive environment will increase.

Bargaining power of buyers. Buyers have higher bargaining power when there is a greater number of suppliers than buyers. This can be seen in the housing market. When the housing market is a "buyer's" market, there are more sellers than buyers. Thus, the buyers have bargaining power. Greater bargaining power of buyers makes an industry less attractive. The internet has greatly increased buyer bargaining power.

Bargaining power of suppliers. The bargaining power of suppliers refers to the ability of an organization's suppliers to have power. When there are limited suppliers, the suppliers have greater bargaining power. When there are numerous suppliers, the suppliers have less bargaining power.

Industrial Organization Approach

The Industrial Organization Theory is an alternative approach to understanding the competitive environment. The Industrial Organizational Approach considers interaction of the competitive environment and aligns to Game Theory, which studies conflict and cooperation. The focus of the Industrial Organizational Approach is that there is an interdependence of behavior regarding the competitive environment. Porter's model fails to consider interdependence of the players and thus must exist inside a perfectly functioning competitive environment. The Industrial Organization Approach, however, suggests that players behave competitively and strategically. Thus, retaliatory situations can arise.

Resource-Based Perspective

In the Resource-Based Perspective of the competitive environment, organizations differ in their competitive advantage because of their level of resources. Thus, a firm could maintain a competitive advantage, given enough resources. Firms that have a greater competitive advantage have a greater level of resources. Resources are contingent on an organization's efficient use of their current resources and their ability to control prices within a competitive industry.

LEARNING GOAL 3: Understand Management's Use of Strategy

Strategy is used by management in a variety of ways, including decisions regarding pricing. For the purposes of the discussion, we will focus on management's use of strategy as a way to position an organization in a competitive environment and distinguish the organization

GIVE IT A WHIRL 4-1

1. The Five-Forces model and the QCT model differ in many ways. Relate each term below to the correct model. Use "F" for Five-Forces and "Q" for QCT.
   Three-dimensional_____
   Cost_____
   Cost Leadership_____
   Quality_____
   Product Differentiation_____
   Broad_____
   Time _____
   Focus_____
   Narrow_____
   Two-dimensional _____

(Answers: Q, Q, F, Q, F, F, Q, F, F, F)

2. The Five-Force Model of the competitive environment involves the following forces. Match the description to the forces.
   1. Threat of entry _____
   2. Intensity of rivalry among existing competitors _____
   3. Pressure from substitute products _____
   4. Bargaining power of buyers _____
   5. Bargaining power of suppliers _____
      a. Growth rates, cost structures, and concentration of leading players impact this force.
      b. Having a greater number of suppliers impacts this force.
      c. This force relates to the level of barriers that exist to entry into the industry.
      d. Refers to a customer's ability to look outside the industry.
      e. Having more buyers impacts this force.

(Answers: c, a, d, e, b)

from its competitors. Managers refer to developing position and distinction as the value proposition, the promise of delivering value to the customer. Strategy must run throughout an organization, being consistent in its development, execution, and evaluation so that management can gain the benefits competitive strategy has to offer.

Position

The position of an organization in a competitive market refers to how the company is perceived in the marketplace. Considering an organization's position means identifying 1) the target market (how the product is positioned in the minds of the chosen target market), 2) frame of reference (that which defines the market), and 3) point of difference (how the company's organization is different from others in the marketplace).

According to Moore and Helstein (2007), six criteria determine an organization's position:

- Relevance: Does it matter to the customers?
- Clarity: Is it clear to the consumer?
- Credibility: Will the consumers believe it?
- Uniqueness: Is it set apart from the competition?

- Attainability: Can claims be delivered?
- Sustainability: Can the position be maintained over time?

Distinction

Offering distinction to customers allows an organization to differentiate itself from its competitors. The essence of distinction is that customers buy benefits, not products. Differentiation can be physical or perceptual. For example, if all a consumer wants is a cheeseburger, why does it matter where they go? Don't McDonald's, Five Guys Burgers, Red Robin, and Culvers all offer cheeseburgers? If a consumer wants a cheeseburger, he or she should be able to go to any restaurant that offers cheeseburgers. However, different consumers have different preferences for where they go because of differentiations that meet their needs. When a client has a car full of children and needs a cheeseburger quickly along with a toy to entertain the children, he or she will go to McDonald's. At McDonald's, the client is buying quick service and the convenience of drive-through, which distinguishes it from Red Robin. When the client who is going to Red Robin is buying a cheeseburger, the client is buying the experience of dining out. The differentiation in the two burger options is in the attributes of the burger as well as the positioning of the restaurant in the marketplace.

For each strategy, whether it be a strategy focused on low cost or one that is focused on product differentiation, the distinction element must be present. Thus, in a low-cost strategy, low cost would not be enough for product distinction. McDonald's and Burger King offer burgers that are comparatively priced. However, consumers still select one over the other due to physical or perceptual differences other than price.

Strategy Map

A strategy map is used by managers as an organizational method to ensure that their operations match their strategy plan (Figure 4.5). A strategy map should describe the strategy, measure the strategy, and provide opportunities to obtain feedback regarding the elements. The strategy map is a planning tool for that which will be evaluated by use of the Balanced Scorecard during the Evaluation Phase. The strategy map is divided into four categories: 1) learning and growth processes, 2) internal business processes, 3) customer processes, and 4) financial processes. The overarching strategy should be mapped to each of the four processes (perspectives). Each process provides an objective that aligns with the competitive strategy and a way to quantitatively measure the objective.

Learning and Growth Processes

The learning and growth process stresses employee competencies and process innovation. The process considers the human capital, the information capital, and the organizational capital. If the corporate strategy is a cost-leadership strategy, the processes should reinforce cost leadership by making the product better, cheaper, and faster. Using improvements such as total quality management (TQM), Six Sigma, just in time, and activity-based management, an organization should be able to align the processes of learning and growth with the overall strategy for cost leadership.

If the corporate strategy is that of product differentiation, the process should reinforce distinctions of the product, making the product original. Therefore, the learning and growth process would focus on innovation and creativity of the workforce.

General objectives and corresponding measurement criteria are described below. The following objectives and measures could be tweaked to accommodate cost leadership, product differentiation, or a focus strategy:

TABLE 4.1 Learning and Growth Processes: Objective and Measurement

Objective	Measurement
1. **Build competencies (human capital)**	Key business processes empowered to lower levels
2. **Integrate IT (information capital)**	IT effectiveness survey
3. **Create an atmosphere of empowerment (organizational capital)**	Empowerment index

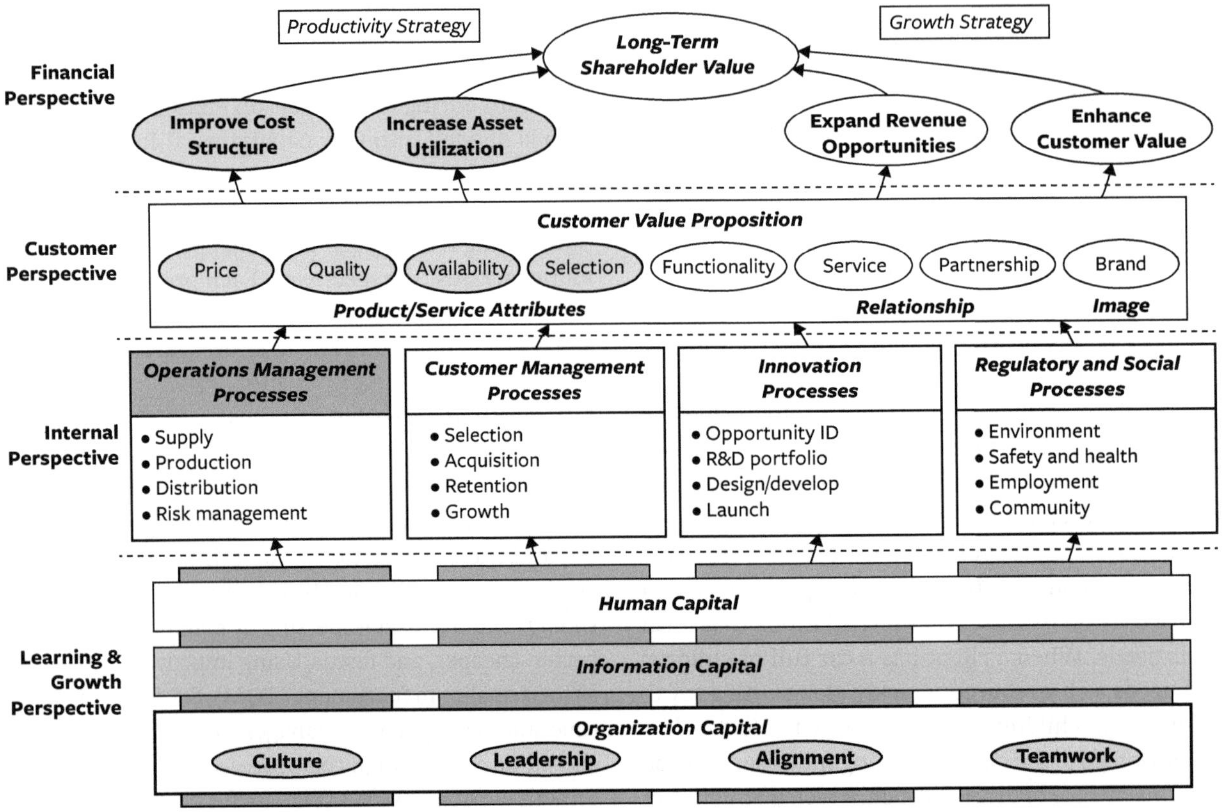

FIGURE 4.5 Generic Strategy Map.

Internal Business Process

The internal business processes consider four areas that relate to the functioning of a business. The four areas include 1) operations of the business, 2) customer management, 3) innovation of the business process, and 4) regulation and social aspects of the organization. An organization with a cost-leadership strategy would focus on streamlining the processes, whereas the organization with a product-differentiation strategy would focus on providing high performance products and innovative ways of developing products.

General objectives and measurement criteria are described below. The following objectives and measures could be tweaked to accommodate cost leadership, product differentiation, or a focus strategy:

TABLE 4.2 Internal Business Process: Objective and Measurement

Objective	Measurement
1. Upgrade manufacturing process	Percentage reduction of wait times
2. Upgrade delivery process	Percentage reduction of delivery time
3. Reduce rework	Percentage reduction of rework

Customer Processes

The customer processes focus on three areas as they relate to customers: 1) product/service attributes, 2) relationship, and 3) image. When customers consider product/service attributes, they look at price, quality,

MAKE IT REAL 4-2

Even when the strategy is that of cost leadership, quality cannot be completely disregarded. Likewise, when the strategy is differentiation, cost cannot be completely disregarded. One such example of a cost-leadership strategy that completely disregarded quality is the Yugo. The Yugo has been touted as the worst car in history, at least the worst car in American history. The vehicle was sold in 1985 for $3,995, while maintaining a substantial profit in the U.S. market. Vuic (2010), author of a book that discussed the mistakes made with the Yugo, said that the Yugo is an example of an inability to understand the techniques for competing and succeeding in an open capitalist society. The car was cheap and poorly made, even a safety hazard. Clearly, cost leadership was the strategic goal upper management was trying to capture. However, with a complete disregard for quality, the strategy and the vehicle were a failure.

Reference

Vuic,. *The Yugo: The Rise and Fall of the Worst Car in History*. Canada: D&M Publishers, Inc, 2010.

availability, and selection. When customers evaluate relationships, they do so via functionality, service, and partnership. When customers consider image, they reflect on brand.

General objectives and measurement criteria are provided below. The following objectives and measures could be tweaked to accommodate cost leadership, product differentiation, or a focus strategy:

TABLE 4.3 Customer Processes: Objective and Measurement

Objective	Measurement
1. Increased customer satisfaction	Customer satisfaction surveys
2. Expansion of new customers	Number of new customers
3. Increase products used per customer	Number of products used by each customer

Financial Process

The financial process relates to areas of longer-term shareholder value by concentrating on improved cost structure, increased asset utilization, expanding revenue opportunities, and enhancing customer value.

General objectives and measurement criteria are described below. The following objectives and measures could be tweaked to accommodate cost leadership, product differentiation, or a focus strategy:

TABLE 4.4 Financial Process: Objective and Measurement

Objective	Measurement
1. Increased market share	Percent increase over base year
2. Increased profit margins	Margin percent
3. Maximum asset utilization	Asset turnover ratio

LEARNING GOAL 4: Discuss How Responsibility Accounting Is a Function of Strategy

As strategy is implemented throughout organizations, one must consider decentralization. Decentralization refers to the decision-making authority that is spread throughout the organization instead of remaining with upper management. For many organizations, the growth of the organization makes decentralization necessary. When decentralization occurs, however, strategy must be maintained for different levels of responsibility.

When organizations spread out the decision-making responsibilities, lower-level management, now charged with decision-making capabilities, must be

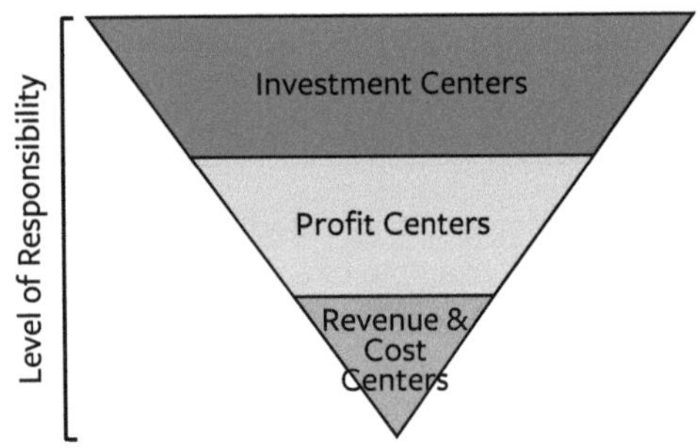

FIGURE 4.6 Responsibility Centers.

able to link into the strategic goals of the organization. The term reasonability center refers to different areas of an organization for which management is accountable (Figure 4.6). The four responsibility centers typically considered are 1) cost center, 2) revenue center, 3) profit center, and 4) investment center.

Cost Center

The manager of a cost center is concerned only with costs. Cost centers consist of service departments and manufacturing areas of an organization. Examples of costs centers include the accounting department, general administration departments, purchasing departments, and various areas of manufacturing. The expectations for a cost center manager are to lower costs. In the process of controlling costs, however, a cost center manager must make decisions that are in line with the strategic goals of an organization. Cost center managers may have success for their area measured both quantitatively and qualitatively.

Revenue Center

The manager of a revenue center is concerned only with revenues. Revenue centers consist of sales departments, where the expectations are for revenues to be increased. As with the cost managers, revenue center managers must make decisions regarding increase in revenue that adhere to the company goals. Revenue center manager's success may be measured based on qualitative customer feedback in addition to revenue dollars brought into the company.

Profit Center

The manager of a profit center is concerned with both costs and revenues but not investments. Profit centers are typically branch, division, and department managers. Such managers track both income and costs to ascertain whether their area of responsibility is meeting goals and maintaining strategy.

Investment Center

The manager of an investment center holds the highest level of responsibility of the four responsibility centers. The manager has control over costs, revenues, and investments in operating assets. Typically, an investment center manger would be located in the corporate office as an upper-level manager. Such managers may be instrumental in helping to develop corporate strategy.

TOPIC 4 REFERENCES

Ansari, S., Bell, J., Klammer, T., and Lawrence, C. *Management Accounting: A strategic focus.* United States of America: Houghton, Co,2004.

Child, G. "Illustration of Porter's 5 Forces." Retrieved from https://upload.wikimedia.org/wikipedia/commons/6/66/Porters_five_forces.PNG (2006).

Fadeev, D. "Michael Porter's Three Generic Strategies." Retrieved from https://upload.wikimedia.org/wikipedia/commons/0/0b/Michael_Porter%27s_Three_Generic_Strategies.svg (2014).

Garrison, R.H., Noreen, E.W., and Brewer, P.C. *Managerial Accounting.* New York, NY: McGraw-Hill Companies, Inc., 2012.

Hicks, K., and Moseley, J.L. "Developing and Executing Strategy: Using the Balanced Scorecard for Alignment and Accountability." *Performance Improvement,* 50(8), 41–47. doi:10.1002/pfi.20240 (2011).

Kaplan, R.S. and Norton, D.P. "Strategy Maps." *Strategic Finance.* p. 27–33. (2004)

GIVE IT A WHIRL 4-2

1. Sara owns a nail salon in which she has decided to use a cost-leadership strategy, offering quality nail service at a low cost. Address Sara's position and distinction in the competitive market.

(Answer: Sara needs to address relevance, clarity, credibility, uniqueness, attainability, and sustainability.

Position

1. *Relevance: Does it matter? Yes, because people who normally couldn't afford such service may be able to be pampered.*
2. *Clarity: Is it clear? Sara should bring attention to her lower rates.*
3. *Credibility: Will the consumer believe it? If people check her rates with other nail techs, she will lose credibility if her prices are higher than other nail techs.*
4. *Uniqueness: Is it set apart from the competition? Is there something other than price that can distinguish Sara from her competitors?*
5. *Attainability: Can your claims be delivered? Sara must either accept a lower profit margin than her competitors or find a supplier who offers lower costs than her competitors have.*
6. *Sustainability: Can the position be maintained over time? Is Sara willing to continue having low profit margins?*

Distinction

Sara may offer other distinctions than a low-cost service. Such distinctions could include specialized hours or a free service with every ten services purchased.)

1. Match the entity to the given responsibility center.

TABLE 4.5 Responsibility Center

Responsibility Center	Entity
1. Cost Center ________	a. A retail store.
2. Revenue Center ________	b. The corporate office for the retail store.
3. Profit Center ________	c. The retail store's stocking department.
4. Investment Center ________	d. The retail store's sales department.
	e. The retail store's accounting department.
	f. The distribution center for the retail store.

(Answer: Cost- c,e,f, Revenue – d, Profit – a, Investment – b)

McGrath, J. "Five Failed McDonald's Menu Items." *Money.* Retrieved from http://money.howstuffworks.com/5-failed-mcdonalds-menu-items3.htm (n.d.).

Moore M.C. and Helstein, R.L. (2007). *Positioning: The Essence of Marketing Strategy.* Charlottesville, VA: Darden Business Publishing, 2009.

Ormanidhi, O. and Stringa, O. "Porter's Model of Generic Competitive Strategies." *Business Economics*, 43(3), 55-64. (2008).

Porter, M. *Competitive Strategy: Techniques for Analyzing Industries and Competitors.* New York, NY: Free Press, 1980.

Sheaffer, Z. Landau, D., and Drori, I. "Mission Statement and Performance: An Evidence of 'Coming of Age.'" *Organizational Development Journal, 26*(2). p. 49-62. (2008).

Vuic, J. *The Yugo: The Rise and Fall of the Worst Car in History.* New York: Hill and Wang, 2010.

Zimmermann, J. "Strategy Map." Wikipedia. Retrieved from https://upload.wikimedia.org/wikipedia/commons/9/96/Strategy-maps-overview-image3_%283597259677%29.jpg (2009).

TOPIC 4 FIGURE CREDITS

TOPIC 5 Cost Behavior

LEARNING GOALS

1. Investigate the behavior of fixed, variable, and mixed costs.
2. Use cost behavior to predict costs.
3. Separate fixed and variable components from mixed costs.
4. Explain how the contribution margin format income statement is driven by cost behavior.

INTRODUCTION

Topic 5 is focused on cost behavior. Because the income statement is more valuable for predicting outcomes when it is arranged in the contribution format, the contribution format income statement is arranged by cost behavior. Managerial accountants should be familiar with the different nuances associated with cost behavior.

Learning Goal 1 takes a closer look at cost behavior as a way to define costs. Although Topic 3 discussed the behaviors of fixed, variable, and mixed costs, this topic seeks to convey a full understanding for the behaviors at an individual level as well as in total. Relevant range is discussed as a function of fully understanding behaviors of both fixed and variable costs.

Learning Goal 2 further analyzes fixed and variable costs by explaining the predictive qualities of the costs. Learning Goal 3 expands on the predictability of fixed and variable costs by explaining how mixed costs can be broken down into the fixed and variable components. Finally, Learning Goal 4 takes a closer look at the income statement arranged under the contribution format. Cost behavior is a foundation of the contribution format income statement.

LEARNING GOAL 1: Investigate the Behavior of Fixed, Variable, and Mixed Costs

Cost Behavior

As discussed in Topic 3, costs can be defined in terms of their behavior as either fixed or variable. Variable costs vary in total in relation to the level of activity while fixed costs do not vary in total with the level of activity.

Fixed and Variable Cost

In order to fully understand fixed and variable costs, we must first understand the cost object. As explained in Topic 3, the cost object is anything for which we wish to gather costs. Let's say the cost object for which we are measuring costs is an appliance manufacturer. We want to measure costs specific to the refrigerator manufacturing department within this appliance manufacturing company. Within the refrigerator manufacturing department, the level of activity for which we will consider variable costs is the number of refrigerators produced. As noted in Figure 5.1 below, the variable costs will increase/decrease in total (Y axis) as the number of refrigerators produced increases/decreases (X axis), and the fixed costs will be unaffected in total as the number of refrigerators increases/decreases.

However, if we look deeper at the cost behavior, we learn that how a cost behaves in total is not how that cost behaves per unit. Therefore, when we look at

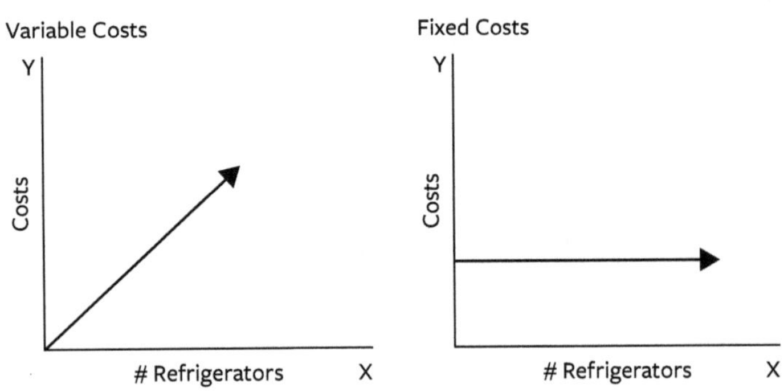

FIGURE 5.1 Variable and Fixed Costs.

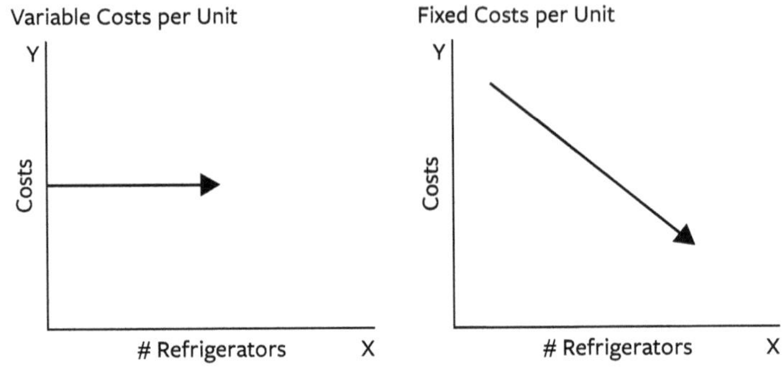

FIGURE 5.2 Variable and Fixed Costs per Unit.

the per unit values of the variable costs as compared with the fixed costs, the per-unit behavior will look like the graphs in Figure 5.2. As the number of refrigerators increases/decreases, the per unit *variable* cost will remain unchanged, while as the number of refrigerators increases/decreases, the *fixed* cost per unit will decrease/increase, inversely with the level of activity.

Relevant Range. A concept associated with the behavior of costs is that of relevant range. Relevant range refers to the range of activity for which variable costs behave as variable costs and fixed costs behave as fixed costs. Outside the relevant range, costs may take on different cost behaviors. For example, a manager may pay rent of $2,000 per month for 3,000 square feet of space. The rent expense is a fixed cost. The manager is able to produce 1,500 refrigerators in the 3,000 square feet of space. If the need for more square feet arises due to an increase in the number of refrigerators produced, the fixed cost will change. Perhaps the manager will need to enter into a new contract for more space. The cost will be $4,000 for 7,000 square feet. The manager can produce a total of 2,500 refrigerators in 7,000 square feet. In this example, the fixed cost behaves similar to a variable cost, but instead of a gradual line, it is a stair-step. The relevant range refers to level of activity associated with each horizontal cost level. In the example of the refrigerators, the relevant range for fixed costs of $2,000 is 0-1,500 refrigerators, and the relevant range for 0-2,500 refrigerators would become $3,000. See Figure 5.3.

Variable costs are also impacted by relevant range. Although variable costs discussed in this text are

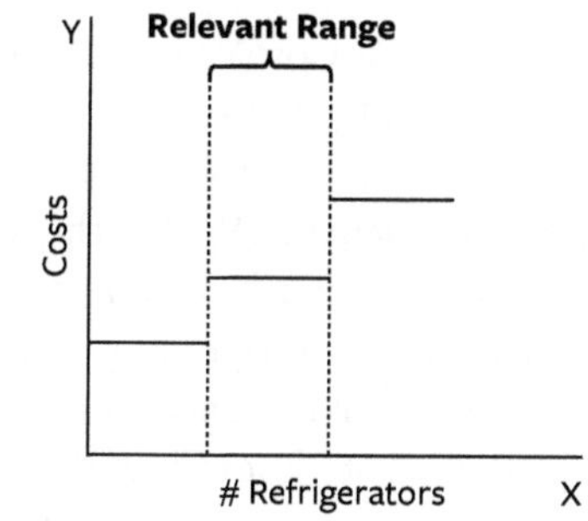

FIGURE 5.3 Fixed Costs and the Relevant Range.

assumed to be linear (represented by a straight line), many variable costs are not linear but are curvilinear. Costs that are curvilinear behave as variable within a given relevant range. See Figure 5.4.

Types of Fixed Costs. Although fixed costs are not impacted by levels of activity within a specific relevant range, fixed costs are impacted by commitment. The managerial accountant may encounter fixed costs that cannot be reduced or significantly changed in any way because they are committed fixed costs. Such costs include things like real estate taxes, insurance costs, long-term rent contracts or mortgage investments, investments in equipment, and similar types of costs that cannot be changed in the short term.

Other fixed costs are not of such a high level of commitment. Fixed costs that have greater capacity for short-term changes are called discretionary fixed costs. Such costs arise from management decision and include costs such as advertising and other management-focused fixed-cost decisions.

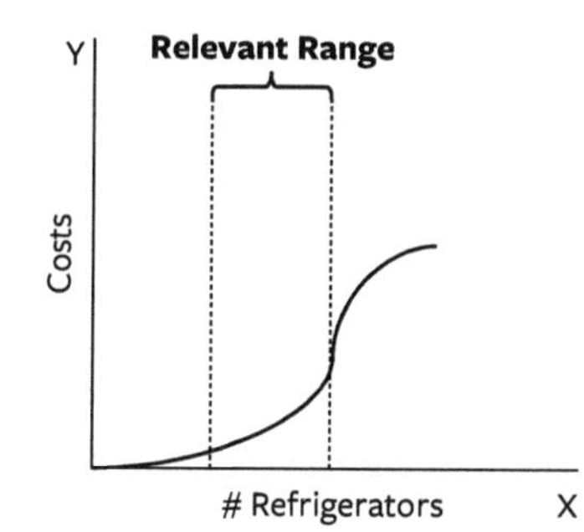

FIGURE 5.4 Variable Costs and the Relevant Range.

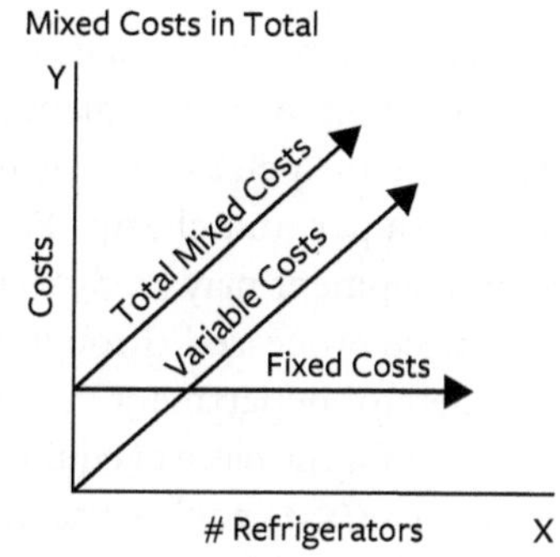

FIGURE 5.5 Mixed Costs in Total.

Mixed Costs

Although some costs are purely fixed and other costs are purely variable, certain costs are a mix of each. Mixed costs contain behaviors of both fixed and variable costs. The behavior of a mixed cost will increase in total with the level of activity but will decrease per unit with the level of activity. See Figure 5.5 and Figure 5.6.

Notice that on the mixed costs graph in Figure 5.5, the total cost does not start at zero. Instead, the total cost starts at the level of the fixed cost. When you have mixed costs, your total costs cannot go below the amount of fixed cost. If, in the example of the refrigerators, with fixed costs of $20,000 per month, total costs cannot decrease below $20,000 because those costs are fixed; the company will have them regardless of whether it produces 100 refrigerators or no refrigerators. Thus, in this mixed costs scenario, the total cost starts at the $20,000 level and goes up from there.

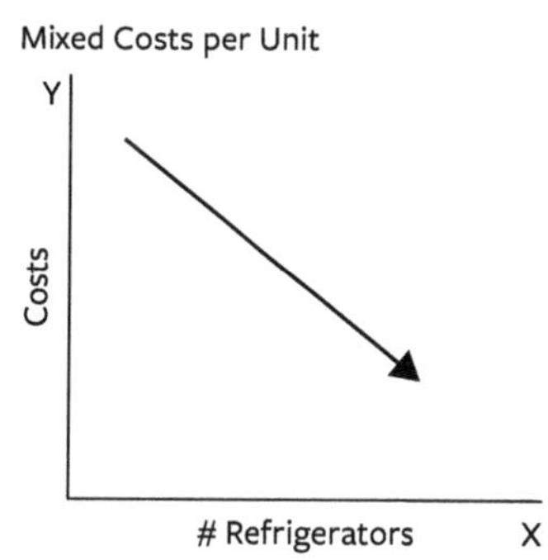

FIGURE 5.6 Mixed Costs per Unit.

For the refrigerator department, a mixed cost may be the cost of leasing a piece of equipment used in the refrigerator department. Such a cost may have a base lease price and also a per unit charge. For example, a leased piece of equipment may be $500 per month plus $3 for each piece processed through the equipment. If the refrigerator department processes 1,500 refrigerators, the cost for the piece of equipment would be $5,000 per month (($3*1,500) + $500). Breaking the cost down per unit would result in a per-unit cost of $3.33 ($5,000/1,500) per refrigerator. If the refrigerator department increases to 1,700 refrigerators, the total cost would be $5,600 (($3*1,700) + $500), and the per-unit cost would be $3.29 per refrigerator ($5,600/1,700). If, instead, the refrigerator department produces 1,200 refrigerators, the total cost would be $4,100 (($3*1,200) + $500), and the per-unit cost would be $3.42 ($4,100/1,200). Note that as the number of refrigerators increases, the total cost also increases while the per-unit cost decreases.

See the summary table below for how fixed, variable, and mixed costs will change in total and per unit in relation to level of activity. Note that mixed costs contain elements of both fixed and variable costs.

TABLE 5.1 If... Then...

Cost	Activity	Cost Per Unit	Cost In Total
Variable	Increases/ Decreases	**Stays the same**	**Increases/ Decreases**
Fixed	Increases/ Decreases	**Decreases/ Increases**	**Stays the same**
Mixed	Increases/ Decreases	**Decreases/ Increases**	**Increases/ Decreases**

LEARNING GOAL 2: Use Cost Behavior to Predict Costs

As the managerial accountant seeks to help managers have a better understanding of costs and be more competitive, the managerial accountant uses an understanding of cost behavior to predict costs. Predicting costs means that when levels of activity change, management knows how the variable costs will change and how the fixed costs will change. One tool used for predictive purposes is Cost Volume Profit analysis. Topic 6 will discuss CVP analysis.

Let's return to the refrigerator division of the appliance manufacturing company. Within the refrigerator manufacturing department, the organization may typically manufacture 1,500 refrigerators every month. Management may receive a special order for 500 refrigerators and needs to know how the increase in refrigerators will impact costs. Knowing that variable costs change with the level of activity, the managerial accountant can predict that the variable costs in total will increase directly and proportionately with the increased number of refrigerators. Likewise, if circumstances occur and the department is only able to manufacture 1,000 refrigerators, 500 below the typical amount, the managerial accountant knows that the variable costs will decrease in total.

Also, knowing the behavior of fixed costs will give management insight into how the fixed costs may or may not be impacted. Thus, if the department produces 500 more refrigerators within the relevant range, fixed costs in total will not be impacted. Likewise, if the department produces 500 fewer refrigerators within the relevant range, the fixed costs will not be impacted in total.

Understanding the behavior of costs is not isolated to the costs in total, however. The refrigerator manufacturing department may also want to understand the per unit cost amounts. To understand per unit cost amounts, you must understand that variable costs do not change per unit while fixed costs vary inversely with the number of units produced. Therefore, when the refrigerator manufacturing department produces 500 more refrigerators, the variable cost per unit will be unchanged. Although the variable cost in total increases with the level of activity, the cost per unit amount remains unchanged. Likewise, when the number of refrigerators is reduced by 500 units, the variable cost in total will decrease while the per-unit amount will remain unchanged.

Fixed costs will have an inverse relationship with the level of activity. When the number of refrigerators increases, the cost per unit of fixed cost will decrease, and when the number of units of refrigerators decreases, the cost per unit of fixed costs will increase. One should be careful when relying on fixed costs per unit, however, because the per-unit amounts can be misleading. When units produced increases, the

MAKE IT REAL 5-1

Every company can benefit from understanding cost behavior. For example, in order to be competitive, Pizza Hut expanded its menu choices, expanded its ordering capabilities into digital markets, and offered a clothing line. Before introducing new products, companies must understand the costs that are going to exist in the new product line and how those costs are going to behave. Before Pizza Hut decided to offer a line of clothing, it would want to consider the fixed and variable costs that would become part of cost structure for the company. Variable costs would include the cost of the raw materials to make the clothing and the wages of those producing the clothing, whereas the fixed costs would include the rent on the facility that produces and houses the clothing line as well as the management team in charge of the product line. The added menu choices also come with additional cost, including the expanded ingredients needed to make the flavored sauces and flavor crusts, as well as the cost of the new additional topping choices.

References

Kramer, J. "A Pizza Hut Express in San Marcos, Texas." Wikimedia. Retrieved from https://commons.wikimedia.org/wiki/File%3APizza_hut_express.jpg (2006).

"Pizza Hut Dishing Disappointment." *Food Business News*. Retrieved from http://www.foodbusinessnews.net/articles/news_home/Financial-Performance/2015/04/Pizza_Hut_dishing_disappointme.aspx?ID={4E15C742-3CB2-4DB2-A0D0-8524035BEE84}&cck=1 (2016).

"Pizza Hut Releases Their 2016 Clothing Line." *Mental Floss*. Retrieved from http://mentalfloss.com/article/72835/pizza-hut-releases-their-2016-clothing-line (2016).

FIGURE 5.7 Pizza Hut.

fixed costs will be spread over more units; therefore, the per-unit costs decrease. However, the fixed costs do not truly fluctuate with level of activity.

This ability to predict costs allows management to perform CVP analyses and predict profit. Understanding how costs behave can save organizations from making bad decisions based on gut-level feelings and "shots in the dark." When we discuss CVP in Topic 6, it will be assumed that you have an understanding for fixed and variable cost behavior both in total and per unit.

GIVE IT A WHIRL 5-1

1. Review the following costs and define them as fixed (F) or variable (V).
   a. Shoe strings for a shoe manufacturing company.______
   b. Rent for a manufacturing company.______
   c. A factory manager's salary.______
   d. The maintenance staff's hourly wages of a manufacturing plant.______
   e. The night security guard's salary of a manufacturing plant.______
   f. The cost of pianos for a piano retailer.______
   g. Depreciation of machinery using the straight-line method.______
   h. Depreciation of machining using units-of-production method.______
   i. Plastic for a manufacturing company producing plastic water bottles. ______
   j. Wood for a picture frame store.______
   k. Dirt for a greenhouse.______

(Answers: V, F, F, V, F, V, F, V, V, V, V)

2. Predict the costs for the following scenario:

Pet Meals on Wheels is a company that delivers pet food to clients who cannot get out of the house to purchase nutritious meals for their pets. The company sells the food by the pound as a cost of $1.25 per pound. The fuel costs are directly related to the miles driven, and the cost of the dog food is directly related to the pounds sold. The owner of Pet Meals on Wheels must also pay for liability insurance at $75 per month, insurance for the vehicles at $750 per year, and rent for the storage unit where the food is kept at $100 per month. The company typically delivers 750 pounds of food to 105 clients each week. In delivering the food, Pet Meals on Wheels owner Lori Johnson drives 1,600 miles. The cost of gas is currently at $1.89 per gallon. Lori has just taken on six new clients. One of the clients has three big dogs which eat a total of 35 pounds of food a week. The other five clients have small dogs each eating five pounds of food each week. The client with the three dogs lives fifteen miles from Lori's home base (round trip), and the other five clients live within ten miles each (round trip). Predict the additional costs of taking on the six new clients.

(Answers:

Variable costs:

Fuel (1.89 per mile): $(1.89 \times 15 \text{ miles}) + (1.89 \times 50) = \$122.85$
Dog food (1.25 per lb): $(1.25 \times 35) + (1.25 \times 25) = \$75$
Fixed costs: Will not change with the increase in the new clients.)

LEARNING GOAL 3: Separate Fixed and Variable Components from Mixed Costs

Mixed Cost

Costs that are mixed are difficult to predict because they don't follow any relative predictable behavior. Although total costs may increase with level of activity and per-unit costs may decrease with increased level of activity, by looking at the cost in its combined form, the breakdown is not apparent.

In order for mixed costs to be useful to management, mixed costs need to be separated into their fixed and variable components. Thus, in a mixed-costs scenario, a mathematical equation can be used to separate the components and the fixed and variable costs. The following equation represents the relationship between fixed and variable costs.

$$Y = a + bx$$

Y = Total mixed cost
a = Total fixed cost
b = Total variable cost per unit of activity
x = Level of activity

Returning to the example of the refrigerator, fixed costs, represented by a horizontal straight line, are $20,000, and variable costs per unit are $150 each refrigerator. At 500 units, the total cost would be $95,000. Once we understand the equation, we can remove any of the amounts and solve for the unknown.

$$Y = \$20{,}000 + \$150(500)$$

There are numerous methods to separate mixed costs into their fixed and variable components including the use of scatter plots, the high-low method, and regression analysis. The two methods discussed below are the high-low method and regression analysis.

High-Low Method

The high-low method is one way to solve for unknown fixed and variable amounts with a known total mixed-cost amount.

To use the high-low method, I need to have various points of data with which to work. See the data below. In the appliance manufacturing company, the refrigerator department provided data from January through June. Costs are presented in total. Therefore, we will use the high-low method to help break down the costs into fixed and variable components.

TABLE 5.2 Refrigerator Department Cost Data

Month	Activity Level	Total Costs
January	595	$109,250
February	695	$124,250
March	700	$125,000
April	625	$113,750
May	600	$110,000
June	500	$95,000

High Level of Activity
Low Level of Activity

Step 1: Solve for Variable Costs

From the data provided above, the highest and lowest *months of activity* are selected. The highest month is March, and the lowest month is June. Once the highest and lowest months are selected, the difference in rise (Y axis) is divided by the difference in run (X Axis). This will provide the amount of variable cost per unit.

$$Rise = slope\ of\ the\ line(total\ costs, Y\ axis)$$

$$Run = activity\ level(X\ axis)$$

$$Variable\ Cost\ per\ Unit = \frac{Rise}{Run}$$

$$= \frac{\$125{,}000 - \$95{,}000}{700 - 500} = \frac{\$30{,}000}{200}$$

$$= \$150\ per\ Unit$$

Step 2: Solve for Fixed Costs

Once the variable cost per unit has been established, we can then plug it into the formula, using either the highest or the lowest level of activity. The objective is to solve for fixed costs, using the cost equation.

$$Y = a + bx$$

$$\$125{,}000 = a + \$150(700)$$

$$\$125{,}000 = a + \$105{,}000$$

$$\$125{,}000 - \$105{,}000 = a$$

$$\$20{,}000 = a$$

By using the high-low method, we have learned that fixed costs are $20,000, and variable costs are $150 per unit. The high-low method is a simple formula that can be computed relatively quickly and easily. Other methods are more accurate, however. One such method is regression analysis. Regression analysis can be computed by hand, but it is best to use a calculator or Excel.

Regression Analysis

Regression analysis is another way to solve for unknown fixed and variable amounts, but a known total mixed-cost amount. Regression analysis is superior to the high-low method because regression analysis uses all the points of data, not just the high and low amounts of activity.

Using the same example as I used in the high-low method, I will use the data from the refrigerator department to solve for fixed and variable costs using regression analysis within an Excel spreadsheet.

Step 1: Set Up Excel to Perform a Regression Analysis

Go to:

1. File,
2. Options,
3. Add-Ins,
4. Manage: Select Excel Add-ins at the bottom of the page from the drop down, click "Go," and
5. Ensure "Analysis Toolpack" is selected, Click "OK."

Step 2: Add Data to the Spreadsheet

You can simply cut and paste or add the information manually. In the screenshot below, I cut and pasted from the provided table.

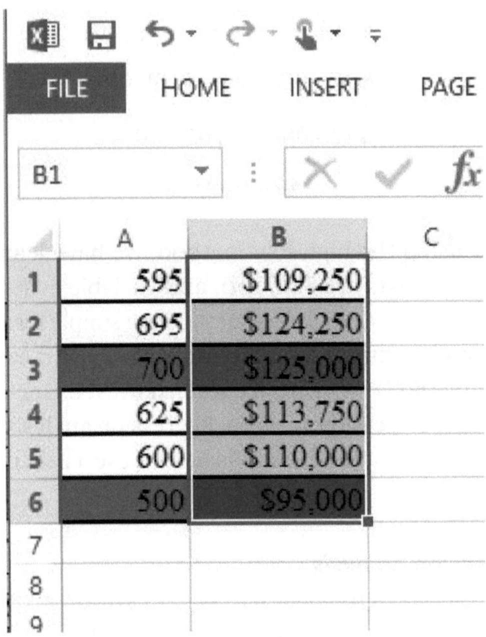

FIGURE 5.8 Data Added to Spreadsheet.

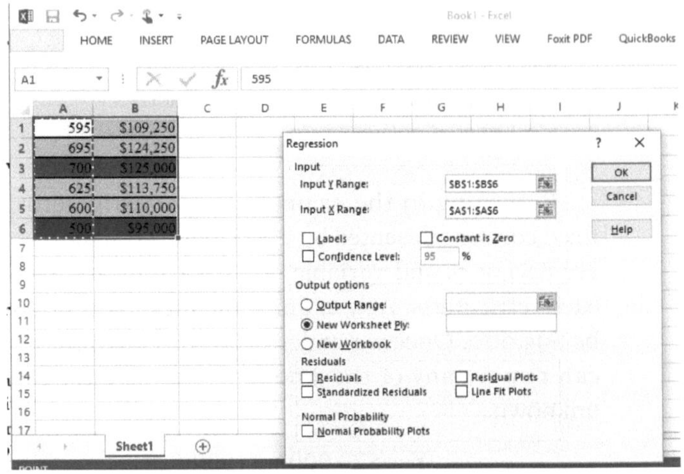

FIGURE 5.9 Viewing the Output.

Once the information is in the spreadsheet click on:

1. Data,
2. Data analysis,
3. Select "Regression," Click "OK," and
4. Add your inputs.

Your "Y" inputs will be the total costs.

Your "X" inputs will be your levels of activity, as noted below.

To add inputs simply select the data and paste it directly into the appropriate input area.

Once the data is added, click "OK" to view the output.

From the output noted above, the following three amounts are the relevant amounts in separating fixed and variable components of a mixed cost:

1. R Square = Goodness of fit. This number should be between 0 and 1. "0" indicates no fit and "1" indicates a perfect fit.
2. Intercept = Fixed amount
3. X Variable = Variable amount

Note that in this example there was a perfect fit. In real life, there will never be a perfect fit. Also note that the results of the regression analysis

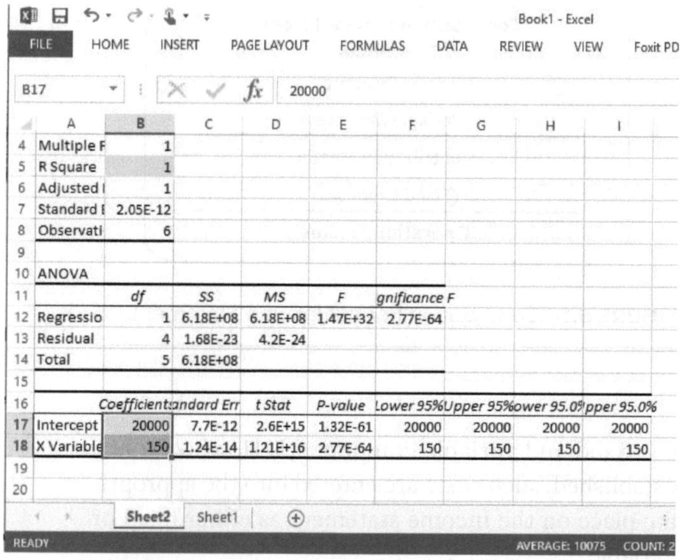

	A	B	C	D	E	F	G	H	I
4	Multiple F	1							
5	R Square	1							
6	Adjusted I	1							
7	Standard E	2.05E-12							
8	Observati	6							
9									
10	ANOVA								
11		df	SS	MS	F	gnificance F			
12	Regressio	1	6.18E+08	6.18E+08	1.47E+32	2.77E-64			
13	Residual	4	1.68E-23	4.2E-24					
14	Total	5	6.18E+08						
15									
16		Coefficient	:andard Err	t Stat	P-value	Lower 95%	Upper 95%	ower 95.0%	pper 95.0%
17	Intercept	20000	7.7E-12	2.6E+15	1.32E-61	20000	20000	20000	20000
18	X Variable	150	1.24E-14	1.21E+16	2.77E-64	150	150	150	150
19									
20									

FIGURE 5.10 The Output.

were exactly the same as the high-low method. In real life, the high-low method results and the regression analysis may be close but not exact. Regression analysis is a more accurate way to determine fixed costs and variable costs from a mixed-cost scenario because regression analysis uses all the data, not just the high and low amounts of activity. However, in the absence of access to Excel or a calculator that performs regression analysis, the high-low method does an adequate job.

LEARNING GOAL 4: Explain How the Contribution Margin Format Income Statement Is Driven by Cost Behavior

As discussed in Topic 3, the contribution-format income statement is arranged by how costs behave. Instead of using a traditional income statement, the managerial accountant rearranges the contribution-format income statement. The contribution-format income statement can only be used for internal reporting purposes because the format is not GAAP compliant. However, it may be well worth taking time to prepare a contribution-format income statement because of the value that the statement holds in predicting outcomes.

As with the traditional-format income statement, the contribution-format income statement starts with sales. There are no differences between the traditional format and the contribution format as related to revenue data. The differences occur when expenses begin to reduce sales. Under the traditional income statement of a manufacturing organization,

MAKE IT REAL 5-2

The contribution-format income statement creates considerable value for those who seek to understand how the functioning of the manufacturing process truly impacts costs. Whether the manufacturing process is one of manufacturing pharmaceuticals or automobiles, the manufacturing process can fall victim to disruptions. Disruptions occur when there is human error or mechanical breakdowns. Such disruptions decrease the output level and thus cost the organization by decreasing the contribution margin. The contribution margin indicates how much of sales revenue is available to cover the fixed expenses. Disruptions decrease the number of units produced and thus decreases the contribution margin. Although never formally tracked on the financial statements, a disruption that slows production by 1,000 units at a contribution margin of $5 per unit costs the company $5,000 in contribution margin.

Reference

Bai, G., Kajwara, T., and Liu, J. "The Cost of Manufacturing Disruptions." *Strategic Finance*. Retrieved from http://sfmagazine.com/post-entry/december-2015-the-cost-of-manufacturing-disruptions/ (2015).

the expenses that are associated with the manufacturing process would be the first to reduce sales because the expenses are not operating expenses, they are manufacturing expense. Both fixed and variable manufacturing costs would be included in this amount. Such expenses are called "cost of goods sold." Under the contribution-format income statement, cost of goods is also the first thing used to reduce sales, but for a different reason. Costs that are part of cost of goods sold when using the contribution-format income statement are variable costs. Fixed costs are not included as part of cost of goods sold. This concept will be discussed in greater detail in Topic 13.

When using a contribution margin-format income statement, after cost of goods sold is entered on the income statement, other variable costs are subtracted. The only criteria needed for a cost to be subtracted here is that the cost must be variable, must vary with the level of units sold.

Once all variable costs have been subtracted from revenue, the resulting amount is the contribution margin. Contribution margin represents the amount that the items sold contribute to the fixed expenses once the variable expenses have been recovered. A contribution margin that is negative would imply that the variable costs exceed the revenue.

Once the contribution margin has been calculated, fixed costs are subtracted. It doesn't matter if the cost is related to the manufacturing process or not related to the manufacturing process. If the cost is fixed, it is subtracted in this part of the contribution-format income statement. See Figure 5.11 for a view of a contribution-format income statement in its simplest form.

The contribution-format income statement boils down to little more than a separation of fixed costs and variable costs. All costs have a fixed or a variable component. Costs that are mixed will need to be broken down to establish the fixed and variable components. However, once established, such costs are entered into the appropriate place on the income statement as either fixed or variable.

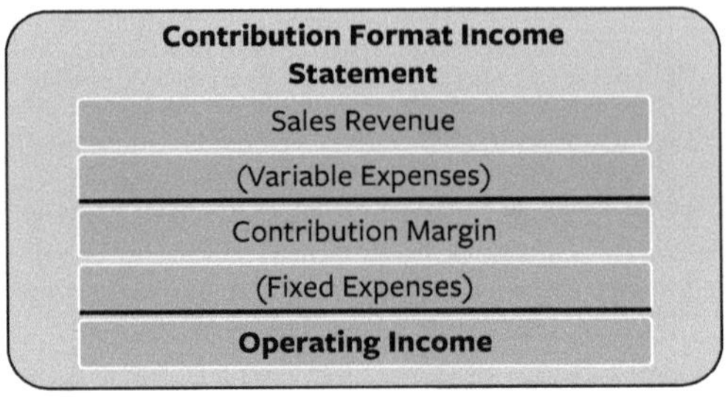

FIGURE 5.11 Contribution Format Income Statement.

On the contribution-format income statement, variable costs include cost of goods sold. Cost of goods sold is the way in which inventory moves from the balance sheet to the income statement once the inventory is sold. Inventory is different for a merchandising company as compared with a manufacturing company. Service companies do not have inventory. See Figures 5.12 through 5.14 for the balance sheet and the income statement for each of the types of businesses below.

Service Company

Service Company
Balance Sheet
December 31, 20XX

Assets:

No Inventory

Service Company
Contribution Format Income Statement
January 1 – December 31, 20XX

Sales...$$
Variable Expenses:
Variable Selling....................$$
Variable Administration....$$

Contribution Margin......................$$

Fixed Expenses:
Fixed Selling........................$$
Fixed Administration.........$$

Operating Income..............................$$

FIGURE 5.12 Service Company.

Merchandising Company

Merchandising Company
Balance Sheet
December 31, 20XX

Assets:

Merchandise Inventory............................$$ → (Cost of Goods Sold)

Merchandising Company
Contribution Format Income Statement
January 1 – December 31, 20XX

Sales..$$
Variable Expenses:
Cost of Goods Sold*........$$
Variable Selling.................$$
Variable Administration..$$

Contribution Margin......................$$

Fixed Expenses:
Fixed Selling.......................$$
Fixed Administration.......$$

Operating Income..........................$$

**Cost of Goods Sold Calculation:*
Beginning Inventory
Purchases
(Ending Inventory)
Cost of Goods Sold

FIGURE 5.13 Merchandising Company.

Manufacturing Company

Manufacturing Company
Balance Sheet
December 31, 20XX

Assets:

Inventory

Raw Materials Inventory.........................$$
Work in Process Inventory.....................$$
Finished Goods Inventory.......................$$ → (Cost of Goods Sold)

Manufacturing Company
Contribution Format Income Statement
January 1 – December 31, 20XX

Sales..$$
Variable Expenses:
Cost of Goods Sold*..........$$
Variable Selling..................$$
Variable Administration....$$

Contribution Margin......................$$

Fixed Expenses:
Fixed Selling.......................$$
Fixed Administration.........$$

Operating Income..........................$$

**Cost of Goods Sold Calculation:*
Beginning Inventory
Purchases
(Ending Inventory)
Cost of Goods Sold

FIGURE 5.14 Manufacturing Company.

GIVE IT A WHIRL 5-2

1. Given the following data, use the high-low method and regression analysis to separate fixed and variable costs from the mixed cost data.

TABLE 5.3 Department Cost Data

Month	Activity Level	Total Costs
January	17,800	$140,000
February	14,550	$139,000
March	25,100	$208,100
April	18,330	$176,300
May	13,450	$125,000
June	18,900	$177,000

Step 1: Solve for variable costs

Variable Cost per Unit =

Step 2: Solve for fixed costs

$$Y = a + b(x)$$

Answers

High-Low method

$$\text{Step 1: } \frac{(\$208,100 - \$125,000)}{(25,100 - 13,450)} = \frac{\$83,100}{11,650} = \$7.13$$

$$\text{Step 2: } \$208,000 = a + \$7.13(15,100)$$

$$\$208,100 - \$178,963 = \$29,137$$

Regression

1. R Square = .8632
2. Intercept = $32,608
3. X Variable = $7.12

2. Put the elements of the contribution-format income statement in the correct order:

TABLE 5.4 contribution-format income statement order

a. Contribution Margin
b. Operating Income (loss)
c. Variable Costs
d. Revenue
e. Fixed Costs
f. Fixed Costs

(Answer: Revenue, Variable Costs, Contribution Margin, Fixed Costs, Operating Income (loss))

TOPIC 5 REFERENCES

Meunier, A. "Autocaricatura de Adri." Wikipedia. Retrieved from: https://upload.wikimedia.org/wikipedia/commons/b/be/Adri_Meunier.jpg (2015).

"Accounting Cost Behavior." *Simple Studies Accounting Made Simple*. Retrieved from http://simplestudies.com/accounting-cost-behavior.html/page/6 (2016).

TOPIC 5 FIGURE CREDITS

Fig. 5.7: Copyright © Jeff Kramer (CC by 2.0) at https://commons.wikimedia.org/wiki/File%3APizza_hut_express.jpg.

Fig. 5.8: Copyright © by Microsoft.

Fig. 5.9: Copyright © by Microsoft.

Fig. 5.10: Copyright © by Microsoft.

TOPIC 6 CVP Analysis

LEARNING GOALS

1. Describe the basics of CVP within the planning phase.
2. Calculate contribution margin.
3. Understand the benefits of CVP in performing sensitivity analysis.
4. Calculate break-even and target income.
5. Determine risk in a company by calculating margin of safety and operating leverage.

INTRODUCTION

Topic 6 is focused on using cost behavior to predict profit or loss. Learning Goal 1 begins by covering the basics of Cost-Volume-Profit (CVP) regarding the interaction of the elements. CVP is intended to demonstrate how changes in volume and in costs can flow through to profit. In the contribution-format income statement, the flow of cost behavior can be predicted when the managerial accountant interchanges various elements. By understanding the relationships that exist, shortcuts can be used to make estimates as to how operating income will change based on changes in volume of sales, variable costs, contribution margin, or fixed costs. Once a clear understanding of the relationships has been established, sensitivity analysis is a way to answer managers' "what if" questions. "What if" questions can revolve around changes in sales volume, variable costs, and fixed costs. Managerial accountants can calculate multiple "what-if" scenarios to predict costs simply by understanding how costs behave. Learning Goals 4 and 5 address levels of risk in a company with calculations of break-even analysis, target-income analysis, margin of safety, and operating leverage. Making changes in the sensitivity analysis could impact company risk levels. The interrelationship of parts involved in this chapter is fundamental to advising management.

LEARNING GOAL 1: Describe the Basics of CVP Within the Planning Phase

Cost-Volume-Profit (CVP) analysis is a tool used by managerial accountants to help predict profitability. Many times in the course of making decisions managers may wonder what will happen to profit if certain changes occur. CVP analysis builds upon cost behavior and uses the relationship among the volume of items sold, the selling price of the items, and the variable and fixed costs to determine potential profits. See Figure 6.1 for a detailed look at how CVP works.

Let's look at an example. Suzy sells T-shirts from a kiosk in the mall for $5.00 a shirt. Suzy usually sells 250 shirts a month. Suzy buys the shirts for $3.00 per shirt and pays $500 a month to rent the kiosk.

$$\begin{aligned}&\textit{Revenue} - \textit{Variable Costs}\\&\quad = \textit{Contribution Margin}\\&\qquad - \textit{Fixed Costs} = \textit{Profit}(\textit{Loss})\end{aligned}$$

$$\begin{aligned}&(\$5.00 \textit{ per shirt} \times 250 \textit{ Shirts})\\&\quad - (\$3.00 \textit{ per shirt} \times 250 \textit{ Shirts})\\&= \textit{Contribution Margin} - \$500\\&= \textit{Profit Loss}\end{aligned}$$

$$\$1{,}250 - \$750 = \$500 - \$500 = \$0$$

Under the current scenario, Suzy is not making any money in her shirt business. What would happen if Suzy raised the price of each shirt by $.50?

$$\begin{aligned}&\textit{Revenue} - \textit{Variable Costs}\\&\quad = \textit{Contribution Margin}\\&\qquad - \textit{Fixed costs} = \textit{Profit}(\textit{Loss})\end{aligned}$$

$$\begin{aligned}&(\$5.50 \textit{ per shirt} \times 250 \textit{ Shirts})\\&\quad - (\$3.00 \textit{ per shirt} \times 250 \textit{ Shirts})\\&= \textit{Contribution Margin} - \$500\\&= \textit{Profit}(\textit{Loss})\end{aligned}$$

$$\$1{,}375 - \$750 = \$500 - \$625 = \$125$$

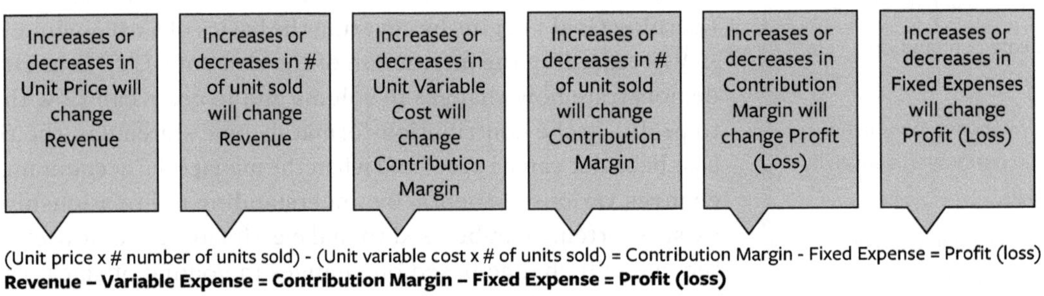

FIGURE 6.1 CVP relationships.

MAKE IT REAL 6-1

Bridgestone Behavioral Health Center is an organization that provides prevention, intervention, and treatment services for individuals with substance abuse problems. After experiencing a loss and then mediocre profits, the health center decided to investigate cost data. Exhibit 1 and Exhibit 2 of the following report depict the organization's contribution margin format income statement. The contribution margin format income statements helped the center to hone in on costs and make the needed adjustments.

Find report at:
http://www.csus.edu/indiv/p/pforsichh/documents/Volume3_Issue4_BridgestoneBehavioralHealthCenter-CVPAnalysisforPlanningandControl.pdf

By adjusting the price for each shirt sold, Suzy learned that the slight increase in selling price could lead to $125 in profit.

LEARNING GOAL 2: Calculate Contribution Margin

Although calculating Suzy's income (loss) was easy because of the simplicity of the scenario, some scenarios become more involved and, thus, require a greater level of analysis. Learning how to use contribution margin to make such calculations helps in more complex circumstances. Contribution margin can be calculated for a single product as noted below.

Single Product

Contribution margin can be broken down by unit or expressed as a percentage. See the following table regarding Suzy's T-Shirt Kiosk business:

TABLE 6.1 Single Product Contribution Margin

	In Total	Per Unit	Percent
Revenue (250 shirts)	$1,250	$5.00	100%
Less: Variable Expenses	$750	$3.00	60%
Contribution Margin	$500	$2.00	40%*
Less: Fixed Expenses	$500		
Profit (Loss)	**$0**		

*$2.00/$5.00 or $500/$1,250

In the table above, note that $2.00 is 40% of $5.00 and $500 is 40% of $1,250. Whether contribution margin is expressed as a unit or is expressed in total, the contribution margin percent will still be the same percentage of sales. Breaking down contribution margin into a percentage allows for greater flexibility regarding CVP.

Let's return to Suzy's T-shirt kiosk. See the table below for an analysis of the revised amounts with the higher selling price.

TABLE 6.2 Single Product Contribution Margin 2

	In Total	Per Unit	Percent
Revenue (250 shirts)	$1,375	$5.50	100%
Less: Variable Expenses	$750	$3.00	55.54%
Contribution Margin	$625	$2.50	45.45%
Less: Fixed Expenses	$500		
Profit (Loss)	**$125**		

Instead of going through the work of rebuilding the information, we could have started from contribution margin. If we knew that selling price would increase by $.50 per unit, we could have focused on adjusting contribution margin. By adjusting contribution margin per unit, we would know that the contribution percentage per unit would be the same as the contribution margin in total. Therefore, we could have used the new contribution margin rate of 45.45% and applied it to the 250 units to come up with the new profit (loss).

$$250\ units \times \$5.50 \times 45.45\%$$
$$= \$625(rounded) - \$500 = \$125$$

By using contribution margin we can make changes to any area of sales or variable expense and quickly determine the outcome. For example, if Suzy didn't change the selling prices, but instead increase sales by fifty shirts, we'd use the following calculation:

$$300\ units \times 5.00 \times 40\% = \$600 - \$500 = \$100$$

If Suzy sold 300 shirts at $5.00 per shirt, having a 40% contribution margin percent, she would make $100 per month.

Here is the proof:

TABLE 6.3 Single Product Contribution Margin 3

	In Total	Per Unit	Percent
Revenue (300 shirts)	$1,500	$5.00	100%
Less: Variable Expenses	$900	$3.00	60%
Contribution Margin	$600	$2.00	40%
Less: Fixed Expenses	$500		
Profit (Loss)	**$100**		

Multiple Products

Usually, companies don't sell just one product. Therefore, contribution margin needs to be calculated for multiple products, based on a product mix. A product mix is the combination of products that make up total sales. For example, Suzy may decide to sell tank tops as well as T-shirts. If Suzy sells three tank top for every seven T-shirts, her product mix is 3:7. When calculating the contribution margin, product mix will weigh the contribution margin, based on the ratio. Consider the following information regarding the T-shirt kiosk:

TABLE 6.4 Multiple Products Contribution Margin

	Tank Tops	T-Shirts	Total	Percent
Sales price per unit	$3.00	$5.00		
Less: Variable expense per unit	$1.50	$3.00		
Contribution margin per unit	$1.50	$2.00		
Sales Mix	3	7	10	
Total Sales	$9.00	$35.00	$44.00	100%
Sales Mix Contribution Margin	$4.50	$14.00	$18.50	42.04%
Weighted Average Contribution Margin			$1.85	

$$*\frac{18.50}{10} = 1.85$$

MAKE IT REAL 6-2

Cat and Joe's Pig Rig is a food truck specializing in barbeque food. The company is a mobile company that provides barbeque foods, such as pulled port sandwiches to various events. The company has variable costs that include food, packaging, and various variable overhead costs. The fixed costs include gas for the generator, maintenance, business licenses and truck depreciation. Variable costs are 40% of the company's revenue, while fixed costs total about $10,000 per year. While the owners contemplate the events they will attend, CVP helps them make well informed decisions.

Bell, T., & Fergus, A (2014). Cat and Joe's Pig Rig: Should we stay or should we go? *IMA Educational Case Journal* 7(3). 1-6

https://upload.wikimedia.org/wikipedia/commons/9/97/BBQ_Pulled_Pork.jpg

FIGURE 6.2

Suzy's contribution margin for the "basket" is $1.85 per basket. Individually, the tank tops would have $1.50 contribution margin based on the sale of one tank top while the T-shirts would have a $2.00 contribution margin based on the sale of one T-shirt. Combined, however, the contribution margin is totaled and weighted according to the sales mix.

LEARNING GOAL 3: Understand the Benefits of CVP in Performing Sensitivity Analysis

Now that you have a greater understanding of the benefits of CVP, let's use CVP to perform sensitivity analysis. Sensitivity analysis is a term used for performing various "what-if" calculations: $\frac{18.50}{10} = 1.85$ What if sales volume changes? What if variable costs change? What if fixed expenses change?

Here is a list of variations to Suzy's scenario. Consider each change independently:

Suzy's current situation:

1. Suzy's current situation is that she sells 250 T-shirts at $5.00 per shirt and has $500 of fixed costs and $3.00 per shirt variable costs.

Changes:

2. Suzy increases sales by 100 units.

$$350\ units \times 5.00 \times 40\% = \$700 - \$500 = \$200$$

or

$$Contribution\ margin\ of\ \$2.00\ per\ unit \times 350\ units = \$700 - \$500$$

3. Suzy decreases sales by 100 units.

$$150\ units \times 5.00 \times 40\% = \$300 - \$500 = (\$200)$$

or

$$Contribution\ margin\ of\ \$2.00\ per\ unit \times 150\ units = \$300 - \$500 = (\$200)$$

4. Suzy increases variable costs by $.50 per unit.

$$Contribution\ margin = \$5.00 - \$3.50 = \$1.50$$

$$Contribution\ percentage = \frac{\$1.50}{\$5.00} = 30\%$$

$$250\ units \times 5.00 \times 30\% = \$500 - \$375 = (\$125)$$

or

$$Contribution\ margin\ of\ \$1.50\ per\ unit \times 250\ units = \$375 - \$500 = (\$125)$$

5. Suzy decreases variable costs by $.50 per unit.

$$Contribution\ margin = \$5.00 - \$2.50 = \$2.50$$

$$Contribution\ percentage = \frac{\$2.50}{\$5.00} = 50\%$$

$$250\ units \times \$5.00 \times 50\% = \$625 - \$500 = \$125$$

or

$$Contribution\ margin\ of\ \$2.50\ per\ unit \times 250\ units = \$635 - \$500 = \$125$$

6. Suzy increases fixed costs by $50 per month.

$$250\ units \times 5.00 \times 40\% = \$500 - \$550 = (\$50)$$

7. Suzy decreases fixed costs by $50 per month.

$$250\ units \times 5.00 \times 40\% = \$500 - \$450 = \$50$$

8. Suzy increases sales by 10%.

$$Contribution\ percentage = 40\% \times 1.10 = 44\%$$

$$250\ units \times 5.00 \times \$550 - \$500 = \$50$$

9. Suzy decreases sales volume by 10%

$$Contribution\ percentage = 40\% \times .90\% = 36\%$$

$$250\ units \times 5.00 \times 36\% = \$450 - \$500 = (\$50)$$

10. Suzy increases selling price by $.50 per unit.

$$Contribution\ margin = \$5.50 - \$3.00 = \$2.50$$

$$Contribution\ percentage = \frac{\$2.50}{\$5.50} = 45.45\%$$

$$250\ units \times 5.50 \times 45.45\% = \$625\ (rounded) - \$500 = \$125$$

or

(continued)

Contribution margin of $2.50 *per unit*

= $625 – $500 = $125

11. Suzy decreases selling price by $.50 per unit.

$$Contribution\ margin = \$4.50 - \$3.00 = \$1.50$$

$$Contribution\ percentage = \frac{\$1.50}{\$4.50} = 33.33\%$$

$$250\ units \times 4.50 \times 33.33\% = \$375\ (rounded) - \$500 = (\$125)$$

or

Contribution margin of $1.50 *per unit* × 250 *units* = $375 – $500 = ($125)

12. Suzy increases selling price by $.50 per unit, but sales decrease by 50 shirts.

$$Contribution\ margin = \$5.50 - \$3.00 = \$2.50$$

$$Contribution\ percentage = \frac{\$2.50}{\$5.50} = 45.45\%$$

$$200\ units \times 5.50 \times 45.45\% = \$500\ (rounded) - \$500 = \$0$$

or

Contribution margin of $2.50 *per unit* × 200 *units* = $500 – $500 = $0

13. Suzy invests in advertising, increasing her fixed costs by $100 per month, but the advertising helps her to sell an additional 100 shirts.

$$Contribution\ margin = \$5.00 - \$3.00 = \$2.00$$

$$Contribution\ percentage = \frac{\$2.00}{\$5.00} = 40\%$$

$$350\ units \times 5.00 \times 40\% = \$700 - \$600 = \$100$$

or

Contribution margin of $2.00 *per unit* × 350 *units* = $700 – $600 = $100

TABLE 6.7 Proof

Proof:	**In Total**	**Per Unit**	**Percent**
1. Revenue (250 shirts)	$1,250	$5.00	100%
Less: Variable Expenses	$750	$3.00	60%
Contribution Margin	$500	$2.00	40%
Less: Fixed Expenses	$500		
Profit (Loss)	$0		
	In Total	**Per Unit**	**Percent**
2. Revenue (350 shirts)	$1,750	$5.00	100%
Less: Variable Expenses	$1,050	$3.00	60%
Contribution Margin	$700	$2.00	40%
Less: Fixed Expenses	500		
Profit (Loss)	$200		
	In Total	**Per Unit**	**Percent**
3. Revenue (150 shirts)	$750	$5.00	100%
Less: Variable Expenses	$450	$3.00	60%
Contribution Margin	$300	$2.00	40%
Less: Fixed Expenses	$500		
Profit (Loss)	($200)		
	In Total	**Per Unit**	**Percent**
4. Revenue (250 shirts)	$1,250	$5.00	100%
Less: Variable Expenses	$875	$3.50	70%
Contribution Margin	$375	$1.50	30%
Less: Fixed Expenses	$500		
Profit (Loss)	($125)		
	In Total	**Per Unit**	**Percent**
5. Revenue (250 shirts)	$1,250	$5.00	100%
Less: Variable Expenses	$625	$2.50	50%
Contribution Margin	$625	$2.00	50%
Less: Fixed Expenses	$500		
Profit (Loss)	$125		
	In Total	**Per Unit**	**Percent**
6. Revenue (250 shirts)	$1,250	$5.00	100%

	In Total	Per Unit	Percent
Less: Variable Expenses	$750	$3.00	60%
Contribution Margin	$500	$2.00	40%
Less: Fixed Expenses	$550		
Profit (Loss)	($50)		

	In Total	Per Unit	Percent
7. Revenue (250 shirts)	$1,250	$5.00	100%
Less: Variable Expenses	$750	$3.00	60%
Contribution Margin	$500	$2.00	40%
Less: Fixed Expenses	$450		
Profit (Loss)	$50		

	In Total	Per Unit	Percent
8. Revenue (275 shirts)	$1,375	$5.00	100%
Less: Variable Expenses	$825	$3.00	60%
Contribution Margin	$550	$2.00	40%
Less: Fixed Expenses	$500		
Profit (Loss)	$50		

	In Total	Per Unit	Percent
9. Revenue (225 shirts)	$1,125	$5.00	100%
Less: Variable Expenses	$675	$3.00	60%
Contribution Margin	$450	$2.00	40%
Less: Fixed Expenses	$500		
Profit (Loss)	($50)		

	In Total	Per Unit	Percent
10. Revenue (250 shirts)	$1,375	$5.50	100%
Less: Variable Expenses	$750	$3.00	54.54%
Contribution Margin	$625	$2.50	45.45%
Less: Fixed Expenses	$500		
Profit (Loss)	$125		

	In Total	Per Unit	Percent
11. Revenue (250 shirts)	$1,125	$5.50	100%
Less: Variable Expenses	$750	$3.00	66.67%
Contribution Margin	$375	$1.50	33.33%
Less: Fixed Expenses	$500		
Profit (Loss)	($125)		

	In Total	Per Unit	Percent
12. Revenue (200 shirts)	$1,100	$5.50	100%
Less: Variable Expenses	$600	$3.00	54.54%
Contribution Margin	$500	$2.50	45.45%
Less: Fixed Expenses	$500		
Profit (Loss)	$0		

	In Total	Per Unit	Percent
13. Revenue (350 shirts)	$1,750	$5.00	100%
Less: Variable Expenses	$1,050	$3.00	60%
Contribution Margin	$700	$2.00	40%
Less: Fixed Expenses	$600		
Profit (Loss)	$100		

If Suzy wanted to make at least $100 per month, what should she do?

- She could invest in advertising, hoping that it would help her to increase unit sales.
- She could increase selling price by $.50 per unit.
- She could decrease variable costs by $.50.
- She could increase sales by one hundred shirts without any advertising.

The best option for Suzy may not be possible. If Suzy could have increased sales by one hundred units without the help of any advertising, she would have already done that by now. The next best option would be to either increase her unit price or decrease her unit cost. If she increases her selling price, she may lose customers, and if she decreases her cost per unit, she may end up with a lesser-quality product. If Suzy spends $100 on advertising but does not experience any increase in sales, she will have lost $100 and gained no benefits. Suzy would have to weigh the benefit and the drawbacks of each alternative and select the one she is most comfortable in handling.

(continued)

GIVE IT A WHIRL 6-1

1. Leon sells jewelry at the craft mall. Among the items sold are hand-crafted rings made out of steel. The rings can be sold for $10.00 a ring. On average, Leon sells twenty-five rings a week. He works at various craft malls throughout the country and is usually working at a craft mall three weeks out of the four each month. The metal for each ring costs Leon $.50. On average booth rental is $150 per show. A.) Use CVP to calculate Leon's profit for one show. B.) Perform sensitivity analysis in which Leon charges $8.00 for each ring and pays $.30 for the raw material. C.) Prepare a contribution margin income statement for the year using the original data and the updated data.

Answer:

A.

$$\$250 - \$12.50 = \$237.50 - \$150 = \$87.50$$

B. $(\$8.00\ per\ ring \times 25\ rings) - (\$.30\ per\ ring \times 25\ rings) = Contribution\ Margin - \$150 = Profit\ (Loss)$

C. Leon works three weeks out of every 4 weeks or ¾ of the year, which is 39 weeks.

TABLE 6.5 Give It a Whirl 6-1

Sales (39 weeks × $250 each week):	**$9,750.00**
Variable Expenses (39 weeks × $12.50 each week):	$487.50
Contribution Margin:	$9,262.50
Fixed Costs (39 weeks × $150)	$5,850.00
Operating Income (loss)	$3,412.50
Sales (39 weeks × $200 each week):	$7,800.00
Variable Expenses (39 weeks × 7.50 each week):	$292.50
Contribution Margin:	$7,507.50
Fixed Costs (39 weeks × 150)	$5,850.00
Operating Income (loss)	$1,657.50

2. Continue with Leon's Rings:
Leon does not just make rings in his business, he also makes necklaces. The necklaces require more raw material, but he can sell them for a higher price. The necklaces can be sold for $15.00. The raw materials total $1.50. Assume that Leon sells one necklace for every three rings. Determine the weighted contribution margin for the rings and the the necklaces.

LEARNING GOAL 4: Calculate Break-Even and Target Income

Break Even

Understanding the relationships that exist in CVP analysis allows for management to also understand their point of break-even. Understanding at what point of sales the company breaks even is a valuable tool that allows for an even deeper understanding of the interactions that occur between volume of items sold, the selling price of the items, and the variable and fixed costs.

Break-even can be established by both units sold and dollar of revenues. Selling above break-even produces a profit while selling under break-even produces a loss. See the Figure 6.3 above for a graphed representation of break-even.

Break-Even in Units

Establishing a firm's break-even point in units means that management will understand how many units must be sold in order to produce a profit. The formula is as follows:

$$\frac{\textit{Fixed Expenses}}{\textit{Contribution Margin per Unit}}$$

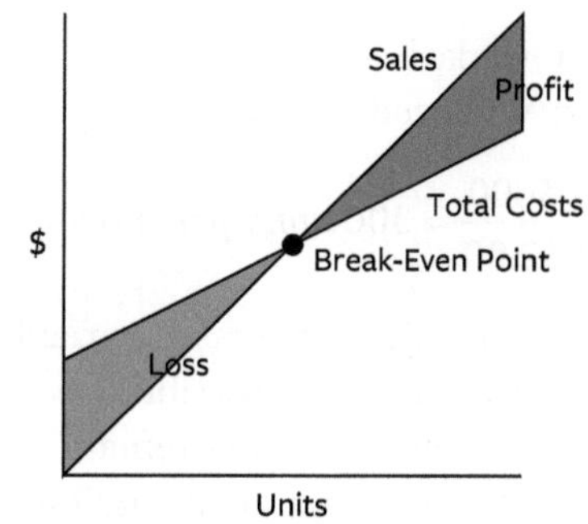

FIGURE 6.3 Break-Even.

Let's look at Suzy's T-shirt kiosk again. Suzy had $500 of fixed expenses and a contribution margin in units of $2.00 ($5.00–$3.00). Therefore, the formula to calculate break-even is:

$$\frac{\$500}{\$2.00} = 250 \textit{ units per month}$$

Note that the result is reported in number of units. If either the fixed expenses or the contribution margin per unit changes, break-even point will also change.

In scenario #13, Suzy purchased advertising, increasing her fixed costs from $500 to $600 per

GIVE IT A WHIRL 6-1 (CONT.)

TABLE 6.6 Give It a Whirl 6-1 Part 2

	Rings	Necklaces	Total	Percent
Sales price per unit	*$10.00*	*$15.00*		
Less: Variable expense per unit	*$.50*	*$1.50*		
Contribution margin per unit	*$9.50*	*$13.50*		
Sales Mix	3	1	4	
Total Sales	$30.00	$15.00	$45.00	100%
Sales Mix Contribution Margin	$28.50	$13.50	$42.00	93.33%
Weighted Average Contribution Margin			$10.50	

month. The reworked calculation increases the number of units Suzy will need to break-even.

$$\frac{\$600}{\$2.00} = 300 \text{ units per month}$$

In scenario #4, Suzy increased variable costs by $.50, thus decreasing her contribution margin per unit to $1.50. When fixed costs remain unchanged, decreasing contribution margin per unit will increase the number of units needed to break even. Using $500 of fixed costs and the new contribution margin of $1.50 per unit, break-even will be calculated as follows.

$$\frac{\$500}{\$1.50} = 333.33 \text{ units per month}$$

When the answer produces a partial amount, we round up because a partial unit cannot be sold. Therefore, the break-even point when variable costs increase per unit increases to 334 units because the contribution margin per unit decreased.

Now, let's combine the two circumstances of increased fixed costs and decreased unit contribution margin:

$$\frac{\$600}{\$1.50} = 400 \text{ units per month}$$

You can see, from the progression of circumstances that Suzy went from needing 250 units to break even each month to needing 400 units per month to break even. This is a valuable piece of information to Suzy because it determines whether she is operating at a profit or a loss.

Break-Even in Dollars

Calculating break-even in dollars tells a manager how many dollars in revenue he or she will need to break even. There are two ways to calculate break-even in dollars. The first way is simply to take the unit break-even calculation and multiply it by selling price. In the case of Suzy's T-shirt kiosk, Suzy determined that she needed 250 units to break even. The way to determine break-even is as follows:

$$250 \text{ units} \times \$5.00 \text{ per unit} = \$1{,}250$$

The second way to calculate break-even in revenues is to us the following formula:

$$\frac{\text{Fixed Expenses}}{\text{Contribuiton Margin Percent}}$$

Let's look at Suzy's T-shirt kiosk again. Suzy had $500 of fixed expenses and a contribution margin percent of 40%. Therefore, the formula to calculate break-even is

$$\frac{\$500}{40\%} = \$1{,}250 \text{ in sales per month}$$

Note that in using this formula, the result is reported in dollars. If either the fixed expenses or the contribution margin percentage changes, break-even point in dollars will also change.

In scenario #13, Suzy purchased advertising, increasing her fixed costs from $500 to $600 per month. The reworked calculation increases the number of units Suzy will need to break even.

$$\frac{\$600}{40\%} = \$1{,}500 \text{ in sales per month}$$

or

$$300 \text{ units per month} \times \$5.00 \text{ per unit}$$
$$= \$1{,}500 \text{ in sales per month}$$

In scenario #4, Suzy increased variable costs by $.50, thus decreasing her contribution margin percentage to 30%. When fixed costs remain unchanged, decreasing contribution margin percent will increase the number of units needed to break even. Using $500 of fixed costs and the new contribution margin percent of 30%, break-even will be calculated as follows.

$$\frac{\$500}{30\%} = \$1{,}667 \text{ in sales per month}^*$$

or

$$334 \text{ units per month} \times \$5.00 \text{ per unit}$$
$$= \$1{,}670 \text{ in sales per month}^*$$

*A slight difference exists due to rounding.

Now, let's combine the two circumstances of increased fixed costs and decreased contribution margin percent.

$$\frac{\$600}{30\%} = \$2{,}000 \text{ in sales per month}$$

or

$$400 \textit{ units per month} \times \$5.00 \textit{ per unit} = \$2{,}000 \textit{ in sales per month.}$$

Again, the progression of sales dollars increases as the fixed expenses increase and the contribution margin percent decreases.

Break-Even for Multiple Products

When calculating break-even for multiple products, the contribution margin per unit is based on the weighted amount. When Suzy decided to sell T-shirts and tank tops, the weighted contribution margin amount was \$1.85. Thus, \$1.85 would be used in the break-even calculation:

$$\frac{\$500}{\$1.85} = 271 \textit{ units per month}$$

Without understanding the sales mix, there is no way to understand how many units of each will make up the 271 units. The following method breaks down how many tank tops and how many T-shirts are included in the 271 units.

$$271 \times \frac{3}{10} = 82 \textit{ tank tops}$$

$$271 \times \frac{7}{10} = 190 \textit{ T-shirts}$$

$$\textit{Total} = 272 \textit{ shirts}*$$

*Calculation is one shirt off due to rounding.

$$82 \textit{ tank tops} \times \$1.50 \textit{ per tank} = \$123$$

$$190 \textit{ T-shirts} \times \$2.00 \textit{ per T-shirt} = \$380$$

$$\textit{Total} = \$503*$$

Proof:

TABLE 6.8 Break-Even Multiple Products

Total Contribution Margin:	\$503
Less: Fixed Expenses:	\$500
Operating Income	\$3

*Calculation is off \$3.00 due to rounding.

When calculating the break-even in dollars, the contribution margin percent must be used.

$$\frac{\$500}{42.04} = \$1{,}189 \textit{ (rounded) in sales per month}$$

$$\frac{\$500}{42.04} = \$1{,}189 \textit{ (rounded) in sales per month}$$

Proof:

TABLE 6.9 Revenue

Revenue:		
$\$1{,}189 \times \frac{3}{10} = \$356.70$		
$\$1{,}189 \times \frac{7}{10} = \$832.30$	\$1,189	
Less variable expenses		
Tank tops:	$82 \times \$1.50$	\$123
T-Shirts	$190 \times \$3.00$	\$693
Contribution Margin:	\$496	
Less: Fixed Expenses:	\$500	
Operating Income:	(\$4)*	

*Calculation is \$4 off due to rounding.

Target Operating Income

Although understanding break-even is of great importance to management, management may want know what point the company will reach a desired level of sales. Shareholders in a company don't want a company to simply break even; they want to see the company operate at a profit. Therefore, a similar calculation involves determining the point at which target profit is reached. Like break-even, the result is conveyed in either dollars or units. See the following formulas:

$$\textit{Target Operating Income in Units} = \frac{(\textit{Fixed Expenses} + \textit{Target Operating Income})}{\textit{Unit Contribution Margin}}$$

$$Target\ Operating\ Income\ in\ Dollars = \frac{(Fixed\ Expenses + Target\ Operating\ Income)}{Contribution\ Margin\ Percent}$$

Let's say that Suzy would like to make a profit of $1,000 every month. Given Suzy's current scenario, how many T-shirts must Suzy sell, and how many sales dollars must Suzy have?

In units:

$$\frac{(\$500 + \$1{,}000)}{\$2.00} = 750\ units\ per\ month$$

In dollars:

$$\frac{(\$500 + \$1{,}000)}{40\%} = \$3{,}750\ in\ sales\ or\ month$$

or

$$750\ units\ per\ month \times \$5.00\ per\ unit = \$3{,}750\ in\ sales\ per\ month$$

Again, understanding what amount of sales in units and/or dollars is an important piece of information for management to have. Management can better plan when the break-even point and/or target operating income levels are known. Multiple products would be calculated in the same way as break-even, with the added component of target operating income.

LEARNING GOAL 5: Determine Risk in a Company by Calculating Margin of Safety and Operating Leverage

When companies consider fixed and variable expenses within their organization, they are considering how much risk they are comfortable taking. Risk involves the distribution of expenses between variable and fixed components. When variable expenses are high, risk is low because if there are not sales, there is no expense. However, when fixed expenses are high, risk is high because if there are no sales, there is still expense. Certain calculations are used to determine the risk in an organization.

Margin of Safety

Margin of safety is used to calculate how far over break-even the company is. The interaction between fixed and variable expenses are part of the break-even calculation and, thus, become part of the margin of safety analysis. The calculation is completed both for units and dollars:

$$Margin\ of\ safety\ in\ units = expected\ /\ actual\ sales\ in\ units - break\ even\ sales\ in\ units$$

$$Margin\ of\ safety\ in\ dollars = expected\ /\ actual\ sales\ in\ dollars - break\ even\ sales\ in\ dollars$$

For example, if Suzy has T-shirt sales of 300 units, she has sales revenue of $1,500 (300 units × $5.00 per unit). Break-even sales for Suzy were 250 units or $1,250 dollars (250 units × $5.00) The margin of safety calculation would be as follows:

$$Margin\ of\ Saftey\ in\ units = 300\ units - 250\ units = 50\ units$$

$$Margin\ of\ Safety\ in\ dollars = \$1{,}500 - \$1{,}250 = \$250$$

If Suzy's sales are 300 units ($1,500 dollars), Suzy will drop below break-even if she sells 51 fewer shirts. Break-even is useful as a raw dollar amount but is also useful as a percentage. The percentage is calculated as follows:

$$Margin\ of\ Safety = \frac{Margin\ of\ Safety}{Expected\ Sales}$$

The margin of safety percent will result in the same percent regardless of whether dollars or units are used.

$$Margin\ of\ Safety\ Percent\ in\ dollars = \frac{(\$1{,}500 - \$1{,}250)}{\$1{,}500} = 16.67\%$$

$$Margin\ of\ Saftey\ Percent\ in\ units = \frac{(300 - 250)}{300} = 16.67\%$$

Operating Leverage

Operating leverage is also a measure of risk that uses fixed and variable expenses. The calculation for operating leverage calculates the variable expenses compared with the fixed expenses and how that comparison relates back to operating income. The resulting amount is a factor that is further used to make predictions The calculation is as follows:

$$\textit{Operating Leverage Factor} = \frac{\textit{contribution margin}}{\textit{operating income}}$$

GIVE IT A WHIRL 6-2

1. **Break-Even Analysis with Leon's Rings.**
Leon, from Give It A Whirl 6-1 would like to know when he will break even if he just sells rings. He would also like to know when he will break even if he keeps selling one necklace for every three rings. Provide Leon with an answer in both dollars and in units.
Answer.
Contribution Margin in Units:
Rings: $\$10.00 - \$.50 = \$9.50$
Rings/Necklaces: Weighted Average Contribution Margin = \$10.50
Break-even for the year:

$$\frac{\text{Fixed costs}}{\text{unit contribution margin}}$$

Rings:

$$\frac{\$5{,}850}{\$9.50} = 616 \textit{ rings} \div 39 \textit{ shows} = 16 \textit{ rings per show}$$

$$616 \textit{ rings per show} \times \$10 \textit{ per ring} = \frac{\$6{,}160 \textit{ in revenues per year}}{39 \textit{ shows}} = \$157.95$$

Rings/Necklaces Mix:

$$\frac{\$5{,}850}{\$10.50} = 557 \textit{ rings/necklaces}$$

Rings: $557 \times \frac{3}{4} = 418 \textit{ Rings}$ *and* $557 \times \frac{1}{4} = 139 \textit{ necklaces}$ *or 11 rings and 4 necklaces at each show*

2. **Margin of Safety:**
Compute the margin of safety for Leon's Rings, based on the original data of \$10 sales price per ring and \$.50 variable cost per ring against his break-even in Give It a Whirl 6-2 #1.
Answer:

$$\textit{Current Sales} - \textit{Break even sales} = \textit{Margin of safety}$$

$$(25 \textit{ rings} \times 39 \textit{ shows}) - 616 \textit{ rings} = 359 \textit{ rings} \quad \text{– Units}$$

$$\$9{,}750 - \$6{,}160 = \$3{,}590 \quad \text{– Dollars}$$

$$\frac{\$3{,}590}{\$9{,}750} = 37\% \quad \text{– Percent}$$

When calculating operating leverage, the lowest possible result will be a 1, with increasing amounts indicated increasing risk. The following is Suzy's operating leverage factor at an expected/actual level of sales of 300 units.

TABLE 6.10 Operating Leverage

Revenue (300 units):	$1,500
Less: Variable Expense:	$900
Contribution Margin:	$600
Fixed Expenses:	$500
Operating Income:	$100

$$Operating\ Leverage\ Factor = \frac{\$600}{\$100} = 6$$

At an operating Leverage Factor of 6, Suzy can determine how operating income will be impacted with a 10% increase in revenue and a 10% decrease in revenue. If revenue increases / decreases by 10%, operating income will increases / decrease by 60%. See the proof below:

To determine if a factor is high or not, one would compare the factor with others in the industry and with prior years.

TOPIC 6 REFERENCES

Bell, T. and Fergus, A. "Cat and Joe's Pig Rig: Should We Stay or Should We Go?" *IMA Educational Case Journal.* 7(3). 1-6. (2014).

Braun, K.W. and Tietz, W.M. *Managerial Accounting* (4th ed.). Upper Saddle River: Prentice Hall, 2014.

"Pulled Pork in BBQ Sauce sSndwich with Slaw." Wikipedia. Retrieved from https://upload.wikimedia.org/wikipedia/commons/9/97/BBQ_Pulled_Pork.jpg (2008).

Horngren, C.T, Datar, S, M. and Rajan, M.V. *Cost Accounting: A Managerial Emphasis* (15ed.). Upper Saddle River, NJ. Pearson Education, Inc., 2015.

Kucic, A.R., Sorensen, J.E., and Victoravich, L.M. "Bridgestone Behavioral Health Center: Cost-Volume-Profit (CVP) Analysis for Planning and Control." *IMA Educational Case Journal.* 3(4). Retrieved from http://www.csus.edu/indiv/p/pforsichh/documents/Volume3_Issue4_BridgestoneBehavioralHealthCenter-CVPAnalysisforPlanningandControl.pdf (2010).

TABLE 6.11 Operating Leverage Proof

Current		**10% increase**		**10% decrease**	
Revenue (300 units):	$1,500	Revenue (330 units):	$1,650	Revenue (270 units):	$1,350
Less Variable Expense	$900	Less Variable Expense:	$990	Less Variable Expense:	$810
Contribution Margin:	$600	Contribution Margin:	$660	Contribution Margin:	$540
Fixed Expenses:	$500	Fixed Expenses:	$500	Fixed Expenses:	$500
Operating Income:	$100	Operating Income:	$160	Operating Income:	$40
		$*\$100 \times 1.60 = \$160$		$*\$100 \times (1-60\%) = \$40$	

TOPIC 6 FIGURE CREDITS

Fig. 6.2: Copyright © Buck (CC by 2.0) at https://commons.wikimedia.org/wiki/File:BBQ_Pulled_Pork.jpg.

Fig. 6.3: Source: https://commons.wikimedia.org/wiki/File%3ACVP-TC-Sales-PL-BEP.svg.

TOPIC 7 Master Budgeting

LEARNING GOALS

1. Discuss the goals and benefits of budgeting.
2. Investigate the framework of the master budget.
3. Differentiate the operating and financial budgets.
4. Create the individual budgets for the master budget.

INTRODUCTION

Topic 7 is focused on the master budget. The master budget is a collection of a number of smaller budgets. As you learn this topic, Learning Goal 1 will focus on the benefits of budgeting and the types of budgets. Learning Goals 2-4 will focus on understanding the parts of the master budget and how the master budget fits together. Learning Goal 4 will specifically focus on each part of the operating budgets and each part of the financial budget. Learning the calculations for such budgets will help you to understand the value of the budget.

LEARNING GOAL 1: Discuss the Benefits of Budgeting and the Types of Budgets

The word budget is an unpleasant word in the minds of most individuals because budgeting is seen as restrictive. For the managerial accountant, however, budgeting is not a restriction but a tool for how to help businesses achieve goals. Budgeting is a quantitative reflection of strategy that provides a way to communicate strategy to all individuals at different levels within the organization.

Budgets help to answer questions such as

- What are the trends that are occurring in our organization/industry?
- What financial structures work best for our company?

- What areas/costs add value for our clients?
- Where are the resources being spent?

Benefits

The benefits of an organization participating in a budgeting process are numerous and include a way to provide 1) communication, 2) a framework, 3) motivation, and 4) benchmarks.

Communication

As a quantitative expression of strategy, the budget has capabilities of communicating to various levels of the organization. Budgets involve communication between sales, production, purchasing, accounts payable, accounts receivable, marketing, and human resources. Each area is impacted by the budget, and each area impacts the budget.

Framework

When sorting out all of the details for the functioning of a company, planning helps to create a framework through which the company can track progress. Budgeting links the planning phase to the evaluating phase because it provides a framework against which performance can be measured and evaluated. With a framework intact, a company is able to learn about its performance, having a framework upon which to base performance.

Motivation

Goals are necessary to keep employees motivated. A budget provides financial goals an organization seeks to meet, which are reflections of strategic goals. Goals are reflected company-wide but can be narrowed to departmental goals and even individual goals. Budgets serve motivational purposes as long as the budgets are attainable. Budgets that are out of reach do not motivate but instead de-motivate. Therefore, in order for budgets to serve their motivational purposes, the budgets need to be within reach.

Benchmarks

The budget provides a grounded area to which a company can return and reflect upon. By using the budget as a benchmark, a company knows if it is spending too much per unit for parts or labor, or if laborers are taking too much time to produce a product. When hiring a new employee, hiring personnel would refer back to the budget to determine the rate of pay for a new employee. Likewise, the purchasing agent would use the budget as a benchmark for costs to purchase materials.

Types of Budgets

Budgets come in various forms, covering different time frames and purposes.

Calendar Year/Fiscal Year Budgets

Many companies create budgets to coincide with the calendar/fiscal year. Such budgets can be broken down into smaller components, helping to create short-term goals. Annual or fiscal year budgets may be beneficial if broken down into monthly or quarterly reports.

Rolling Budgets/Continuous Budgets

Businesses may find value in using a rolling budget. A rolling budget is always for a twelve-month period of time. A company using a rolling budget may break its budget down by quarter or month. Thus, at the end of every quarter, the next quarter would be added, or at the end of every month, the next month would be added. For example, a budget may run from January to December. At the end of January, the budget would cover the time period from February to January, the next from March to February, and so forth and so on. A budget prepared in this way forces management to be constantly thinking about the next twelve months.

Zero-Based Budgets

Companies that used a zero-based budget do not rely upon the prior year's budget in creating the next year's budget. Each year begins at zero, and departments build their budgets from scratch. The benefit for such type of budgeting is that budgeted amounts are not simply chosen because that was the amount budgeted last year. Instead, department managers must contemplate each year individually. The drawback to such a budget is that each year, managers reinvent the wheel, and valuable information from the past is overlooked. Additionally, building a budget according to zero-based budgeting is extremely time consuming.

MAKE IT REAL 7-1

Budgets are used in every walk of life. Whether for personal use, corporate use, or government use, budgets help organizations to carry out their strategy and provide a road map for success but only if implemented properly. A budget that is not appreciated nor implemented properly is not of any benefit. In response to arguments that the budget process was useless, Vaznoniene (2012) completed a study that addressed the major complaints of budgeting: 1) Budgets are not related to corporate strategy, 2) budgets are not adjusted during implementation, 3) budgets are subject to a top-down approach, 4) budgeting is time consuming and expensive, 5) the budget system is rarely upgraded, 6) employees try to prepare a budget that is easier to implement, 7) employees report false budget implementation results, 8) budgets encourage unreasonable spending, 9) employees do not understand the budgeting system, 10) budgeting tools are inconvenient, and 11) there is not enough educational literature on budgeting issues. Each of the above-noted complaints were investigated to find that many organizations did not establish budgets because they did not recognize their value. The Vaznoniene (2012) study supported the fact that a budget that is not properly implemented will not serve its intended purpose. By using the concepts discussed in this topic, the budget process can be a success to those who use it.

Reference

Vaznoniene, M. "Corporate Budgets and Their Limitations: A Case Study of Meat and Poultry Producers." *Economics & Rural Development, 8*(2), 37–49. (2012).

Participative Budget

A participative budget requires engagement from management at several levels, not just upper-level management. Using participative budgets offers benefits in that individuals are more likely to feel "ownership" for the budget and will be more likely to see it as a motivational tool. One of the negative consequences associated with participative budgets is that of budgetary slack. Budgetary slack is the practice of underestimating revenues or overestimating expenses to make the budget easier to achieve. Companies that use participative budgeting take measures to account for such slack by using budgets as a planning tool, not as a basis for a reward system and/or by using external benchmarks as a basis for budgeting. Budgets cannot serve as a proper planning tool if they are misleading.

LEARNING GOAL 2: Investigate the Framework of the Master Budget

The Master Budget is the starting point for the budgeting process. The Master Budget is made up of several different smaller budgets that combined, reflect the overall goals of an organization. Throughout the various topics that will be discussed in the planning phase, variations on the master budget will help the master budget to become a useful tool beyond communication. The master budget is made up of two distinct types of budgets: 1) the operating budgets and 2) the financial budgets. See Figure 7.1 below to understand how the various small budgets make up the master budget.

Note in the figure above that the budgeting process begins with the Sales and Revenues Budget. Marketing and sales are part of creating the Sales and Revenues Budget. Once the Sales and Revenues Budget has been established, the Production Budget can be built. The Production Budget will require the input of the production manager and conveys how many units should be produced, based on the amount of sales in units. Factors involved in creating the production budget include how much safety stock a company wishes to maintain and how much finished goods inventory is already in beginning inventory. A company will produce the amount needed to cover sales, plus the amount the company requires to keep on hand as finished goods ending inventory.

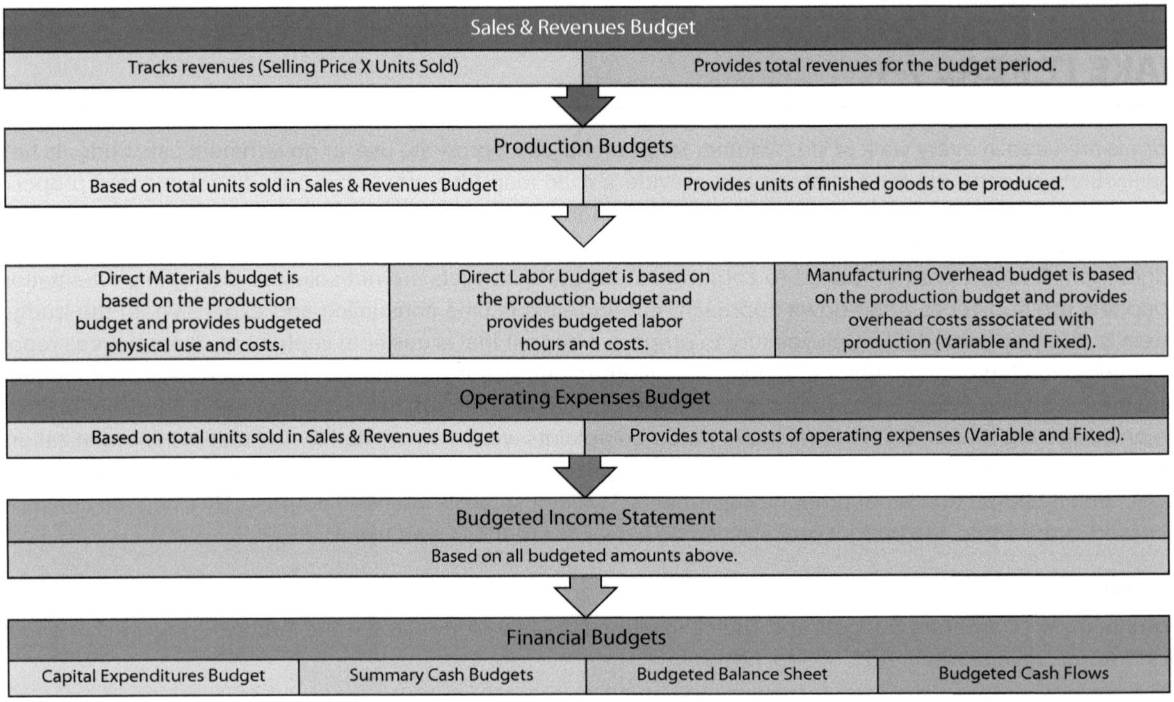

FIGURE 7.1 Master Budget.

Once the company establishes how much to produce, the purchasing department will need to determine the raw material needed to produce that which production has decided will need to be produced. Therefore, the purchasing department becomes involved when creating the Direct Materials Budget. Purchasing needs to calculate how many pieces of raw material are used by each unit and order appropriately. Each type of raw material will have a desired level of ending inventory, which must be factored into the amount needing to be purchased.

The Direct Labor Budget is also based on the Production Budget and would include the production manager's analysis of how many labor hours are needed to complete the job as well as human resources recommendation as to how much to pay the laborers.

The Manufacturing Overhead Budget is based on the Production Budget but is also a reflection of cost behavior. The budget is broken down into fixed and variable components. The variable component is driven by a cost driver, based on budgeted amounts. For example, if the variable component of overhead is based on direct labor hours, the direct labor hours from the Direct Labor Budget would be used to calculate variable overhead.

The Operating Expense Budget includes amounts that fall outside of the manufacturing process, including items such as marketing costs, distribution costs, general office costs, etc. Finally, the budgeted income statement can be built once the above costs have been determined. The budgeted income statement is nothing more than a reflection of all the operating budgets.

The financial budgets, then, involve accounting for asset purchases the company will make, a summary of the flow of cash (inflow and outflow), a budgeted cash flows statement, and the budgeted balance sheet. The budgeted balance sheet and the budgeted cash flows will be a reflection of the calculated prior budget amounts.

LEARNING GOAL 3: Differentiate the Operating and Financial Budgets

Operating Budgets

Operating budgets are what the name implies, the budgets for the various operating parts of the company.

GIVE IT A WHIRL 7-1

1. **Match the advantages and the disadvantages to each type of budget.**

TABLE 7.0A Give It a Whirl 7-1

Type	Advantage	Disadvantage
Calendar Year/Fiscal Year Budgets		
Rolling Budgets/Continuous Budgets		
Zero-Based Budgets		
Participative Budget		

Advantages

1. Involves participation from various areas and levels of the organization.
2. Coincides with "normal" business activity.
3. Does not encourage the use of preconceived notions regarding budgeted amounts.
4. Encourages management to always be looking ahead.

Disadvantages

1. Does not encourage management to think beyond the current budget period.
2. Can cause confusion, due to the continuous nature.
3. Can result in budgetary slack.
4. Time-consuming and costly.

Answer:

TABLE 7.0B Give It a Whirl 7-1, part 2

Type	Advantage	Disadvantage
Calendar Year/Fiscal Year Budgets	2	1
Rolling Budgets/Continuous Budgets	4	2
Zero-Based Budgets	3	4
Participative Budget	1	3

2. Match the budget with its role in the budgeting process. Also, indicate whether the budget is part of the Operating Budget (O) or the Financial Budgets (F).

TABLE 7.0C Give It a Whirl 7-1, part 3

Budget	O or F	Description
Sales and Revenues Budget		
Production Budget		
Raw Materials Budget		
Direct Labor Budget		

(continued)

Manufacturing Overhead Budget
Operating Expenses Budget
Budgeted Income Statement
Capital Expenditures Budget
Summary Cash Budgets
Budget Balance Sheet
Budgeted Cash Flows

1. Based on units sold in the Sales and Revenues Budget and provides total operating costs, both variable and fixed.
2. Based on the production budget and provides overhead costs, both variable and fixed.
3. Tracks revenue by taking selling price X units sold.
4. Based on total units sold in the Sales and Revenues Budget. Provides units of finished goods to be produced.
5. An operating budget that is based on all other budgets.
6. Reflects a budgeted statement of cash flows.
7. Tracks capital purchases.
8. Based on the production budget and provides budgeted physical use and costs.
9. Summarizes all cash flows (inflows and out flows).
10. Based on the production budget and provides budgeted labor hours and costs.
11. Based on prior budget data to reflect a budgeted balance sheet.

Answer:

TABLE 7.0D Give It a Whirl 7-1, part 4

Sales and Revenues Budget	*O*	*3*
Production Budget	**O**	4
Raw Materials Budget	**O**	8
Direct Labor Budget	**O**	10
Manufacturing Overhead Budget	**O**	2
Operating Expenses Budget	**O**	1
Budgeted Income Statement	**O**	5
Capital Expenditures Budget	**F**	7
Summary Cash Budgets	**F**	9
Budget Balance Sheet	**F**	11
Budgeted Cash Flows	**F**	6

The operating budgets begin with the Sales & Revenues Budget and move through all the small budgets, including the Production Budget, the Direct Materials Budget, the Direct Labor Budget, the Overhead Budget, and the Operating Expenses Budget, until arriving at the budgeted income statement. The operating budgets help to provide the information needed for the financial budgets.

MAKE IT REAL 7-2

In a TED Talk, Roy Sutherland (2010) discusses how sweating the small stuff is important. This is the concept of the master budget. Corporations need to work out the small details that will ultimately have a big impact. To view the video, see the link in the reference below.

Reference

Sutherland, R. "Sweat the Small Stuff." *TED: Ideas Worth Spreading*. Retrieved from http://www.ted.com/talks/rory_sutherland_sweat_the_small_stuff?language=en (2010).

When creating a budget, many companies start with the financial budgets, not truly understanding the value of the operating budgets. By starting with the financial budgets, a company misses the detail that the operating budgets provide. The operating budgets specifically answer questions, such as:

- What are the expected sales, in volume?
- How do the volume sales transfer over to revenue?
- What amount of finished goods does the company desire to keep on hand?
- How many units must be produced to ensure sales needs and inventory amounts are maintained?
- How much raw material should be kept in ending inventory?
- How much raw material is needed to produce that which is required for sales and finished goods ending inventory levels?
- How many hours of work will the expected sales require?
- At what rates of pay can the company afford to hire laborers?
- What is the overhead rate?
- What is the expected level of the cost driver(s) for overhead?
- What are the various administration and marketing costs?

Financial Budgets

The financial budgets have a different purpose than the operating budgets. The financial budgets seek to provide the big picture and seek to answer the following questions:

- What major capital expenditures will the company be making?
- Will the company need to borrow money?
- If the company borrows money, what is the plan for repayment?
- What are the company's assets, liabilities, and equity at the end of the year?

LEARNING GOAL 4: Create the Individual Budgets for the Master Budget

Operating Budgets

The master budget, in its entirety, conveys a story of strategy, highlighting those things within an organization that are important to management.

Sales and Revenues Budget

The Sales and Revenues Budget is the first budget to be completed. The Sales and Revenues Budget is the easiest budget to complete in terms of computations but is the most difficult budget because it is the starting point for all other budgets. If the Sales and Revenues Budget is not correct, all other calculations will be off.

Wine Country Wine Racks' Sales and Revenues Budget is listed below. The company has estimated the amount of wine racks that can be sold for the first quarter of 2018.

Wine Country Wine Racks
Master Budget
Year Ending December 2018

Sales & Revenues Budget				
	January	February	March	1st Quarter
Unit Sales:	4,000	4,900	5,400	14,300
Sales price per unit:	$125	$125	$125	$125
Sales Revenue:	500,000	612,500	675,000	1,787,500
Payment Type				
Cash (25%)	125,000	153,125	168,750	446,875
Credit (75%)	375,000	459,375	506,250	1,340,625
Total	500,000	612,500	675,000	1,787,500

Extra Data	
December	April
5,000	5,500
$125	$125
$625,000	$687,500
$156,250	$171,875
$468,750	$515,625
$625,000	$687,500

FIGURE 7.2 Sales and Revenues Budget.

In Figure 7.2 the budget is conveyed for one quarter, with the detail of each month provided. Additional information for December and April has also been included as may be needed for subsequent calculations. Some companies may require or need the detail provided from the monthly amounts. The budget could also be reported for the quarter or the year, ignoring the monthly detail and simply stating the quarterly amounts.

TABLE 7.1 First Quarter Sales and Revenue Budget, 2018

Units	Selling Price	Total Revenues
14,300	$125	$1,787,500

*Cash sales = 25%, Credit sales = 75%.

The needs of the company should rule when it comes to formatting the budget.

No matter the formatting method, the formula used to complete the sales and revenue budget is

$$Units \times Selling\ Price = Budgeted\ Revenue$$

Production Budget

The Production Budget must follow the Sales and Revenues Budget and should be a reflection of the finished product. The amount to be produced cannot be determined without first determining how much product can be sold. Production is based on that which the Sales and Revenues Budget revealed can be sold. Additionally, the Production Budget will estimate a certain percent of ending finished goods inventory that the company likes to remain on hand as safety stock in the event sales are greater than expected. Wine Country Wine Racks has decided to account for ten percent of the following month's sales as their desired ending inventory amount.

As with Figure 7.2, in Figure 7.3 the budget is conveyed for one quarter, with the detail of each month provided. Additional information for December and April has also been included because the quarterly data draws from April amounts to determine ending inventory for March. The budget could also be reported for the quarter, ignoring the monthly detail and simply stating the quarterly amounts.

TABLE 7.2 First Quarter Production Budget, 2018

Wine Racks	
Budgeted unit sales:	14,300
Add: Target ending inventory:	550
Total required units	14,850
Less: Beginning inventory:	400
Units of finished goods to produce:	14,450

*Desired ending inventory = ten percent of the following month's sales

Production Budget (in units)	January	February	March	1st Quarter
Budgeted Unit sales:	4,000	4,900	5,400	**14,300**
Add: Target ending inventory:	490	540	550	**550**
Total required units:	4,490	5,440	5950	**14850**
Less: Beginning inventory:	400	490	540	**400**
Units of finished goods to be produced:	4,090	4,950	5410	**14450**

Extra Data	December	April
Budgeted Unit sales	5,000	5,500
Add: Target ending inventory	400	650
Total required units	5,400	6,150
Less: Beginning inventory	500	550
Units of finished goods to be produced	4,900	5,600

FIGURE 7.3 Production Budget.

No matter the formatting method, the formula used to complete the production budget is

Budgeted Unit Sales + Target Ending Inventory – Beginning Inventory = Units of Finished Goods to Produce

Direct Materials Budget

The Direct Materials Budget transitions the amount of finished product into raw materials needed to create the finished product. Each direct material would need its own Direct Materials Budget (Figure 7.4). In order to keep the problem simple, in the example of Wine Country Wine Racks, only one direct material has been used for the Direct Materials Budget. Board feet of oak is the raw material required to make the wine racks. Each wine rack uses ten board feet, and board feet can be purchased for $5 a board foot. As with the finished goods inventory, raw material inventory should account for a desired ending inventory amount. In the case of Wine Country Wine Racks, desired ending inventory of board feet is fifteen percent of the following month's raw material needs.

If reflecting the quarter as a whole, the budget would look like the following:

TABLE 7.3 First Quarter Raw Materials Budget, 2018

Oak	
Units to be produced	14,450
Quantity of DM used per unit (in board feet):	10
Quantity of DM (board feet) needed for production:	144,500
Add: Target ending DM inventory:	8,400
Total Quantity of DM needed:	152,900
Less: Beginning inventory of DM:	6,135
Quantity of DM to purchase:	146,765
Cost per unit:	$ 5
Total Cost:	$733,825

*Desired DM ending inventory = fifteen percent of the following month's DM needs.

Direct Materials (DM) Budget	January	February	March	1st Quarter
Units to be produced:	4,090	4,950	5,410	14,450
Qty of DM used per unit (in board feet):	10	10	10	10
Qty of DM (board feet) needed for production:	**40,900**	**49,500**	**54,100**	**144,500**
Add: Target ending DM inventory:	7425	8115	8400	8400
Total Qty of DM needed:	48,325	57,615	62,500	152,900
Less: Beginning inventory of DM:	6135	7425	8115	6135
Qty of DM to purchase:	**42,190**	**50,190**	**54,385**	**146,765**
Cost per unit:	$5	$5	$5	$5
Total Cost:	$210,950	$250,950	$271,925	$733,825

Extra Data	December	April
Units to be produced	4,900	5,600
Qty of DM used per unit	10	10
Qty of DM needed for production	**49,000**	**56,000**
Add: Target ending DM inventory	6135	9900
Total Qty of DM needed	55,135	65,900
Less: Beginning inventory of DM	7350	8400
Qty of DM to purchase	**47,785**	**57,500**
Cost per unit	$5	$5
Total Cost	$238,925	$287,500

FIGURE 7.4 Direct Materials Budget.

Direct Labor (DL) Budget				
	January	February	March	1st Quarter
Units to be produced:	4,090	4,950	5410	14,450
DL Hours per unit:	3.5	3.5	3.5	3.5
Total Hours:	**14,315**	**17,325**	**18,935**	**50,575**
Cost per DL Hour:	$12	$12	$12	$12
Total Cost:	$171,780	$207,900	$227,220	$606,900

Extra Data	
December	April
4,900	5,600
3.5	3.5
17,150	**19,600**
$12	$12
$205,800	$235,200

FIGURE 7.5 Direct Labor Budget.

No matter the formatting method, the formula used to complete the Raw Materials budget is

$$\begin{aligned} &\textit{Units To Be Produced} \times \textit{Per Unit Quantity} \\ &\quad + \textit{Target DM Ending Inventory} \\ &\quad - \textit{Beginning DM Inventory} \times \textit{Cost Per Unit} \\ &= \textit{Total Cost of DM} \end{aligned}$$

Direct Labor Budget

Like the Direct Materials Budget, the Direct Labor Budget follows the Production Budget. The Direct Labor Budget will determine how much labor will cost to complete the amount of units that need to be produced (figure 7.5). Wine Country Wine Racks pays laborers $12 per hour, and each wine rack takes 3.5 hours to complete.

If reflecting the quarter as a whole, the budget would look like the following:

TABLE 7.4 First Quarter Direct Labor Budget, 2018

Labor	
Units To Be produced:	14,450
DL Hours Per Unit:	3.5
Total Hours	50,575
Cost Per DL Hour:	$ 12
Total Cost:	$606,900

* Laborers are paid $12 per hour, and each wine rack takes 3.5 hours to complete.

No matter the formatting method, the formula used to complete the Direct Labor budget is

$$\begin{aligned} &\textit{Units To Be Produced} \times \textit{DL Hours Per Unit} \\ &\quad \times \textit{Cost per DL Hour} = \textit{Total DL Costs} \end{aligned}$$

Manufacturing Overhead Budget

The Manufacturing Overhead Budget is broken down into two components: fixed and variable overhead (Figure 7.6). Variable overhead is variable according to a cost driver that drives up the cost. Fixed overhead is a fixed amount. In order to determine the variable overhead rate, the company must estimate the total amount of variable overhead for the year and the total amount of the driver consumed during the year. In the case of Wine Country Wine Racks the driver that drives up overhead is Direct Labor Hours. Direct Labor Hours are estimated to be 202,300 hours per year, and variable overhead is estimated to be $535,000, breaking down to $2.64 per direct labor hour. Fixed overhead is budgeted based on the fixed rate. Wine Country Wine Racks has depreciation of machinery, plant rent, direct fixed labor, utilities, and property taxes as fixed amounts. Property taxes are due twice a year, in January and July, and are considered to be prepayments of the following six months.

If reflecting the quarter as a whole, the budget would look like the following:

Manufacturing Overhead (MOH) Budget					Extra Data	
	January	February	March	1st Quarter	December	April
Units to be produced:	4,090	4,950	5,410	**14,450**	4,900	5,600
Hours needed to produce:	14,315	17,325	18,935	**50,575**		
Variable MOH						
Based on DL Hour (2.64 [rounded] per DL Hour)	$37,857	$45,817	$50,075	**$133,750**	$45,355	$51,834
Fixed MOH						
Depreciation of Machinery:	$3,600	$3,600	$3,600	**$10,800**	3,600	3,600
Plant Rent:	$8,000	$8,000	$8,000	**$24,000**	$8,000	$8,000
Direct Fixed Labor:	$6,000	$6,000	$6,000	**$18,000**	$6,000	$6,000
Utilities:	$3,400	$3,400	$3,400	**$10,200**	3400	3400
Property Taxes:	$6,000			**$ 6,000**		
Total Fixed MOH:	$27,000	$21,000	$21,000	$69,000	21,000	21,000
Total MOH:	$64,857	$66,817	$71,075	$202,750	$66,355	$72,834

*Calculation for variable MOH requires that the $2.64 not be rounded.

FIGURE 7.6 Manufacturing Overhead Budget.

TABLE 7.5 First Quarter Manufacturing Overhead Budget, 2018

Labor	
Variable MOH:	$133,750
Fixed MOH:	
Depreciation of Machinery:	$ 10,800
Plant Rent:	$ 24,000
Direct Fixed Labor:	$ 18,000
Utilities:	$ 10,200
Property Taxes	$ 6,000
Total Fixed MOH:	$ 69,000
Total Overhead	$202,750

*Based on the wine racks taking 3.5 hours to produce and a variable overhead rate of $\frac{\$535{,}000}{202{,}300}$ (approximately $2.64) that is driven by DL Hours. Fixed overhead is based on monthly detail.

No matter the formatting method, the formula used to complete the Manufacturing Overhead budget is

Variable Overhead (based on variable rate × driver)
+ Fixed Overhead (based on budgeted amounts)
= Manufacturing Overhead

Operating Expenses Budget

The Operating Expenses Budget consists of expenses that are not related to the manufacturing process. Both variable and fixed expenses are budgeted for the Operating Expenses Budget (Figure 7.7).

If reflecting the quarter as a whole, the budget would look like the following:

TABLE 7.6 First Quarter Operating Expenses Budget, 2018

Operating Expenses	
Variable Expenses:	
Commissions (ten percent of sales):	$178,750
Shipping Expenses ($2 per unit sold):	$ 28,600
Total Variable Expenses:	$207,350

(continued)

Operating Expenses Budget					Extra Data	
	January	February	March	1st Quarter	December	April
Units to be sold:	4,000	4,900	5,400	**14,300**	5,000	5,500
Variable Expenses						
Commissions (10% of sales)	$50,000	$61,250	$67,500	**$178,750**	$62,500	$68,750
Shipping Expense ($2.00 per wine rack)	8,000	9,800	10,800	**28,600**	10,000	11,000
Total Variable Expense:	58,000	71,050	78,300	**207,350**	72,500	79,750
Fixed Expense						
Depreciation of office Equipment:	$800	$800	$800	**$2,400**	800	800
Office Rent:	$1,500	$1,500	$1,500	**$4,500**	$1,500	$1,500
Salaries	$12,000	$12,000	$12,000	**$36,000**	$12,000	$12,000
Utilities:	$750	$750	$750	**$2,250**	750	750
Property Taxes	$3,000			**$3,000**		
Total Fixed Expenses	$18,050	$15,050	$15,050	**$48,150**	15,050	15,050
Total Operating Expenses:	$76,050	$86,100	$93,350	**$255,500**	$87,550	$94,800

FIGURE 7.7 Operating Expenses Budget.

Fixed Expenses:	
Depreciation of Office Equipment:	$ 2,400
Office Rent:	$ 4,500
Salaries:	$ 36,000
Utilities:	$ 2,250
Property Taxes	$ 3,000
Total Fixed Expenses:	$ 48,150
Total Operating Expenses:	**$255,500**

*Variable Expenses based on units sold from the Sales and Revenues Budget. Fixed Expenses as detailed in monthly budget.

No matter the formatting method, the formula used to complete the Manufacturing Overhead Budget is:

Variable Expenses (based on units sold)
+ Fixed Expenses (based on budgeted amounts)
= Operating Expenses

Budget Income Statement

Before the Budgeted Income Statement can be prepared, including cost of goods sold, the cost per unit needs to be calculated. As noted in Figure 7.8, each wine rack costs $106 to make.

Once the calculation for per unit amount has been completed, the budgeted income statement can be prepared. The budgeted income statements pull the revenues from the Sales and Revenues Budget, the cost of goods sold amount from the number of units reported in the Sales and Revenues Budget times the cost per unit, and the operating expenses from the Operating Budget. By understanding the detail of materials, labor, and overhead, the Budgeted Income statement can reflect a fairly accurate estimation for the operating income amount.

The budgeted income statement is the final step of the Operating Budget. Once complete, the financial budgets can be completed. The Budgeted Income statement can be reflected for each month,

DM (10 BF per rack × $5 per BF):	$50
DL (3.5 hours per rack × $12 per hour):	$42
Variable MOH (2.64 × 3.5 hours):	$9
Fixed MOH (69000 for the qtr / 14450 units produced):	$5
Total cost per Wine Rack	$106

FIGURE 7.8 Unit Cost.

Budgeted Income Statement (Traditional Format)					
	January	February	March	1st Quarter	
Sales Revenue:	$500,000	$612,500	$675,000	$1,787,500	From Sales & Revenues Budget
Less: Cost of Goods Sold:	$424,000	$519,400	$572,400	$1,515,800	Revenue Budget & Per Unit Costs
Gross Profit:	$76,000	$93,100	$102,600	$271,700	
Less Operating Expenses:	$76,050	$86,100	$93,350	$255,500	From Operating Budget
Operating Income:	$(50)	$7,000	$9,250	$16,200	

FIGURE 7.9 Budgeted income Statement.

as noted in Figure 7.9, or for the quarter or the year as follows:

TABLE 7.7 Budgeted Income Statement

Quarter ending 03/30/18	
Revenue:	$1,787,500
Cost of Goods Sold: (14,300 × $106)	$1,515,800
Gross Profit:	$271,700
Operating Expenses:	$255,500
Operating Income:	$16,200

Financial Budgets

The financial budgets are comprised of the Capital Purchases Budget, the Cash Flows Budget, and the Budgeted Balance Sheet.

The Capital Purchases Budget is built from various decision-making tools that will be discussed later in the course. In the case of Wine Country Wine Racks, all capital purchases are taking place in January, during the first quarter of the year (Figure 7.10).

Capital Budget

The capital purchases can be reflected with monthly detail or for the quarter as follows:

TABLE 7.8 First Quarter Operating Expenses Budget, 2018

Equipment purchases	$200,000
Total quarterly purchases:	$200,000

	January	February	March	1st Qtr
Equipment	$20,000			$20,000
Total Capital Investment	$20,000			$20,000

FIGURE 7.10 Capital Purchases Budget.

Cash Summary

To prepare for the Cash Flows Budget, accountants should summarize all inflows and outflows, as noted below in Figure 7.11. Cash receipts and disbursements follow certain rules relating to when collection occurs or is paid. For Wine Country Wine Racks, the rule for receipts is that cash sales are collected in the month of the sale, and credit sales are collected the month following the sale. For material purchases, the company pays fifty percent in the month of the purchase and fifty percent in the following month. All labor is paid as incurred. Cash disbursements for manufacturing overhead and for operating expenses have the amounts of depreciation removed when calculating disbursements because depreciation is a non-cash expense. Due to the variable nature of cash flows, when completing the cash summary, it may be easier to track cash flows monthly as noted in Figure 7.11.

Cash Flows Budget

The Cash Flows Budget (Figure 7.12) can be calculated once cash disbursements and collections have been totaled. There are rules associated with the cash

Cash Collections and Disbursements Summary

	January	February	March	1st Quarter
Cash Collections				
25%	$125,000	$153,125	$168,750	**$446,875**
75%	$468,750	$375,000	$459,375	**$1,303,125**
Total Collections:	$593,750	$528,125	$628,125	**$1,750,000**

Cash Disbursements for Raw Materials	January	February	March	1st Quarter
50% month of	$105,475	$125,475	$135,963	**$366,913**
50% month after	$119,463	$105,475	$125,475	**$350,413**

Total Disbursements from Raw Material Purchase:	$224,938	$230,950	$261,438	**$717,325**

Cash Disbursements for Labor	January	February	March	1st Quarter
Total Disbursements for Labor:	$171,780	$207,900	$227,220	**$606,900**

Cash Disbursements for Manufacturing Overhead	January	February	March	1st Quarter
Total Overhead:	$64,857	$66,817	$71,075	**$202,750**
Less: Depreciation:	$3,600	$3,600	$3,600	**$10,800**
Total Cash Disbursements for MOH:	$61,257	$63,217	$67,475	**$191,950**

Cash Disbursements for Operating Expenses	January	February	March	1st Quarter
Total Expenses:	$76,050	$86,100	$93,350	**$255,500**
Less: Depreciation:	$800	$800	$800	**$2,400**

Total Cash Disbursements for Operating Expenses:	$75,250	$85,300	$92,550	**$253,100**

Total Disbursements	January	February	March	1st Quarter
Disbursements other than Raw Materials	$308,287	$356,417	$387,245	**$1,769,275**

FIGURE 7.11 Cash Collections/Disbursements.

Budgeted Cash Flows

	January	February	March	1st Quarter
Beginning Cash Balance	$5,000	$5,463	$161,870	$5,000
Cash Collections	$593,750	$528,125	$628,125	$1,750,000
Total Cash Available	$598,750	$533,588	$789,995	$1,755,000
Less: Cash Disbursements	$308,287	$356,417	$387,245	$1,051,950
Less: Equipment Purchases	$300,000	$0	$0	$300,000
Cash Balance	–$9,537	$177,170	$402,750	$403,050
Financing:				
New Borrowing	$15,000	$0	$0	$15,000
Debt Repayment	$0	$15,000	$0	$15,000
Interest	$0	$300	$0	$300
Ending Cash Balance	$5,463	$161,870	$402,750	$402,750

FIGURE 7.12 Budgeted Cash Flows.

flows. The rules for Wine Country Wine Racks are as follows:

- Account must maintain a bank balance of $5,000 and borrow in $1,000 increments.
- Borrowings take place at the end of the month.
- Interest payments take place at the end of the month at a two percent monthly rate.
- Repayment takes place at the end of the month.

Budgeted Balance Sheet

The Budgeted Balance Sheet (Figure 7.13) has to be the last budget completed because it requires input from all the other budgets. For the March 31 Wine Country Wine Racks Budgeted Balance Sheet:

- The cash balance is a result of the March 31 cash balance listed on the budgeted Cash Flows.
- The Accounts Receivable Balance is a result of the amount outstanding from the Sales and Revenues Budget on March 31.
- Raw Materials Inventory is the target ending inventory for March multiplied by the cost per unit.
- The Finished Goods Inventory is the target ending inventory from productions budget multiplied by the per-unit cost.
- The prepaid property tax amount for March 31 is the remaining six months of property taxes. Property taxes are paid in January and July for the manufacturing plant and for the office buildings. Therefore, amounts are taken from the Manufacturing Overhead Budget and from the Operating Budget. January's payment signified a prepayment of six months. As of March 31, three months are still outstanding.
- Although a given amount, the property plant and equipment amount would consist of all property, plant, and equipment already on the balance sheet plus newly purchased equipment, net of any accumulated depreciation.
- The Accounts Payable is the fifty percent due from March.
- The Income Tax Liability amount is based on operating income from the budgeted income statement, calculated at a thirty-five percent tax rate.
- Although a given amount, the Stockholders' Equity amount would be based on the prior year's Stockholder's Equity amount + net income (operating income – taxes) – dividends.

Period Ended 03/31/18				
Assets:				
Cash	$402,750			From Budgeted Cash Flow
Accounts Receivable	$506,250			From Sales & Revenues Budget
Raw Materials Inventory	$42,000			From Direct Materials Budget
Finished Goods Inventory	$58,089			From Production Budget at per unit rate
Prepaid Property Taxes	$4,500			From Operating Budget and Overhead Budget
Total Current Assets		$1,013,589		
Property, Plant, and Equip.		$1,023,200	(given)	
Total Assets		$2,036,789		
Liabilities and Equity:				
Accounts Payable		$135,963		From Cash Budget
Income Tax Liability (35%)		$3,963		From Budgeted Income Statement
Other Current Liabilities		$0		
Stockholders' Equity		$1,896,863	(given)	
		$2,036,789		

FIGURE 7.13 Budgeted Balance Sheet.

TOPIC 7 REFERENCES

Sutherland, R. "Sweat the Small Stuff." *TED*. Retrieved from: http://www.ted.com/talks/rory_sutherland_sweat_the_small_stuff?language=en (2010).\

Vaznoniene, M. "Corporate Budgets and Their Limitations: A Case Study of Meat and Poultry Producers." *Economics & Rural Development*, 8(2), 37-49. (2012).

TOPIC 8 Standard Costs

LEARNING GOALS

1. Explain the need for standard costs.
2. Explain the significance of standard costs to the budgeting process.
3. Use direct material, direct labor, and manufacturing overhead standards for computing standard costs.
4. Introduce variances derived from the use of standards

INTRODUCTION

Topic 8 is focused on standard costs. Standards are part of the budgeting process as companies seek to provide a benchmark for inputs and motivation for employee behavior. Learning Goal 1 provides an overview of standards and the types of standards a company may use. Learning Goal 2 introduces the standard cost card and the use of standards in the budgeting process. Learning Goal 3 looks specifically at the process of standardization. What questions need to be answered in the process of creating standards and how standards are tracked and maintained? Learning Goal 4 will complete the discussion of standards by introducing the concept of variance analysis.

LEARNING GOAL 1: Explain the Need for Standard Costs

Before investigating the topic of standard costs, one must truly understand the concept of standards in general. Merriam-Webster states that a standard is a "level of quality, achievement, etc., that is considered acceptable or desirable." There are standards for just about everything in life. If you investigate the topic of standards, you can find standards for music, sports, mathematics, education, and any other topic imaginable. There are standards of conduct and standards of performance. You know from your own experience that at times in your life you have been held to certain standards. What was the purpose of those standards? How did the standards help you? Standards can be low or high; they can motivate or they can discourage.

In the managerial accounting context, standards are needed for a variety of reasons including establishing costs of products and amount of input. According to the Kaplan Financial Knowledge Bank, authors of accounting exam preparation material, standards come in four forms: 1) attainable, 2) basic, 3) current, and 4) ideal.

Attainable Standards

An attainable standard provides a realistic goal for employees to reach during the manufacturing process. The standards allow for normal allowances of machine breakdowns, worker fatigue and breaks, and material waste. Because the standards are attainable, they serve as a motivational tool for employees. Such standards are frequently used because of their applicability to most job environments and because of their reasonable allowance for "less-than-perfect" performance.

Basic Standards

Unlike attainable standards, basic standards are not used to evaluate current efficiency. Instead, such standards serve as long-term measures used to show trends regarding material pricing, labor rates, and labor efficiency.

Current Standards

Current standards are used for current working circumstances. When current conditions fall outside of "normal" activity, current standards serve as an intermediary between "normal" activity and activity that is currently being experienced.

Ideal Standards

Ideal standards are based on perfect operations. Ideal standards do not allow room for breakdowns, labor downtime, wasted material, or stoppages of any kind. Although ideal standards may serve as motivational for some employees, most employees are discouraged by a constant standard of perfection that may not be attainable on a consistent level.

Why Have Standards

Managerial accountants need standards for two purposes: 1) benchmarks and 2) motivation. As Merriam-Webster points out, standards provide a desirable level of quality or achievement. Thus, by definition, standards serve as a benchmark, something that provides a basis of measurement. Motivation is a second purpose for having standards. Motivation can be a difficult activity to attain in the manufacturing environment. However, by providing benchmarks that are within reach, such standards can serve the purpose of motivation. There are advantages and disadvantages of using standards. See Figure 8.1 to understand the implications for the use of standards.

The idea of standards is grounded in the work of Frederick Winslow Taylor, who is said to be the father of time-motion studies. "Taylorism," as it has come to be called, has received bad press in that the concept has been seen as a way to make a manufacturing workforce scientific, causing human resources to work harder and faster, squeezing as much out of each laborer as possible. Thus, standardization is said to be the death of creativity and a demotivating

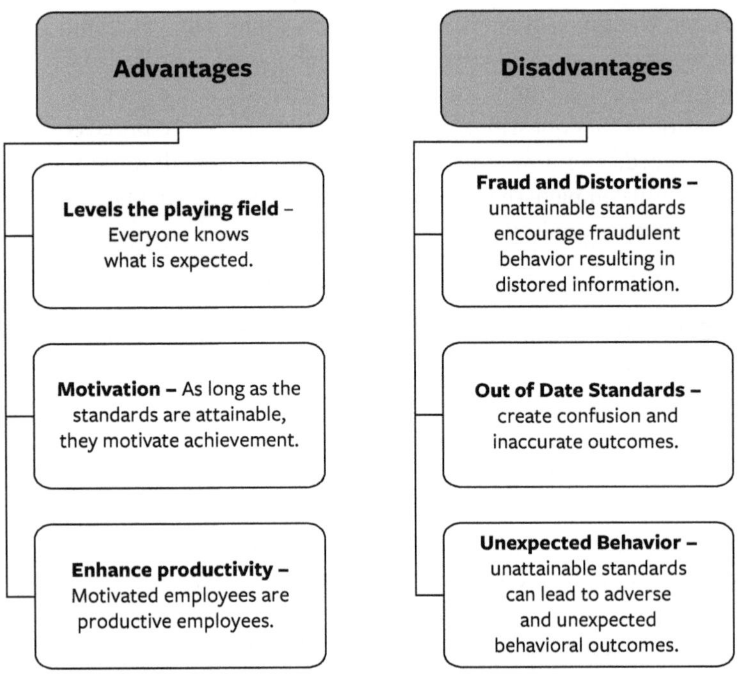

FIGURE 8.1 Advantages and Disadvantages of Standards.

force for employees. The truth is, however, standards do quite the opposite than proposed above. Standards can actually increase the power of both management and workers. Instead of demotivating employees, the use of standards can actually empower them by helping them work smarter, not harder.

Approaches to Implementing Standards

Standards can be implemented in a variety of ways. Standards may come from past performance, where the standard is built from what the organization successfully did in the past. The problem with implementing standards from past performance is that past performance mistakes may accompany the standards, leaving such standards out of date. Standards may also be implemented by using the current marketplace. The current marketplace would provide for up-to-date standards and address any nuances that may be taking place as a result of the current environment. Competitor standards could also be used, in which an organization gains an understanding for what the competitor is using as a standard practice within their organization. Competitor information, however, may or may not be readily available. Many standards that competitors use are protected as trade secrets. Ideally, the best approach to creating standards is to combine the approaches noted above, using the past but tweaking for the future.

LEARNING GOAL 2: Explain the Significance of Standard Costs to the Budgeting Process

What is the point of standards, where are they used, and what purpose do they serve? Standards are used in the budgeting process. When you were building the master budget, you were given information as to the time the laborer should take to complete one unit, the amount of input (material) that was used, the cost of the material, and the cost of labor. Such amounts are derived from standards. A standard cost card, then, houses the standards for materials, labor, and overhead in one location. See Figure 8.3 below for information contained in a standard cost card.

In the above standard cost card, the company has used a standard of five yards of material for the product being made. The standard may be based on an attainable standard that allows for waste; a current standard, based on special circumstances; a basic standard that is in place primarily to track the standards over the long term; or an ideal standard, which does not allow for any waste. Additionally, the company has a standard of .75 hours to make the product and variable overhead that is driven by direct labor. In terms of standard prices/rates, the cost standard for the material is $1.50 per yard, a labor standard that is $12.00 per hour, and a variable overhead standard that is $4.50 per labor hour. Such standards outline the expected amounts of input at the expected pricing. Any deviations from the standards will result in a variance. Many companies use standards. UPS, for example, uses standards relating to deliver driver routes. Pizza restaurants have standards relating to how much ingredient to put on a pizza. Standards keep the end product uniform and provide a benchmark for which workers can follow.

LEARNING GOAL 3: Use Direct Material, Direct Labor, and Manufacturing Overhead Standards for Computing Standard Costs

When referring to material standards, the standard can be for quantity or price. When referring to labor standards, the standard can be for quantity or rate. When referring to overhead standards, the standard can be for rate or quantity. When referring to overhead, the quantity standard refers to the amount of the input that drives up overhead. Many times overhead is driven by labor hours or machine hours. If the overhead is driven by labor hours, the quantity of input will be the same for overhead as the quantity of input for the labor standard.

Let's look at the example of a pizza restaurant and how the use of standards can benefit the organization. Paul's Pizza Parlor is a local restaurant that makes pizza. Paul would like to franchise the pizza parlor and wants to ensure that his process is

MAKE IT REAL 8-1

UPS is an example of a company that has found the value in implementing standards. The company has developed standards for driver safety, timely package delivery, and cost-saving techniques by implementing policies that require that drivers complete their routes using no left turns. Drivers are also required to use twelve steps to retrieve packages out of the truck in under 15.5 seconds. Such rigorous standards are not achievable by everyone. To work for UPS, a driver must be able to meet the standards.

To naysayers who doubt that UPS saves money by making no left turns, the TV show *Mythbusters* checked it out and confirmed the cost-saving technique.

https://www.youtube.com/watch?v=cTuqgr8vd7o
https://www.youtube.com/watch?v=HV_bJxkdNDE
http://www.discovery.com/tv-shows/mythbusters/videos/right-turn-only-minimyth/
https://upload.wikimedia.org/wikipedia/commons/6/6a/2010_NCCBF_Grand_Parade_2010-04-18_30.JPG

References

Beesburg. "UPS Driver Training." YouTube. Retrieved from https://www.youtube.com/watch?v=cTuqgr8vd7o (2012).

"Right Turn Only Minimyth." *Mythbusters*. Retreived from http://www.discovery.com/tv-shows/mythbusters/videos/right-turn-only-minimyth/ (n.d.).

Stoffel, B. "Why UPS Trucks Never Turn Left." *CNN Money*. Retrieved from https://www.youtube.com/watch?v=HV_bJxkdNDE (2010).

Image

"The Grand Parade of the 2010 Northern California Cherry Blossom Festival in San Francisco, California." Broken Sphere. Retrieved from https://upload.wikimedia.org/wikipedia/commons/6/6a/2010_NCCBF_Grand_Parade_2010-04-18_30.JPG (2010).

FIGURE 8.2 UPS.

Inputs	Qty Hours / Materials	Qty Price / Rate	Total Standard Cost
Materials	5 yards	$1.50 per yard	$7.50
Labor	.75 hours	$12.00 per hour	$9.00
Variable Manufacturing Overhead	.75 hours	$4.50 per labor hour	$3.38
Total Standard			$19.88

FIGURE 8.3 Standard Cost Card (per unit).

MAKE IT REAL 8-2

Toyota is a company that has refined the art of understanding standard costs. In order to make a vehicle with the least amount of cost as possible, waste must be eliminated. By eliminating waste and controlling costs, Toyota is able to sell their vehicles at an affordable price. The Toyota Production System (TPS) is known for its efficiency. By applying concepts of Kaizen manufacturing and a Just in Time (JIT) approach, Toyota is able to define the tasks that go into manufacturing an automobile and standardize the process.

https://upload.wikimedia.org/wikipedia/commons/4/45/HK_Wan_Chai_39_Gloucester_Road_Harcourt_House_sign_Toyota_logo_Crown_Motors_Nov-2012.JPG
http://www.toyota.com.au/toyota/company/operations/toyota-production-system

FIGURE 8.4

standardized. Paul needs to consider the following information.

Dough:

1. How much of each ingredient goes into the dough?
2. How long should the dough be kneaded?
3. How long does the dough need to rise?
4. How much should the ingredients costs?
5. At what temperature should the dough rise?

Sauce:

1. How much of each ingredient goes into the sauce?
2. How much should the ingredients costs?

Pizza-making process:

1. How much dough is used for various size pizzas?
2. How many ounces of sauce go on the various size pizzas?
3. How much of each ingredient goes on the pizza? For example, how many pepperonis go on a pepperoni pizza, or how many ounces of black olives go on a pepperoni and black olive pizza? How many ounces of cheese go on each pizza?
4. In what order do the ingredients go on the pizza?
5. How long should the pizza bake?
6. How many pieces should the pizza be cut into?
7. How much should Paul pay for each of the ingredients?

Packaging:

1. How will the pizza be packaged for pickup or delivery?
2. How will the pizza be packaged for dine in?

Overhead:

1. What costs are included in overhead?
2. What drives overhead costs?

Once Paul is able to answer each of the above questions, he will have a standardized process which will become a part of his master budget. Let's create a cost card of standards for the pepperoni pizza of Paul's Pizza Parlor.

TABLE 8.1 Paul's Pizza Parlor Standard Cost Card (per pepperoni pizza)

Inputs	(A) Quantity Hours/ Materials	(B) Quantity Rate/Price	(A × B) Total Standard Cost
Materials			
*Dough	10 ounces	$.10 per ounces	$1.00
**Sauce	3 ounces	$.50 per ounces	$1.50
Pepperoni	25 pieces	$.01 per piece	$.25
Labor	.05 hours	$12.00 per hour	$.60
****Variable Manufacturing Overhead*	.05 hours	$5.40 per labor hour	$.27
Total Standard			$3.62

*Dough would require its own standard cost card, and price for the pepperoni pizza cost card would be determined by the dough cost card.
**Sauce would require its own standard cost card, and price for the pepperoni pizza cost card would be determined by the sauce cost card.
***Variable overhead:

$$\frac{\$90{,}000 \textit{ estimated annual variable overhead}}{16{,}640 \textit{ estimated annual direct labor hours}}$$

Benefits of Standardizing

As you can see, once Paul standardizes his work flow, he will have a clearer idea of the amounts of his inputs and the costs of making one product. Realistically, Paul would want to complete a cost card for each item on his menu so that he would understand the standard costs of each product. By breaking down the standards into material, labor, and overhead, Paul will understand each input of making the product and how total costs will change in relation to the number of inputs.

LEARNING GOAL 4: Introduce Variances Derived From the Use of Standards

When creating budgets with the use of standards, such standards can be used to calculate variances. Once a company has made a product, it may find that actual costs do not match the budgeted amounts. The differences between the actual costs and the budgeted amounts (represented by standards) are considered to be variances. Every company will have variance because it is impossible to perform exactly as was budgeted. Variances may exist because the actual activity either over-performed or under-performed in comparison to the budgeted standards. The difference may be attributable to the actual performance level or to the standard itself. If a standard is out of date, the variance may be caused by an inaccurate standard. If the standards in place are ideal standards, the variance may be caused from actual performance that is less than the ideal performance expected.

Variance exists at several levels for material, labor, and overhead. Ultimately, a manager wants to get to the heart of if the variance lies at the level of a difference in price/rate paid for materials or laborers, or a difference in quantity used or time taken. Variances are part of the controlling phase and will, therefore, be discussed as part of Topic 15. However, in understanding standards, one must understand that costs of inputs (labor and material) and the amounts of inputs (labor and material) are measured by either attainable standards, basic standards, current standards, or ideal standards. Such measurement will eventually impact the variance.

TOPIC 8 REFERENCES

Bakie, K. "Birdhouse. Cincinnati, OH." Wikimedia, Retrieved from: https://commons.wikimedia.org/wiki/File:Birdhouse_073.jpg (2005).

"Basic Vanilla Cake. Food Network Kitchen." *Food Network Magazine*. Retrieved from http://www.foodnetwork.com/recipes/food-network-kitchens/basic-vanilla-cake-recipe.html (n.d.).

"Build a Birdhouse in 7 Easy Steps." *Popular Mechanics*. Retrieved from http://www.popularmechanics.com/home/how-to-plans/how-to/g1528/build-a-birdhouse-in-7-easy-steps/ (n.d.).

"Buttercream Icing for Wedding Cakes." Allrecipes.com. Retrieved from http://allrecipes.com/recipe/7410/wedding-cake-frosting/ (n.d.)

Ferroni, L. "Classic Glazed Donuts." *Epicurious*. Retrieved from http://www.epicurious.com/recipes/food/views/classic-glazed-doughnuts-51160200 (2013).

Sady, S. "How to Make Pizza Dough." *Susan's Cooking School*. Retrieved from https://www.youtube.com/watch?v=C-2C6v9mGuR0 (2009).

"Standard." *Merriam-Webster.com*. Retrieved from: http://www.merriam-webster.com/dictionary/standard (n.d.).

Stoffel, B. "Why UPS Trucks Never Turn Left." *CNNMoney*. Retrieved from https://www.youtube.com/watch?v=HV_bJxkdNDE (2010).

"UPS Driver Training." *ABC News*. Retrieved from https://www.youtube.com/watch?v=cTuqgr8vd70 (2012).

TOPIC 8 FIGURE CREDITS

TOPIC 9 Capital Budgeting

LEARNING GOALS

1. Recognize management's use of various capital investment decisions.
2. Describe capital budgeting decision techniques.
3. Define strengths and weakness of capital budgeting decisions.
4. Integrate capital budgeting decision techniques with the budget.

INTRODUCTION

Topic 9 is focused on capital investment decisions. Capital investment decisions are part of the budgeting process but are not part of the operating budget. Whereas the operating budget addresses day-to-day flow of an organization's resources, capital budgeting decisions deal with long-term choices such as investing in a project or purchasing a new piece of equipment. Capital budgeting decisions must factor in considerations of time because the assets are long term. Thus, the operating budget considers costs that flow through the income statement, whereas capital budgeting considers costs that flow through the balance sheet.

LEARNING GOAL 1: Recognize Management's Use of Various Capital Investment Decision

Depending on their level of management, managers may or may not be concerned with capital investment decisions. Not all managers make capital budgeting/investment decisions. Managers of cost centers and revenue centers are concerned with controlling costs or revenues that are within their scope of responsibility. Managers of profit centers are also not concerned with capital budgeting decisions but are concerned with the overall revenues and costs. Managers of investment centers, however, make decisions that use large sums of money and impact the company at broad levels. See the master budget below (Figure 9.1) for areas

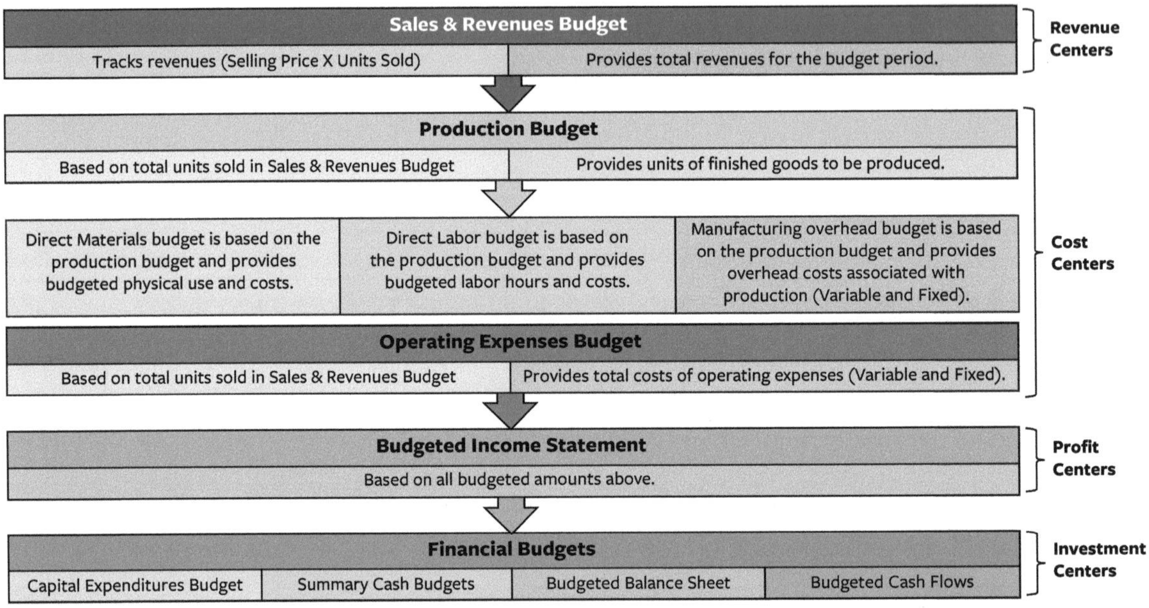

FIGURE 9.1 Master Budget Areas of Management Responsibility.

of responsibility and the management levels impacted by capital budgeting decisions.

Because capital budget decisions are long-term decisions that involves large amounts of money, management should follow a series of steps to make the decisions (Figure 9.2). The steps include:

- Recognize that a capital investment must be made.
- Investigate options.
- Perform analyses.
- Screening analysis
- Decision analysis

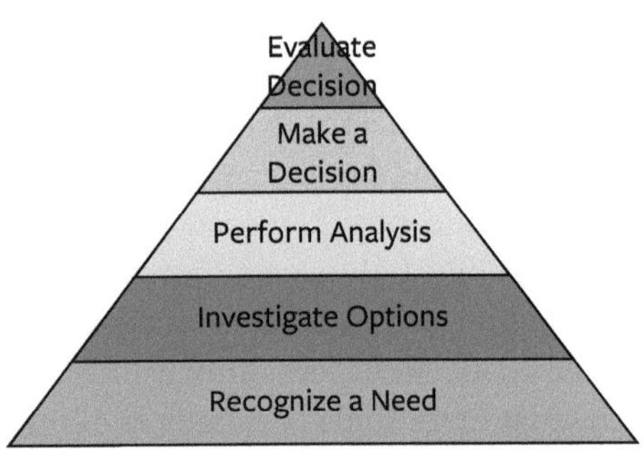

FIGURE 9.2 Capitol Budgeting Decision Steps.

- Make a decision.
- Evaluate the decision.

Recognize a Capital Investment Needs to be Made

Management will recognize that a capital investment decision needs to be made in a variety of ways. A new piece of equipment may need to be purchased or refurbished, a new building may need to be purchased, or the company may want to invest in a new project. Situations that give rise to making a capital budgeting decision include expanding operations, having equipment that has come to the end of its useful life, or increasing efficiency within the operation. At the point of recognition, management would need to begin investigating options.

Investigate Options

Investigating options involves looking at decisions such as those concerning purchasing new equipment, refurbishing existing equipment, renting the equipment instead of purchasing it, or doing nothing. By investigating all options available, management can make a clear and informed decision.

Perform Analysis

In performing analysis, managers use various techniques that help them make the best decision for the company. Such techniques will be discussed in Learning Goal 2. Regardless of technique, however, managers need to make decisions that impact cash flows. Even if a company operates on the accrual basis, capital budgeting decisions are converted to cash flow because such decisions impact cash flow.

Cash Inflows. When management considerers the cash inflow of a capital investment, inflows may include future revenue. In purchasing an item that has revenue capabilities, the inflow of such item needs to be considered. For example, let's say that a piece of equipment will produce $100,000 in revenue each year for the next five years. The $100,000 is an inflow of cash to be considered in purchasing the capital expenditure. Other inflows could include the lack of an outflow. If the same piece of equipment will also save the company $2,000 per year, the lack of the outflow is considered an inflow. Additionally, let's say that the piece of equipment can be resold at the end of its useful life of five years for $25,000. The $25,000 would be considered residual value and is considered an inflow.

Cash Outflows. Cash outflows are a little more obvious than cash inflows. Cash outflows include the purchase price of the equipment and any other installation costs that could be incurred to make the piece of equipment ready for use. Cash outflows could also include maintenance costs that must be incurred each year to keep the equipment in good working condition. Perhaps the piece of equipment purchased requires annual maintenance of $5,000 each year. Thus, in considering outflows, all cash that is expended to purchase or keep the equipment running is considered an outflow of the capital investment.

Net Cash Flows. Net cash flow is a term that is used simply to reflect the inflow of cash netted with the outflow.

Screening vs. decision analysis. Once cash flows have been determined, the analysis can begin. Screening analysis uses analysis tools to determine if an investment is feasible or logical whereas decision analysis is used to arrive at a final decision. A company may have five options that are up for debate. After performing a screening analysis, only three of the five may be determined to be feasible. Decision analysis can be performed on the three remaining options to determine which of the three options is the best choice.

Make a Decision

When making a decision about a capital investment, management needs to be thorough in order to make a well-informed decision. After analyzing the cash flows and applying a decision-making tool, management can be sure to make a decision that has considered all available options.

Evaluate the Decision

Although the decision-making process may take some time, the process should produce the best decision for the company. Sometimes, however, even the best thought-out decision process results in a decision that is not optimal. In such a case, management must be aware of how the decision could have been better. Thus, analyzing the decision is an important step in order to improve the process.

LEARNING GOAL 2: Describe Capital Budgeting Decision Techniques

As noted above, the analysis stage of capital budgeting can be divided into two types of analysis (Figure 9.3). The first type of analysis is a screening analysis. The intent of screening is to take all the options that were gathered during the investigation process and determine which options will make the best starting point for making a decision. Although a multitude of tools

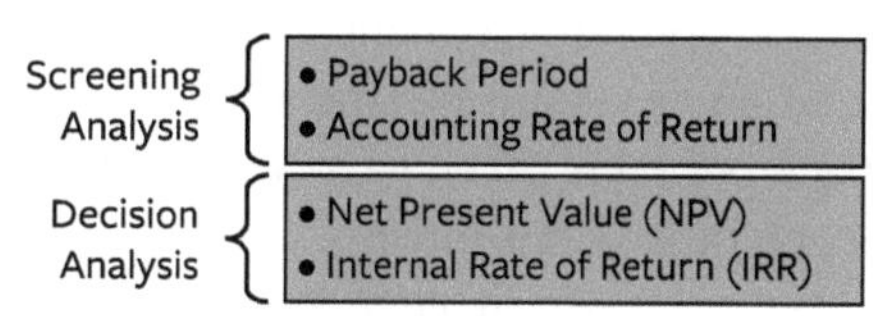

FIGURE 9.3 Analysis Tools.

exist to analyze capital investments, this textbook will focus on two tools of screening and two tools for making decisions. The two tools used for screening include the payback period and the accounting rate of return (simple rate of return). The two tools used for making decisions include the Net Present Value (NPV) method and the Internal Rate of Return (IRR).

Screening Analysis

When screening for potential capital budgeting decisions, management wants to find out if the investment is feasible. Two tools that will provide information as to the feasibility of a project include the payback period and the accounting rate of return. Such tools provide surface data, but this data will be helpful for either short-term capital budgeting decisions or screening for longer-term capital budgeting decisions.

Payback Period. The payback period is the period of time that it would take to recover from an investment. The payback period can be calculated in two ways. The first way to calculate the payback period involves an equal amount of expected annual net cash inflows for every year. Let's say the company was contemplating investing in investment project A. The formula used to determine if project A is an acceptable project under the payback period is:

$$\textit{Payback period} = \frac{\textit{Amount Invested}}{\textit{Expected Annual Net Cash Inflow}}$$

If the investment in project A is $120,000, and the expected annual net cash inflow is $20,000 each year for the next ten years, the project will be paid back in six years ($\frac{\$120,000}{\$20,000}$). If the company had criteria that allowed for investments to be accepted if the payback period is five years or less, the company would rule out this capital investment. If the company had criteria that allowed for investments to be accepted if the payback period is seven years or less, the capital investment would be accepted.

Now let's say for project B that the amount invested remains the same, but the expected annual net cash inflow is not the same year after year. In this case, the formula does not work. Thus, in order to determine the payback period, net cash inflows will need to accumulate until the original investment is paid back.

TABLE 9.1 Project B

Year	Annual Cash Inflow	Accumulated Annual Cash Inflow
1	$3,000	$3,000
2	$5,000	$8,000
3	$10,000	$18,000
4	$15,000	$33,000
5	$20,000	$53,000
6	$20,000	$73,000
7	$20,000	$93,000
8	$20,000	$113,000
9	$20,000	$133,000
10	$20,000	$153,000

As noted above for project B, the original investment is paid back some time in year 9. We want to be more exact than indicting that the investment is paid back some time in year 9, however. Therefore, we need to determine how much of year 9 is needed to complete the payback of the investment. The following formula is used:

Initial Investment –
Cumulative Amount Received in the Year
Before the Payback Year = Total Left

$$\$120,00 - \$113,000 = \$7,000$$

Once the total amount left has been calculated, the total amount left is divided by the amount that will be received in the year of the payback. The resulting amount is the percentage of the payback year that will be needed to payback the original investment

$$\frac{\$7,000}{\$20,000} = .35 \textit{ years}$$

Based on the uneven net annual inflows, the investment will be paid back in 8.35 years or just over eight years and four months.

Accounting Rate of Return (Simple Rate of Return). The accounting rate of return is the second tool that is a good screening tool. Management would use this tool to find out what type of return the asset would have over its useful life. As mentioned earlier, the focus for capital investments is on cash flow. However, the accounting rate of return begins with net operating income.

$$\textit{Accounting Rate of Return} = \frac{(\textit{Average Annual Net Cash Flow} - \textit{Annual Depreciation})}{\textit{Initial Investment}}$$

If Project A was being evaluated by the Accounting Rate of Return, the company would need to have an acceptable rate of return over which the investment would need to surpass. Let's say the investment in project A is $120,000 and the expected annual net cash inflow is $20,000 each year for the next ten years. If the annual depreciation is $12,000 and the salvage value is $0, the Accounting Rate of Return is 6.67% ($20,000-$12,000)/$120,000). If the company had criteria that allowed for investments to be accepted if the rate of return is 7% or greater, the company would rule out this capital investment. If the company had criteria that allowed for investments to be accepted if the rate of return is 6% or greater, the capital investment would be accepted.

Now, let's say that the amount invested remains the same, but the annual depreciation is $10,000, and the salvage value is $20,000. The Accounting Rate of Return calculation would look like this:

$$\textit{Accounting Rate of Return} = \frac{(\$20{,}000 - \$10{,}000)}{\$120{,}000}$$

$$\textit{Accounting Rate of Return} = \frac{\$10{,}000}{\$120{,}00}$$

$$\textit{Accounting Rate of Return} = 8.3\%$$

$${}^{*}\textit{Depreciation} = \frac{(\$120{,}000 - \$20{,}000)}{10\ \textit{years}} = \$10{,}000$$

Note that the Accounting Rate of Return was increased once salvage value was considered.

Now, let's consider project B, which has uneven cash flows (Figure 9.4). If project B is the same as project A in all regards except for cash flow, let's say the Accounting Rate of Return first considers no salvage value. The formula might look like this:

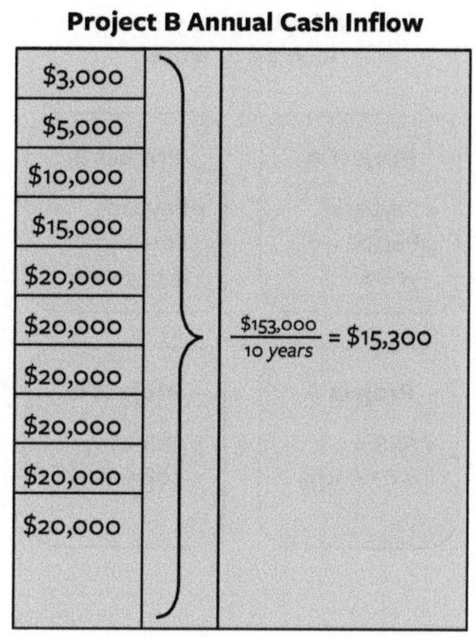

FIGURE 9.4 Project B Annual Cash Flow.

$$\textit{Accounting Rate of Return} = \frac{(\$15{,}300 - \$12{,}000^{**})}{\$120{,}000}$$

$$\textit{Accounting Rate of Return} = \frac{\$3{,}300}{\$120{,}000}$$

$$\textit{Accounting Rate of Return} = 2.75\%$$

$$^{**}\textit{Depreciation} = \frac{(\$120{,}000 - \$0)}{10\ \textit{years}} = \$12{,}000$$

Now, if we use the uneven cash flow amounts and a salvage value of $20,000, the formula would look like this:

$$\textit{Accounting Rate of Return} = \frac{(\$15{,}300 - \$\,10{,}000^{**})}{\$120{,}000}$$

$$\textit{Accounting Rate of Return} = \frac{\$5{,}300}{\$120{,}000}$$

$$\textit{Accounting Rate of Return} = 4.42\%$$

$$^{**}\textit{Depreciation} = \frac{(\$120{,}000 - \$20{,}000)}{10\ \textit{years}} = \$10{,}000$$

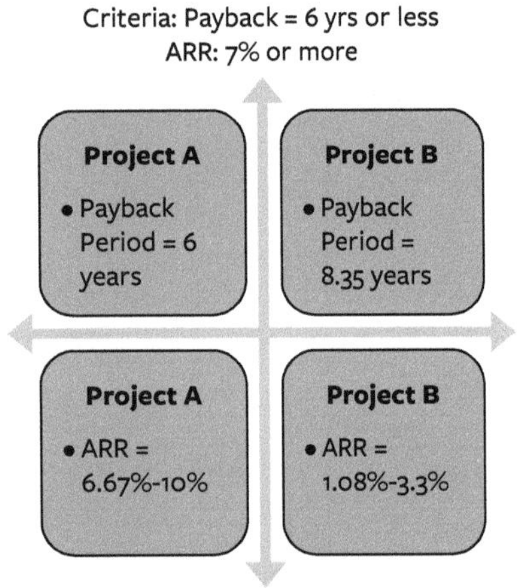

FIGURE 9.5 Screening Summary.

As expected, by increasing salvage value, the Accounting Rate of Return was also increased.

Summary of screening tools. As a summary for the screening tools of payback period and accounting rate of return, consider Project A and Project B under the scenario that the company accepts investments that are paid back in six years or less and have a rate of return of 7% or more (Figure 9.5). When the net annual inflow values are the same every year under Project A, the company would accept the investment under the payback period but not under the Accounting Rate of Return. When the cash flows are not even as in Project B, the company would accept the investment under neither the payback method nor under the Accounting Rate of Return method. Screening investments in this way may provide inconsistent results under the two methods. A company could have criteria in place where one or both of the initial screening tools must elicit an acceptable result for the project to move on to decision analysis.

Decision Analysis

Once the project/investment has passed the screening tool(s), it moves into a position where management must rate it against other tools that have also passed the screening process. The goal of management in using decision analysis is to hone in on the best decision. Two tools will be discussed as common tools for decision making: Net Present Value and Internal Rate of Return. In order to use the tools that are part of decision analysis, the time value of money must be taken into consideration.

Time Value of Money. Time value of money is the concept that a dollar today is worth more than a dollar tomorrow because the dollar today can be invested. Therefore, it is preferable to receive cash sooner rather than later.

Time value of money can be calculated manually, with the help of tables, with the use of a calculator, or in Excel. For the purposes of this textbook, we will use Excel to perform TVM calculations.

As it relates to making capital investment decisions, the purpose in understanding the TVM is to be able to bring future inflows and outflows to the present so that all projects can be judged from present dollars. For example, if a project or an investment will be producing income in years 1-3, the time value is needed to bring year 1 income to present dollars, year 2 income to present dollars, and year 3 income to present dollars. Whether the amounts in year 1-3 are consistent or different will determine how we perform the calculation.

Five variables will always be needed in time value of money calculation: 1) PV (present value), 2) FV (future value), 3) N (number of periods), 4) i (interest rate), and 5) PMT (payment amount). One of the five variables is that which we need to solve for, and one of the variables may be zero.

Let's return to Project A. Project A has cash inflows of $20,000 for ten years. When considering the TVM, one cannot simply take $20,000 multiplied by ten years to determine the present value as each year is weighted differently. Receiving the same amount of cash inflow every year is considered an annuity, so we'd have to solve for the present value of an annuity.

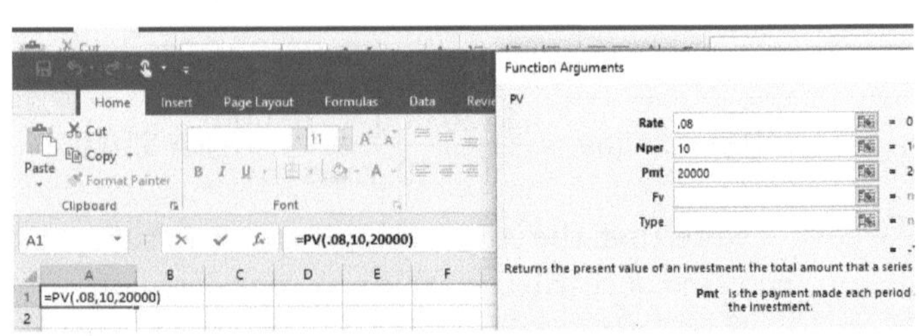

FIGURE 9.6 Excel Calculation.

In this case, the variables used would look like this if we calculate at an 8% interest rate:

PV = Solving for
FV = 0 (not used)
N = 10
i = 8% (.08)
PMT = $20,000

The Excel calculation is as follows:

The total amount of $20,000 each year for the next ten years in present dollars is $134,201.63. This amount is different than the $20,000 multiplied by 10 years $\$20{,}000 \times 10 = 200{,}000$) because of the interest rate, otherwise known as the discount rate, hurdle rate, or required rate of return. The amount of $200,000 has been discounted to the present value.

Now, let's return to Project B. Project B had uneven inflows, so using the present value of annuity would not be possible. Each year has to be calculated individually. Let's calculate for each of the ten years.

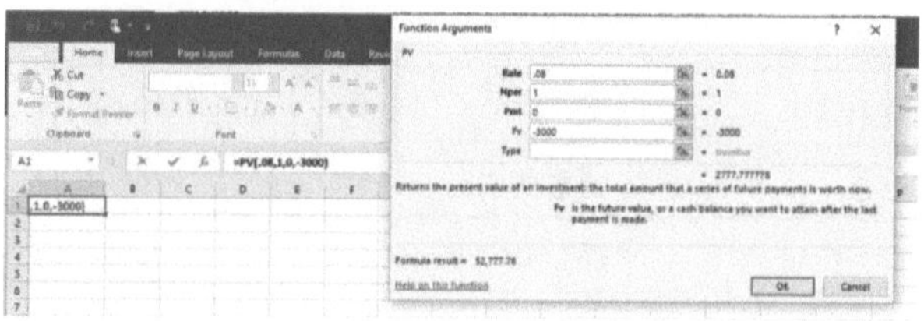

FIGURE 9.7 Year 1.

Note that the "Pmt" field has not been used because we are simply trying to find the present value of a single future amount, not of an annuity. Instead, the "FV" has an amount entered. The "FV" amount must be entered as a negative amount in order to remit a positive result.

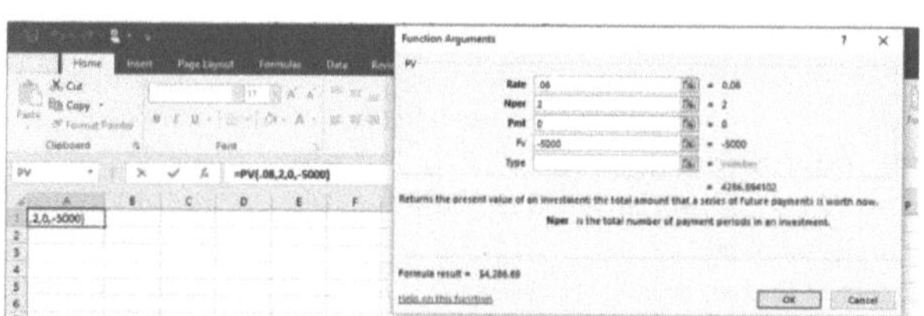

FIGURE 9.8 Year 2.

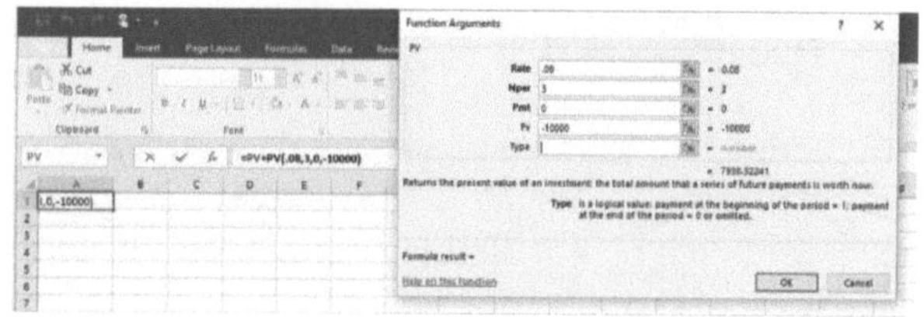

FIGURE 9.9 Year 3.

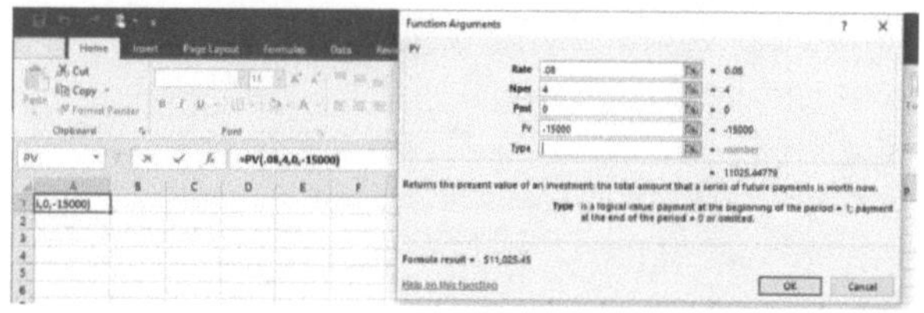

FIGURE 9.10 Year 4.

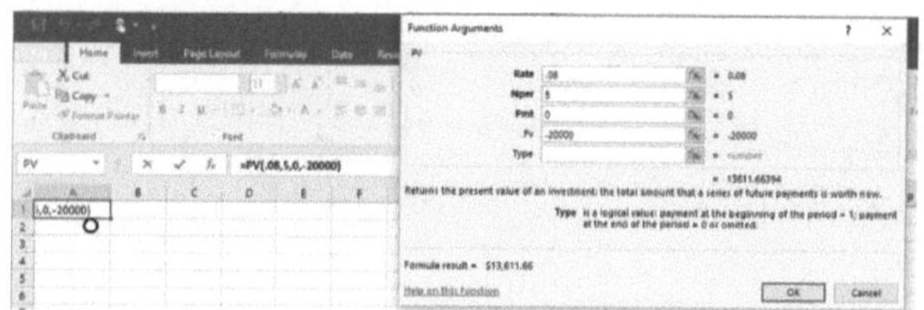

FIGURE 9.11 Year 5.

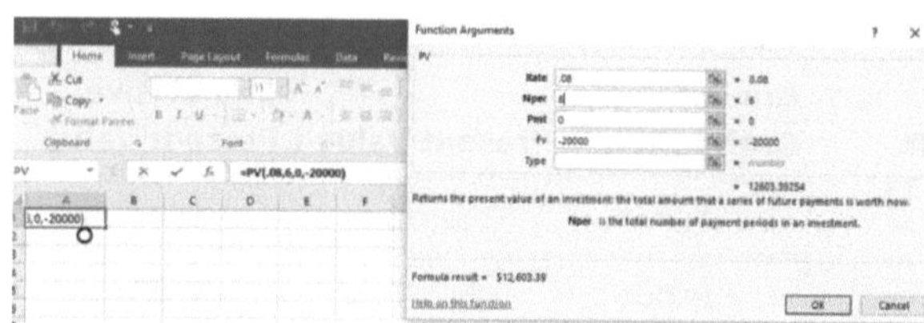

FIGURE 9.12 Year 6.

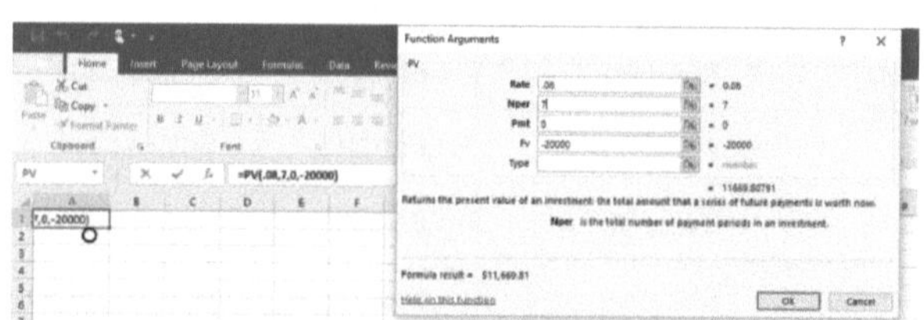

FIGURE 9.13 Year 7.

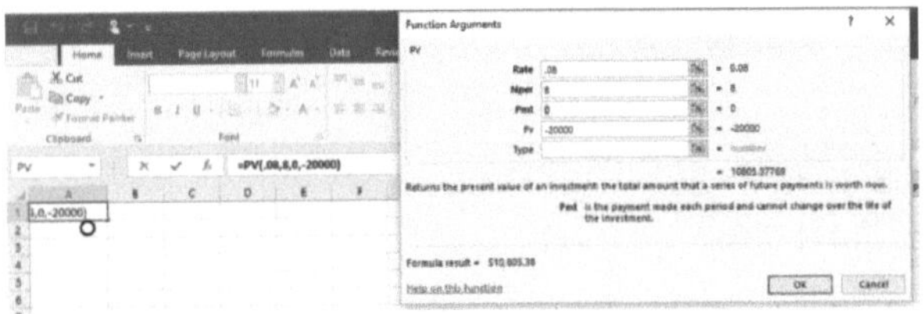

FIGURE 9.14 Year 8.

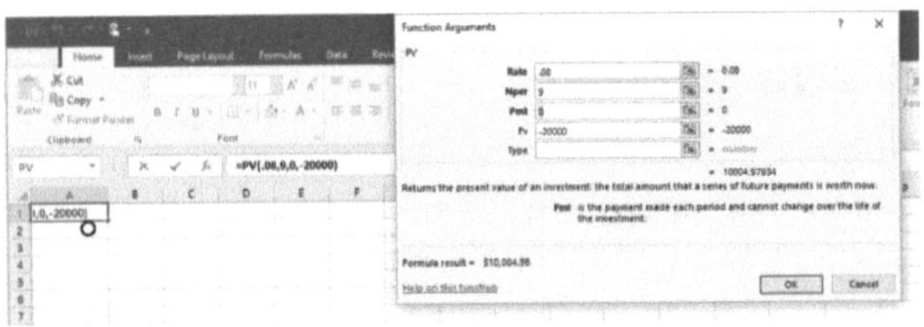

FIGURE 9.15 Year 9.

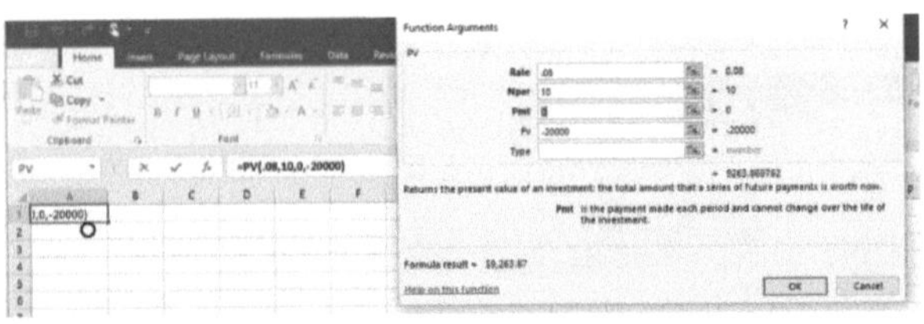

FIGURE 9.16 Year 10.

TABLE 9.2 Years 1-10

Yr.	Annual Cash Inflow	Present Value	Cumulative Present Value
1	$3,000	$2778.78	$2,778.78
2	$5,000	$4,286.69	$7,065.47
3	$10,000	$7,938.32	$15,003.79
4	$15,000	$11,025.45	$26,029.24
5	$20,000	$13,611.66	$39,640.90
6	$20,000	$12,603.39	$52,244.29
7	$20,000	$11,669.81	$63,914.10
8	$20,000	$10,805.38	$74,719.48
9	$20,000	$10,004.98	$84,724.46
10	$20,000	$9,263.87	$93,988.33
Total	$153,000	$93,988.33	$93,988.33

Note that the total of all amounts, not considering the TVM, would be $153,000, whereas the total amount considering the TVM is $93,988.33. The amounts considering the TVM are significantly less because of the discount rate.

Net Present Value (**NPV**). Now that you understand how the TVM works, let's apply the concept to the decision tool of NPV. The concept behind NPV is that all inflows and outflows are brought to the present and then netted. Let's look at Project C. The details of Project C are as follows:

Investment $ = $100,000
Useful life = five years
Residual Value (year 5) = $15,000
Annual income = $50,000
Annual maintenance = $5,000

TABLE 9.3 Net Present Value

When? (N)	$ Inflow/ (outflow)	rate (*i*)	present value (PV)
Now	($100,000)	6%	($100,000.00)
Yr 1-5	$50,000	6%	$210,618.19
Yr 5	$15,000	6%	$11,208.87
Yr 1-5	($5,000)	6%	($21,061.82)
NPV			**$100,765.24**

Otherwise stated:

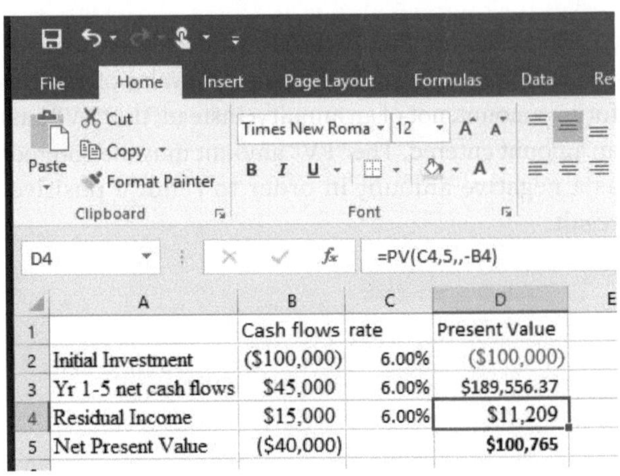

FIGURE 9.17 Net Present Value.

Because the NPV for this project is positive, it is a good investment.

Now, let's compare Project C to Project D.

The details of Project D are as follows:

Investment $ = $120,000

Useful life = five years

Residual Value (year 5) = $25,000

Annual income = $60,000

Maintenance in year 1 = $5,000

Maintenance in year 2 = $7,000

Maintenance in year 3 = $7,000

Maintenance in year 4 = $10,000

Maintenance in year 5 = $12,000

TABLE 9.4 Net Present Value, part 2

When? (N)	$ Inflow/ (outflow)	rate (i)	present value (PV)
Now	($120,000)	6%	($120,000.00)
Yr 1-5	$60,000	6%	$252,741.83
Yr 5	$25,000	6%	$18,681.45
Yr 1 Maintenance	($5,000)	6%	($4.716.98)
Yr 2 Maintenance	($7,000)	6%	($6,229.98)
Yr 3 Maintenance	($7,000)	6%	($5,877.33)
Yr 4 Maintenance	($10,000)	6%	($7,920.94)
Yr 5 Maintenance	($12,000)	6%	($8,967.10)
NPV			**$117,710.95**

Otherwise stated as:

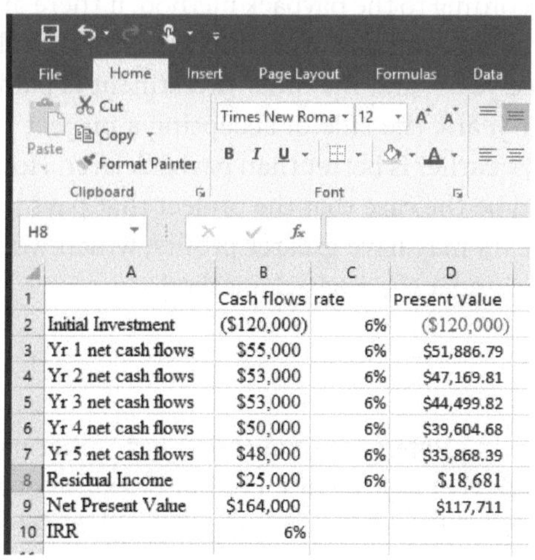

	A	B	C	D
1		Cash flows	rate	Present Value
2	Initial Investment	($120,000)	6%	($120,000)
3	Yr 1 net cash flows	$55,000	6%	$51,886.79
4	Yr 2 net cash flows	$53,000	6%	$47,169.81
5	Yr 3 net cash flows	$53,000	6%	$44,499.82
6	Yr 4 net cash flows	$50,000	6%	$39,604.68
7	Yr 5 net cash flows	$48,000	6%	$35,868.39
8	Residual Income	$25,000	6%	$18,681
9	Net Present Value	$164,000		$117,711
10	IRR	6%		

FIGURE 9.18 Net Present Value 2.

Project D is also a good investment. However, is Project D a better investment than Project C because it has a higher NPV? Not necessarily. Project C and Project D cannot be compared simply by reviewing their NPV because the investment amounts are not the same. If both projects had investment amounts equal to one another, the projects could be compared simply by looking at NPV. When projects have different investment amounts, however, management must calculate the profitability index.

The profitability index is calculated by comparing the NPV amounts to the amount invested.

Present Value of Cash Flows/Initial Investment = Profitability Index

$$\frac{\textit{Present Value of Cash Flows}}{\textit{Initial Investment}} = \textit{Profitability Index}$$

Using the formula above, project C's profitability index is: $\frac{\$100{,}765.24}{\$100{,}000} = 1.01$

Using the formula above, project D's profitability index is: $\frac{\$117{,}710.95}{\$120{,}000} = .98$

According to profitability index, project C is a better project to invest in, even though project D has a higher NPV. Project C delivers greater profitability when compared with the amount of the investment.

Internal Rate of Return (**IRR**). IRR is a method closely linked to NPV in that IRR seeks to find the discount rate that will cause the NPV to be $0 or as close to $0 as possible. Trial and error is easily used with the help of Excel. When calculating IRR, annual inflows and outflows are netted for each year, and then the discount rate that allows for net present value to be as close to $0 as possible is calculated. For example, the discount rate that would bring net present value as close to zero as possible without going negative for project C is 36.73% and 36.21% for project D (see screenshots below). The discount rate calculated means that at a discount rate of 36.73% for project C and 36.21% for project D, the present value would be zero. The higher the discount rate, the greater the freedom. For example, if the IRR was 2%, it would mean that the project would require a maximum interest rate of 2% to break even. Anything higher than 2% would cause the NPV to be negative. With an IRR of 36%, a company could pay up to 36% for the investment and still not suffer a loss. See the spreadsheets below.

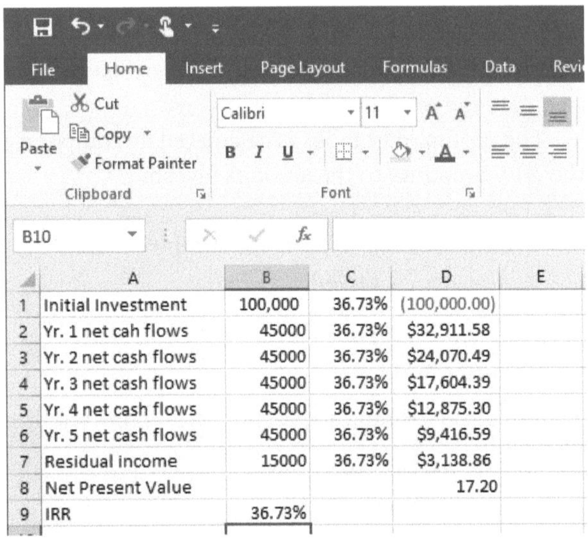

	A	B	C	D	E
1	Initial Investment	100,000	36.73%	(100,000.00)	
2	Yr. 1 net cah flows	45000	36.73%	$32,911.58	
3	Yr. 2 net cash flows	45000	36.73%	$24,070.49	
4	Yr. 3 net cash flows	45000	36.73%	$17,604.39	
5	Yr. 4 net cash flows	45000	36.73%	$12,875.30	
6	Yr. 5 net cash flows	45000	36.73%	$9,416.59	
7	Residual income	15000	36.73%	$3,138.86	
8	Net Present Value			17.20	
9	IRR	36.73%			

FIGURE 9.19 Project C.

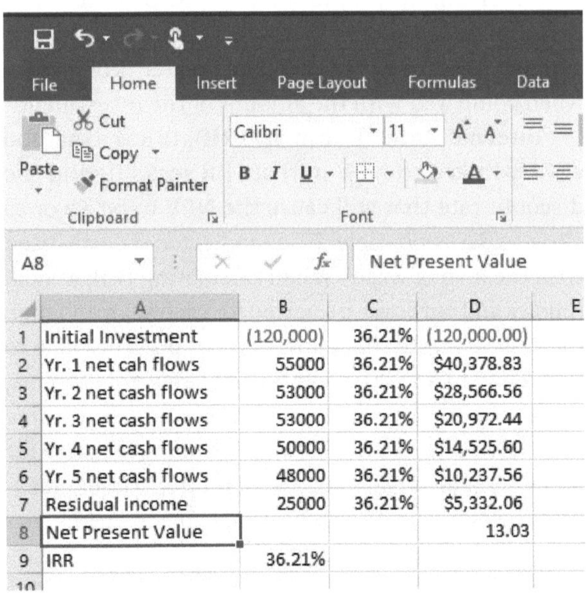

	A	B	C	D	E
1	Initial Investment	(120,000)	36.21%	(120,000.00)	
2	Yr. 1 net cah flows	55000	36.21%	$40,378.83	
3	Yr. 2 net cash flows	53000	36.21%	$28,566.56	
4	Yr. 3 net cash flows	53000	36.21%	$20,972.44	
5	Yr. 4 net cash flows	50000	36.21%	$14,525.60	
6	Yr. 5 net cash flows	48000	36.21%	$10,237.56	
7	Residual income	25000	36.21%	$5,332.06	
8	Net Present Value			13.03	
9	IRR	36.21%			

FIGURE 9.20 Project D.

IRR is an important tool so that a company knows at what interest rate they'd be willing to borrow to invest in a project.

LEARNING GOAL 3: Define Strengths and Weakness of Capital Budgeting Decisions

The process of making decisions is only as strong as the decision tools used. There are strengths and weaknesses to each of the tools noted above.

Payback Period

The payback method is one of the easiest tools to use, but that is where its benefits stop. There are far more criticisms about the payback method than there are benefits. One of the most notable criticisms is that the payback method is focused only on time, not profitability. Under the payback method, something is worth investing in if it is paid back within a specific time period. Although such information has merit in establishing the risk of an investment, it should not be the only criteria. Secondly, the payback method ignores cash flows that occur after the item has been paid back. If a project is paid back within three years, cash flows that would occur in years four and beyond are not relevant to the decision. Such cash flows may include residual value of the investment or significant amounts of return.

According to the payback method, if there are two investments, and one of the investments is paid back in three years, and the other investment is paid back in four years, the rule of accepting a project is that payback earlier is better than payback later. However, it could be the case that the project that pays back in four years may have greater profits, which would be ignored under the payback method.

ARR

Accounting Rate of Return (ARR) is another method that is fairly easy to compute but does not consider important information needed in making decisions. ARR converts accrual accounting to cash accounting by removing depreciation from the net cash flows and determining the rate of return of the asset over the entire life of the asset. However, in determining the rate of return over the life of the asset, TVM is not taken into consideration. Because the value of the dollar today must be discounted to the present, ARR provides an inaccurate reflection of an asset's return when the assets are long term.

Screening Tools

Because of the criticisms of the above two methods, payback method and ARR are both best used as screening tools or on shorter-term capital investment decisions. The effects of not using TVM would not be as drastic over one or two years as they would be over five or ten years. Because of the weaknesses, such methods are rarely used as the only method of decision making.

The weaknesses of the payback method can be overcome by the strengths of the ARR, and the weaknesses of the ARR can be overcome by the strengths of the payback method. Thus, used together, both methods are stronger tools but still do not consider the TVM.

NPV

Although considered a superior method to either the payback method or the ARR, NPV has both strengths and weaknesses. One of the most significant strengths of NPV is that NPV incorporates TVM in reviewing cash flows over the life of the asset. Secondly, NPV ties the required rate of return to the present value, showing excess or deficiency in the present value cash flow. The weakness of NPV is that it cannot be compared to other investments that are not of equal value without using the profitability index.

IRR

Like NPV, IRR incorporates the TVM into the cash flows over the life of the asset. Also, IRR allows a company to learn the unique rate of return required for the investment to be profitable. Finally, IRR results are comparable between projects without any additional steps. A weakness of the method is that without the use of technology, IRR trial and error can be tedious.

Decision Tools

The most significant difference between the screening tools and the decision tools is the use of TVM. Without considering TVM, a tool does not provide long-term dependability. Therefore, managers will usually use multiple tools in decision making. Because each of the tools has strengths and weaknesses (Figure 9.21), the hope is that by using more than one tool, the strengths and weaknesses will be leveled and a good decision can be made.

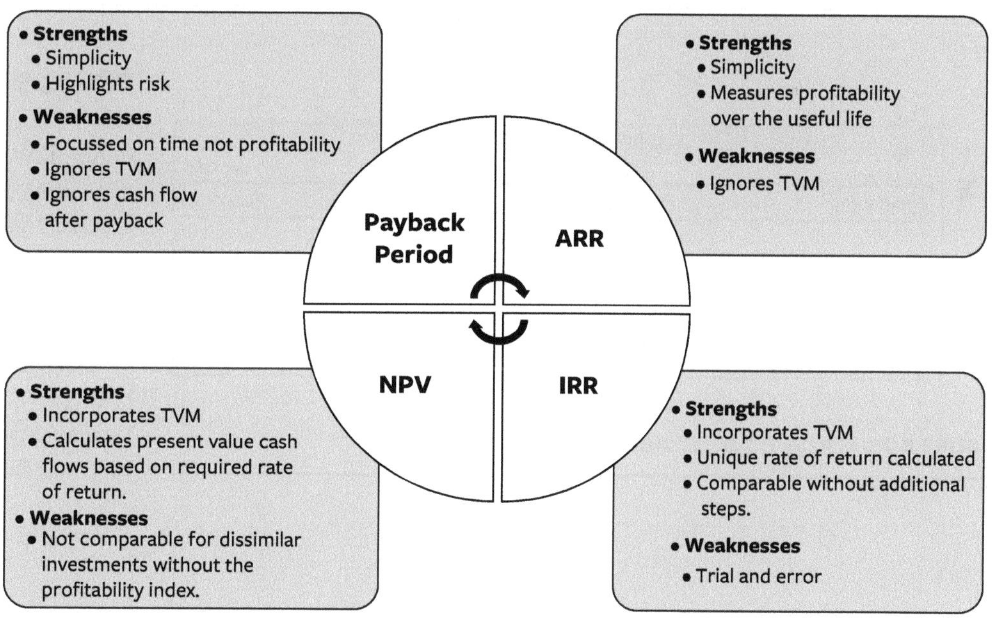

FIGURE 9.21 Strengths and Weaknesses of Tools.

LEARNING GOAL 4: Integrate Capital Budgeting Decision Techniques with the Budget

As noted in Topic 7, capital budgeting is part of the financial budgets. Recall that financial budgets seek to provide the big picture regarding the financial situation of the company and encompass any major capital expenditures the company will be making. Integrating capital budgeting techniques with the master budget involves following the steps noted in Learning Goal 1 to: 1) recognize a need, 2) investigate options, 3) perform analysis, 4) make a decision, and 5) evaluate the decision. Once a company makes a decision, the cash flow must be accounted for in the budgeted cash flow so that the company knows it has the cash available to support the decision to make a capital purchase. In some cases, making the capital purchase may include borrowing funds. The borrowing rate would be reflected as the discount rate applied when using the NPV method. All capital expenditures must be analyzed on a cash basis so that the expenditures can be evaluated as part of cash flow.

Figure 9.22 shows the budgeted statement of cash flows through which the total from the capital budget would flow. Figure 9.23 shows the supporting "capital budget" where the purchases would be tracked in the given month.

Budgeted Cash Flows

	January	February	March	1st Quarter
Beginning Cash Balance	$5,000	$5,463	$161,870	$5,000
Cash Collections	$593,750	$528,125	$628,125	$1,750,000
Total Cash Available	$598,750	$533,588	$789,995	$1,755,000
Less: Cash Disbursements	$308,287	$356,417	$387,245	$1,051,950
Less: Equipment Purchases	$300,000	$0	$0	$300,000
Cash Balance	-$9,537	$177,170	$402,750	$403,050
Financing:				
New Borrowing	$15,000	$0	$0	$15,000
Debt Repayment	$0	$15,000	$0	$15,000
Interest	$0	$300	$0	$300
Ending Cash Balance	$5,463	$161,870	$402,750	$402,750

FIGURE 9.22 Budgeted Cash Flows.

Capital Purchases Budget

	January	February	March	1st Qtr
Equipment	$20,000			$20,000
Total Capital Investment	$20,000			$20,000

FIGURE 9.23 Capital Purchases Budget.

TOPIC 9 REFERENCES

Braun, K.W. and Tietz, W.M. *Managerial Accounting* (4th ed.). Upper Saddle River: Prentice Hall, 2014.

Garrison, R.H., Noreen, E.W., and Brewer, P.C. *Managerial Accounting.* New York, NY: McGraw-Hill Companies, Inc., 2012.

Horngren, C.T., Datar, S.M. and Rajan, M.V. (2015). *Cost Accounting: A Managerial Emphasis* (15th ed.). Upper Saddle River, NJ. Pearson Education, Inc., 2015.

SECTION III

THE PERFORMING PHASE

The Performing Phase addresses the competency of:

Demonstrate an understanding for how companies implement that which was planned and report necessary information.

The following topics have been introduced in Section 3 as topics imperative to learning the tasks involved in the Performing Phase.

- Job Costing
- Process Costing
- Activity-Based Costing (ABC)
- Absorption Costing vs. Direct Costing
- Short-Term Decision Making

Competency 3 is all about performing that which was planned. The managerial accountant's role is to provide timely and relevant feedback regarding the performance of an organization. Therefore, students must achieve an understanding for the costing systems used and the ways in which such information can be applied to decision making.

FIGURE III.1 Theory: Planning, Evaluating, Performing.

TOPIC 10 Job Costing

LEARNING GOALS

1. Describe the differences between job costing and process costing.
2. Understand the types of organizations that would use a job-cost system.
3. Describe the flow of inventory through a job-cost system.
4. Discuss the source documents in a job-cost system.
5. Allocate overhead in a job-cost system.
6. Make journal entries for a job-cost system.
7. Account for under-allocated and over-allocated overhead in a job-cost system.

INTRODUCTION

Topic 10 is the start of Section 3, which analyzes the Performing Phase of managerial accounting. A company must first plan how to carry out business within the company and then act on such plans. The Performing Phase represents such action. The managerial accountant's role inside the performing phase is to keep management informed as to the success or failure to carry out the plans from the Planning Phase. To keep management informed, the managerial accountant creates reports that analyze current performance. In order to determine the types of reports that management will need, the costing system used must be fully understood by the managerial accountant.

LEARNING GOAL 1: Describe the Differences Between Job Costing and Process Costing

Process Costing

When a company tracks the cost of making its product, there must be a logical way of keeping track of such costs. Usually, the way that will be the most logical is the way that represents the physical flow of the units. Two main costing systems are used to keep track of an organization's costs: a) job costing and b) process costing. The difference between the two costing systems depends on the type of product.

A process-costing system is generally used for products that are mass produced into similar products. In a process-costing system, each individual unit cost is measured by an average of all costs including direct materials, direct labor, and manufacturing overhead. Because products that are mass produced are identical, each individual product does not have individual costs associated with it and therefore can be averaged.

Many of the foods purchased in the grocery store would use a process-costing system. For example, when you purchase a bag of cookies or a box of cereal, you would assume that each bag of cookies or box of cereal purchased will taste exactly the same as the last bag of cookies you purchased or the last box of cereal. The cookies and the cereal are produced in a process where the exact amounts of the same ingredients are added to every bag or box. Non-food items can be processed in the same way. Consider the dry erase markers used in a classroom. Although there may be multiple colors such as red, blue, black, and green, the markers are processed in the same way. A difference such as a color change would not impact or change the process.

Job Costing

A job-costing system differs from a process-costing system in that each product is not necessarily identical in a job-cost system. A job-cost system is used for unique products that are specially made for an individual "job." Alternatively, a job-cost system would also be used for small batches of identical products that are made for a specific client or "job."

The costs associated with the job include the same costs as those used in process costing: direct materials, direct labor, and manufacturing overhead. However, instead of the costs of an individual item being averaged over a number of identical products, the costs are tracked for each job.

A job-cost system would be used for any product that requires individual and unique tracking of costs. Examples of products that would use a job-cost system include homes built custom-made for the owners, hospital visits, advertising agencies, custom-built furniture, and movies. Such items are not identical and do not have the same input amounts of each product. Imagine going to a doctor and following a specific process that did not consider your individual needs but followed the process. Everyone gets checked in, weighed, measured, blood drawn, and a couple of shots before being sent home. The price everyone paid would be identical because the costs would be identical and could be averaged to arrive at an individual cost. Such a costing system would not make sense. Therefore, a job-costing system is better suited to industries that require individual differentiations.

LEARNING GOAL 2: Understand the Types of Organizations That Would Use a Job-Cost System

Since a job-cost system is used for products that are unique and individual in some way, the managerial accountant should be familiar with the variety of products that could fall under the job-cost system. This learning goal will discuss the two reasons why a product would use job costing.

Small Batches

A manufacturing company could mass produce items that are specific to individual clients. For example, a company that prints logos on a variety of products such as T-shirts, hats, and jackets may receive an order for 5,000 T-shirts from a client. Costs would be tracked for the job of 5,000 T-shirts because it would be considered a small batch. Such costs would include the direct materials of the ink for the logo, the direct labor for the individuals who work on the batch, and the overhead allocated to the job.

Unique Products

Unique products may be made specifically for a client based on client preference. For example, a client of a custom-made clothing shop may order an article of clothing that requires a special pattern to be sewn to fit the size and design the client wants from the clothing. Job-order costing would be used to track the direct materials such as the fabric, the direct labor such as the individual who designs and sews the clothing item, and the overhead allocated to the job.

Products That Use Job Costing and Process Costing

Certain products may have qualities of being mass produced and specialty made. Such products could use process costing for part of the product and job costing for part of the product. For example, a company may make pens of various colors and may print company information on the exterior of the pen. The process of making the pen would be considered process costing because all the pens are exactly the same. However, the point at which the pens would leave the mass production process and receive special imprinting may be part of a small batch or a job, thus requiring that the pens become part of a job-costing system.

LEARNING GOAL 3: Describe the Flow of Inventory Through a Job-Cost System

Inventory in a job-cost system involves raw materials, work in process, and finished goods (Figure 10.1). The flow of inventory is important to master in understanding costing systems. Inventory items flow into the balance sheet when they are purchased as raw materials. The raw materials, both direct and indirect, are then used to make the product. Hence, raw materials become part of work in process. Items remain in work-in-process inventory until they are finished, at which point they become finished goods. Finally, the finished-good costs move to the income statement as cost of goods sold when they are sold to the end user. The flow of inventory helps to determine the cost of producing a product.

Note that in the figure above, costs move through each of the inventory accounts before leaving the balance sheet. The costs flow from raw materials to work in process to finished goods before leaving the balance sheet.

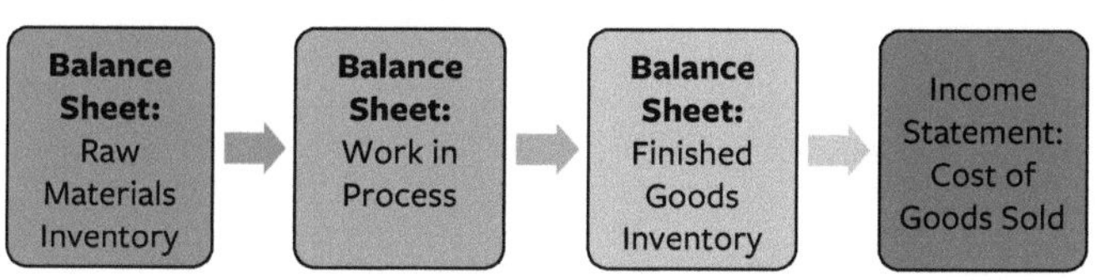

FIGURE 10.1 Flow of Inventory: Job Costing.

LEARNING GOAL 4: Discuss the Source Documents in a Job-Cost System

In order for costs to flow through the proper inventory accounts, certain documents must initiate the transactions.

Raw Materials

In a job-costing system, purchasing needs are determined by the purchasing department which issues a purchase order for the required materials according to the production schedule. The materials are ordered and received by the receiving department, where they are entered into inventory as a raw material. The raw materials can be a variety of items that are used during the production process. The items could be direct and/or indirect items used in production, but all raw materials needed are entered on a raw materials record and tracked for items received and used. Each item of raw materials has its own record (see Figures 10.2–10.4).

Raw Materials Documents

1. Production Schedule
2. Purchase Order
3. Raw Materials Record

July

Job	Product	Customer #	Qty	Start Date
780	Small Wine Racks	ABC101	50	07/16
781	Small Wine Racks	XYZ203	100	07/20
782	Large Wine Racks	MNO300	75	07/30

FIGURE 10.2 Production Schedule.

Shipping Method	Shipping Terms	Delivery Date
UPS	Net 30	06/15

Qty	Item #	Description	Job	Unit Price	Total
30	Oak01	Board Feet of OAK01	780	5.75/BF	172.50
				Subtotal	172.50
				Sales Tax	14.23
				Total	186.73

FIGURE 10.3 Purchase Order.

Work in Process

Once the job is ready to start, the start of the job is recorded on a job-cost sheet where each job receives a number. The production department begins to requisition materials. Materials requisitioned enter into work-in-process inventory where they are combined with labor and overhead in the production process. When materials are requisitioned, each individual raw materials record is recorded to ensure accurate records are kept for the amount of materials available for use. The requisitioned materials are then recorded on the job-cost sheet so that management knows how much the job's direct materials cost (see Figures 10.5–10.7).

The job-cost sheet also tracks the amount of direct labor attributed to the job. Labor costs are tracked on a time card for each employee who directly works on the job. Finally, overhead is applied based on the overhead rate applied to the amount of the driver used.

Work in Process Documents

1. Raw Materials Record
2. Materials Requisition
3. Time Record
4. Job Cost Sheet

Finished Goods

Once a job is finished, the items leave the work-in-process inventory account and move into finished

Item Number: OAK01

Date	Received			Used				Balance	
	Units	Cost	Total	Requisitioned	Units	Cost	Total	Units	Total
06/15	30 BF	5.75/BF	172.50					30 BF	172.5
06/25	120 BF	6.20/BF	744.00					150 BF	916.5
06/30	75 BF	5.95/BF	446.25					225 BF	1362.75
07/15				#8550	50 BF	30@ 5.75 20 @ 6.20	296.50	175 BF	1066.25
07/18	100 BF	6.00/BF	600.00					275 BF	1666.25
07/19				#8551	50 BF	50@6.20	310.00	225 BF	1356.25

FIGURE 10.4 Raw Materials Record.

Date: 07/15		**Job: 780**		**Req #: 8550**
Part No.	**Description**	**Qty**	**Unit Cost**	**Amount**
OAK01	Board Feet of Oak	30 BF	5.75	172.50
OAK01	Board Feet of Oak	20 BF	6.20	124.00
SCR55	3 inch screws	15 screws	0.12	1.80
STA36	Dark Stain	1 qt	3.60	3.60
Total:				301.90

FIGURE 10.5 Materials Requisition.

Employee: Joy Cline
Hourly Rate: 12.50
Week: 06/15-06/21
Record #:556

Date	**Job**	**Start Time**	**End Time**	**Total Hours**	**Cost**
06/16	780	2:00 pm	4:00 pm	2.00	25.00
06/17	780	10:00 am	12:30 pm	2.50	31.25
Total:					56.25

FIGURE 10.6 Labor Hours.

goods, where they await sale. Finished goods is the final inventory destination for the costs associated with making the product.

Cost of Goods Sold

Cost of goods sold is an income statement account and the place where finished goods leave the balance and enter the income statement. A finished item that

Job: #780
Date Started: 06/15
Date Completed: 06/17
Description: 50 Units
Manufacturing Costs

Direct Materials		Direct Labor		Manuacturing Overhead	
Req. # 8550		No. 556	56.25	*$12.50 per DLH × 4.50	
	301.90				56.25
Total	301.90	Total	56.25	Total	56.25

Total Job Cost	414.40
Number of Units	50.00
Cost per Unit	8.29

*Overhead Rate = Estimated Overhead / Esimated Driver = $10,000 / 800 = 12.50

FIGURE 10.7 Job Cost Sheet.

is not sold will remain on the balance sheet as finished goods inventory until it is sold.

LEARNING GOAL 5: Allocate Overhead in a Job-Cost System

Overhead can be a confusing area because all the items that cannot be labeled direct labor or direct materials fall under overhead. Therefore, overhead contains a myriad of items that must somehow be applied to a job. In Topic 7, the overhead rate was discussed as part of the budgeting process. The rate that was established for the budget would be the same rate applied to the job here. Let's say that the overhead rate is $14.00 per direct labor hour. If a specific job actually used ten direct labor hours, $140.00 of overhead would be applied to the job. Just like direct labor and direct materials, overhead is tracked on the job-cost record.

The cost driver for overhead is anything the company decides will drive up the cost of overhead.

Many times a company uses machine hours or labor hours. However, a cost driver can be anything the company deems as something that drives up the overhead costs. When applying overhead to a job, the amount of overhead applied, then, will be contingent on the amount of the driver that the job uses.

$$Overhead\ Rate = \frac{Estimated\ amount\ of\ overhead}{Estimated\ amount\ of\ driver}$$

LEARNING GOAL 6: Make Journal Entries for a Job-Cost System

As a managerial accountant, it is not enough to calculate the cost of the job. The proper journal entries must also be made to ensure proper accounting for the costs.

Purchase Raw Materials

The first entry for the cost of a job is the purchase of raw materials. Raw materials may include direct materials and indirect materials. There is no distinction in the materials at this point, however.

TABLE 10.1 Raw Materials Inventory

Raw Materials Inventory	$XX	
Accounts Payable		$XX

To record the purchase of raw materials

Use of Raw Materials

When raw materials are used, the distinction is made as to the direct and indirect nature of the materials. Direct raw materials enter work in process, while indirect raw materials enter overhead.

TABLE 10.2 Work in Process Inventory

Work in Process Inventory	$XX	
Raw Materials Inventory		$XX

To record use of direct raw materials into work in process

TABLE 10.3 Manufacturing Overhead

Manufacturing Overhead	$XX	
Raw Materials Inventory		$XX

To record the use of indirect raw materials into manufacturing overhead

Use of Labor

Like raw materials, labor comes in two forms, direct and indirect. The distinction for labor between direct and indirect is made at the point of entry.

TABLE 10.4 Work in Process Inventory, part 2

Work in Process Inventory	$XX	
Wages Payable		$XX

To record the use of direct labor into work in process

TABLE 10.5 Manufacturing Overhead, part 2

Manufacturing Overhead	$XX	
Wages Payable		$XX

To record the use of indirect labor into manufacturing overhead

Allocation of Overhead

When entering overhead, there are two amounts to consider: the amount of actual overhead and the amount of allocated overhead. Actual overhead is always debited while allocated overhead is always credited.

Consider actual overhead first:

TABLE 10.6 Manufacturing Overhead, part 3

Manufacturing Overhead	$XX	
Accounts payable		$XX
Cash		$XX
Prepaid insurance		$XX
Accumulated depreciation		$XX

To record actual overhead incurred

When overhead is allocated, it is based on the overhead rate used in the job-cost record and applied to the job(s).

TABLE 10.7 Work in Process

Work in Process	$XX	
Manufacturing Overhead		$XX

To allocate overhead applied to jobs

Move to Finished Goods

Once the job is finished, it is no longer a work in process and must be moved to finished goods. The movement represents the final journal of the balance sheet out of work in process inventory and into finished goods inventory.

TABLE 10.8 Finished Goods Inventory

Finished Goods Inventory	$XX	
Work in Process Inventory		$XX

To record completed goods

Sale of Goods

The sale of the items represents a movement of costs off the balance sheet and into the income statement. Under a perpetual system, costs of goods sold is recorded at the same time the sale is recorded.

TABLE 10.9 Accounts Receivable

Accounts Receivable	$XX	
Sales Revenue		$XX

To record the sale of goods

TABLE 10.10 Cost of Goods Sold

Cost of Goods Sold	$XX	
Finished Goods Inventory		$XX

To record costs of sold goods

LEARNING GOAL 7: Account for Under-Allocated and Over-Allocated Overhead in a Job-Cost System

Typically, once all transactions have been entered, one more final entry must be made to close out manufacturing overhead. Manufacturing overhead is a temporary account that does not have a normal balance and must be closed at the end of the period.

Note that in the above transactions listed under Learning Goal 6, the manufacturing overhead account has debit entries for actual amounts of materials, labor, and overhead, and a credit entry for allocated overhead. Depending on whether actual amounts of overhead were greater or less than allocated amounts, the manufacturing overhead account will either have a debit or credit balance. A debit balance means that manufacturing overhead has been under-allocated, and a credit balance means that manufacturing overhead has been over-allocated. Whether over-allocated or under-allocated, the manufacturing overhead account must be closed out. A debit balance would require a credit entry while a credit balance would require a debit entry.

Manufacturing Overhead

TABLE 10.11 Overhead Allocated

Actual Mat.	$XX	$XX	**Overhead Allocated**
Actual Lab.	$XX		
Actual OH.	$XX		

Underallocated or Overallocated

TABLE 10.12 Manufacturing Overhead, part 4

Manufacturing Overhead	$XX	
Cost of Goods Sold		$XX

To close out manufacturing overhead with over-allocated overhead

OR

TABLE 10.13 Cost of Goods Sold, part 2

Cost of Goods Sold	$XX	
Manufacturing Overhead		$XX

To close out manufacturing overhead with under-allocated overhead

Typically, the over-allocated or under-allocated amounts are closed out to cost of goods sold. Although there are other methods for how to close out the over-allocated or under-allocated amounts, the easiest way is to close them out to cost of goods sold because eventually all costs will pass through cost of goods sold. The other methods are beyond the scope of this text.

TOPIC 10 REFERENCES

Braun, K.W. and Tietz, W.M. *Managerial Accounting* (4th ed.). Upper Saddle River, NJ: Prentice Hall, 2014.

Garrison, R.H., Noreen, E.W., and Brewer, P.C. *Managerial Accounting.* New York: McGraw-Hill Companies, Inc., 2012.

Horngren, C.T., Datar, S.M. and Rajan, M.V. *Cost Accounting: A Managerial Emphasis* (15th ed.). Upper Saddle River, NJ: Pearson Education, Inc., 2015.

TOPIC 11 Process Costing

LEARNING GOALS

1. Describe the differences between job costing and process costing.
2. Describe the flow of inventory through a process-cost system.
3. Build a process-cost report.
4. Make journal entries for a process-cost system.
5. Account for under-allocated and over-allocated overhead in a process-cost system.
6. Discuss process costing as it relates to service types of companies.

INTRODUCTION

Topic 11 covers an alternative costing system to job costing. In a job-costing system, we learned that job costing would apply as the costing method for a company that completed orders by the job or in small batches. Process costing, on the other hand, is more appropriate in situations where there is no way of separating and defining the project into small components. As such, the process-costing system relies on broad averages for its per-unit calculations.

LEARNING GOAL 1: Describe the Differences Between Job Costing and Process Costing

Understanding when to use job costing and when to use process costing is important to the managerial accountant in the performing phase. In the performing phase, what becomes important to management is the need to know how much it costs to make the product. If management understands the costs involved in making the product, all sorts of decisions can be made such as the amount the company should bid for the job, the price the company should charge for their product, and the potential need to find cheaper suppliers. Such issues can be addressed with either a job-costing system or a process-costing system. However, given the nature of the product, one costing system will be a better fit to address such issues over the other costing system.

In Topic 10, we learned that a process-costing system would be used for companies that maintained a steady flow of production in building a product that is identical in terms of the process used to produce it. Items that would fall in this category include most food items found in a grocery store such as cookies, crackers, cereal, rice, etc. Service items and specialty products, on the other hand, would more appropriately use job costing. There is also a mix that could occur when a product has elements of a process system and a job system. In such a case, management would use both a job-costing system and a process-costing system. Such a mix, however, is beyond the scope of this textbook.

To track the costs in the job-costing system, managers use a job-cost record where materials, labor, and overhead are tracked on the cost sheet. In a process-costing system, costs are not tracked on a job-cost sheet where the cost of the job can be totaled, but instead costs are tracked on a process-cost report completed for each process for a given period of time.

As an example, let's say you purchase some bags of potato chips at the supermarket. You expect each bag to taste the same. Each bag of potato chips does taste the same because the potato chips go through an identical process where each potato chip receives the same treatment. In order to determine how much it costs to produce each case of chips, the managerial team would break down the procedure into processes. The process of producing potato chips could include four different processes: 1) washing and slicing, 2) frying, 3) seasoning, and 4) packaging (Figure 11.1).

Costs are tracked for a given period for each of the four processes instead of for a job because there is no start or end of a job. Instead, the process continues non-stop.

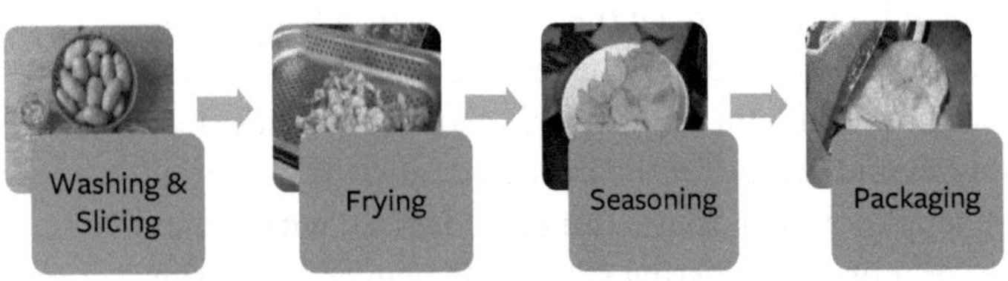

FIGURE 11.1 Processes: a. potatoes; b. production homemade chips; c. potato chips; d. salt and vinegar chips.

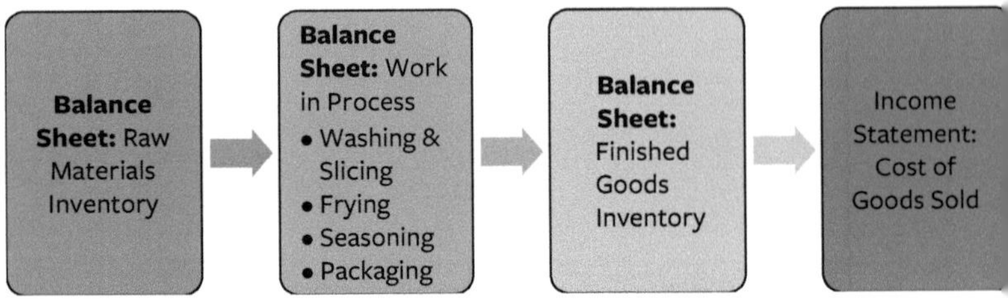

FIGURE 11.2 Flow of Inventory: Process Cost.

LEARNING GOAL 2: Describe the Flow of Inventory Through a Process-Cost System

Inventory flows in relatively the same way in a process-costing system as in a job-cost system, with some nuances specific to process costing. In a job-cost system, inventory flows from raw materials to work in process to finished goods. In a process costing system, inventory still flows from raw materials to work in process to finished goods. However, the material that flows from raw materials into work in process moves into work in process for each process. Let's return to the example of the potato chips.

Note that in Figure 11.2, the raw materials flow into work in process for the washing and slicing department, for the frying department, for the seasoning department, and for the packaging department. Raw materials for the washing and slicing department could include a washing solution. Raw materials for the frying department would include the oil used to fry the chips. Raw materials for the seasoning department would include the seasonings. The fact that the seasonings may be different does not disrupt the flow of the processes. Finally, the packaging department would include raw materials that consist of the bag and any other materials required to properly package the chips. Hence, each department receives some form of raw material. Each department also receives labor and overhead as noted in Figure 11.3.

LEARNING GOAL 3: Build a Process-Cost Report

The output report in a process-cost system involves materials, labor, and overhead just as in a job-cost

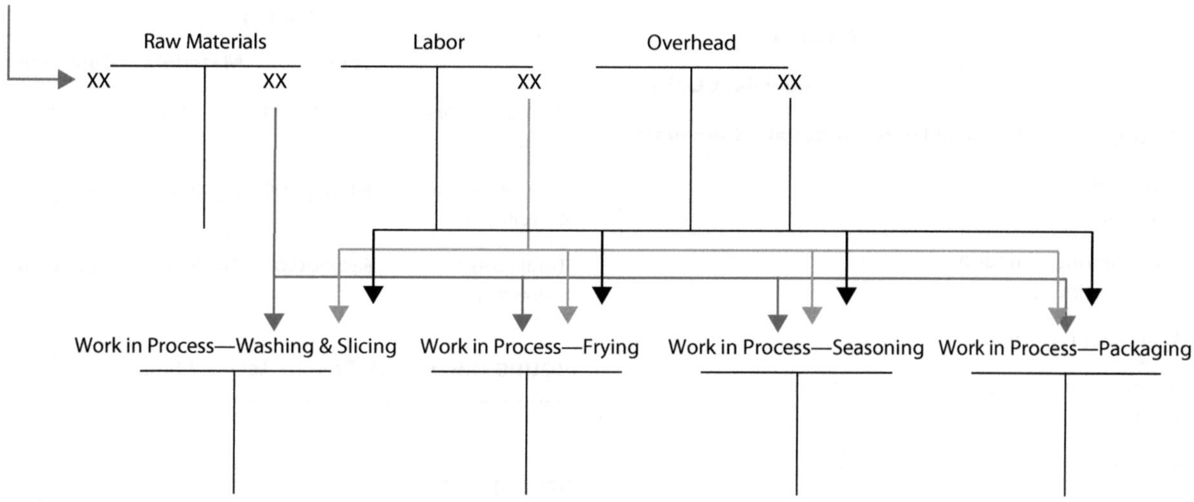

FIGURE 11.3 T-Accounts.

system, but the application of the three elements looks slightly different because of the broad averaging that must take place. The process is described below in five steps. Note that labor and overhead are generally combined and referred to as conversion costs in a process-costing report. There are five steps involved in the process as outlined below.

Step 1: FLOW OF PHYSICAL UNITS

The first step in completing a process-cost report is to determine the physical flow of the units. To determine the physical flow, the managerial accountant must understand the number of units that need to be accounted for and then account for such units. For example, if the washing and slicing department has 0 units in beginning work in process and adds 60,000 units, there are 60,000 units to account for. If 20,000 of those units are completed and transferred to the frying department, and 40,000 remain in work in process, all 60,000 units have been accounted for. On the report, it looks like Figure 11.4.

Note that the total units to account for match the total units accounted for. These must always match, or you've made a mistake.

(Step 1)	**Physical Units**
Work in process, beginning	0
Started during current period	60000
To Account for	**60000**
Completed and transferred out	20000
Work in process, ending	40000
Accounted for	**60000**

FIGURE 11.4 Step 1: Flow of Physical Units.

Step 2: EQUIVALENT UNITS

In step 2, the physical units must be recalculated in terms of equivalent units. Equivalent units equal the amount of partially completed units at the percentage complete. For example, if I have two glasses of water that are each 50% full, I essentially have one equivalent unit. Hence, if raw materials are added during the *beginning* of the period, and labor and overhead (conversion costs) are added equally throughout the period, the 40,000 units left in ending inventory are only partially completed. If the ending inventory items have only moved 25% of the way through the conversion process, the equivalent units for conversion equal

		(Step 2)	
		Equivalent Units	
(Step 1)	**Physical Units**	**Materials**	**Conversion**
Work in process, beginning	0		
Started during current period	60000		
To Account for	60000		
Completed and transferred out	20000	20000	20000
Work in process, ending	40000	40000	10000
Accounted for	60000	60,000	30,000

FIGURE 11.5 Step 2: Equivalent Units.

only 10,000 equivalent units (40,000 × 25% complete), while the equivalent units for materials equals 40,000 units (40,000 × 100% complete). The 20,000 that moved out of washing and slicing and on to frying are 100% complete in all regards. The report would look like Figure 11.5.

Note that units are calculated in terms of materials and conversion costs. Conversion costs are a combination of labor and overhead. When understanding the equivalent units in ending inventory, the managerial accountant must know how complete the ending inventory items are. They may have all of their material, none of their material, or a percentage of material. In terms of conversion costs, they may have all of their conversion, none of their conversion, or a percentage of their conversion. Every scenario will be different.

Step 3: SUMMARIZE TOTAL COSTS

In step 3, the focus moves from units to dollars. The flow of physical units that took place in step 1, must now be reflected as costs in step 3. Since there was no beginning inventory, there would also be no costs. However, since 60,000 units were started into inventory, there were $10,000 of material costs and $30,000 of conversion costs. See Figure 11.6.

(Step 3)	**Total**	**Materials**	**Conversion**
Work in process, beginning	$0.00	$0.00	$0.00
Costs added in current period	$40,000.00	$10,000.00	$30,000.00
Total costs to account for	**$40,000.00**	**$10,000.00**	**$30,000.00**

FIGURE 11.6 Step 3: Cost to Account For.

Step 4: COST PER EQUIVALENT UNIT

Step 4 is the step in which the total costs to account for in step 3 are calculated on a per-equivalent-unit basis. The point is to understand how much each unit costs in material and how much each unit costs in conversion costs (labor and overhead). Step 4 is just the division of total materials and total conversion costs divided by the equivalent units for materials and conversion respectively (Figure 11.7).

Note that in Figure 11.7, each unit of product in the washing and slicing department costs $.17 for materials and $1.00 for conversion costs. The total cost of each unit is $1.17 for materials, labor, and overhead.

Step 5: ASSIGNMENT OF COSTS

Step 5 is the final step on the report and provides the data needed to make the journal entries regarding transferred amounts from the washing and

(Step 4)			
Costs incurred to date	$40,000.00	$10,000.00	$30,000.00
Divide by equivalent units of work done in current period		60,000	30,000
Costs per equivalent unit of work done in current period	**$1.17**	**$0.17**	**$1.00**

FIGURE 11.7 Step 4: Cost per Equivalent Unit.

(Step 5)	Total	Materials	Conversion
Assignment of costs:			
Completed and transferred out	$23,333.33	$3,333.33	$20,000.00
Work in process, ending	$16,666.67	$6,666.67	$10,000.00
Total costs accounted for	$40,000.00	$10,000.00	$30,000.00

FIGURE 11.8 Step 5: Assignment of Costs.

slicing department to the frying department. Based on the cost per unit, step 5 assigns costs to the units completed and transferred out to the frying process and to the units left in ending inventory. See Figure 11.8.

Note that the total costs assigned in step 5 match the total costs to account for in step 3. These must always match (except for rounding issues), or you've made a mistake.

Final Analysis

In reviewing the final report as noted in Figure 11.9, the data the managerial accountant needs for the journal entries for ending work in process inventory and costs transferred to the next department is reflected in step 5.

The amount credited to work in process for washing and slicing and debited to work in process for frying is $23,333.33. The amount that should be left in ending work in process for washing and slicing is $16,666.67.

Second and Subsequent Processes

The report above was prepared for the first process in the potato chip factory. Subsequent processes would look slightly different because you have to account for the transferred costs. See Figure 11.10 for the report of the frying department in the following month.

LEARNING GOAL 4: Make Journal Entries for a Process Cost System

For a managerial accountant, calculating the cost report is not enough. The proper journal entries must also be made to ensure proper accounting for the costs. Conversion costs reflected on the report are the combined amounts of labor and overhead. However, when making the journal entries, the amounts need to be separated into their proper accounts.

Purchase Raw Materials

Like a job-costing system, the first entry for completing entries in a process-costing system is for the purchase of raw materials. Raw materials may include direct materials and indirect materials. There is no distinction in the materials at this point.

TABLE 11.1 Raw Materials Inventory

Raw Materials Inventory	$XX	
Accounts Payable		$XX

To record the purchase of raw materials

Use of Raw Materials

When raw material is used, a distinction is made as to the department in which the raw materials are used and the nature of the raw materials. Materials either go directly into the work in process account for a given process or to manufacturing overhead.

TABLE 11.2 Work in Process—Washing and Slicing

Work in Process Inventory—Washing and Slicing	$XX	
Raw Materials Inventory		$XX

To record use of direct raw materials into work in process—Washing and Slicing

Work in Process Inventory—Frying	$XX	
Raw Materials Inventory		$XX

To record use of direct raw materials into work in process—Frying

Weighted Average Method		**(Step 2)**	
		Equivalent Units	
(Step 1)	Physical Units	Materials	Conversion
Work in process, beginning	0		
Started during current period	60000		
To Account for	**60000**		
Completed and transferred out	20000	20000	20000
Work in process, ending	40000	40000	10000
Accounted for	**60000**	**60,000**	**30,000**

(Step 3)

	Total	Materials	Conversion
Work in process, beginning	$0.00	$0.00	$0.00
Costs added in current period	$40,000.00	$10, 000. 00	$30, 000. 00
Total costs to account for	$40,000.00	$10,000.00	$30,000.00

(Step 4)

Costs incurred to date	$40,000.00	$10,000.00	$30,000.00
Divide by equivalent units of work done in current period		60, 000	30, 000
Costs per equivalent unit of work done in current period	$1.17	$0.17	$1.00

(Step 5)

	Total	Materials	Conversion
Assignment of costs:			
Completed and transferred out	$23,333.33	$3,333.33	$20,000.00
Work in process, ending	$16,666.67	$6,666.67	$10,000.00
Total costs accounted for	**$40,000.00**	**$10,000.00**	**$30,000.00**

FIGURE 11.9 Total Report.

Manufacturing Overhead—Washing and Slicing	$XX	
Raw Materials Inventory		$XX

To record the use of indirect raw materials into manufacturing overhead for the washing and slicing department.

Manufacturing Overhead—Frying	$XX	
Raw Materials Inventory		$XX

To record the use of indirect raw materials into manufacturing overhead for the frying department.

Weighted Average		(Step 2)			(Step 3)				
Subsequent department		**Equivalent Units**							
(Step 1)	**Physical Units**	**Washing & Slicing**	**Materials**	**Conversion**					
						Total	**Washing & Slicing**	**Materials**	**Conversion**
Work in process, beginning	15000*				Work in process, beginning	$19,850.00	$17,550.00	$0.00	$2,300.00
Transferred in	20000				Costs added in current period	$33,133.33	$23,333.33	$6,000.00	$3,800.00
To Account for	**35000**				Total costs to account for	$52,983.33	$40,883.33	$6,000.00	$6,100.00
Completed and transferred out	25000	25000	25000	25000					
Work in process, ending	10000	10000	10000	5000					
Accounted for	**35000**	35,000	35,000.0	30000					

*This information would have been obtained from the prior month ending inventory for the frying department.

*Materials are added in beginning of period and conversion is added throughout. Conversion is 50% complete.

(Step 4)				
Costs incurred to date	$52,983.33	$40,883.33	$6,000.00	$6,100.00
Divide by equivalent units of work done in current period		35,000	35, 000	30, 000
Costs per equivalent unit of work done in current period	$1.54	**$1.17**	**$0.17**	**$0.20**

(Step 5)				
	Total	**Washing & Slicing**	**Materials**	**Conversion**
Assignment of costs:				
Completed and transferred out	$38,571.43	$29,202.38	$4,285.71	$5,083.33
Work in process, ending	$14,411.90	$11,680.95	$1,714.29	$1,016.67
Total costs accounted for	$52,983.33	**$40,883.33**	**$6,000.00**	**$6,100.00**

FIGURE 11.10 Total Report: Subsequent Processes.

Use of Labor

Like raw materials, labor comes in two forms, direct and indirect. The distinction for labor between direct and indirect is made at the point of entry. Labor is applied to the given work in process, and overhead accounts for the process.

TABLE 11.3 Work in Process—Washing and Slicing, part 2

Work in Process Inventory—Washing and Slicing	$XX	
Wages Payable		$XX

To record the use of direct labor into work in process—washing and slicing

Work in Process Inventory—Frying	$XX	
Wages Payable		$XX

To record the use of direct labor into work in process—frying

Manufacturing Overhead—Washing and Slicing	$XX	
Wages Payable		$XX

To record the use of indirect labor into manufacturing overhead for washing and slicing

Manufacturing Overhead—Frying	$XX	
Wages Payable		$XX

To record the use of indirect labor into manufacturing overhead for frying

Allocation of Overhead

When entering overhead, there are two amounts to consider: the amount of actual overhead and the amount of allocated overhead. Actual overhead is always debited while allocated overhead is always credited.

Consider actual overhead first:

TABLE 11.4 Manufacturing Overhead—Washing and Slicing

Manufacturing Overhead—Washing and Slicing	$XX	
Accounts payable		$XX
Cash		$XX
Prepaid insurance		$XX
Accumulated depreciation		$XX

To record actual overhead incurred in the washing and slicing department

Manufacturing Overhead—Frying	$XX	
Accounts payable		$XX
Cash		$XX
Prepaid insurance		$XX
Accumulated depreciation		$XX

To record actual overhead incurred in the frying department

When overhead is allocated in a job-costing system, it is based on the overhead rate. Nothing changes in a process-costing system. Overhead is still allocated based on an overhead rate.

TABLE 11.5 Work in Process—Washing and Slicing, part 3

Work in Process—Washing and Slicing	$XX	
Manufacturing Overhead—Washing and Slicing		$XX

To allocate overhead applied to the washing and slicing Department

Work in Process—Frying	$XX	
Manufacturing Overhead—Frying		$XX

To allocate overhead applied to the frying department

Move to Subsequent Departments and to Finished Goods

Once the product works its way through one department, it moves on to the next department as noted below:

TABLE 11.6 Work in Process—Frying

Work in Process—Frying	$XX	
Work in Process—Washing and Slicing		$XX

To record costs leaving the washing and slicing process and moving to the frying process.

Work in Process—Seasoning	
Work in Process—Frying	

To record costs leaving the frying process and moving to the seasoning process.

Work in Process—Packaging	
Work in Process—Seasoning	

To record costs leaving the seasoning process and moving to the packaging process.

Once the product moves into the last department, it is finished and is no longer a work in process. Thus, the costs must be moved to finished goods. The movement represents the final journal entry of the balance sheet out of work in process inventory and into finished goods inventory.

TABLE 11.7 Finished Goods Inventory

Finished Goods Inventory	$XX	
Work in Process—Packaging		$XX

To record completed goods

Sale of Goods

The sale of the items represents a movement of costs off the balance sheet and into the income statement. Under a perpetual system, costs of goods sold is recorded at the same time the sale is recorded.

TABLE 11.8 Accounts Receivable

Accounts Receivable	$XX	
Sales Revenue		$XX

To record the sale of goods

Cost of Goods Sold	$XX	
Finished Goods Inventory		$XX

To record costs of sold goods

LEARNING GOAL 5: Account for Under-Allocated and Over-Allocated Overhead in a Process-Cost System

As with job costing, overhead must be allocated to the different processes. In the process of allocating overhead, there will be overallocation and underallocation, just as in a job-costing system. Overhead in a process-costing system will be allocated via a plant-wide rate or may be broken down into a more refined rated as will be discussed in Topic 12.

The entry is the same as with job costing, however.

TABLE 11.9 Manufacturing Overhead

Actual Mat.	$XX	$XX	**Overhead Allocated**
Actual Lab.	$XX		
Actual OH	$XX		

Underallocated or Overallocated

Manufacturing Overhead—Washing and Slicing	$XX	
Cost of Goods Sold		$XX

To close out manufacturing overhead—washing and slicing with over-allocated overhead

Manufacturing Overhead—Frying	$XX	
Cost of Goods Sold		$XX

To close out manufacturing overhead—frying with over-allocated overhead

OR

TABLE 11.10 Cost of Goods Sold

Cost of Goods Sold	$XX	
Manufacturing Overhead—Washing and Slicing		$XX

To close out manufacturing overhead—washing and slicing with under-allocated overhead

Cost of Goods Sold	$XX	
Manufacturing Overhead—Frying		$XX

To close out manufacturing overhead—frying with under-allocated overhead

Typically, the over-allocated or under-allocated amounts are closed out to cost of goods sold. Although there are other methods for how to close out the over-allocated or under-allocated amounts, the easiest way is to close them out to cost of goods sold because eventually all costs will pass through cost of goods sold. The other methods are beyond the scope of this text.

LEARNING GOAL 6: Discuss Process Costing as it Relates to Service Types of Companies

The use of a process-cost system implies a product that is mass produced. Although mostly used with products, the process-cost system could also be used with a service. The package delivery business is an example of a service-based company that would use a process-costing system. The process of delivering packages is not based on a job but based on a process. UPS, for example has a sorting process and a delivery process. Packages come into the facility and need to be sorted. Although there is no raw material in this scenario, there are conversion costs which would include labor and overhead. The cost of the conversion per unit would be averaged based on the number of packages that enter the facility. The cost per package would move from the sorting process to the delivery process, where additional labor and overhead would be added. Management would be interested to know, on average, how much labor and overhead is applied to each package that comes into the facility. Knowing such information helps management to determine the charge of sending a package and the cost of labor and overhead in that process.

TOPIC 11 REFERENCES

Braun, K.W. and Tietz, W.M. *Managerial Accounting* (4th ed.). Upper Saddle River, NJ: Prentice Hall, 2014.

Garrison, R.H., Noreen, E.W., and Brewer, P.C. *Managerial Accounting.* New York: McGraw-Hill Companies, Inc., 2012.

Horngren, C.T, Datar, S.M. and Rajan, M.V. *Cost Accounting: A Managerial Emphasis* (15th ed.). Upper Saddle River, NJ: Pearson Education, Inc., 2015.

TOPIC 11 FIGURE CREDITS

TOPIC 12 Activity-Based Costing

LEARNING GOALS

1. Describe the use of an activity-based costing system.
2. Compare and contrast activity-based costing with traditional costing and departmental costing.
3. Discuss how activity-based costing is a refined costing system for allocating overhead.
4. Calculate departmental and activity overhead rates and allocate overhead based on activity rates, department rates, and plant-wide rates.
5. Discuss cost distortion, comparing and contrasting job costing, process costing and activity-based costing.

INTRODUCTION

In Topic 12, we will delve into a third costing system known as activity-based costing. Activity-based costing is a complex system that is not used for primary costing but as a supplementary system. Activity-based costing is considered to be a refined costing system in which the overhead rate is more accurately calculated than that of a plant-wide rate you've learned up until this point. The difficulty in calculating the cost of any given product lies in the overhead. The direct cost categories are traceable and are, thus, easily calculated. The overhead component, however, is where problems in costing arise. Some believe that plant-wide rates used in process costing or job costing are not accurate. Activity-based costing refines the plant-wide rate used for overhead and replaces the plant-wide rate with an activity-based rate (see Figure 12.1). All other calculations relating to the direct cost categories are unchanged.

LEARNING GOAL 1: Describe the Use of an Activity-Based Costing System

Not all companies have a need for an activity-based costing system. Companies that would want to add such a supplementary system would include companies that feel that all of overhead is not being driven by a single cost driver. To estimate overhead according to a plant-wide overhead cost rate, estimated overhead is divided by estimated amounts of a driver, which is one thing selected that drives up overhead. What if that

Overhead Rate	
Plant-wide rate = One Cost Driver	ABC rate = Multiple Cost Drivers

FIGURE 12.1 Plant-wide rate vs. ABC overhead rate.

one thing does not truly drive up all of overhead? What if the mismatch of resources causes cost distortions?

A company would want to supplement its existing system and use activity-based costing as a refinement when they recognize that:

- Sales are regularly lost to competition because the competition prices are much lower.
- You've noticed that the competition always prices much higher, and although you seem to sell a lot in terms of quantity, your profits are minimal, or you consistently have a loss.
- Profits and losses are hard to explain.
- Your product has changed over time and has become much more diversified.

LEARNING GOAL 2: Compare and Contrast Activity-Based Costing with Traditional Costing and Departmental Costing

A traditional costing system is known as a plant-wide system in which all overhead is lumped together, and the driver is one thing that drives up all of overhead. See Figure 12.2. In a traditional costing system, management would need to determine what that one cost driver could be. The difference in an activity-based costing system is that there are multiple drivers for multiple categories of overhead. See Figure 12.3.

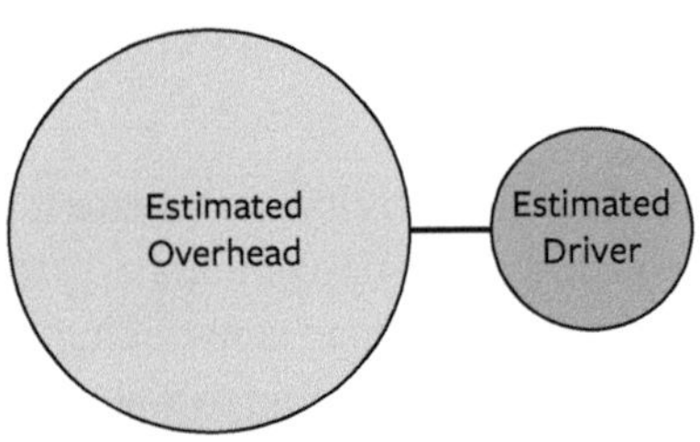

FIGURE 12.2 Traditional Costing System.

Just like a traditional costing system, activity-based costing still traces direct cost categories. Each job or process traces direct materials and direct overhead. The difference is in how the overhead is applied (Figure 12.4).

LEARNING GOAL 3: Discuss How Activity-Based Costing Is a Refined Costing System for Allocating Overhead

Activity-based costing is a refined costing system in that it allocates overhead at a more refined level than the traditional costing system's plant-wide calculation of overhead.

Traditional Costing System

As was already discussed, a traditional costing system lumps all overhead together and determines a rate based on a cost driver for all the overhead:

$$\frac{\textit{Estimated Overhead}}{\textit{Estimated Driver}} = \textit{Plant-Wide Overhead Rate}$$

Activity-Based Costing System

In a traditional costing system, all overhead is lumped together, whereas in a refined system, overhead costs are separated into cost categories based on the type of cost. When using an activity-based costing system, there are four levels into which an overhead cost can be separated: 1) unit-level costs, 2) batch-level costs, 3) product-level costs, and 4) facility-level costs (see Figure 12.5). Such hierarchical cost levels help to separate out overhead into homogenous pools of cost. Once all similar costs are separated out, a driver is established for each cost pool.

Using this system of calculating overhead is more refined because similar costs are pooled together with appropriate cost drivers instead of all overhead being lumped together with a single cost driver.

Facility-level costs. Facility-level costs are a group of costs that are related to keeping the entire facility running. They are the broadest level of costs. These costs cannot be traced to the unit, the batch, or even

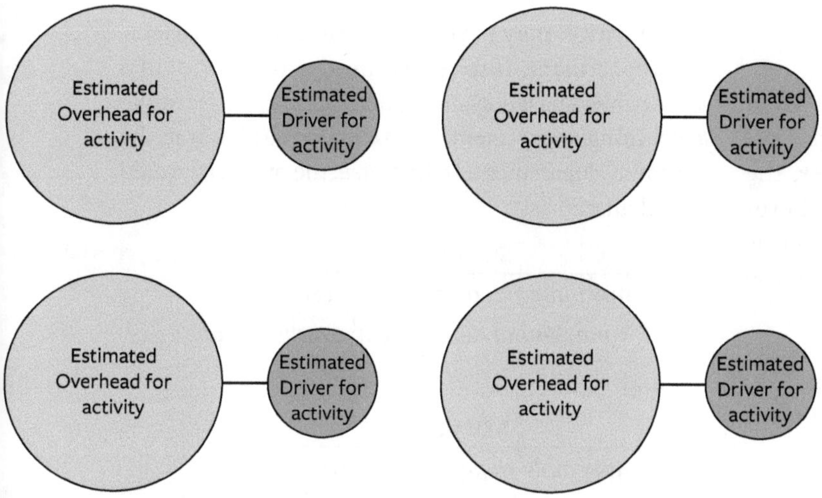

FIGURE 12.3 Activity-Based Costing System: Multiple Activities and Multiple Drivers.

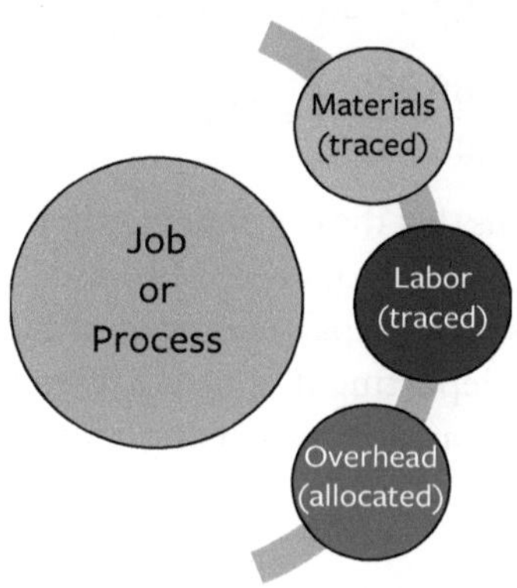

FIGURE 12.4 Materials, Labor, and Overhead.

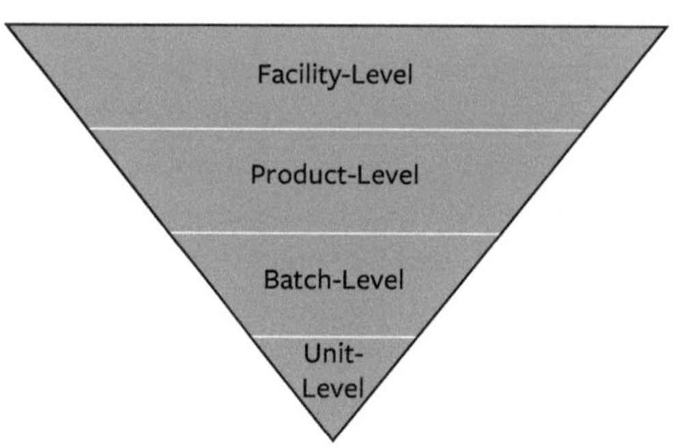

FIGURE 12.5 Cost Hierarchy.

to the product. Such overhead costs may include building rent for the manufacturing facility, utilities of the manufacturing facility, and maintenance of the manufacturing facility.

Product-level costs. Product-level costs are not quite as broad as facility-level costs but still cannot be traced to a product or a batch. Instead these costs are associated with the product. Such costs may include costs relating to product design or storage of a particular product. Product-level costs are overhead costs that support the product of a specific product line.

Batch-level costs. Batch-level costs are costs that are still not able to be traced to a specific unit but can be traced to the batch. A batch is a group of products manufactured together. In job costing, this would be the job, and in process costing, this would be a small batch within the process. All overhead costs associated with the batch would be categorized together. Such costs may include machine setup costs or the costs associated with the purchase orders for the batch, and inspection costs.

Unit-level costs. Unit-level costs are the narrowest type of cost in that they can be traced directly to each unit. Although direct material and direct labor are unit-level costs, they are not overhead costs and thus are not part of overhead costs that would be included in overhead. Such overhead costs may include indirect materials and machine repair costs if such costs are driven by the number of units.

The costs included in the hierarchical areas are not black and white. Some negotiation may be necessary as to what category each cost belongs. Ultimately, however, the goal is to separate out the entire amount of overhead into categories that are driven by relatively the same thing. Each cost pool will have its own cost driver.

$$\frac{\textit{Activity Overhead}}{\textit{Activity Driver}} = \textit{Activity-Based Overhead Rate}$$

Department-Based Costing

Similar to activity-based costing, department-based costing divides all overhead into separate groups. Instead of being driven by activity, however, the rate is calculated for each department. Therefore, all the overhead for each department is lumped together, and the rate is calculated for the department.

$$\frac{\textit{Department Overhead}}{\textit{Department Driver}} = \textit{Department-Based Overhead Rate}$$

LEARNING GOAL 4: Calculate Departmental and Activity Overhead Rates and Allocate Overhead Based on Activity Rates, Department Rates, and Plant-Wide Rates

If the calculation of a plant-wide rate is simply totaling all annual estimated overhead and dividing it by total annual amounts of the driver, a refined system would logically divide out the overhead into groups based on some similarity.

A plant-wide rate based on $100,000 of overhead and 60,000 machine hours (M.H.) would calculate into a plant-wide overhead rate of $1.67 per machine hour.

$$\frac{\$100{,}000}{60{,}000} = \$1.67$$

If product #1 and product #2 each use eight machine hours, the total cost of overhead for each of the products is 8 M.H. × $1.67 or $13.36. Under a plant-wide system, product #1 and product #2 are allocated the same amounts of overhead.

To refine the rate, overhead would need to be divided into separate cost pools. One way to divide overhead is to use activities as defined by their hierarchies. A second way is to use departments. Let's review using departments first.

Departments

In a manufacturing company, products flow in and out of various departments. For example, a manufacturing organization may have a machining and an assembly department. If total overhead is $100,000, in a department-based system $80,000 may be from the machining department and $20,000 may be from the assembly department. In this case, the overhead would be calculated as

$$\frac{\$80{,}000}{\textit{machining department driver}} = \textit{machining department overhead rate}$$

and

$$\frac{\$20{,}000}{\textit{assembly department driver}} = \textit{assembly department overhead rate}$$

If the machining department determines that overhead in the department is driven by machine hours and determines that 50,000 machine hours will be used during the year, the calculation is

$$\frac{\$80{,}000}{50{,}000\ M.H.} = \$1.60\ \textit{per M.H.}$$

This means that the overhead rate in the machining department is $1.60 for every M.H. used.

If the assembly department determines that overhead in the department is also driven by machine hours, and it anticipates using 10,000 M.H, the calculation is:

$$\frac{\$20{,}000}{10{,}000\ M.H.} = \$2.00\ \textit{per M.H.}$$

This means that the rate in the assembly department is $2.00 of overhead for every M.H. used.

To determine the total overhead for each product, we would need to know how much of each department the product actually used. For example, if product #1 uses one hour of M.H. in machining and product #2 uses seven hours of M.H. in machining, the amount of overhead for machining would be applied in different amounts: 1) $1 \times \$1.60$ and 2) $7 \times \$1.60$. If product #1 also uses 7 M.H. in assembly and product #2 uses 2 M.H. in assembly, the amount of overhead for machining would be applied in different amounts: 1) $7 \times \$2.00$ and 2) $2 \times \$2.00$.

TABLE 12.1 Departments

Product	Machining	Assembly	Total Overhead per Unit
#1	1 M.H.	7 M.H.	$(1 \times \$1.60)$ $+(7 \times \$2.00)$ $= \$15.60$
#2	7 M.H	1 M.H	$(7 \times \$1.60)$ $+(1 \times \$2.00)$ $= \$13.20$

Note that the two different products have different amounts of overhead because they use different amounts of each department. Product #1 uses more M.H. in the assembly department, which has a higher rate and product; therefore, the total overhead amount is higher. In the plant-wide rate, the cost of overhead for both products was $13.36, which means that product #1 was under-costed while product #2 was over-costed.

Activities

Using activities is similar to departments, only the rates are based on activities. Let's look at a product with four activities.

In an activity-based system, the manufacturing process may flow in and out of a variety of departments. However, the manufacturing process is broken down into activities, not departments. For example, let's say a company has determined that it has four activities: 1) machine setup, 2) material handling, 3) fabricating parts, and 4) packaging. Remember, these are not departments, they are activities. All costs in machine setup would be considered batch-level costs, driven by number of batches; all costs in the material handling activity would be unit-level costs, driven by number of parts; all costs in fabricating parts activity would be unit-level costs, driven by machine hours; and all costs in the packaging activity would be unit-level costs, driven by number of packages.

Now, let's review our total cost of $100,000, broken down into the four activities.

TABLE 12.2 Activities

Activity	Costs	Driver	Amount of Driver
Machine Setup	$30,000	# of Batches	10,000 batches
Material Handling	$15,000	# of Parts Moved	250,000 parts
Fabricating	$35,000	# Machine Hours	60,000 M.H
Packaging	$20,000	# of units packaged	150,000 units
Total	**$100,000**		

The breakdown of costs into activities involves first deciding on the activities that take place in the company and secondly, deciding on the amount of overhead that is attributable to each activity. Once the dollar amount has been established as overhead, the cost driver must be identified with the amount of the driver that will be used during the period. The following calculation is performed to establish the activity-based overhead rate.

TABLE 12.3 Activity-Based Overhead Rate

Costs		Amount of Driver	Cost per Driver
$30,000	/	10,000 batches	$3 per batch
$15,000	/	250,000 parts	$.06 per part
$35,000	/	60,000 M.H	$.58 per M.H. (rounded)
$20,000	/	150,000 units	$.13 per unit (rounded)
$100,000			

Once the overhead rate is established, the rate is applied to the actual amount of the activity the product uses. If Job A for fifty units of product #1 uses four batches, moves eighty-three parts, uses four hundred M.H., and fifty packages, the overhead would be calculated as follows.

TABLE 12.4 Overhead Calculation

Activity-based overhead rate		Actual use of Activity	Overhead Allocated to Job.
$3	×	4 batches	$12
$.06	×	83 parts	$4.98

(continued)

$.58	× 400 M.H.	$232
$.13	× 50 units	$6.50
$4.13		$255.48 / 50 *units* = 5.11 *per unit (rounded)*

If Job B for 75 units of product #2 uses five batches, moves 125 parts, uses four hundred M.H., and seventy-five packages, the overhead would be calculated as follows.

TABLE 12.5 Overhead Calculation, part 2

Activity-based overhead rate	Actual use of Activity	Overhead Allocated to Job.
$3	× 5 batches	$15
$.06	× 125 parts	$7.50
$.58	× 400 M.H.	$232
$.13	× 75 units	$9.75
$4.13		$264.25 / 75 *units* = 3.52 *per unit (rounded)*

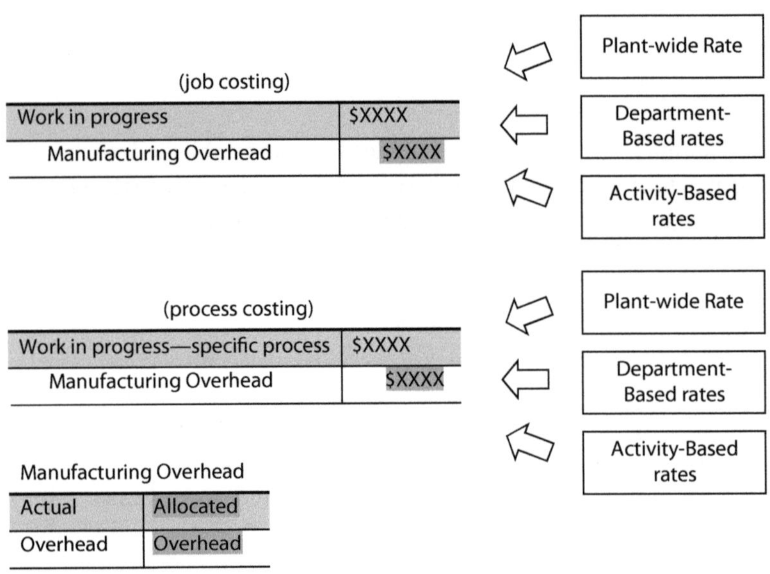

FIGURE 12.6 Job and Process Costing.

As you can see, by dividing the $100,000 of overhead costs over several activities, the cost per unit has dropped even more because of the different amount of resources used.

LEARNING GOAL 5: Discuss Cost Distortion, Comparing and Contrasting Job Costing, Process Costing and Activity-Based Costing

In a job-cost or process-cost system, overhead is allocated to either jobs or processes via an overhead rate. Such a rate can be either calculated from a plant-wide system or from an activity-based system. As noted in Learning Goal 4, there can be significant differences between the overhead applied using a plant-wide system vs. a departmental-based system vs. an activity-based system. Generally, an activity-based system is thought to be the most accurate, given the level of refinement. However, there is also greater room for error in that the amount of estimated overhead applied to the activities must be accurate, the amount of each of the estimated amount of the drivers must be accurate, and the amount of each activity used must be accurate.

Under job costing and process costing, the entry to the Manufacturing Overhead account is a debit to Work in Process and a credit to Manufacturing Overhead. Recall the transaction:

The only difference in using an ABC system is from where the credit to Manufacturing Overhead comes.

Cost distortion can occur at the point where manufacturing overhead is debited because the debited amount represents the allocated amount. Recall that if the debited amount is "off" from the actual amount, the difference will be written off to cost of goods sold. However, also recall that inaccurate amounts under-cost and over-cost our product, making it difficult to price the product or bid on jobs.

ABC is an expensive system to implement, and, thus, the benefits must outweigh the costs. If cost distortion is occurring with products that require different amounts of resources, and the product is in a competitive market, the benefits of using ABC will most likely outweigh the costs. However, if the marketplace is not competitive, and products use resources equally, the costs of implementing ABC may outweigh the benefits.

Each company needs to conduct its own analysis as to whether or not ABC should be implemented.

TOPIC 12 REFERENCES

Braun, K.W. and Tietz, W.M. *Managerial Accounting* (4th ed.). Upper Saddle River, NJ: Prentice Hall, 2014.

Garrison, R.H., Noreen, E.W., and Brewer, P.C. *Managerial Accounting.* New York: McGraw-Hill Companies, Inc., 2012.

Horngren, C.T, Datar, S.M. and Rajan, M.V. *Cost Accounting: A Managerial Emphasis* (15th ed.). Upper Saddle River, NJ: Pearson Education, Inc., 2015.

TOPIC 13 Absorption Costing Vs. Direct Costing

LEARNING GOALS

1. Discuss how fixed manufacturing overhead differentiates absorption costing from variable costing.
2. Calculate an income statement under absorption costing.
3. Calculate an income statement under variable costing.
4. Reconcile absorption costing to variable costing.
5. Explain the source of the difference in the reconciliation of absorption costing to variable costing.
6. Discuss strengths and weaknesses of absorption costing vs. variable costing.

INTRODUCTION

In Topic 13, we will discuss the difference between variable costing and absorption costing. Sometimes these costing methods are referred to under different names such as direct costing and full costing, respectively. Up until this point, we have been using absorption costing, which means that we have absorbed all manufacturing cost into the cost of the product. Now, we will take another look at the costs we include in product cost and investigate variable costing.

LEARNING GOAL 1: Discuss How Fixed Manufacturing Overhead Differentiates Absorption Costing from Variable Costing

Two main costing systems are used to determine which costs will funnel through as product costs in a manufacturing system: absorption costing and variable costing. Absorption costing requires the use of a traditional-format income statement, while variable costing requires the use of a contribution-format income statement. The purpose for differentiating the two is to comply with regulation and to clarify the costs of the products produced.

Under an absorption-costing system, all manufacturing costs are considered to be product costs. For example, in absorption costing all variable and fixed manufacturing costs would flow through as a product cost on the balance sheet and would end up as cost of goods sold on the

Variable Costing (Product Costs)	Direct Materials	Internal Reporting
	Direct Labor	
	Variable Manufacturing Overhead	
Variable Costing (Period Costs)	Fixed Manufacturing Overhead	
	Variable Selling and Admin. Fixed Selling and Admin.	
Absorption Costing (Product Costs)	Direct Materials	GAAP & IRS
	Direct Labor	
	Variable Manufacturing Overhead	
	Fixed Manufacturing Overhead	
Absorption costing (Period costs)	Variable Selling and Admin.	
	Fixed Selling and Admin.	

FIGURE 13.1 Variable vs. Absorption Costing.

income statement. Under a variable costing system, all variable manufacturing costs would flow through as a product cost on the balance sheet and would end up as cost of goods sold on the income statement. Hence, under the variable costing system, the fixed manufacturing overhead would be considered a period cost, and under the absorption costing method it would be considered a product cost.

Why are there two methods? The first method, absorption costing, exists to comply with Generally Accepted Accounting Principles (GAAP) as well as IRS requirements. Absorption is required for GAAP and the IRS because it is a more accurate account of how costs match revenue.

Successful companies, however, use both methods, absorption costing for GAAP and the IRS, and variable costing for internal reporting purposes (Figure 13.1). Each method has its strengths and weakness for its given purpose (see Figures 13.3 and 13.4).

Each method will elicit a different amount for operating income depending on whether inventory rises or falls (Figure 13.2).

LEARNING GOAL 2: Calculate an Income Statement Under Absorption Costing

As noted in Learning Goal 1, the contribution-margin income statement and the traditional-format income statement may elicit a different amount of operating income depending on if inventory increases or

Production vs. Sales	Units produced = Units sold	Units produced > Units Sold	Units Produced < Units Sold
Inventory Effect	No Change	Inventory increases	Inventory Decreases
Variable vs. Absorption Operating Income	Absorption = Variable	Absorption > Variable	Absorption < Variable

FIGURE 13.2 Effects of inventory on operating income.

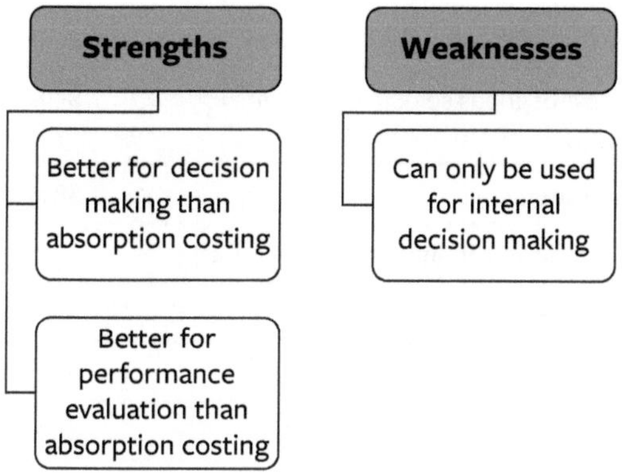

FIGURE 13.3 Strengths and Weaknesses—Variable Costing.

decreases. Learning Goal 2 focuses on the Absorption-Costing Income Statement at various levels of production and sold amounts.

Calculation 1: INVENTORY PRODUCED EQUALS INVENTORY SOLD

Assume the following data for Cline Corporation.

TABLE 13.1 Cline Corp Data

Produced: 20,000 units	
Sold: 20,000 units	
Variable costs per unit: Labor: \$11 Materials: \$3 Overhead: \$2 Selling and administration: \$5	
Fixed costs per year: Manufacturing overhead: \$95,000 Selling and administration: \$75,000	
Selling price: \$55 per unit	
Per unit cost:	
Absorption Costing: Variable Manufacturing Costs: \$16 (\$11+\$3+\$2)	
Fixed Manufacturing Costs: \$4.75 $\left(\frac{\$95{,}000}{20{,}000 \textit{ units produced}}\right)$	
Sales: (20,000 units × \$55)	\$1,100,000
Less cost of goods sold: (20,000 units × (16 + 4.75))	\$415,000
Gross Margin:	\$685,000
Less selling and administrative expenses:	
Variable (20,000 units × \$5):	\$100,000
Fixed:	\$75,000
Net Operating Income:	\$510,000

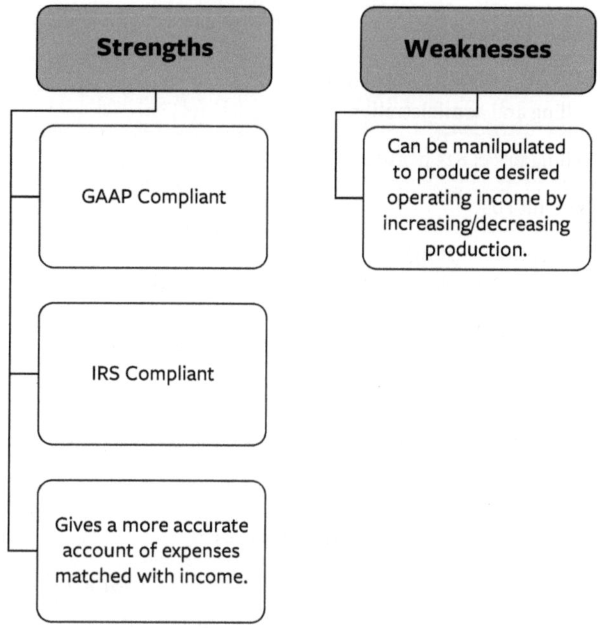

FIGURE 13.4 Strengths and Weakness—Absorption Costing.

Calculation 2: INVENTORY PRODUCED IS GREATER THAN INVENTORY SOLD

Assume the following data for Cline Corporation.

TABLE 13.2 Cline Corp Data 2

Produced: 25,000 units
Sold: 20,000 units
Variable costs per unit: Labor: \$11 Materials: \$3 Overhead: \$2 Selling and administration: \$5

Fixed costs per year:	
Manufacturing overhead: $95,000 Selling and administration: $75,000	
Selling price: $25 per unit	
Per unit cost:	
Absorption Costing: Variable Manufacturing Costs: $16 ($11 + $3 + $2) Fixed Manufacturing Costs: $3.80 ($\frac{\$95{,}000}{25{,}000\ units\ produced}$)	
Sales: (20,000 units × $55)	$1,100,000
Less cost of goods sold: (20,000 units × (16 + 3.80))	$396,000
Gross Margin:	$704,000
Less selling and administrative expenses:	
Variable (20,000 units × $5):	$100,000
Fixed:	$75,000
Net Operating Income:	$529,000

Calculation 3: INVENTORY PRODUCED IS LESS THAN INVENTORY SOLD

Assume the following data for Cline Corporation.

TABLE 13.3 Cline Corp Data 3

Produced: 20,000 units	
Sold: 25,000 units	
Variable costs per unit: Labor: $11 Materials: $3 Overhead: $2 Selling and administration: $5	
Fixed costs per year: Manufacturing overhead: $95,000 Selling and administration: $75,000	
Selling price: $25 per unit	
Per unit cost:	
Absorption Costing: Variable Manufacturing Costs: $16 ($11 + $3 + $2) Fixed Manufacturing Costs: $4.75 ($95,000/20,000 units produced)	
Sales: (25,000 units × $55)	$1,375,000
Less cost of goods sold: (25,000 units × (16+4.75))	$518,750
Gross Margin:	$856,250
Less selling and administrative expenses:	
Variable (25,000 units × $5):	$125,000
Fixed:	$75,000
Net Operating Income:	$656,250

LEARNING GOAL 3: Calculate an Income Statement Under Variable Costing

Learning Goal 3 focuses on the Variable Costing and the Contribution-Format Income Statement at various levels of production and sold amounts.

Calculation 1: INVENTORY PRODUCED EQUALS INVENTORY SOLD

Assume the following data for Cline Corporation.

TABLE 13.4 Cline Corp Data 4

Produced: 20,000 units	
Sold: 20,000 units	
Variable costs per unit: Labor: $11 Materials: $3 Overhead: $2 Selling and administration: $5	
Fixed costs per year: Manufacturing overhead: $95,000 Selling and administration: $75,000	
Selling price: $55 per unit	
Per-unit cost:	
Variable Costing: Variable Manufacturing Costs: $16 ($11 + $3 + $2) Fixed Manufacturing Costs: $0	
Sales: (20,000 units × $55)	$1,100,000
Less cost of goods sold: (20,000 units × $16)	$320,000

Less variable selling and administration (20,000 units × $5)	$100,000
Contribution Margin:	$680,000
Less fixed expenses:	
Selling and Administration	$75,000
Manufacturing Overhead	$95,000
Net Operating Income:	$510,000

Notice that the amount of Net Operating Income is that same amount as it was in Calculation #1 of Learning Goal 2.

Calculation 2: INVENTORY PRODUCED IS GREATER THAN INVENTORY SOLD

Assume the following data for Cline Corporation.

TABLE 13.5 Cline Corp Data 5

Produced: 25,000 units	
Sold: 20,000 units	
Variable costs per unit: Labor: $11 Materials: $3 Overhead: $2 Selling and administration: $5	
Fixed costs per year: Manufacturing overhead: $95,000 Selling and administration: $75,000	
Selling price: $25 per unit	
Per-unit cost:	
Variable Costing: Variable Manufacturing Costs: $16 ($11 + $3 + $2) Fixed Manufacturing Costs: $0	
Sales: (20,000 units × $55)	$1,100,000
Less cost of goods sold: (20,000 units × $16)	$320,000
Less variable selling and administration (20,000 units × $5)	$100,000
Contribution Margin:	$680,000
Less fixed expenses:	
Selling and Administration	$75,000
Manufacturing Overhead	$95,000
Net Operating Income:	$510,000

Notice that the amount of Net Operating Income is less than the amount calculated in Calculation #2 of Learning Goal 2.

Calculation 3: INVENTORY PRODUCED IS LESS THAN INVENTORY SOLD

Assume the following data for Cline Corporation.

TABLE 13.6 Cline Corp Data 6

Produced: 20,000 units	
Sold: 25,000 units	
Variable costs per unit: Labor: $11 Materials: $3 Overhead: $2 Selling and administration: $5	
Fixed costs per year: Manufacturing overhead: $95,000 Selling and administration: $75,000	
Selling price: $25 per unit	
Per-unit cost: Variable Costing: Variable Manufacturing Costs: $16 ($11 + $3 + $2)	
Fixed Manufacturing Costs: $0	
Sales: (25,000 units × $55)	$1,375,000
Less cost of goods sold: (25,000 units × $16)	$400,000
Less variable selling and administration: (25,000 units × $5)	$125,000
Contribution Margin:	$850,000
Less fixed expenses:	
Selling and Administration	$75,000
Manufacturing Overhead	$95,000
Net Operating Income:	$680,000

Notice that the amount of Net Operating Income is greater than the amount calculated in Calculation #3 of Learning Goal 2.

LEARNING GOAL 4: Reconcile Absorption Costing to Variable Costing

In Figure 13.2, the effects of inventory on operating income were displayed in table format. The difference between the operating income amounts can be reconciled and explained. See the reconciliation for each of the calculations noted in Learning Goals #2 and #3.

Dollar Differences

TABLE 13.7 Dollar Differences

	Absorption Costing Operating Income	Variable Costing Operating Income
Calculation #1:	$510,000	$510,000
Calculation #2:	$529,000	$510,000
Calculation #3:	$656,250	$680,000
	Differences	
Calculation #1:	$0	
Calculation #2:	$19,000 (Absorption Costing—Greater)	
Calculation #3:	$23,750 (Variable Costing—Greater)	

Unit Differences

TABLE 13.8 Unit Differences

	Units Produced	Units Sold
Calculation #1:	20,000	20,000
Calculation #2:	25,000	20,000
Calculation #3:	20,000	25,000
Differences		
Calculation #1:	Nothing left in ending inventory/Nothing taken from ending inventory	
Calculation #2:	5,000 units left in ending inventory ($25,000 produced and $20,000 sold)	
Calculation #3:	5,000 units taken from ending inventory ($20,000 units produced and $25,000 units sold)	

Reconciliation

TABLE 13.9 Reconciliation

Calculation #1:	None Required
Calculation #2:	$\frac{\$19,000}{5,000} = \$3.80 \textit{ per unit}$
Calculation #3:	$\frac{\$23,750}{5,000} = \$4.75 \textit{ per unit}$

LEARNING GOAL 5: Explain the Source of the Difference in the Reconciliation of Absorption Costing to Variable Costing

In the reconciliation of the amount of dollars and units in Learning Goal #3, you can see that in calculation #2, the difference of the 5,000 units *left in* ending inventory was calculated at $3.80 per unit, which is the amount of the fixed manufacturing overhead divided by the number of units **produced**. In calculation #3, the difference of the 5,000 units *taken from* ending inventory was calculated at $4.75 per units, which is the amount of the fixed manufacturing overhead divided by the number of units **produced.** The amounts produced were different in calculation #2 and calculation #3.

Thus, the difference has to do with the amounts of fixed overhead as it relates to the number of units left in or taken from ending inventory. As more units are produced, fixed manufacturing overhead is less per unit. This is the nature of a fixed cost. In calculation #2, 25,000 units were produced, whereas in calculation #3, 20,000 units were produced. Under the absorption method, the amount of fixed manufacturing overhead was less per unit when more units were produced.

As fixed overhead is added to inventory, if the amount produced increases, fixed overhead per unit decreases, and cost of goods sold decreases. If cost of goods sold decreases, operating income increases. Therefore, an increase in production can increase operating income. Conversely, as fixed overhead is taken from ending inventory, if the amount produced decreases, fixed overhead per unit increases, and cost of goods sold increases. If cost of goods sold increases, operating income decreases. Therefore, a decrease in production, which would force the units sold to be removed from inventory, would cause an increase in cost of goods sold and a decrease in operating income.

LEARNING GOAL 6: Discuss Strengths and Weaknesses of Absorption Costing vs. Variable Costing

As mentioned earlier, absorption costing is the method required by GAAP and by the IRS. However, a successful company will use variable costing for internal purposes to supplement absorption costing. Because of the weakness found in absorption costing to manipulate operating income by producing more or less, most companies do not want to use absorption costing as a method of evaluating employees or administering bonuses. See Figures 13.3 and 13.4 for a summary of strengths and weaknesses for each of the costing methods discussed within this topic.

TOPIC 13 REFERENCES

Braun, K.W. and Tietz, W.M. *Managerial Accounting* (4th ed.). Upper Saddle River, NJ: Prentice Hall, 2014.

Garrison, R.H., Noreen, E.W., and Brewer, P.C. *Managerial Accounting.* New York: McGraw-Hill Companies, Inc., 2012.

Horngren, C.T, Datar, S.M. and Rajan, M.V. *Cost Accounting: A Managerial Emphasis* (15th ed.). Upper Saddle River, NJ: Pearson Education, Inc., 2015.

TOPIC 14 Short-Term Decision Making

LEARNING GOALS

1. Understand the difference between relevant and not-relevant information in decision making.
2. Discuss the various decisions faced by management.
3. Perform short-term decision calculations such as pricing, make or buy, drop or add a segment, and acceptance of a special order.
4. Investigate special issues associated with decision making.

INTRODUCTION

Managers make decisions on a daily basis. The managerial accountant's role in such decision making is to provide management with relevant data so that informed decisions can be made. Most decisions made by management can be fairly easily calculated but must also be weighed with non-financial data. The whole of decision making involves a quantitative analysis as well as a qualitative analysis. The topic of short-term decision making is a very practical application of how managerial accounting aids management on a daily basis.

LEARNING GOAL 1: Understand the Difference Between Relevant and Not-Relevant Information in Decision Making

One of the foundations to making management decisions is to understand which data is relevant data and which data is not relevant to the decision-making process. As management makes various decisions such as if the company should make or buy a part, if it should drop or add a segment, or if it should accept a special order, a lot of information will be presented, much of which is not relevant.

When management makes decisions, they will make decisions consistent with their strategy. Thus, the decision-making process involves a re-evaluation of goals and a gathering of information. Once an appropriate level of data has been gathered, management can make a decision by choosing that which it feel is the best alternative. Once the decision

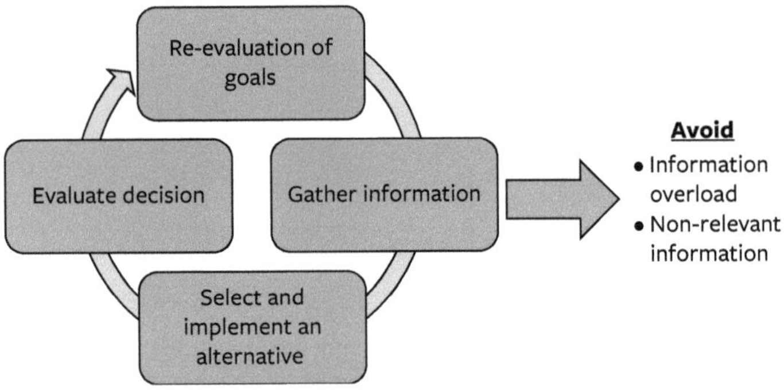

FIGURE 14.1 The decision making process.

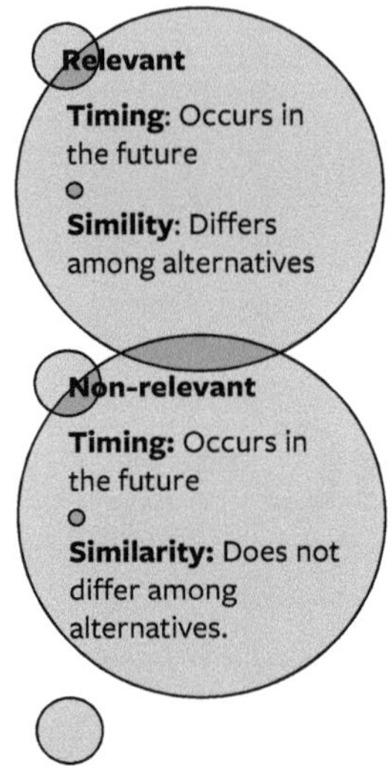

FIGURE 14.2 Relevant vs. non-relevant information.

has been implemented, the process of evaluating the outcome will be beneficial to guide the next decision (see Figure 14.1).

In gathering data to make a decision, it is important to avoid two things: 1) Information overload and 2) using data that is not relevant. Information overload is the overabundance of information. Although gathering information is important to the decision-making process, too much information can be as detrimental to the decision making process as not enough information. Using data that is not relevant confuses the decision-making process and should, thus, also be avoided.

Relevant vs. Non-Relevant Information

When making decisions, even on a personal topic, certain information is relevant and certain information is not relevant (Figure 14.2). For example, let's say you want to go out to eat at a fast food restaurant. Because the prices are fairly similar at all fast food restaurants, the cost of dinner is not relevant to your decision. However, you may prefer burgers over tacos, and, thus, the style of food would be relevant to your decision. Likewise, if you are deciding between dining out at a fast food restaurant and a formal restaurant, cost would be relevant as would the style of food.

To understand the difference between relevant and non-relevant information, the distinction can be made in two categories: 1) timeframe and 2) similarity. Relevant information occurs in the future and differs among alternative choices. Non-relevant information occurs in the past and does not differ among alternatives. Let's return to the dining out example at the fast food restaurants. Paying for the meal occurs in the future; however, the costs will be similar. Thus, the cost of the meal, a financial decision, is not relevant. The food type, on the other hand, both occurs in the future and is different among alternatives. The food type is relevant information and should factor into the decision. However, the food type is non-financial. If you are truly hungry for burgers, and you go to a place that serves tacos, you may not be satisfied. As you evaluate your decision, you may find that your decision was not a good decision based on the nonfinancial data.

Non-Financial vs. Financial

As accountants, we tend to focus on the financial component of decision making. However, when managers exclude non-financial data from the decision, the results can be disastrous. Let's refer, again, to the fast food restaurant example. The type of food is a non-financial alternative that occurs in the future and is different among alternative. Therefore, the information is relevant and should be considered.

What is non-financial data in a business environment? Non-financial data includes information such as:

- Employee morale.
- Quality of work.
- Goodwill in the community.
- Client loyalty.

LEARNING GOAL 2: Discuss the Various Decisions Faced by Management

Management is faced with a host of decisions regarding the way in which the business operates and the best use of resources. Decisions include 1) pricing; 2) outsourcing; 3) discontinuing a product line, department, or a store; 4) selling as is or processing further, and 5) accepting or rejecting a special order.

Pricing

Pricing the product is one of the most important decisions that management will make. A product that is overpriced may lose customers while a product that is underpriced may lose money. Managerial accountants are heavily involved in pricing decisions because pricing the product has a direct relationship with the cost of the product. Additionally, the pricing model used to price one's product is a direct result of the strategy. A company that follows a cost-leadership strategy would use a target-costing pricing model while a company that follows a product-differentiation strategy would follow a cost-plus pricing model.

Once a company establishes the strategy it will use in the marketplace, such a decision will determine the pricing model and the role that strategy will play in pricing (see Figure 14.3).

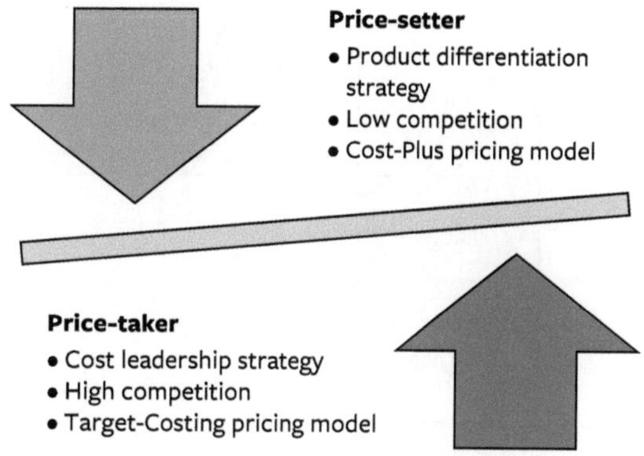

FIGURE 14.3 Price-takers vs. Price-setters.

Price-takers. A company is a price-taker when it has chosen a cost-leadership strategy. As a price-taker, a company offers a product that is not distinct or unique. Thus, there is no justification to sell the product at a higher price than the rest of the players in the marketplace. Usually, competition is heavy for those who are considered price-takers, and price will be a significant factor for clients who are considering buying a product from a price-taker. When pricing their product, a price-taker will use a target-costing model, which begins with the price in the marketplace and ensures that the cost of making the product, combined with the desired profit does not surpass that price charged in the marketplace.

Price-setters. A company is a price-setter when it has chosen a product-differentiation strategy. As a price-setter, a company offers a product that is distinct or unique in some way. Thus, there is justification to sell the product at a higher price than the rest of the players in the marketplace. Competition is not as heavy for price-setters because the product offered is unique and the marketplace is willing to pay a premium for such a product. When pricing their product, a price-setter will use a cost-plus pricing model, which begins with the cost of making the product, adds the desired profit, and prices the product as a total of cost plus desired profit.

Outsourcing

Another decision faced by management is whether to make or buy a product used in the manufacturing process. For a manufacturing company, a variety of resources are available to use in the manufacturing process. Management must decide how to best use the available resources. Sometimes that means it is a better plan to make a product in-house, and other times it is a better plan to outsource a product.

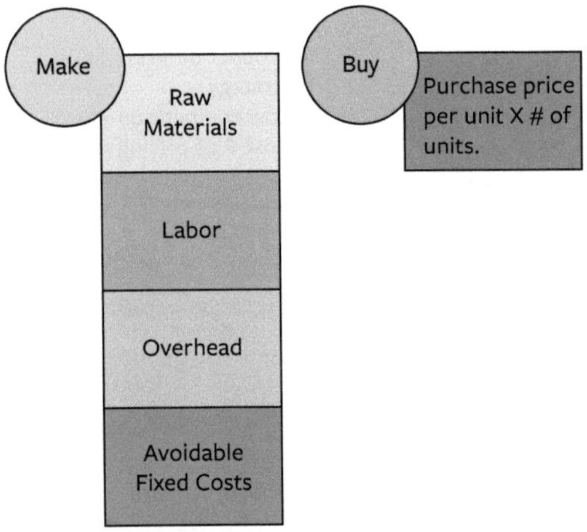

FIGURE 14.4 Outsourcing.

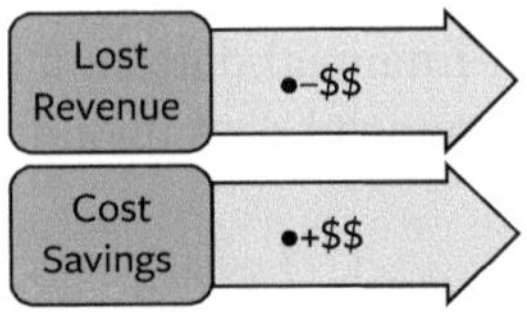

FIGURE 14.5 Discontinue a product line, department, or store.

For example, let's say that Company 1 makes product A. Product A has three components: a, b, and c. The company wants to decide if it would be a better use of resources to make or buy component c. In making such a decision, Company 1 would want to consider the cost involved in making component c in-house and compare such costs to buying component c from another vendor. In making such a decision. financial and nonfinancial considerations must be reviewed (see Figure 14.4).

The financial considerations include the cost of the raw materials used in making the product, the labor used in making the product, and the variable overhead. Non-financial considerations include company morale, the quality of the product, and the timeliness of the component c as needed in the production process.

Discontinuing a Product Line, Department, or Store

Companies must constantly evaluate the profitability of product lines, departments, and stores to determine if such products, departments, or stores are benefiting the overall goals of the company. When considering such decisions, management reviews the variable costs of a given entity but also considers fixed costs that may be able to be avoided should the product, department, or store be discontinued (Figure 14.5).

For example, let's say that the jewelry department of a given store appears to be unprofitable, and the company is considering discontinuing the department. The financial considerations that the management would seek to understand would include the variable costs of running the jewelry department. If the jewelry department goes away, such variable costs would also go away. Additionally, management would need to consider certain fixed costs that would also go away if the department were closed. From a financial perspective, if lost revenue exceeds the absence of costs, the product, department, or store should not be discontinued. However, if the cost savings exceeds the lost revenue, the product, department, or store should be discontinued. From a non-financial perspective, management would want to consider how the unprofitable department helped or hurt other departments. It is possible that an unprofitable product brings in customers that spend money in other departments, making each of those departments profitable.

Sell as Is or Process Further?

In a sell-as-is-or-process-further decision, management is faced with whether the additional revenue brought in by processing a product further is worth the cost of processing a product further (Figure 14.6). For example, if a company sells bags of unprocessed cocoa bean, the company may want to consider whether the cost of processing the beans into cocoa powder or dark chocolate is worth the additional revenue brought in by the further processed product.

Accept or Reject a Special Order

The last decision addressed in this textbook is the decision companies make to accept or reject special orders. On occasion, a company will receive a request for a special order that has somewhat different

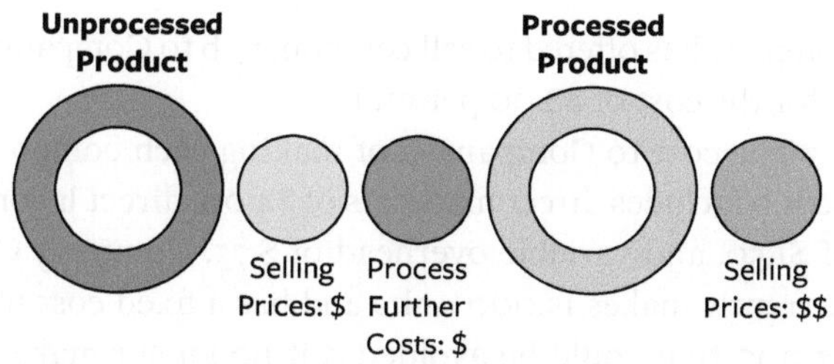

FIGURE 14.6 Sell as is or process further.

characteristics than the typical order received by the company. Management will need to determine if the special order should be accepted or rejected (see Figure 14.7). The financial considerations for accepting the special order begin with the variable costs involved in meeting the request of the special order. Fixed costs are also a consideration as management determines whether additional fixed costs will be needed or if the special order will simply use fixed costs that will be incurred regardless of whether the special order is accepted or not. Non-financial considerations include whether there is capacity for the special order and whether such special order will impact regular business.

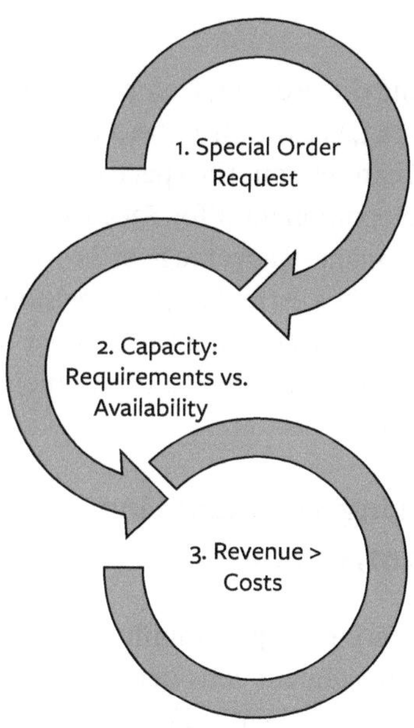

FIGURE 14.7 Accept or Reject Special order.

LEARNING GOAL 3: Perform Short-Term Decision Calculations Such as Pricing, Make or Buy, Drop or Add a Segment, and Acceptance of a Special Order

Understanding the methodology behind the various decisions management makes is important before learning to make the calculations associated with the decision. Once the calculations are performed, both financial and nonfinancial considerations must be made before a final decision is reached.

Pricing

Pricing, as determined by whether a company is a price-taker or a price-setter, is calculated by way of target costing or cost-plus pricing.

Target Costing. Target costing is a method of calculating the target cost of making the product. Target costing is used for price-takers because the cost of their product cannot exceed the market price. Therefore, the pricing model solves for cost of making the product with the understanding that the price of the product cannot exceed the market price.

Example: Company A is a company that sells a product common in the marketplace. There is nothing unique or distinct about the product. The marketplace sells the product for $10 each unit. Company A anticipates selling 10,000 units. Shareholders want a return of 5% of total assets. Total assets equal $500,000.

TABLE 14.1 Target Cost

Revenue at market price (10,000 × $10):	$100,000
Less: Desired Profit (.05 × $500,000):	$25,000
Target Cost:	**$75,000**

In the above scenario, Company A's total cost cannot exceed $75,000 if the item is sold at market price. Therefore, the price of each item would be $10.00 while the cost of making 10,000 units could not exceed $75,000. If $50,000 is fixed cost, $25,000 would be left as a variable cost. Variable cost would be $2.50 per unit ($\frac{\$25,000}{10,000}$).

The managerial accountant who gathers costs for Company A would be responsible for ensuring that total costs did not exceed $75,000.

Cost-Plus Pricing. Cost-plus pricing is a method of calculating selling price of the product based on the cost of making the product. Cost-plus pricing is used for price-takers because the cost of their product may exceed the market price. The pricing model solves for the price of the product, building upon the cost.

Example: Company B is a company that sells a product that is unique in the marketplace. The marketplace sells a similar product for $10 each unit. Company B can rise above the $10.00 per unit because it has a product-differentiation strategy and is considered to be a price-setter. Company B anticipates selling 10,000 units. Shareholders want a return of 5% of total assets. Total assets equal $500,000. The total cost of making the product is $3.00 variable cost per unit and $60,000 fixed costs.

TABLE 14.2 Fixed Cost

Fixed Cost:	$60,000
Variable Cost (10,000 × $3.00):	$30,000
Plus: Desired Profit (.05 × $500,000):	$25,000
Cost-Plus Price:	$115,000
Divided by number of units ($\frac{\$115,000}{10,000}$):	$11.50

In the above scenario, Company B's cost-plus price can exceed the market price of $10.00 because of its unique qualities. Total price per unit would be $11.50.

The managerial accountant who gathers costs for Company B would be responsible for ensuring that the additional costs add value to the product and make the product unique.

Outsourcing

In a make-or-buy decision, the calculation involves a comparison of the cost to make the product with the cost of buying the product.

Example: Company C currently makes component b as part of its manufacturing process. Another company has offered to sell component b to Company C for the cost of $8.00 per unit.

The cost to Company C of making each component b includes direct materials of $4.00, direct labor of $1.50, and variable overhead of $.75. Company C currently makes 15,000 units and has a fixed cost of $3,000 that could be avoided if it no longer makes component b.

TABLE 14.3 Outsourcing

	Make (per unit)	Buy (per unit)	Make (15,000 units)	Buy (15,000 units)
Purchase Price	$0	$8.00	$0	$120,000
Direct Materials	$4.00		$60,000	
Direct Labor	$1.50		$22,500	
Variable Overhead	$.75		$11,250	
Fixed Costs	$.20 ($\frac{\$3,000}{15,000\ units}$)		$3,000	
Total	**$6.45**	**$8.00**	**$96,750**	**$120,000**

By making the product, Company C will save $1.55 per unit or $23,250 for all 15,000 units. However, if Company C can rent out the space it would otherwise use to make component b for $30,000, the company would have a financial advantage of $6,750 to outsource component b. Thus, in making the decision to make or buy, managers must consider the best use of resources and make the decision based on financial and non-financial data.

Discontinuing a Product Line, Department, or Store

When considering the profitability of a segment of the company, management considers the amount of revenue lost as compared with the amount of cost saved.

Example: Company D sells product line f, which appears to be unprofitable (See Column B). However, upon analysis of the costs, Company D learns that none of the fixed operating costs are avoidable, and $25,000 of the fixed manufacturing costs would be avoidable. In Column D, the company considers the lost revenue and the cost savings.

TABLE 14.4 Discontinuing Product Line

Column A	Column B	Column C	Column D
Revenue	$500,000	Lost Revenue	($500,000)
Less Variable Expenses:		Saved Variable Expenses:	
Variable Manufacturing	($275,000)	Variable Manufacturing	$275,000
Variable Operating	($125,000)	Variable Operating	$125,000
Contribution Margin	$100,000	Lost Contribution Margin	($100,000)
Less Fixed Expenses:		Saved Fixed Expense:	
Fixed Manufacturing	($75,000)	Fixed Manufacturing	$25,000
Fixed Operating	($35,000)	Fixed Operating	$0
Operating Income	**($10,000)**	**Lost Operating Income**	**($75,000)**

According to the scenario above for Company D, if product line f were dropped, the loss in revenue would be greater than the cost savings. From a financial perspective, product line f should not be dropped.

Sell as Is or Process Further?

Making the decision to sell as is or process further is a decision made by several managers and must be calculated correctly to ensure that it does not cost more to process further than the revenue received.

Company E sells cocoa beans in individual sixteen-ounce bags. The company is considering selling the cocoa beans as cocoa powder. To sell the beans as ground power, the company will need to process the cocoa beans into power, causing additional expense.

On an annual basis, the company sells 50,000 bags of cocoa beans. The cocoa beans sell for $5.00 per bag. The company anticipates that if it sells the same number of bags but instead sells cocoa power, it will be able to sell the bags for $7.50 per bag. However, it anticipates added cost of $40,000.

TABLE 14.5 Cocoa Beans

	Beans	Powder
Revenue		
($5.00 × 50,000)	$250,000	
$7.50 × 50,000)		$375,000
Further Processing Costs:	($0)	($40,000)
Net Benefit:	**$250,000**	**$335,000**

In the scenario for Company E, the additional revenue brought in by selling the cocoa as powder instead of beans creates a net benefit of $85,000 more. From a financial perspective, it would be better to expend the extra costs of processing the beans into power.

Accept or Reject a Special Order

When managers decide whether or not to accept a special order, they have two considerations. The first consideration is whether they have the capacity to fill the special order. The second consideration is whether or not the benefit of accepting the special order exceeds the cost. If there is not enough capacity to fill the special order, there is no reason to further consider the special order. However, if there is enough capacity, further consideration should be made.

Company F receives a call about a special order for product g. Product g normally sells for $9.00. The requested special order is offering to pay $7.75 for an order of 15,000 units. Company F has a capacity to make 75,000 units and current sales are 50,000 units. The special order will require the purchase of a $10,000 piece of equipment that will not be used again. Company F needs to know if it should accept the special order. The cost of direct material per unit is \$5.50, labor is \$1.75 per unit, and variable overhead is \$.25 per unit for a total variable cost per unit of \$7.50 per unit. Below is the data for the special order:

TABLE 14.6 Special Order

	Per Unit	Total (15,000 units)
Revenue	\$7.75	\$116,250
Less Variable Costs	\$7.50	\$112,500
Contribution Margin	\$.25	\$3,750
Additional Costs (\$20,000/15,000 units)	\$.67 ($\frac{\$10,000}{15,000\ units}$)	\$10,000
Increase (decrease) in operating income	(\$.42)	(\$6,250)

In the scenario above, accepting the special order would actually cost the company money if the special order is accepted for \$7.75. The lowest amount that the company would be able to accept is \$8.17 (7.75+\$.42). If the purchasing company increased the number of units to 40,000 units, the company would be able to accept the special order at the requested price. However, it does not have capacity for an additional 40,000 units.

TABLE 14.7 40,000 Units

	Per Unit	Total (40,000 units)
Revenue	\$7.75	\$310,000
Less: Variable Costs	\$7.50	\$300,000
Contribution Margin	\$.25	\$10,000
Additional Costs (\$20,000/15,000 units)	\$.25 ($\frac{\$10,000}{40,000\ units}$)	\$10,000
Increase (decrease) in operating income	\$0	\$0

LEARNING GOAL 4: Investigate Special Issues Associated With Decision Making

Joint Product Costs in Sell-As-Is-or-Process-Further Decisions

When making a decision to sell as is or process further, managers consider the costs that are relevant to the decision-making process. This means that managers consider future costs that differ among alternatives. Joint product costs are costs that occur before the split-off point and are, therefore, not considered relevant.

Let's return to the example of the cocoa beans sold by Company E. In Figure 14.8, note that the cost of washing the beans (\$30,000) is not factored into the manager's decision to sell as is or process further.

The cost of washing the cocoa beans is a joint product cost that occurs before the split-off point. Such costs must be allocated to the various products but cannot be directly traced and, therefore, do not enter into the decision to sell as is or process further.

Transfer Pricing

When making decisions regarding pricing of a product, at times the product being sold is for internal purposes. Assume that Company Z makes product #1. There are two divisions of the company, division X and

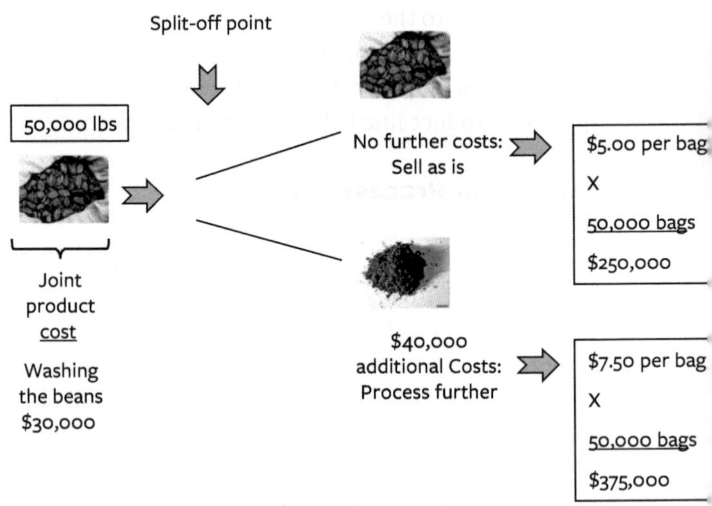

FIGURE 14.8 Joint Product Costs.

Y. Division X makes product #1, while division Y uses product #1. In order to track the costs for each individual division, division X must "sell" the product to division Y. Because the product is being sold internally, there are three choices for how to "price" the product.

- Market price
- Negotiated price
- Cost
- Cost Plus

Pricing the product via market pricing means that division X would sell the product to division Y for the same price as division Y could buy the product externally. Such pricing is fair to both divisions because division X would still report a profit from the sale of the product, and division Y would pay a price equivalent to what it would pay to go outside the company.

Pricing the product via a negotiated price empowers both divisions to act in their own best interest. However, such a form of pricing can result in haggling, which could create "bad blood" between the two divisions.

Pricing the product via cost or cost plus a small markup means that division X would ensure the cost of making the product is covered, while division Y pays less than the market price. Understanding the cost of making the product is essential in using this form of transfer pricing. Also, division X would need to decide which form of cost would be used: variable costing or absorption costing.

Global Considerations of Transfer Pricing. Pricing a product internally becomes more complex when the company is a global company. Considerations in a global company include

- Taxes
- Import duties/Tariffs
- Free Trade agreements
- Exchange rate

In a global company, division X may be located in the United States while division Y may be located in Germany. To determine a fair price of transfer for both divisions, each division must consider the cost of transferring the product across country borders. Such transfers are not as straightforward as domestic transfers.

Constrained resources and product mix. Many times, when making a product, certain resources are constrained such as machine hours or other resources. The demand for a product could also be considered a restraint.

In such cases, the contribution margin needs to be calculated with consideration of the constrained resource. For example, product #9 and product #10 both use machine M. Machine M has a limited number of hours it can run. The contribution margin per machine hour is calculated below.

TABLE 14.8 Contribution Margin per Machine Hour

	Product #9	Product #10
Unit Contribution Margin	$15	$20
Number of units produced per hour	20	10
Contribution Margin per Machine Hour	$300 ($15 × 20)	$200 ($20 × 10)

In the above example, the contribution margin per machine hour (constrained resource) is higher for product #9 than for product #10. If there are a total of 2,500 machine hours in each given year, the contribution margin at full capacity would be $750,000 ($300 × 2,500) for product #9 and $500,000 ($200 × 2,500) for product #10. Thus, product #9 would be the product that management would want to focus on, given demand for both products.

Now let's look at an example of when a product takes more than one machine hour to complete. Product #11 and Product #12 are reflected below. They use a different machine that also has 2,500 available machine hours.

TABLE 14.9 Product 11 and 12

	Product #11	Product #12
Unit Contribution Margin	$25	$30
Number of units produced per hour	.75	.50
Contribution Margin per Machine Hour	$18.75 ($25 × .75)	$15.00 ($30 × .50)

In the above example, the contribution margin per machine hour (constrained resource) is higher for product #11 than for product #12. If there are a total of 2,500 machine hours in each given year, the contribution margin at full capacity would be $46,875 ($18.75 × 2,500) for product 11 and $37,500 ($15.00 × 2,500) for product 12. Thus, product #11 would be the product management would want to focus on, given demand for both products.

What if there is not equal demand for the products under consideration? In reviewing product #9 and product #10, let's say that there is demand for 40,000 units of product #9 and 30,000 units of product #10. That would mean that product #9, which has the highest contribution margin per constrained resource, would be the first product to fulfill the maximum demand. Product #11 would fulfill as much of the demand as available on the constrained resource. See the table below.

TABLE 14.10 Product 9 and 10

	Product #9	**Product #10**
Contribution Margin Per Machine Hour	$300	$200
Number of Machine Hours Needed to Meet Demand or Available	2,000 ($\frac{40,000}{20}$)	500 (2,500 − 2,000)
Total Contribution Margin at Full Capacity	**$600,000** ($300 × 2,000)	**$100,000** ($200 × 500)

Obviously, it is better to have full demand of all products; however, some things within each given market influence demand. Pricing and competition may play a role in the demand for products.

TOPIC 14 REFERENCES

Braun, K.W. and Tietz, W.M. *Managerial Accounting* (4th ed.). Upper Saddle River, NJ: Prentice Hall, 2014.

Garrison, R.H., Noreen, E.W., and Brewer, P.C. *Managerial Accounting.* New York: McGraw-Hill Companies, Inc., 2012.

Horngren, C.T, Datar, S.M. and Rajan, M.V. *Cost Accounting: A Managerial Emphasis* (15th ed.). Upper Saddle River, NJ: Pearson Education, Inc., 2015

Houmøller, M. "Cocoa Beans." Wikimedia. Retrieved from https://commons.wikimedia.org/wiki/File:Cocoa_beans.jpg. (2015).

Rillke. "Theobromae Cacaois Seminis Pulvis." Wikimedia. Retrieved from https://commons.wikimedia.org/wiki/File:Theobromae_cacaois_seminis_pulvis_308294.jpg#-file (2011).

TOPIC 14 FIGURE CREDITS

SECTION IV

THE EVALUATING PHASE

The Evaluating Phase addresses the competency of:

Demonstrate an understanding of how the evaluation of an organization relates back to the planning phase and is linked by the performing phase.

The following topics are introduced in Section 4 as topics imperative to learning the tasks involved in the Evaluating Phase.

- Flexible Budgeting and Cost Variance Analysis
- Non-Traditional Performance Evaluation
- Traditional Performance Evaluation

Competency 4 connects that which was planned and performed to the evaluation of such processes. The process of planning, performing, and evaluating is a cyclical process in which the effectiveness of evaluation process will lead to more refined planning the next time around.

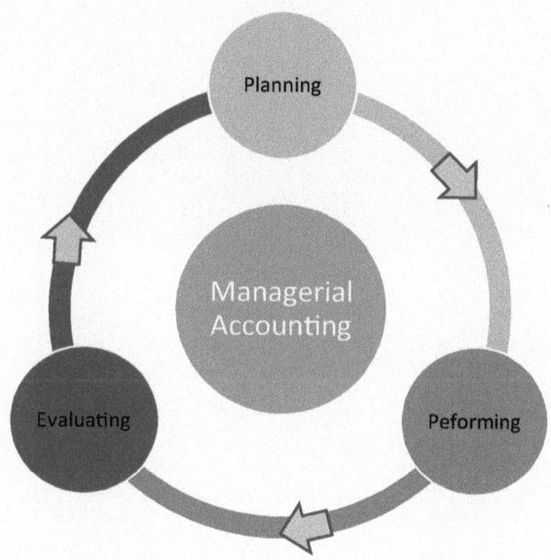

FIGURE IV.1 Theory: Planning, Evaluating, Performing.

TOPIC 15 Flexible Budgeting and Cost Variance Analysis

LEARNING GOALS

1. Discuss the benefits and role of a flexible budget.
2. Calculate flexible budgets based on various levels of activity.
3. Introduce variances derived from preparing flexible budgets.
4. Compute direct material variances: Quantity and Price.
5. Compute direct labor variances: Hours and Rate.
6. Compute overhead variances: Hours and Rate.
7. Understand the differences between "favorable" or "unfavorable" variances.
8. Investigate potential causes for variances.

INTRODUCTION

The importance of the evaluating stage is that it provides managers an opportunity to find out what needs to change as they move forward. Management learns how that which was planned in the planning phase was carried out. The master budget is a static budget, however, and serves as a starting point for the evaluation process. As you will learn in this topic, the flexible budget gives wings to the master budget as it opens up an ability to apply budgeted amounts to various levels of activity. From the introduction of the flexible budget, management can analyze the actual performance with budgeted performance, had the budget been based on the actual level of activity. Flexible budgeting and variance analysis are keys to predicting future performance.

LEARNING GOAL 1: Discuss the Benefits and Role of a Flexible Budget

Flexible budgets are part of the budgeting process and expand upon the master budget as a tool of evaluation. In a master budget, there is no wiggle room for a different level of activity than for that which was planned. For example, if in the process of creating the master budget it is anticipated that the company would sell 3,200 units, the entire master budget is built around selling the 3,200 units. Raw materials, finished goods, and labor are all calculated based on selling 3,200 units. Consequently, if the company does not sell 3,200 hundred units, there is no way to know if the company did or did not perform as planned.

A flexible budget, then, allows for management to achieve an apples-to-apples comparison with the master budget. The starting point of a flexible budget is the calculations used in the master budget. Both variable and fixed costs can be re-estimated given a new level of activity by understanding how costs behave. For example, the amounts used as variable costs per unit would simply be applied to a new level of units. Budgeted fixed costs would remain unchanged. Revenue, like the variable costs, would be applied to a new level of activity.

Managerial accountants would report the flexible budget amounts alongside the master budget and the actual level of activity as in the table below.

TABLE 15.1 Flexible Budget

	Actual	Flexible Budget Variance		Flexible Budget	Volume Variance		Master Budget
Sales volume in units	35,000	0		35,000	5,000	F	30,000
Revenue ($15 per unit)	$512,000	$13,000	U	$525,000	$75,000	F	$450,000
Variable Expenses:							
Cost of Goods Sold ($6.30 per unit)	$292,000	$71,500	U	$220,500	$31,500	U	$189,000
Shipping Expense ($2.50 per unit)	$92,000	$4,500	U	$87,500	$12,500	U	$75,000
Sales Commission (15% of sales)	$65,200	$13,550	F	$78,750	$11,250	U	$67,500
Total Variable Exp.	$449,200	$62,450	U	$386,750	$55,250	U	$331,500
Contribution Margin	**$62,800**	**$75,450**	**U**	**$138,250**	**$19,750**	**U**	**$118,500**
Fixed Expenses:							
Salaries	$47,000	$1,000	U	$46,000	$0		$46,000
Office Rent	$36,000	$0		$36,000	$0		$36,000
Insurance	$12,000	$0		$12,000	$0		$12,000
Advertising	$3,000	$5,000	F	$8,000	$0		$8,000
Depreciation	$5,500	$0		$5,500	$0		$5,500
Total Fixed Expenses	$103,500	$4,000	U	$107,500	$0	U	$107,500
Operating Income	($40,700)	$71,450	U	$30,750	$19,750	F	$11,000

In addition to reporting the flexible budget amount, the flexible budget variance and the volume variance are reported on the same report.

Characteristics of a Flexible Budget

Flexible budgets have many characteristics that make them valuable in the evaluation process. Some of the characteristics include

- Can be prepared for any level of activity, given the behavior of costs.
- Costs can be compared between what was actually spent and the budget for a given level of activity in an apples-to-apples comparison.
- Gives managers a greater ability to control costs.
- Provides for a greater explanation of performance.
- Allows management to perform in-depth analysis and evaluation.

LEARNING GOAL 2: Calculate Flexible Budgets Based on Various Levels of Activity

Stram Lawn Care Services is located in the Midwest where they treat lawn for weeds in the summer months. Lawns are generally treated on a monthly basis throughout the months of May, June, July, August, September, and October. Certain lawns may require extra treatments, depending on the type of vegetation on the property. Stram Lawn Care Services charges $80 for each treatment and has 350 clients. Stram Lawn Care Services would like to know if the company has met its budget this summer.

The budgeted and actual amounts are listed below.

TABLE 15.2 Budgeted and Actual Amounts

	Budgeted Amounts	Actual Amounts
Number of treatments:	2310	2450
Revenue:	$184,800	$190,300
Wages	$25 per lawn	$62,805
Supplies	$15 per lawn	$32,918
Equipment Maintenance	6% of sales	$8,215
Office Supplies	$500	$350
Equipment Depreciation	$1,200	$1,200
Insurance	$800	$850
Salaries	$25,000	$25,000

We begin by comparing actual amounts with budgeted amounts.

TABLE 15.3 Flexible Budget: Actual and Budgeted

	Actual	Flexible Budget Variance	Flexible Budget	Volume Variance	Master Budget
Sales Volume in Units	2450				2310
Revenue ($80 per lawn)	$190,300				$184,800
Variable Expenses					
Supplies ($15 per lawn)	$32,918				$34,650
Wages ($25 per lawn)	$62,805				$57,750
Equipment Maintenance (6% of sales)	$8,215				$11,088
Total Variable Expenses	$103,938				$103,488
Contribution Margin	**$86,362**				**$81,312**
Fixed Expenses					
Salaries	$25,000				$25,000
Office Supplies	$350				$500
Insurance	$850				$800
Equipment Depreciation	$1,200				$1,200
Total Fixed Expenses	$27,400				$27,500
Operating Income	$58,962				$53,812

Based on the above figures, it's difficult to know if Stram Lawn Care Services met its budget. The difference between the master budget and the actual amount is called the Master Budget Variance. All we really know from this is that the company didn't perform at the planned level of activity. We have to create a flexible budget so that we can move on with the analysis.

TABLE 15.4 Flexible Budget: Actual and Budgeted part 2

	Actual	Flexible Budget Variance	Flexible Budget	Volume Variance	Master Budget
Sales Volume in Units	2450		2450		2310
Revenue ($80 per lawn)	$190,300		$196,000		$184,800
Variable Expenses					
Supplies ($15 per lawn)	$32,918		$36,750		$34,650
Wages ($25 per lawn)	$62,805		$61,250		$57,750
Equipment Maintenance (6% of sales)	$8,215		$11,760		$11,088
Total Variable Expenses	$103,938		$109,760		$103,488
Contribution Margin	**$86,362**		**$86,240**		**$81,312**
Fixed Expenses					
Salaries	$25,000		$25,000		$25,000
Office Supplies	$350		$500		$500
Insurance	$850		$800		$800
Equipment Depreciation	$1,200		$1,200		$1,200
Total Fixed Expenses	$27,400		$27,500		$27,500
Operating Income	$58,962		$58,740		$53,812

The flexible budget is based on the actual level of activity and the budgeted inputs. The budgeted inputs are per unit inputs for variable expenses and total budgeted fixed amounts for fixed expenses. For example, to arrive at the variable expense amounts, the actual number of units is multiplied by the budgeted per unit amounts. To arrive at the fixed expense amounts, the master budget fixed amounts are simply moved into the flexible budget column. No calculations are needed here.

LEARNING GOAL 3: Introduce Variances Derived from Preparing Flexible Budgets

After having developed the flexible budget, management is now better able to understand the financial performance of the company and better able to compare and control for costs. Two variances exist that allow management to take a preliminary look at actual performance compared with budgeted performance. The first variance is the volume variance. The volume variance conveys little more than the fact that the actual level of activity was not the same as the planned level of activity. Each variance calculated is either favorable or unfavorable. An unfavorable variance is one in which revenues reflected in the flexible budget are lower than budgeted or expenses were higher than budgeted. A favorable variance is one in which revenues reflected in the flexible budget were higher than budgeted or expenses were lower than budgeted. See the calculations below in the "Volume Variance" column.

TABLE 15.5 Variances

	Actual	Flexible Budget Variance	Flexible Budget	Volume Variance		Master Budget
Sales Volume in Units	2450		2450	140	F	2310
Revenue ($80 per lawn)	$190,300		$196,000	$11,200	F	$184,800
Variable Expenses						
Supplies ($15 per lawn)	$32,918		$36,750	$2,100	U	$34,650
Wages ($25 per lawn)	$62,805		$61,250	$3,500	U	$57,750
Equipment Maintenance (6% of sales)	$8,215		$11,760	$672	U	$11,088
Total Variable Expenses	$103,938		$109,760	$6,272	U	$103,488
Contribution Margin	**$86,362**		**$86,240**	**$4,928**	F	**$81,312**
Fixed Expenses						
Salaries	$25,000		$25,000	$0		$25,000
Office Supplies	$350		$500	$0		$500
Insurance	$850		$800	$0		$800
Equipment Depreciation	$1,200		$1,200	$0		$1,200
Total Fixed Expenses	$27,400		$27,500	$0		$27,500
Operating Income	$58,962		$58,740	$4,928	F	$53,812

Note that in the above table, level of activity is higher than was planned. Therefore, revenues are favorable and variable expenses are unfavorable. Fixed expenses will never see a volume variance.

The second preliminary review of the performance of the company involves the flexible budget variance. The flexible budget variance provides a greater depth of information in that it now compares what the budget should have been based on the actual level of activity with that actual performance. An unfavorable variance would indicate that actual revenues were lower than the flexible budget or that actual expenses were higher than the actual budget. A favorable variance would indicate that actual revenues were higher than the flexible budget or that actual expenses were lower than the flexible budget. See the table below:

TABLE 15.6 Favorable Variance

Fixed Overhead		Actual	Flexible Budget Variance		Flexible Budget	Volume Variance		Master Budget
	Sales Volume in Units	2450	0		2450	140	F	2310
	Revenue ($80 per lawn)	$190,300	$5,700	U	$196,000	$11,200	F	$184,800
	Variable Expenses							
Labor	Supplies ($15 per lawn)	$32,918	$3,832	F	$36,750	$2,100	U	$34,650
Variable Overhead	Wages ($25 per lawn)	$62,805	$1,555	U	$61,250	$3,500	U	$57,750
Materials	Equipment Maintenance (6% of sales)	$8,215	$3,545	F	$11,760	$672	U	$11,088
	Total Variable Expenses	$103,938	$5,822	F	$109,760	$6,272	U	$103,488
Fixed Overhead	**Contribution Margin**	**$86,362**	**$122**	**F**	**$86,240**	**$4,928**	**F**	**$81,312**
	Fixed Expenses							
	Salaries	$25,000	$0		$25,000	$0		$25,000
	Office Supplies	$350	$150	F	$500	$0		$500
	Insurance	$850	$50	U	$800	$0		$800
	Equipment Depreciation	$1,200	$0		$1,200	$0		$1,200
	Total Fixed Expenses	$27,400	$100	F	$27,500	$0		$27,500
	Operating Income	$58,962	$222	F	$58,740	$4,928	F	$53,812

Note that in the above table, the variance of operating income is still favorable but not as favorable as that which was originally calculated for the master budget variance or the volume variance.

The flexible budget variance becomes the starting point for various other variances such as the materials variance, labor variance, and overhead variance. We base subsequent variance analysis on the flexible budget variance because of the value the information provides.

LEARNING GOAL 4: Compute Direct Material Variances: Quantity and Price

The material variance allows managers to determine whether the flexible budget variance exits due to the price paid for the materials or the efficient/inefficient use of materials. Hence, the materials variance is broken down into two variances: 1) price variance and quantity variance.

In order for management to find out how much of the total flexible budget variance exists as it relates to material (in this case supplies), the following formula is used:

DM Price Variance $= \textbf{\textit{Actual Quantity Purchased}}$ $\textbf{\textit{(Actual Price − Standard Price)}}$

$= \textbf{\textit{AQP(AP − SP)}}$

Assume that Stram Lawn Care Services purchased 6,930 gallons of weed control. Each gallon was budgeted to cost $5.00 ($34,650). The actual price paid was $4.75 ($32,918).

DM Price Variance $= \textbf{Actual Quantity Purchased (Actual Price − Standard Price)}$

$= 6{,}930\ (\$4.75 - \$5.00)$

$= \mathbf{\$1{,}733\ F}$

Part of the flexible budget variance, then, is related to price. To determine the portion of the variance related to quantity used, we'd need to perform the following calculation:

DM Qty Variance $= \textbf{Standard Price (Actual Quantity Used − Standard Quantity Allowed)}$

$= \mathbf{SP\ (AQU - SQA)}$

Assume that Stram Lawn Care Services purchased 6,930 gallons of weed killer based on a standard of using three gallons per yard. They actually used the full 6,930 gallons purchased. However, they should have used three gallons per yard times the actual number of treatments (3 × 2,450).

DM Qty Variance $= \textbf{Standard Price (Actual Quantity Used − Standard Quantity Allowed)}$

$= \$5.00(6{,}930 - 7{,}350)$

$= \mathbf{\$2{,}100\ F}$

*The dollar difference is due to rounding.

LEARNING GOAL 5: Compute Direct Labor Variances: Hours and Rate

The labor variance is similar to the material variance but focuses on the cost of the workforce. The labor variances are broken down into two variances: 1) rate variance and 2) efficiency variance.

In order for management to find out how much of the total flexible budget variance exists as it relates to labor, the following formula is used:

DL Rate Variance $= \textbf{Actual Hours (Actual Rate − Standard Rate)}$

$= \mathbf{AH(AR - SR)}$

Assume that Stram Lawn Care Services budgeted to pay the labor $12.50 per hour, and each treatment would take two hours. The workforce actually took 5,300, hours and Stram Lawn Care Services spent $62,805 on labor.

DL Rate Variance $= \textbf{Actual Hours (Actual Rate − Standard Rate)}$

$= 5{,}300\ (\$11.85 - \$12.50)$

$= \$3{,}445\ F$

DL Efficiency Variance $= \textit{Standard Rate (Actual Hours − Standard Hours Allowed)}$

$= \$12.50(5{,}300 - 4{,}900)$

$= \mathbf{\$5{,}000\ U}$

LEARNING GOAL 6: Compute Overhead Variances: Hours and Rate

Variable Overhead

Variable Overhead is based on direct labor hours as a driver of overhead.

Variable Overhead Rate Variance $= \textbf{Actual Hours} \times \textbf{(Acutal Rate − Standard Rate)}$

$= AH(AR - SR)$

$= 5{,}300(\$1.55 - \$2.40)$

$= \mathbf{\$4{,}505\ F}$

Variable Overhead Efficiency Variance $= \textbf{Standard Rate} \times \textbf{(Actual Hours − Standard Hours Allowed)}$

$= SR(AH - SHA)$

$= 2.40(5{,}300 - 4{,}900)$

$= \mathbf{\$960\ U}$

Fixed Overhead

Budget Variance = ***Actual Fixed Overhead − Budgeted Fixed Overhead***

$$= \$27{,}400 - \$27{,}500$$

$$= \mathbf{\$100}\ \boldsymbol{F}$$

Volume Variance = ***Budgeted Fixed Overhead − (Standard Hours Allowed × Standard Rate)***

$$= 27{,}500 - (4{,}900 \times 5.95)$$

$$= \mathbf{\$1{,}655}\ \boldsymbol{F}$$

LEARNING GOAL 7: Understand the Differences Between "Favorable" and "Unfavorable" Variances

The terms "favorable" and "unfavorable" can be confusing when defining a variance. Such a label would imply that "favorable" is good and "unfavorable" is bad. The truth is that it is not the direction of the variance that is important to management. Instead, it is the percentage of the variance. For example, a direct labor rate variance that is 2% favorable is not as big of a concern as a direct labor variance that is 10% favorable. Likewise, if that same variance is unfavorable instead of favorable, the concern would again be for the percentage difference, not the direction of the variance.

A favorable variance means that expenses were lower than budgeted and that revenue was higher than budgeted. An unfavorable variance means that expenses were higher than budgeted and revenue was lower than expected. An expense being lower than expected may be fully as detrimental to a company as an expense being higher than expected.

Management by Exception

When management views the managerial accounting reports and notes the variances that exist, a certain level can be tolerated. For example, management may be willing to tolerate any variance that is 2% or less. Anything over 2% is thoroughly investigated, whether favorable or unfavorable. Such management by exception is based on the amount the company feels is a material difference.

Managing in such a way is called management by exception. Management by exception means that management uses their limited resource of time in an efficient way. If management had to investigate every variance, they would end up spending time on things that are not impactful to future decisions.

LEARNING GOAL 8: Investigate Potential Causes for Variances

If management does not want to spend time investigating every variance that falls under their materiality threshold, they need to investigate those things that may make a difference in future decisions. The managerial accountant must become skilled at analyzing and interpreting why differences occur. Let's imagine that a company has a 10% favorable material price variance and a 20% unfavorable direct labor efficiency variance. If management investigates any variance greater than 5%, both of these variances would need to be investigated.

Upon the initial analysis, this would appear to be a problem with efficiency of the direct labor workforce. We need to review several other variances, however. What if we further analyze the material variance and learn that the material variance has an unfavorable quantity variance of 8%. Now, in terms of material, we have less than we anticipated but used more than we anticipated. In order to find out why we paid less than the budged amount, we would seek the insights provided by the purchasing manager (Figure 15.1). The purchasing manager may let us know that she was able

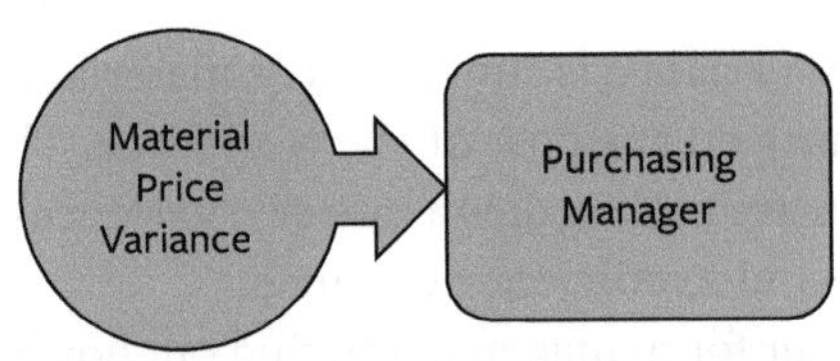

FIGURE 15.1 Material Price Variance Analysis.

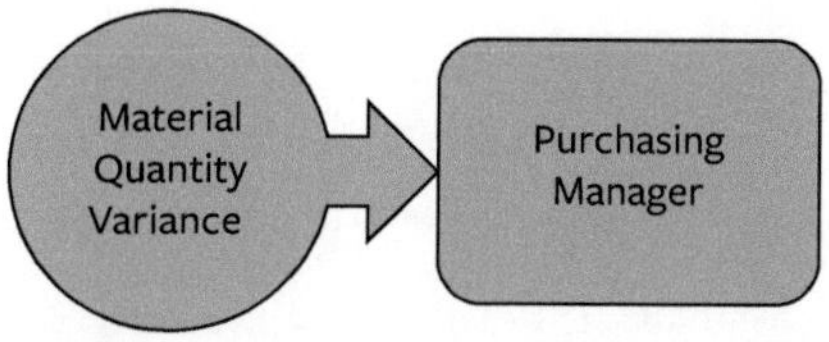

FIGURE 15.2 Material Quantity Variance Analysis.

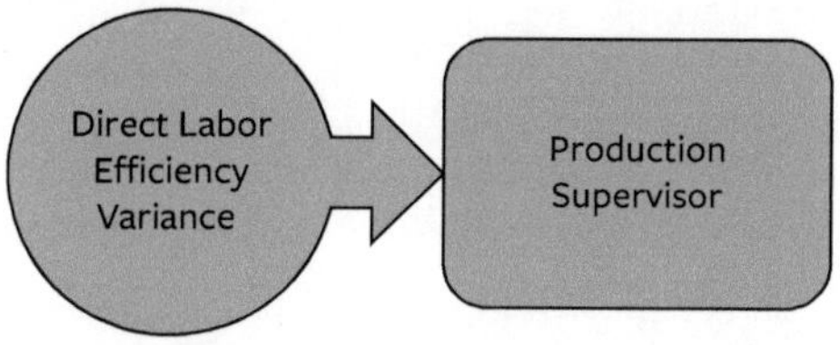

FIGURE 15.3 Direct Labor Efficiency Variance Analysis.

to get a deal on materials the vendor was trying to get rid of.

Next, further investigation would bring us to a discussion with the production manager. The production manager would have answers to questions regarding both the unfavorable quantity variance and unfavorable efficiency variance (Figures 15.2 and 15.3).

The production supervisor may inform us that the materials were cheap and kept breaking. Therefore, the workers had large amounts of waste. Such breakage of the materials also slowed them down.

As we continue to unravel what has happened with the production of our product, there is one rock left unturned, the direct labor rate variance (the analysis of the overhead variances is beyond the scope of this textbook). We may review the direct labor rate variance to also find a favorable rate variance of 5%. For the answer to the questions regarding direct labor rate variance, we would need to talk with the director of human resources (Figure 15.4).

In talking with human resources, we may learn that human resources was able to hire an unskilled workforce for a lower rate than was budgeted. Now, this gives us a complete picture.

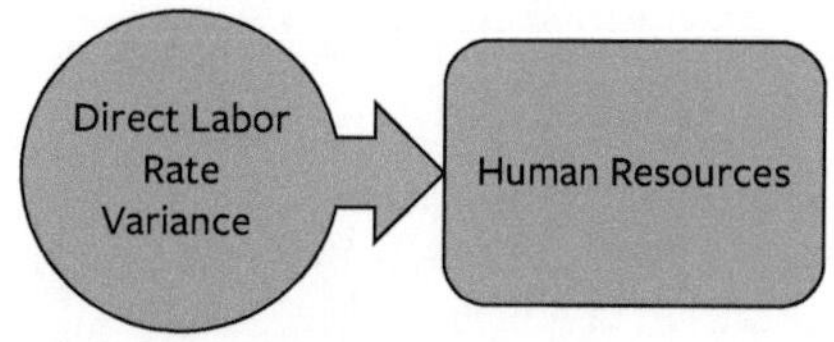

FIGURE 15.4 Direct Labor Rate Variance Analysis.

The analysis has revealed that cheap materials caused waste and inefficiency in production. However, such waste and inefficiency was further exasperated by the fact that the workforce was not experienced and did not know how to handle the low-quality materials. In this scenario, there seems to be a perfect storm brewing within the company.

The goal of evaluating the current circumstances is to improve upon such circumstances. At this point, both management and the managerial accountants know where the problems exist. They could determine that the financial cost savings in buying the cheaper material and paying the workforce less outweighed the increased costs of inefficiency and waste and do nothing. However, the financial results could reveal that the cost of the cheaper materials and the inefficient workforce was more expensive than the savings. In such a case, management would be able to make a plan for improvement.

TOPIC 15 REFERENCES

Braun, K.W. and Tietz, W.M. *Managerial Accounting* (4th ed.). Upper Saddle River, NJ: Prentice Hall, 2014.

Garrison, R.H., Noreen, E.W., and Brewer, P.C. *Managerial Accounting.* New York: McGraw-Hill Companies, Inc., 2012.

Horngren, C.T, Datar, S.M. and Rajan, M.V. *Cost Accounting: A Managerial Emphasis* (15th ed.). Upper Saddle River, NJ: Pearson Education, Inc., 2015.

TOPIC 16 Non-Traditional Performance Evaluation

LEARNING GOALS

1. Discuss the perspectives of the Balanced Scorecard together and individually.
2. Discuss the flow of the Balanced Scorecard.
3. Understand the relationship of the Balanced Scorecard to strategy.
4. Identify key performance indicators and measurement criteria for each perspective of the Balanced Scorecard.
5. Build a Balanced Scorecard.

INTRODUCTION

Companies have numerous ways of evaluating employees and the organization. The first thought of management is usually to evaluate based on financial data. Such a form of evaluation, however, may not necessarily be the best or the only form of evaluation that should be used. Topic 4 discussed the use of a strategy map during the planning phase. Building a strategy map during the planning phase is the first step for evaluating based on the balanced scorecard. When using a strategy map, managers can be assured that their operations match their strategy plan. Following up with the use of a Balanced Scorecard, managers can be further assured that their form of evaluation aligns with their strategy. All components must work together for the good of the organization.

LEARNING GOAL 1: Discuss the Perspectives of the Balanced Scorecard Together and Individually

The perspectives of the Balanced Scorecard are the same as the processes of the strategy map. When creating the strategy map, four processes were created: 1) learning and growth processes, 2) internal business processes, 3) customer processes, and 4) financial processes. Such processes become the perspectives from which the organization is evaluated during the evaluation phase. Let's review each of the processes and discuss how the process will become a perspective of evaluation.

Learning and Growth Processes

The learning and growth process stressed employee competencies and process innovation. Human capital was considered as well as information and organizational capital. The learning and growth process aligned with the strategy of either cost leadership or product innovation.

When considering the evaluation from the perspective of learning and growth, the evaluator is looking toward the objectives and measurements outlined during strategy mapping. In Topic 4, we highlighted three objectives and measurements of those objectives. The objectives would be linked to the strategy but would also need to measure performance according to the measurements established. The following objectives and measurements were included in Topic 4.

TABLE 16.1 Learning and Growth Processes

Objective	Measurement
1. **Build competencies (human capital)**	Key business processes empowered to lower levels
2. **Integrate IT (information capital)**	IT effectiveness survey
3. **Create an atmosphere of empowerment (organizational capital)**	Empowerment index

For the first objective selected, "build competencies," the focus is on human capital, and the measurement includes key business processes empowered to lower levels. In this case, management would be looking to see if lower-level management was empowered to take on tasks within key business processes. Performance for such an objective could be measured by a percentage of lower-level managers who have performance tasks relating to key business processes. Perhaps a target-level performance would start out at 25%. Thus, if 25% or more of lower-level managers were assuming key business process functions, the objective has been reached. If not, management would need to reevaluate the objective, the measurement, or the motivators in place to achieve such an objective.

For the second objective selected, "integrate IT," the focus is on information capital and the measurement includes an IT effectiveness survey. In this case, management would be looking to see if the integration of IT within the company is effective by surveying the employees. The results of the survey would indicate the effectiveness of IT. The survey could be something as simple as a Likert scale, where employees would rate effectiveness of IT within their respective departments from 1-5 (with 1 being the least effective and 5 being the most effective). Perhaps the target level of performance would be that 95% of the responses were 4s and 5s.

The third objective selected, "create an atmosphere of empowerment," is focused on organizational capital, and the measurement includes an empowerment index. In this case, empowerment would be measured by a composite index in which management defines behaviors that indicate empowerment. Such behaviors may include things such as offering suggestions for new products or helping other employees.

Each of the above objectives were established during the planning phase and are measured during the evaluation phase. The learning and growth perspective is a perspective that helps companies determine if business processes are helping employees perform at optimum levels of performance (Figure 16.1). Optimum levels of performance are achieved when human, information, and organization capital are used efficiently and effectively. The measurements that take place during evaluation will indicate the effectiveness of such resources.

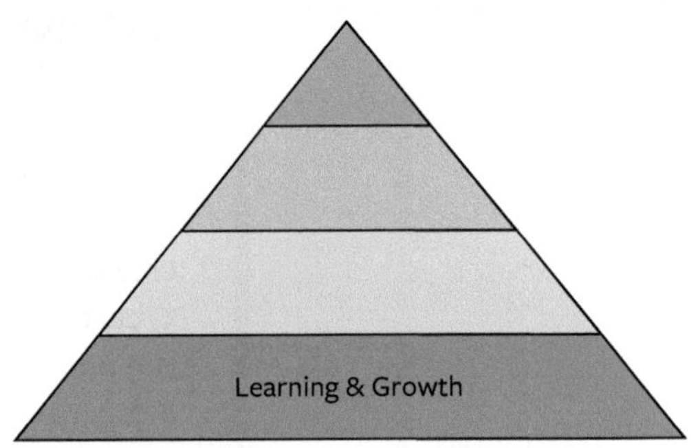

FIGURE 16.1 Learning and Growth Perspective.

Internal Business Process

The Internal Business Process stresses internal business functioning. When considering the evaluation from the perspective of the internal business perspective, the evaluator is looking toward the objectives and measurements outlined during strategy mapping. In Topic 4, we highlighted three objectives and measurements of those objectives. The objectives would be linked to the strategy but would also need to measure performance according to the measurements established. The following objectives and measurements were included in Topic 4.

TABLE 16.2 Internal Business Process

Objective	Measurement
1. **Upgrade manufacturing process**	Percentage reduction of wait times
2. **Upgrade delivery process**	Percentage reduction of delivery time
3. **Reduce rework**	Percentage reduction of rework

For the first objective selected, "upgrade manufacturing process," the focus is on reducing wait times within the business process. Performance for such an objective could be measured by a percentage decrease of wait times. If within the internal business process, a product typically incurs five hours of wait time, the organization may use a target percentage decrease of 20%. If a decrease of 20% or more is achieved, the target performance has been met. If a performance level of less than 20% is achieved, the organization may need to review the objective, the measurement, or the motivators put in place to reach the objective.

For the second objective selected, "upgrade delivery process," the focus is on reducing delivery time. While the focus is different than in objective #1, the way to measure the objective could be based on similar criteria of a measurement of delivery time. If within the internal business process, delivery time is usually two days, the company may be seeking a 50% decrease.

For the third objective selected, "reduce rework," the focus is on a percentage reduction of rework. Typically rework is tracked by number of hours spent on rework. The company may determine that they want rework to be reduced by 10%. If ten minutes of rework is typically attributed to each product, a 10% reduction would decrease rework to nine minutes for each product.

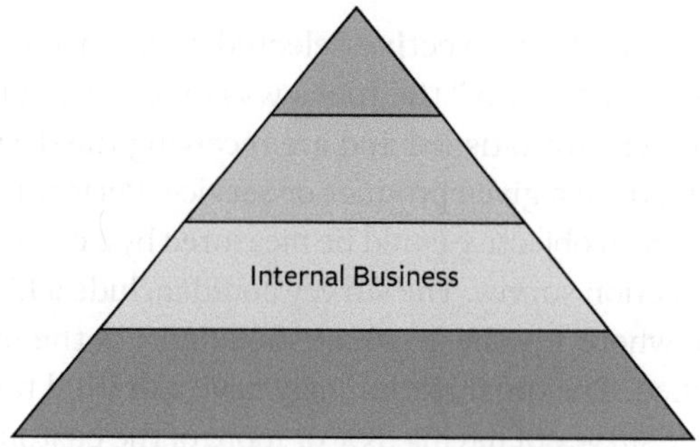

FIGURE 16.2 Internal Business Perspective.

The internal business process perspective helps companies determine if their business processes are functioning efficiently (Figure 16.2). Based on the evaluation of the measures established during strategy mapping, the Balanced Scorecard will reveal areas of struggle within the internal business processes.

Customer Processes

The customer process stresses the perspective of the customer. When considering the customer perspective, the organization wants to know if customers are happy, will return, or will recommend the product/service to their friends and family. In Topic 4, we highlighted three objectives and measurements of those objectives within the customer process. The objectives would be linked to the strategy but would also need to measure performance according to the measurements established. The following objectives and measurements were included in Topic 4.

TABLE 16.3 Customer Processes

Objective	Measurement
1. **Increased customer satisfaction**	Customer satisfaction surveys
2. **Expansion of new customers**	Number of new customers
3. **Increase products used per customer**	Number of products used by each customer

For the first objective selected, "increased customer satisfaction," the focus was on ensuring that customers are satisfied and are receiving the desired results from a given product or service. Performance for such an objective could be measured by a customer satisfaction survey. The survey could include a Likert scale where 1 is the least satisfied and 5 is the most satisfied. The organization may have a desired target for the survey of having 85% or more of the customers surveyed respond with a 4 or 5. If the desired target measurement is not reached, the company may need to review the objective, the measurement, or survey itself.

For the second objective selected, "expansion of new customers," the focus is on increasing the customer base. Such a focus would be measured numerically by the number of new customers or as a percentage of increase over existing customers. A company seeking increases by way of number of new customers may seek five new customers every month. If the five customers per month are achieved, the organization may seek to increase the measurement goal or maintain and focus on a new measurement goal.

For the third objective selected, "increase products used per customer," the focus is expanding integration of customers within the company. Such a goal would stress cross-sales within the existing customers. The objective may be measured by number of products/services used by existing customers. Measuring the objective could seek a target goal of three products used by 80% of the customers.

The customer process perspective helps companies determine if their perception of their organization matches the customer perception (Figure 16.3). The company may learn that their customers are not as satisfied as the company thought they were, or it may learn that customers were not aware of everything the company offered. Regardless of the outcome, the company has new information and can make adjustments to better serve customers.

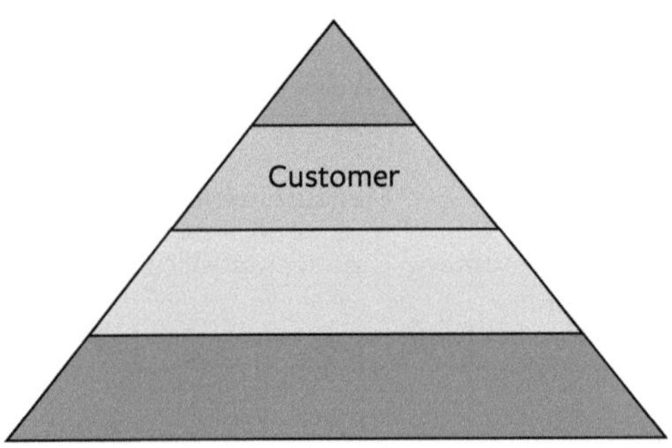

FIGURE 16.3 Customer Perspective.

Financial Process

The financial process stresses the financial functioning of the organization. When considering the evaluation from the perspective of the shareholders, the financial perspective is of great importance. Thus, the financial perspective highlights three objectives and measurements of those objectives. The objectives would be linked to the strategy but would also need to measure performance according to the measurements established. The following objectives and measurements were included in Topic 4.

TABLE 16.4 Financial Process

Objective	Measurement
1. **Increased market share**	Percent increase over base year
2. **Increased profit margins**	Margin percent
3. **Maximum asset utilization**	Asset turnover ratio

For the first objective selected, "increased market share," the focus is on ensuring that the company is growing by increasing the percentage of the market share achieved. The measurement as a percent over base year would measure whether the company achieved continual growth. Shareholders are interested in investing in a company that is growing.

For the second objective selected, "profit margins," the focus is on not just increasing revenues but also potentially decreasing expenses. Profit margin is a function of the relationship between revenues and expenses. The margin percent takes into account the cost of purchasing the items sold and/or the expenses associated with selling the item. For a margin percent to increase, either revenues must increase and expenses must stay the same, or revenues must stay the same and expenses must decrease. A combination of the two would also deliver increased profit margins.

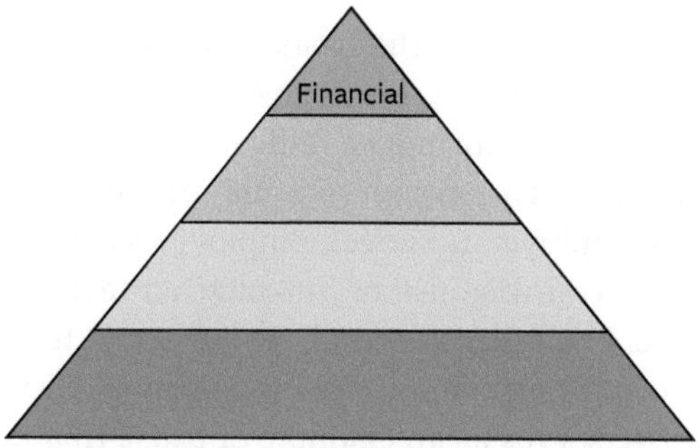

FIGURE 16.4 Financial Perspective.

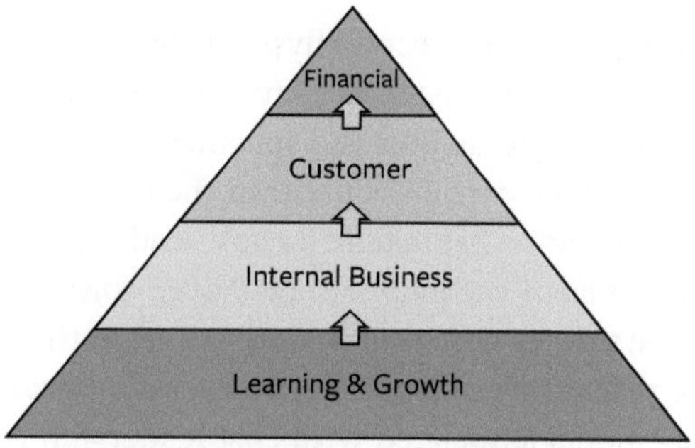

FIGURE 16.5 Balanced Scorecard Pyramid.

An organization would measure such profit margins by a simple calculation.

For the third objective selected, "maximum asset utilization," the focus is on the specific use of assets. By measuring and tracking the asset-turnover ratio, organizations can determine if their use of assets is becoming more or less efficient. The asset-utilization ratio may trend upward by a desired percent increase.

The financial process perspective helps companies determine if they are keeping shareholders happy (Figure 16.4). The objectives and measurements would be based on that which the shareholders are requiring/accepting as desired levels of performance.

Integration

Although each of the perspectives above has individual components and measurements, the Balanced Scorecard is an evaluation process that sees the perspectives from an integrated assessment. Although each perspective has its own objectives and measurement, the management within an organization must realize that the perspectives are intended to work together from the bottom up.

LEARNING GOAL 2: Discuss the Flow of the Balanced Scorecard

The Balanced Scorecard integrates all perspectives from the bottom up. The first perspective of learning and growth is a necessary starting point for the Scorecard. Instead of starting with financial goals, an organization begins by starting with that which drives the organization forward into success. An organization cannot be successful without efficient use of human capital, information capital, or organizational capital. All pieces of the learning and growth perspective ensure that a company can have effective internal business functioning, satisfied customers, and financial success. However, the first perspective must address the foundation in order for all other areas to find success.

Although there may or may not be direct links between the four perspectives, it is important to note that the relationship between the perspectives. For example, a company that fails to provide training to employees may find that internal business functions are not smoothly run. Thus, customers become frustrated with long waits and stop supporting the organization with their loyalty. Once customers stop coming to the organization, market share drops, as does profit. To focus on market share profit would be starting at the wrong end. The organization must begin with ensuring that employees are properly trained. See Figure 16.5 below.

LEARNING GOAL 3: Understand the Relationship of the Balanced Scorecard to Strategy

From the beginnings of the Balance Scorecard as a strategy map, the Balanced Scorecard has seen a direct link with strategy. According to Porter (1980), strategy is determined as a direct analysis of the competitive market. However, once strategy has been resolved, the strategy map defines the specifics for how such strategy will be carried out within the organization. If an organization has taken on a cost-leadership strategy, all areas of the map will be driven towards the initiative to keep costs as low as possible. In the topic where pricing was discussed, you learned that the pricing model associated with cost leadership was a model that began with the market price and focused on decreasing costs so that pricing could remain at or below the market price. The learning and growth, internal business, customer, and financial perspectives would all seek to lower costs to maintain a competitive advantage.

Likewise, if an organization has taken on a product-differentiation strategy, all areas of the map will be driven towards the initiative of differentiating the product and keeping the product as unique as possible. In the topic where pricing was discussed, you learned that the pricing model associated with product differentiation was a model that began with the needed costs to ensure the product was unique. Each of the perspectives within the Balanced Scorecard would seek to keep the product differentiated at whatever cost it takes.

Managerial accountants measure performance at many levels as they seek to supply managers with the information they need to be competitive. The role of the managerial accountant in the strategy map and the Balanced Scorecard is to help to set up measurements and report such measurements back to management.

LEARNING GOAL 4: Identify Key Performance Indicators and Measurement Criteria for Each Perspective of the Balanced Scorecard

In the example noted within this topic, three objectives were selected to reflect key performance indicators for each perspective. A key performance indicator is a metric used to assess how well a company is doing at achieving its strategic goals. The objectives, then, are based on the key performance indicators that form the basis of acceptable levels of performance within the given perspective. For example, key performance indicators for the learning and growth perspective may include things such as employee turnover, employee satisfaction, employee training, use of information technology, and use of organizational resources. Although many other performance measures may exist, the list above serves as an example of those that could take place within the learning and growth perspective. The key performance indicators for the internal business perspective may include things such as number of new products, lead times, wait times, defect rates, customers rework hours, and delivery times. The key performance indicators would be based on the type of business under evaluation. Key performance indicators from the customer perspective could include customer satisfaction ratings, repeat business, customer penetration, and number of customers. Finally, key performance indicators for the financial perspective could include gross margin, sales margin, return on investment, return on assets, and other ratios used in financial analysis.

Measurement of such indicators noted above would allow for each key performance indicator to be quantitatively measured so that management can effectively assess whether the key performance indicators are being met. Key performance indicators are, in essence, that which management feels are necessary to the success of the organization.

No maximum or minimum number of objectives should be used for the various perspectives. Additionally, key performance indicators may have more than one objective associated with each indicator. It's important to keep in mind that the more objectives a perspective has, the more difficult it becomes to measure success. A company that has three key performance measures may be better able to focus on the success of the performance measures than a company that has ten objectives. As noted above, however, there is no set amount of objectives. A company should meet the key performance measures important to its own success with objectives that define that success.

For success in using the Balanced Scorecard, a company may want to begin with a small number of objectives that define the most important key performance indicators. The Balanced Scorecard can grow, shrink, and change over time, based on management need.

LEARNING GOAL 5: Build a Balanced Scorecard

See the Balanced Scorecard below for the data provided in Learning Goal 1.

TABLE 16.5 Annual Balanced Scorecard

Key Performance Indicator (KPI)	Objective	Measurement	Target	Actual
		Learning and Growth Perspective		
Employee Empowerment	Build Competencies	Key business processes empowered to lower levels	25% of lower level management assuming key business process functions	?
Technology Enhancement	Integrate IT	IT effectiveness survey	95% of responses indicate 4 or 5	?
Corporate Culture	Create an Atmosphere of Empowerment	Empowerment Index	10% increase in empowerment-type behaviors	?
		Internal Business Perspective		
Manufacturing Times	Upgrade Manufacturing Process	Upgrade manufacturing process	20% reduction in wait times	?
Delivery Times	Upgrade Delivery Process	Upgrade delivery process	50% decrease in delivery time	?
Process Efficiency	Reduce Rework	Reduce rework	10% reduction in rework	?
		Customer Perspective		
Customer Satisfaction	Increases Customer Satisfaction	Customer satisfaction survey	85% of customers give a 4 or 5 rating	?
Increased Customers	Expansion of New Customers	Number of new customers	five new customers per month	?
Customer penetration	Increase Products Used Per Customer	Number of products used by each customer	80% of customers use three or more products	?
		Financial Perspective		
Market Share	Increased Market Share	Percent increase over base year	5% increase over base year	?
Profit Margin	Increased Profit Margins	Profit margin percent increase	10 % profit margin increase	?
Return on Assets	Maximum Asset Utilization	Maximum asset utilization	Asset utilization ratio of 1.5	?

Note that the Balanced Scorecard reflects the KPIs, the objectives, measurements, and goals for each perspective. The number of KPIs and objectives is at the discretion of management. The above card can be used to measure actual performance in the four perspectives against strategic goals outlined in the strategy map.

TOPIC 16 REFERENCES

Braun, K.W. and Tietz, W.M. *Managerial Accounting* (4th ed.). Upper Saddle River, NJ: Prentice Hall, 2014.

Garrison, R.H., Noreen, E.W., and Brewer, P.C. *Managerial Accounting*. New York: McGraw-Hill Companies, Inc., 2012.

Horngren, C.T, Datar, S.M. and Rajan, M.V. *Cost Accounting: A Managerial Emphasis* (15th ed.). Upper Saddle River, NJ: Pearson Education, Inc., 2015.

TOPIC 17 Traditional Performance Evaluation

LEARNING GOALS

1. Examine decentralization.
2. Understand the role of responsibility centers and responsibility accounting in performance evaluation.
3. Discuss and calculate the methods of evaluation for the different responsibility centers.
4. Discuss the strengths and weaknesses of the different forms of performance evaluation.

INTRODUCTION

When evaluating the performance of an organization, the non-traditional methods discussed in Topic 16 and the traditional methods discussed in Topic 17 can be used. Using both methods helps to provide management with a full analysis as to the performance of the organization. Traditional evaluation methods focus on the quantitative side of evaluation, using such tools as performance reports, Return on Investment (ROI), and Residual Income (RI). In this topic, such tools will be discussed in the context of traditional quantitative evaluation.

LEARNING GOAL 1: Examine Decentralization

The concept of decentralization is the idea that one person or one group of people cannot do everything within an organization. Hence, certain responsibilities are delegated to other individuals or to other departments. In delegating responsibilities to others in an organization, the company becomes decentralized and requires an analysis of the organizational structure. According to Clawson and Pitts (1991), the organizational structure reflects the way in which an organization is divided. Such divisions may include accounting, management, marketing, production, purchasing, and any number of other divisions (Clawson and Pitts, 1991). The authors contend that organizational structure is impacted by a number of factors, including:

- Fit: Alignment with the organizational environment.
- Differentiation and integration: The interconnected relationship between the division of labor and the coordination that must occur among the divisions.
- Technology: The type of technology an organization uses can shape the organizational structure.
- Size: Differences in size place different demands on an organization.
- Span of control: How many people report to one supervisor.
- Staffing: The fit of individual skills and talents to the jobs.
- Unity of command: Many individuals in today's organizational environments report to more than one supervisor. Such supervisors must have unity.
- Line vs. staff: Traditional hierarchical organizational structures built a wedge between line vs. staff. As complex companies find new ways of organization, such lines become blurred.

Organizational structures come in a variety of shapes and sizes that move away from the traditional hierarchical model (see Figure 17.1). As reported by Clawson and Pitts (1991), such organizational structures may include:

Functional structures: Functional structures are designed around the functions within an organization. Organizations may have different functions that exist, so every organization is different, depending on the functions that exist inside the organization.

- The advantage of the functional structure is the level of expertise that exists inside the given functions.
- The disadvantage of the functional structure is that individuals can become departmentalized, taking ownership of their own department but not lending a hand to other departments because it is "out of scope" for them.

Product structures: Product structures are designed around products within the organization, with each product having a manager with a supporting staff that may include marketing, sales, and advertising.

- The advantage of the product structure is that each group of individuals working in a specific product line can focus on the given product.
- The disadvantage of the product structure is in the duplication of resources for each product.

Customer structure: Customer structure is organized by assigning a team to particular customers. Such a structure is common in the service industry.

- The advantage of the customer structure is that employees become keenly aware of the source of revenue.
- The disadvantage of such a structure is that meeting client needs can become a source of stress.

Geographic structure: The geographic structure is a hybrid of the customer structure. Companies may have divisions for various geographical regions.

- The advantages of geographic structures are that they are easy to manage and costs are contained to the given geographical region. Travel costs may be minimized as sales staff would be geographically positioned.
- The disadvantage of the geographic structure is that such geographic boundaries can build barriers.

Divisional structure: In the divisional structure, management is in charge of all aspects of their own "business."

- The advantage to such a complex business structure is that the autonomy of the divisions can lead to ownership and ultimately successful operations.

- The disadvantage of the divisional structure is that it can lead to too much independence and not enough interdependence.

Matrix structure: A matrix structure may have several lines of authority, and an employee may report to multiple individuals for various things.

- The advantage of the matrix structure is that the structure services complex business processes well within globalized organizations.
- The disadvantage of the matrix structure is that it is an expensive structure, and individuals could become confused as to who they report.

Amorphous structure: The amorphous structure is undefined and emerges based on the needs of the organization.

- An advantage to the amorphous structure is that new theories and organization emerges as the possibilities become endless. This structural form can become highly motivating.
- What can be viewed as a disadvantage of the amorphous structure is that there is no organizational chart and no clear line of reporting. This structural form can become confusing.

LEARNING GOAL 2: Understand the Role of Responsibility Centers and Responsibility Accounting in Performance Evaluation

As the organization of companies begins to take shape, managerial accountants need to know how to meet the needs of management. Who is management? Who reports to specific areas of management? What type of information does management need? These are all questions that emerge when there is a decentralized working environment. In the context of performance evaluation, managers need to:

- Communicate
- Encourage goal congruence
- Motivate leaders

Performance evaluation can accomplish all of these things within the organizational structure.

A manager cannot be held responsible for something that falls outside of his or her area of responsibility. Thus, the concept of responsibility accounting measures performance within the given area of responsibility. There are four areas of responsibility:

- Cost center
- Revenue center
- Profit center
- Investment center

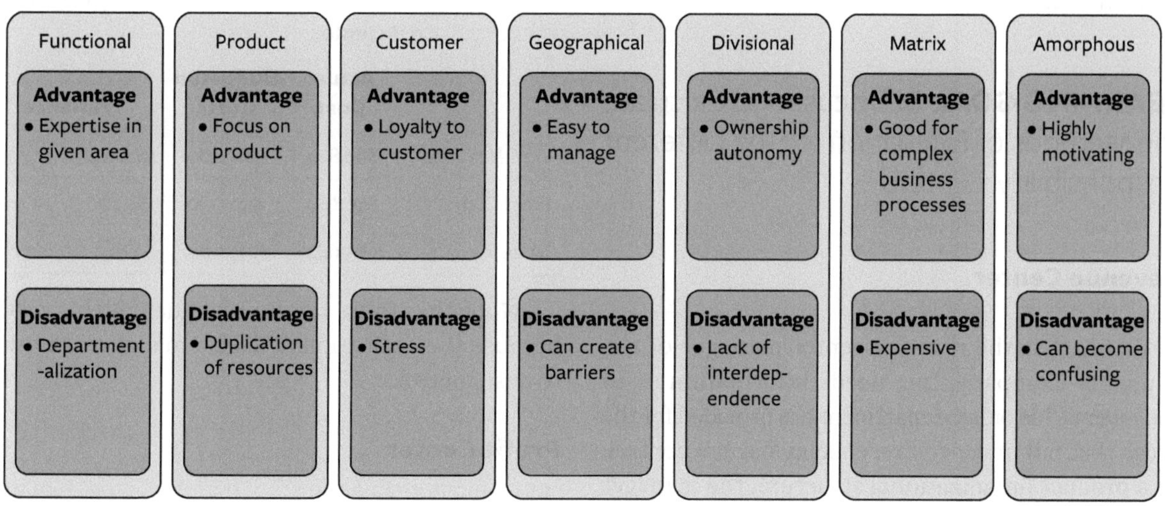

FIGURE 17.1 Organizational Structures.

When evaluating a manager of a cost center, the manager is responsible only for costs and holds no responsibility for revenues. An example of a cost center would be the manager of the manufacturing process within a given company. Conversely, when evaluating a manager of a revenue center, the manager is responsible only for revenues and holds no responsibility for costs. An example of a revenue center manager would be the manager of the sales department.

The manager of a profit center holds a greater level of responsibility than the manager of the cost center or the revenue center. A profit center manager is responsible for costs and revenues, which ultimately means the manager is responsible for profit. An example of a profit center manager would be the manager of an individual store such as the manager of a McDonald's location.

The manager of an investment center holds the highest level of responsibility in that this manager is responsible for profits and investments. An example of an investment center manager would be the manager of the corporate offices of Target.

Managers at various levels within an organization require different reporting mechanisms to let them know how their area is performing. For example, the manager of a revenue center does not need cost data. Therefore, all reports provided to the revenue center manager would reflect only revenue data. The revenue center's supervisor is going to evaluate the revenue manager based on revenue performance, not cost control.

LEARNING GOAL 3: Discuss and Calculate the Methods of Evaluation for the Different Responsibility Centers

Revenue Center

Let's say that the revenue center manager of the Alphabet Company, Inc. needs information as to the revenue his or her department has provided for the areas that fall under the revenue manager's control. In a product organizational structure, the manager may be responsible for the women's clothing product line. The manager would need information as to the budgeted and actual amounts for the various types of clothing that fall under the women's clothing line. See the table below for the type of monthly report such a manager would need.

TABLE 17.1 Revenue Center

Product	Actual Revenue	Budgeted Revenue	Variance	
Shirts	$13,380	$15,000	($1,620)	(10.8%)
Shoes	$14,255	$13,000	$1,255	9.65%
Pants/Skirts	$18,213	$15,000	$3,213	21.42%
Dresses	$16,059	$18,000	($1,941)	(10.78%)
Jewelry	$8,050	$8,000	$50	.63%
Undergarments	$3,962	$4,000	($38)	(.95%)
Total:	$73,919	$73,000	$919	1.26%

Note that there are no costs in this report because the evaluation of such a manager is limited to revenue.

Cost Center

Now let's say that the cost center manager of the Alphabet Company, Inc. needs information as to the costs in his or her department that fall under the cost manager's control. See the table below for the type of monthly report such a manager would need.

TABLE 17.2 Cost Center

	Actual Cost	Budgeted Costs	Variance	
Variable Costs	$69,882	$65,000	($4,882)	($7.51%)
Fixed Costs	$35,800	$40,000	$4,200	10.50%
Total:	$105,682	$105,000	$682	.65%

Note that there are no revenues in this report because the evaluation of such a manager is limited to cost control.

Profit Center

Finally, let's say that the profit center manager is evaluated on both revenues and costs for the entire store. The entire store consists of both the men's and the women's product line revenues and the costs for the various areas of the store. Such a report may look like this:

TABLE 17.3 Profit Center

Revenues	Actual Revenue	Budgeted Revenue	Variance	
Women's Line	$73,919	$73,000	$919	1.26%
Men's Line	$82,448	$90,000	($7,552)	(8.39%)
Total Revenue:	$156,367	$163,000	$6,633	(4.07%)

TABLE 17.4 Profit Center, part 2

Expenses	Actual	Budgeted	Variance	
Variable Costs	$132,000	$135,000	$3,000	2.22%
Contribution margin	$24,367	$28,000	($3,633)	(12.98%)
Fixed Costs	$35,800	$40,000	$4,200	10.50%
Segment Margin	**($11,433)**	**($12,000)**	**$567**	4.73%
Less Common Fixed Costs	$5,000	$5,000	$0	0%
Operating Income	($16,433)	($17,000)	$567	3.34%

Note that both revenues and costs are listed on the profit center's report because the manager is responsible for the overall profit of the organization. Note also that fixed costs are reported for the store as those that belong specifically to the store and those that are shared with other stores. The fixed costs that are shared with other stores are called common fixed costs. Although common fixed costs could make a store or a segment appear unprofitable, such costs are allocated based on a reasonable allocation method.

Fixed Cost Allocation. Fixed costs that occur company-wide may be allocated to various departments or stores based on a method the company feels is reasonable. For example, fixed costs might be allocated on a measure such as square footage, hours of operation, or total sales revenue. In the example noted above, $5,000 of fixed costs is allocated to store A. If total fixed costs, company-wide, are $20,000, Store A may have received an allocation of fixed costs based on square footage. If, for example, Store A has 25% of the square feet of all the stores, the company may feel it's fair to allocate 25% of the total common fixed costs to the store. Likewise, Store C is a larger store and has 50% of the square feet of all the stores. Therefore, the company has allocated 50% of the common fixed costs to Store C as noted below:

TABLE 17.5 Fixed Cost Allocation

Revenues	Store A	Store B	Store C	Total
Women's Line	$73,919	$90,580	$150,880	$315,379
Men's Line	$82,448	$115,216	$146,421	$344,085
Total Revenue:	$156,367	$205,796	$297,301	$659,464

TABLE 17.6 Fixed Cost Allocation, part 2

Expenses	Store A	Store B	Store C	Total
Variable Costs	$132,000	$159,500	$231,990	$523,490
Contribution margin	$24,367	$46,296	$65,311	$135,974
Fixed Costs	$35,800	$36,200	$51,110	$123,110
Segment Margin	**($11,433)**	**$10,096**	**$14,201**	**$12,864**
Less Common Fixed Costs	$5,000	$5,000	$10,000	$20,000
Operating Income	($16,433)	$5,096	$4,201	($7,136)

Keep in mind, that the common fixed costs are allocated. Thus, if the Alphabet Company, Inc. would choose to close Store A, due to its level of unprofitability, such fixed costs would need to be allocated to a different store. If the company allocated them to Store C, then Store C would appear to be unprofitable. If the company decided to close Store C due to its unprofitability, the fixed common costs would then be allocated to the only remaining store, which would appear unprofitable. Such a downward spiral would eventually cause all stores to become unprofitable.

Thus, the profitability of a profit center should be evaluated based on segment margin, not on operating income. Evaluating the profit of the entire company would include the common fixed costs but not the evaluation of each segment.

Investment Center

The corporate offices of the Alphabet Store, Inc. would be considered an investment center. In an investment center, the manager is responsible for the overall profit and loss of the stores but is also responsible for investments. The manager may consider investing in an additional store or an additional product line. Such investments will be evaluated according to their return and their profit potential.

Return on Investment (ROI). ROI is a performance measure that considers the return an investment will deliver. Managers of investment centers are evaluated based on the overall ROI of the organization but also of each individual investment. The formula for ROI is made up of two separate ratios multiplied by one another:

$$Sales\ Margin = \frac{Operating\ Income}{Sales}$$

$$Capital\ Turnover = \frac{Sales}{Total\ Assets}$$

$$ROI = Sales\ Margin \times Capital\ Turnover$$

$$or\ \frac{Operating\ Income}{Sales} \times \frac{Sales}{Total\ Assets}$$

If Alphabet Company, Inc. has sales of $659,464 and operating income of ($7,136), it would have a negative sales margin of .01 ($\frac{(\$7{,}136)}{\$659{,}464}$) or negative 1%.

However, if the company were able to reduce expenses and increase Operating Income to $10,000, it would have a sales margin of 1.5%.

Sales Margin tells a company if it is using revenue dollars efficiently. The margin is expressed in terms of a percent, and the higher the percent, the stronger the margin. Alphabet Company, Inc. has very low margins as indicated by the calculation.

If Alphabet Company, Inc. has total assets of $156,000, its capital turnover would be 4.23 ($\frac{659{,}000}{156{,}000}$).

The capital turnover ratio indicates how many times assets are turned over through sales. Alphabet Company's capital turnover is strong.

In calculating ROI, Alphabet Company, Inc. would multiply its sales margin by its capital turnover.

$$\frac{Operating\ Income}{Sales} \times \frac{Sales}{Total\ Assets}$$

$$-1\% \times 4.23\ times$$

$$-4.23\%$$

Due to the poor sales margin, the Alphabet Company, Inc. has a negative ROI. Let's revisit the computation using the sales margin of 1.5%

$$\frac{Operating\ Income}{Sales} \times \frac{Sales}{Total\ Assets}$$

$$1.5\% \times 4.23$$

$$6.345\%$$

Simply by increasing the sales margin, the company is able to maintain a stronger ROI.

If the manager of the investment center decides to open a new product line, and the product line will have operating income of $8,000, bringing in additional assets of $5,000 and sales revenue of $16,000, the following analysis would reveal that the investment would be a good investment.

$$Sales\ Margin = \frac{Operating\ Income}{Sales}$$

$$= \frac{\$8{,}000}{\$16{,}000} = .50 = 50\%$$

$$Capital\ Turnover = \frac{Sales}{Total\ Assets} = \frac{\$16{,}000}{\$5{,}000} = 3.2$$

$$\frac{Operating\ Income}{Sales} \times \frac{Sales}{Total\ Assets}$$

$$50\% \times 3.2$$

$$160\%$$

Such an investment has a high ROI. Let's see how it impacts the overall condition of the company.

$$Sales\ Margin = \frac{Operating\ Income}{Sales}$$

$$= \frac{(\$7{,}136) + \$8{,}000}{\$659{,}464 + \$16{,}000} = .001 = .1\%$$

$$Capital\ Turnover = \frac{Sales}{Total\ Assests}$$
$$= \frac{\$659{,}464 + \$16{,}000}{\$156{,}000 + \$5{,}000} = 4$$
$$\frac{Operating\ Income}{Sales} \times \frac{Sales}{Total\ Assets}$$
$$.1\% \times 4$$
$$.4\%$$

The investment has helped to move the company in the right direction. Such a manager would want to make several investments that would help to increase ROI. Larger, more impactful investments that have a high ROI will help to increase the company's performance and increase ROI more quickly. Also, working on the current margin for the company will also help to increase the performance as reflected by ROI.

The strength of the ROI calculation is that managers are able to divide the calculation into its two pieces: 1) Sales Margin and 2) Capital Turnover, to see why an ROI calculation is or is not strong. Such a tool gives direction to future decisions.

Residual Income. The residual income calculation is a calculation that should be used in conjunction with ROI, not as a replacement for ROI. Residual income helps a company know if an investment will create any excess income. To use the residual income calculation, a company must have a target rate of return.

If Alphabet Company, Inc. borrows money at 9% interest, the target rate of return would be at least 9%. Let's say the company uses a target rate of return of 9% for our calculation here. The residual income calculation for the new product line would be as follows:

$$Operating\ income$$
$$-(target\ rate\ of\ return \times total\ assets)$$
$$\$8{,}000 - (.09 \times \$5{,}000)$$
$$\$8{,}000 - \$450$$
$$\$7{,}550$$

By combining the use of ROI with Residual Income, we can see that the new product line would have 160% ROI and $7,550 of residual income given a 9% target rate of return.

LEARNING GOAL 4: Discuss the Strengths and Weaknesses of the Different Forms of Performance Evaluation

Each performance method of evaluation has strengths and weakness that management should consider in using the evaluation method (see Figure 17.2). The best analysis involves multiple methods that are able to work together. The following data pertains to the strengths and weaknesses of ROI and Residual Income.

ROI Strengths

- Ensures that investments are made that deliver strong returns.
- Provides for comparative analysis of different internal divisions of an organization.
- Provides for comparative analysis of different investments.
- Allows management to understand where a performance problem exists when the ROI formula is broken down into its component parts of sales margin and capital turnover.
- Can be used from existing financial data.

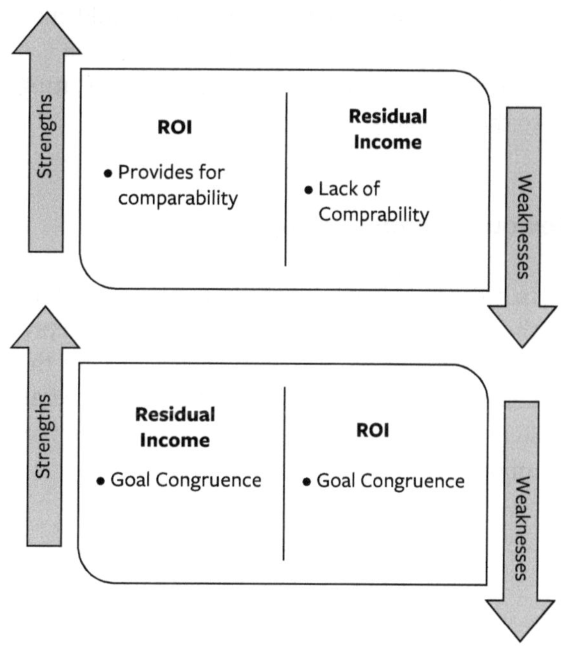

FIGURE 17.2 ROI and Residual Income.

ROI Weaknesses

- Calculations may have discrepancies of income. Operating income was the type of income used in this text; however, net income, income before interest and taxes, or other various forms of income could be used as the income amount needed for calculating sales margin.
- Calculations may have discrepancies in the value of assets. Assets could be entered as current cost, historical cost, or FMV. Other questions may involve whether intangible assets should be included in the calculation.
- ROI may have influence over a decision to invest or not invest in a project that is not in the best interest of the overall company goals. For example, if a manager has a current ROI in his or her division of 15%., investing in a project that has an ROI of 12%, although still a good investment, would lower overall ROI and cause a disconnect in goal congruence.
- Over-concern for ROI could result in short-term profitability but long-term problems. In an effort to increase ROI, a manager could cut costs too drastically in an effort to increase margin. Long-term effects could be devastating to the company.

Residual Income Strengths

- In order to balance out the weaknesses of ROI, the residual income method of analysis will provide a perspective as to goal congruence for the company. An investment that may lower overall ROI may still be a strong investment, given the amount of residual income.

Residual Income Weaknesses

- Residual income cannot be used to compare investments or divisions of different sizes. Larger divisions or investments will more than likely show larger residual income amounts simply because they are larger, not necessarily because they are better investments.

For the purposes of a quantitative analysis, using ROI and Residual Income together helps managers of investment centers make informed decisions. Additionally, the use of both tools to evaluate the existing performance of an organization or division provides a broad picture to best understand areas of strength and struggle within the division or the organization.

TOPIC 17 REFERENCES

Agarwal, R. "Return on Investment (ROI): Advantages and Disadvantages." Your Article Library. Retrieved from www.yourarticlelibrary.com/accounting/return-on-investment-roi-advantages-and-disadvantages/52928/ (2016).

Ahmed, S. "Limitations, Criticism or Disadvantage of Residual Income Method." *Accounting Details.* Retrieved from www.accountingdetails.com/limitations_of_residual_income.htm (2016).

Braun, K.W. and Tietz, W.M. *Managerial Accounting* (4th ed.). Upper Saddle River, NJ: Prentice Hall, 2014.

Clawson, J. & Pitts, T. (1991). *Organizational structure.* Darden Business Publishing.

Garrison, R.H., Noreen, E.W., and Brewer, P.C. *Managerial Accounting.* New York: McGraw-Hill Companies, Inc., 2012.

Horngren, C.T, Datar, S.M. and Rajan, M.V. *Cost Accounting: A Managerial Emphasis* (15th ed.). Upper Saddle River, NJ: Pearson Education, Inc., 2015.

APPENDIX

Andy's Excel Application Problems were inspired by "Andy" who was a student in one of my managerial accounting courses. After class one day, he suggested that I write managerial accounting problems in which students can learn how to use Excel to solve. Thank you, Andy!

Andy's Excel Application Problems have been created to help students master the calculations of management accounting. When management accountants perform such calculations in the "real world", the calculations are completed with the use of a technological resources such as Excel or a similar tool. Students should be learning how to use tools such as Excel to complete problems relating to budgeting, costing, pricing, and numerous other such calculations.

Andy's Excel Application Problems

Calculating Cost of Goods Sold in a Manufacturing Company

Andy has discovered that Excel can come in handy when calculating inventory. Help Andy build an Excel spreadsheet for raw materials available for use, cost of goods manufactured and cost of goods sold. Use the following data:

- Beginning Raw Materials Inventory: $556
- Purchases: $220
- Ending Raw Materials Inventory: $150
- Beginning Work in Process Inventory: $480
- Labor: $10 * 1056 hours
- Overhead: $895
- Ending Work in Process Inventory: $334
- Beginning Finished Goods Inventory: $225
- Ending Finished Goods Inventory: $130

Compute Cost of Goods Sold using Excel.

*Review the Excel training videos for further help with Excel. Link: http://somup.com/cDnlFTTwo

Hints

1. When creating this spreadsheet, it is helpful to use totals from other cells. For example, if B5 contains a total that I will also use in B9, my B9 entry will be "=B5".
2. Let Excel do the math. Many students do the math on their calculator and then enter it into Excel. This defeats the purpose of using Excel.

FIGURE A.0 Andy illustration thumbnail.

Worksheet

High-Low Method & Regression Analysis

Andy has discovered that Excel can come in handy when separating mixed costs into its fixed and variable components. Help Andy build an Excel spreadsheet to separate fixed and variable costs using the high-low method and regression analysis.

TABLE A.1 High-Low Method and Regression

Month	Activity Level	Total Costs
July	550	$110,543
August	725	$131,480
September	675	$127,005
October	580	$109,885
November	603	$109,998
December	496	$93,990

*Review Excel training videos for further help with Excel. Link: http://somup.com/cDn2qpTzD

Hints

1. When performing regression analysis, you will need to ensure that the analysis toolpack is available in Excel. Perform the following steps to complete a summary output:
   1. **Step 1: Set up Excel to perform a regression analysis**
      Go to:
      File,
      Options,
      Add-Ins,
      Manage: Select Excel Add-ins at the bottom of the page from the drop down, Click "Go", and Ensure "Analysis Toolpack" is selected, Click "OK".
   2. **Step 2: Add data to the spreadsheet**
      You can simply cut and paste or add the information manually. In the screenshot below, I cut and pasted from a provided table.

Once the information is in the spreadsheet click on:

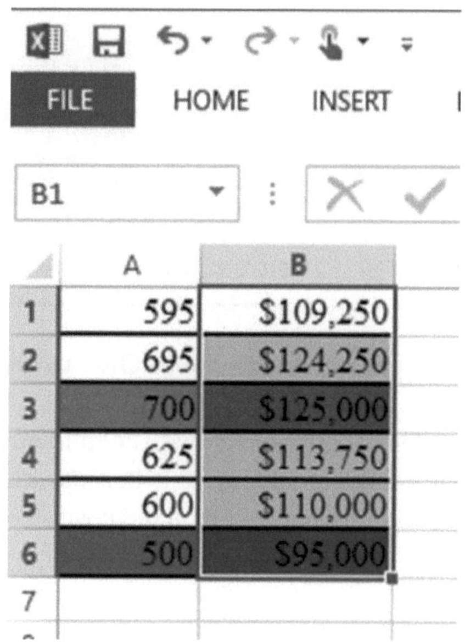

FIGURE A.1

1. Data,
2. Data analysis,
3. Select "Regression", Click "OK", and
4. Add your inputs.

Your "Y" inputs will be the total costs
Your "X" inputs will be your levels of activity, as noted below.
To add inputs simply select the data and paste it directly into the appropriate input area.

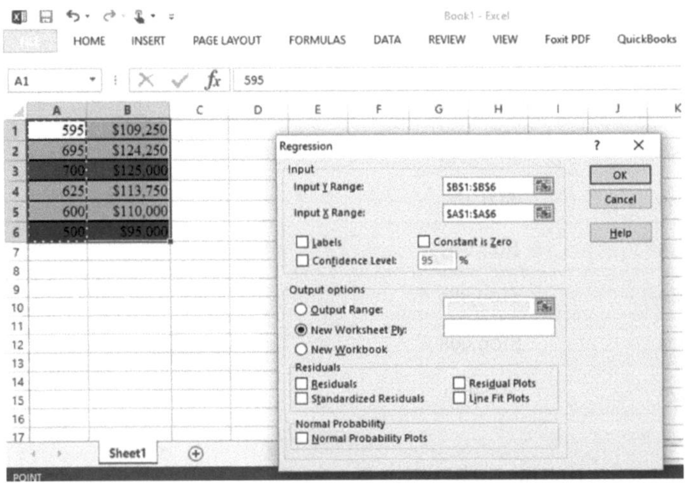

FIGURE A.2

Once the data is added, click "OK" to view the output.

From the output noted above, the following three amounts are the relevant amounts in separating fixed and variable components of a mixed cost:

1. R Square = Goodness of fit. This number should be between 0 and 1. "0" indicates no fit and "1" indicates a perfect fit.
2. Intercept = Fixed amount
3. X Variable = Variable amount

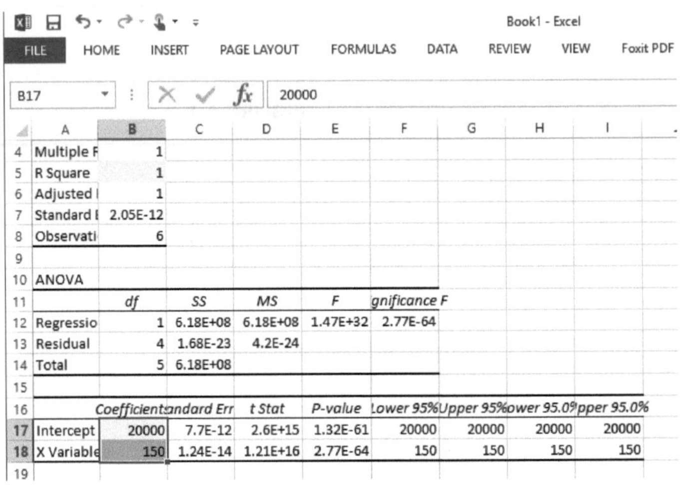

	A	B	C	D	E	F	G	H	I
4	Multiple F	1							
5	R Square	1							
6	Adjusted I	1							
7	Standard I	2.05E-12							
8	Observati	6							
9									
10	ANOVA								
11		df	SS	MS	F	gnificance F			
12	Regressio	1	6.18E+08	6.18E+08	1.47E+32	2.77E-64			
13	Residual	4	1.68E-23	4.2E-24					
14	Total	5	6.18E+08						
15									
16		Coefficient	andard Err	t Stat	P-value	Lower 95%	Upper 95%	ower 95.0%	pper 95.0%
17	Intercept	20000	7.7E-12	2.6E+15	1.32E-61	20000	20000	20000	20000
18	X Variable	150	1.24E-14	1.21E+16	2.77E-64	150	150	150	150
19									

FIGURE A.3

Worksheet

CVP Analysis

Andy has discovered that Excel can come in handy when performing CVP analysis. Help Andy to complete a sensitivity analysis of the following information:

Data

Scott's Hot Chocolate Shoppe owns and operates 8 shops throughout the midwest. Revenue and cost data for the year is as follows:

Revenues	$12,300,000
Fixed costs	$ 1,480,000
Variable costs	$ 5,400,000

Variable costs change based on the number of cups of hot chocolate sold.

Use Excel to compute the budgeted operating income for each of the following deviations from the original budget data. Consider each case independently to determine which results in the highest operating income.

Required

1. A 5% increase in contribution margin when revenues constant
2. A 5% decrease in contribution margin when revenues constant
3. A 2% increase in fixed costs
4. A 2% decrease in fixed costs
5. A 10% increase in units sold
6. A 10% decrease in units sold
7. A 5% increase in fixed costs and a 3% increase in units sold
8. A 3% increase in fixed costs and a 2% decrease in variable costs

*Review Excel training videos for further help with Excel. Link: http://somup.com/cDnontTA6

Hints

1. When you set up this spreadsheet, be sure to place your percentage increases and decreases in their own column so that when you enter the formulas, you can refer to the cell containing the increased or decreased amount. If there are words on the cell with the percentage increases/decreases, you will not be able to reference the cell. For example, if I am trying to calculate an increase of 3%. I want to have a cell (formatted as a percent) that contains 3%. The word increase will be in the next cell over.
2. Let Excel do the math. Many students do the math on their calculator and then enter it into Excel. This defeats the purpose of using Excel.

Worksheet

Master Budgeting

Andy has discovered that Excel can come in handy when building a master budget. Help Andy to complete a master budget in Excel:

Data

Charmelle's Chocolate Shop sells chocolate covered cherries. Each box contains 12 chocolate covered cherries. A unit is one box. The chocolate shop has anticipated sales for each month of the first quarter as follows:

- January: 200 boxes
- February: 350 boxes
- March: 150 boxes
- April: 175 boxes
- May: 175 boxes

In December of the prior year Charmelle budgeted for 400 boxes.

Each unit sales for $15.00. 15% of sales are cash and the rest is on credit. The company requires 15% of the following month's sales in their finished goods ending inventory. Each finished good unit requires 1.5 lbs of chocolate and 1.75 lbs of cherries. The raw material required to be kept on hand in raw materials inventory is 10% of the following months production needs. Chocolate costs $2.75 per lb and cherries cost $5.00 per pound. Each unit takes .25 hours to produce and direct labor is paid $12 per hour. Round all partial units up.

Required

Use Excel to complete the:

1. Sales and revenues budget.
2. Production budget.
3. Raw materials budget for both chocolate and cherries.
4. Labor budget.

*Review Excel training videos for further help with Excel. Link: http://somup.com/cDein8tof

Hints

1. When creating this spreadsheet, it is helpful to use totals from other cells. For example, if B5 contains a total that I will also use in B9, my B9 entry will be "=B5".
2. It is helpful to create a box of variables used in the calculations so that if I change one of the variables, it will change in all the cells in which the variable has been used. This will simplify the process when I make changes to the variables.
3. Let Excel do the math. Many students do the math on their calculator and then enter it into Excel. This defeats the purpose of using Excel.

Worksheet

Standard Costs

Andy has discovered that Excel can come in handy when building Standard Cost Card. Help Andy to complete a standard cost card in Excel:

Data

B.H. Corporation is an online company that makes a variety of products out of wood. One of their products is a birdhouse. There are several different sizes for the birdhouse. B.H. Corporation would like to create standards for their medium sized birdhouse including the packaging material and has provided you with the information below.

Material to make 2 birdhouses:

- 1 in. × 6 in. × 8 ft. Cedar, $14.27
- ¼ inch dowel, $4.71 for 10 dowels
- Shipping boxes are $1.52 per box.

B.H. Corporation pays their employees $16.00 per hour to make the birdhouses. Each birdhouse is scheduled to take 1.5 hours to build and paint. The 1.5 hours accommodates normal work stoppages.

Overhead is applied per labor hour at a rate of $3.75. Overhead includes various items including materials such as wood glue, paint and stain, nails, and packing peanuts.

Each birdhouse is boxed for shipment. Packing peanuts are put in the box to protect during shipment.

*Review Excel training videos for further help with Excel. Link: http://somup.com/cDeQ3JtwQ

Hints

1. When creating this spreadsheet, it is helpful to use totals from other cells. For example, if B5 contains a total that I will also use in B9, my B9 entry will be "=B5".
2. It is helpful to create a box of variables used in the calculations so that if I change one of the variables, it will change in all the cells in which the variable has been used. This will simplify the process when I make changes to the variables.
3. Let Excel do the math. Many students do the math on their calculator and then enter it into Excel. This defeats the purpose of using Excel.

FIGURE A.4 Birdhouse.

Worksheet

Capital Budgeting

Andy has discovered that Excel can come in handy when calculating the payback period and the ARR when there are uneven cash flows. Help Andy to complete a payback and ARR calculation in Excel for even cash flows and for uneven cash flows:

The company Andy works for is considering buying a new machine. They have a choice between two machines:

TABLE A.2 Capital Budgeting

Machine 1	Machine 2
• Initial Investment: $275,000	• Initial Investment: $160,000
• Expected annual cash inflow: $125,000	• Expected annual cash inflow:
• Expected annual cash outflow: $50,000	• Year 1: $75,000
• Useful life: 5 years	• Year 2: $100,000
• Salvage Value: None	• Year 3: $75,000
	• Year 4: $70,000
	• Year 5: $60,000
	• Expected annual cash outflow:
	• Year 1: $20,000
	• Year 2: $30,000
	• Year 3: $50,000
	• Year 4: $55,000
	• Year 5: $55,000
	• Useful life: 5 years
	• Salvage Value $15,000
Rules for acceptance:	
Payback: 4 years or less	
ARR: 5% or greater	

*Review Excel training videos for further help with Excel. Link: http://somup.com/cbVvfuLuN

Hints

1. When creating this spreadsheet, it is helpful to use totals from other cells. For example, if B5 contains a total that I will also use in B9, my B9 entry will be "=B5".
2. It is helpful to create a box of variables used in the calculations so that if I change one of the variables, it will change in all the cells in which the variable has been used. This will simplify the process when I make changes to the variables.
3. Let Excel do the math. Many students do the math on their calculator and then enter it into Excel. This defeats the purpose of using Excel.

Worksheet

Job Costing

Andy has discovered that Excel can come in handy when calculating costs for a job.

The company Andy works for uses a job costing system. Create a job cost sheet and calculate the materials, labor, and overhead for a given job. Determine the cost per unit for each unit in the job. Overhead is allocated based on direct labor hours. At the beginning of the current year, Andy's company determined that overhead would be $8,370 and that the company would use a total of 5,500 direct labor hours for the year. In October, Andy's company started job #365. The following information relates to job #365.

- Material used from requisition #7760: $530.50
- Direct labor tracked from time card record #250: 23 hours at $13.00 per hour.
- State date: 10/17/17
- Completed date: 10/25/17
- Number of units: 2

*Review Excel training videos for further help with Excel. Link: http://somup.com/cbnq3J8JO

Hints

1. When creating this spreadsheet, it is helpful to use totals from other cells. For example, if B5 contains a total that I will also use in B9, my B9 entry will be "=B5".
2. It is helpful to create a box of variables used in the calculations so that if I change one of the variables, it will change in all the cells in which the variable has been used. This will simplify the process when I make changes to the variables.
3. Let Excel do the math. Many students do the math on their calculator and then enter it into Excel. This defeats the purpose of using Excel.

Worksheet

Process Costing

Andy has discovered that Excel can come in handy when calculating costs for a process costing system.

Andy is helping out a friend who works for a company that uses a process costing system. Create a process cost report for the company. The information for the company is as follows:

Joseph's Groovy Guitar Manufacturing Company produces high level guitars for a number of famous artists. The guitars follow several processes to create. The first process is the wood cutting process, the second process is the 1st assembly process, the third process is the painting process, the fourth process is the electronic installation process, and the last process is the final assembly process. Joseph has asked Andy to help him create a process cost report for the first process, wood cutting. In the wood cutting process, materials are added at the beginning of the process while conversion costs are added evenly throughout. (round all partial units up)

Joseph has provided Andy with April data as follows:

TABLE A.3 Process Costing

Guitars:	
Beginning work in process inventory:	70 guitars
Added into production:	25 guitars
Completed and transferred to the 1st assembly process:	50 guitars
Ending work in process inventory:	45 guitars
(80% through the conversion process)	
Costs:	
Beginning WIP Materials Costs:	$3,250
Beginning WIP Conversion Costs:	$4,250
Costs added during April:	
Direct Materials (Wood):	$1,550
Direct Labor:	$2,600
Manufacturing Overhead:	$1,200

Per Andy's request, create a process cost report.

*Review Excel training videos for further help with Excel. Link: http://somup.com/cbnThFPvp

Hints

1. When creating this spreadsheet, it is helpful to use totals from other cells. For example, if B5 contains a total that I will also use in B9, my B9 entry will be "=B5".
2. It is helpful to create a box of variables used in the calculations so that if I change one of the variables, it will change in all the cells in which the variable has been used. This will simplify the process when I make changes to the variables.
3. Let Excel do the math. Many students do the math on their calculator and then enter it into Excel. This defeats the purpose of using Excel.
4. Highlighting cells where there are connections to other cells is helpful to quickly identify those connections.

Worksheet

Activity-Based Costing

Andy has discovered that Excel can come in handy when calculating overhead costs for an activity-based costing system.

Andy's company has determined that the plantwide overhead rate they are using is not sufficient in calculating overhead costs. Thus, the company would like Andy to determine activities and activity rates for their overhead costs. If you recall, Andy's company uses a job cost system in which overhead has been applied based on direct labor hours with a plantwide overhead rate of 1.52 per direct labor hour.

Andy determines that there are three main activities that occur in his organization: 1) Machining, 2) Assembling, and 3) Packaging. The following information is related to the three activities:

TABLE A.4 Allocation Base

Activity	Allocation Base
Machining	Number of machine hours (MH)
Assembling	Direct labor hours (DLH)
Packaging	Number of finished units

TABLE A.5 Amount of Overhead]

Activity	Amount of Overhead	Amount of Allocation Base
Machining	$4,690	9,000 MH
Assembling	$2,800	5,500 DLH
Packaging	$880	88 finished units
	$8,370	

Recall that job #365 had $530.50 in direct materials, $299.00 in direct labor, and $35 in overhead. Recalculate the overhead for the job based on Andy's separation of the overhead costs into various activities. Andy has determined that job #365 uses the following amounts of allocation base:

TABLE A.6 Job #365

Job #365:

Activity	Amount of Allocation Base
Machining	450 MH
Assembling	23 DLH
Packaging	2 finished units

*Review Excel training videos for further help with Excel. Link: http://somup.com/cbe1Y69Ux

Hints

1. When creating this spreadsheet, it is helpful to use totals from other cells. For example, if B5 contains a total that I will also use in B9, my B9 entry will be "=B5".
2. It is helpful to create a box of variables used in the calculations so that if I change one of the variables, it will change in all the cells in which the variable has been used. This will simplify the process when I make changes to the variables.
3. Let Excel do the math. Many students do the math on their calculator and then enter it into Excel. This defeats the purpose of using Excel.

Worksheet

Absorption vs. Variable Costing

Andy has discovered that Excel can come in handy when preparing income statements under variable costing and absorption costing.

Andy's company has a division in which they are considering manufacturing a single product that sells for $75 per unit. The company would like Andy to project its operating income for the first two years of operations. Cost information is below for each unit produced.

- Direct Material: $32 per unit
- Direct Labor: $12 per unit
- Variable Manufacturing Overhead (VOH): $2 per unit
- Variable Operating Expenses: $3 per unit

Cost information for annual fixed costs are noted below:

- Fixed manufacturing overhead (MOH) for each year: $142,000
- Fixed operating expenses each year: $79,000

During its first year of operations, the company plans to manufacture 20,000 units and anticipates selling 15,000 units. During the second year of its operations, the company plans to manufacture 20,000 units and anticipates selling 25,000 units.

Help Andy to create a variable costing income statement and an absorption costing income statement. Be sure to reconcile the differences for the difference in operating income.

*Review Excel training videos for further help with Excel. Link:

Hints

1. When creating this spreadsheet, it is helpful to use totals from other cells. For example, if B5 contains a total that I will also use in B9, my B9 entry will be "=B5".
2. It is helpful to create a box of variables used in the calculations so that if I change one of the variables, it will change in all the cells in which the variable has been used. This will simplify the process when I make changes to the variables.
3. Let Excel do the math. Many students do the math on their calculator and then enter it into Excel. This defeats the purpose of using Excel.

Worksheet

Pricing Decisions

Andy has discovered that Excel can come in handy when deciding how to price a product.

Andy's company is a price-taker and wants to analyze the price consumers pay for their product. They are also wondering if it would be in their best interest to make their product unique in some way to justify their position as a price-setter. Compute the company's current pricing structure and then adjust based on becoming a price-setter.

Cost to manufacture one unit of product:

- Direct Material: $265.25
- Direct Labor: $149.50
- Overhead: $133.11
- Operating Costs: $142,000 per year
- Estimated number of units sold: 10,000
- Required return on investment for shareholders: 5% of total assets of $1,000,000
- The marketplace is charging $549 per unit.

*Review Excel training videos for further help with Excel. Link: http://somup.com/cbejYo9GJ

Hints

1. When creating this spreadsheet, it is helpful to use totals from other cells. For example, if B5 contains a total that I will also use in B9, my B9 entry will be "=B5".
2. It is helpful to create a box of variables used in the calculations so that if I change one of the variables, it will change in all the cells in which the variable has been used. This will simplify the process when I make changes to the variables.
3. Let Excel do the math. Many students do the math on their calculator and then enter it into Excel. This defeats the purpose of using Excel.

Worksheet

Flexible Budgeting

Andy has discovered that Excel can come in handy when preparing a flexible budget and when determining variances.

Andy's company would like to perform a variance analysis of their actual data compared with their master budget data. Help Andy prepare a report that will contain the actual and budgeted data information as well as the flexible budget information. Once the data is entered into Excel, perform a flexible budget variance analysis and a volume variance analysis. The following information exists for the budgeted amounts:

TABLE A.7 Sales Volume, 10,000 Units

Sales Volume:	**10,000 units**
Sales Revenue:	$599 per unit
Cost of Goods Sold	$460 per unit
Fixed Manufacturing Overhead:	1,000,000
Variable Operating Expenses	
Sale Expense:	$3 per unit
Shipping Expense:	$4 per unit
Fixed Operating Expenses	
Salaries:	$46,000
Office Rent:	$26,000

The actual data is as follows:

TABLE A.8 Sales Volume, 8,850 Units

Sales Volume:	**8,850 units**
Sales Revenue:	$4,543,000
Cost of Goods Sold	$4,710,000
Fixed Manufacturing Overhead:	$940,000
Variable Operating Expenses	
Sale Expense:	$28,330
Shipping Expense:	$33,680
Fixed Operating Expenses	
Salaries:	$47,000
Office Rent:	$26,000

*Review Excel training videos for further help with Excel: Link: http://somup.com/cbeQ3m9N1

Hints

1. When creating this spreadsheet, it is helpful to use totals from other cells. For example, if B5 contains a total that I will also use in B9, my B9 entry will be "=B5".
2. It is helpful to create a box of variables used in the calculations so that if I change one of the variables, it will change in all the cells in which the variable has been used. This will simplify the process when I make changes to the variables.
3. Let Excel do the math. Many students do the math on their calculator and then enter it into Excel. This defeats the purpose of using Excel.

Worksheet

Andy's Excel Application Problems: Answer Key

FIGURE A.0 Andy illustration thumbnail.

Calculating Cost of Goods Sold in a Manufacturing Company

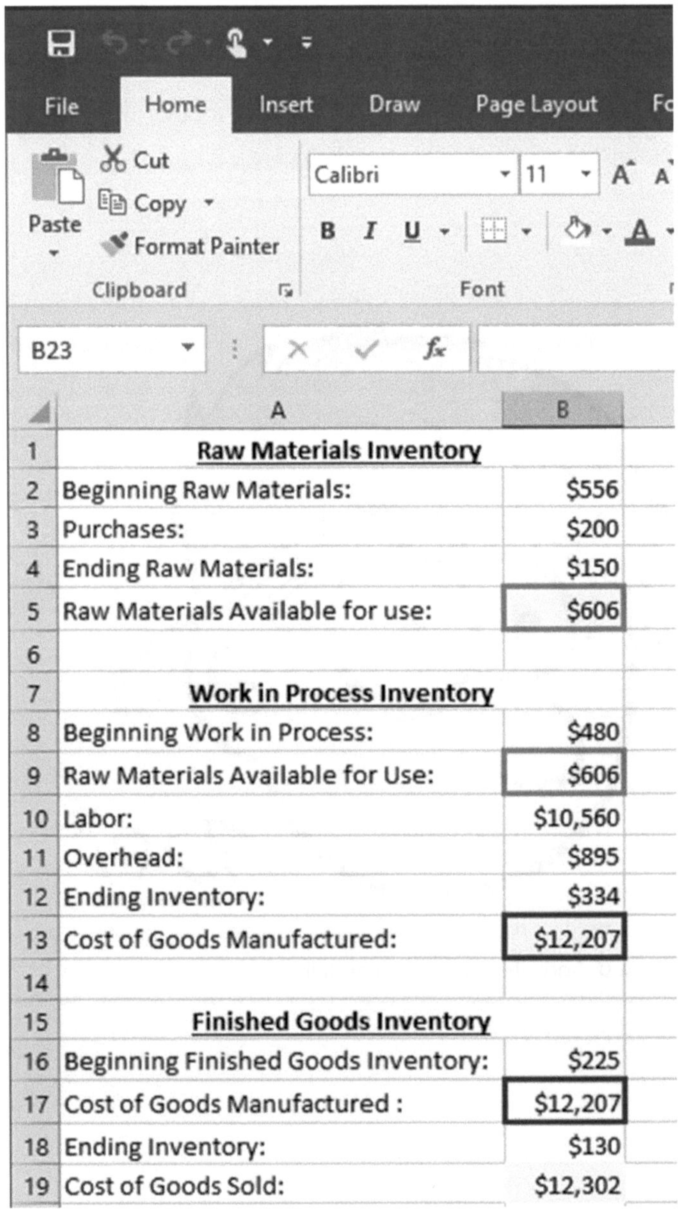

	A	B
1	**Raw Materials Inventory**	
2	Beginning Raw Materials:	$556
3	Purchases:	$200
4	Ending Raw Materials:	$150
5	Raw Materials Available for use:	$606
6		
7	**Work in Process Inventory**	
8	Beginning Work in Process:	$480
9	Raw Materials Available for Use:	$606
10	Labor:	$10,560
11	Overhead:	$895
12	Ending Inventory:	$334
13	Cost of Goods Manufactured:	$12,207
14		
15	**Finished Goods Inventory**	
16	Beginning Finished Goods Inventory:	$225
17	Cost of Goods Manufactured :	$12,207
18	Ending Inventory:	$130
19	Cost of Goods Sold:	$12,302

FIGURE A.5

High-Low method and Regression Analysis

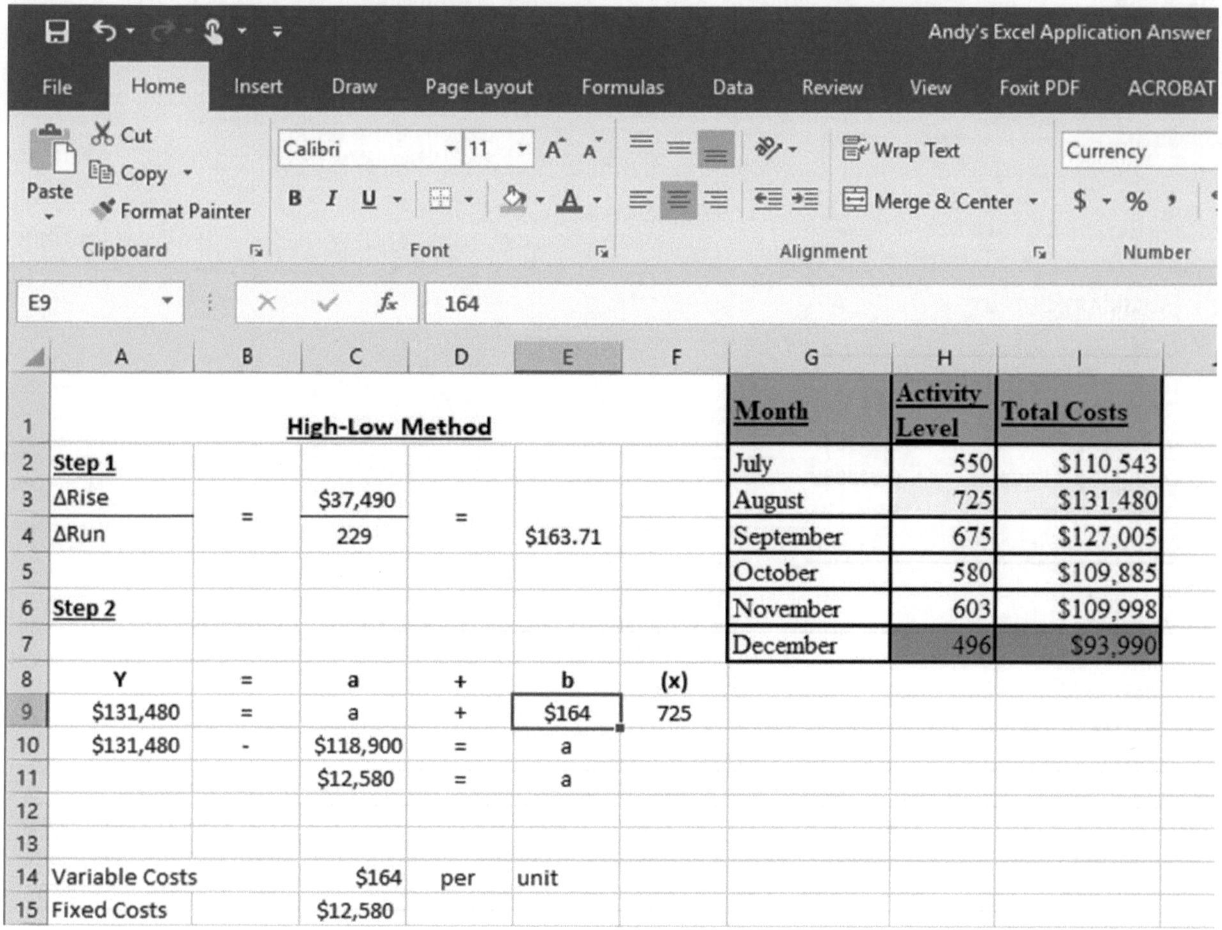

	A	B	C	D	E	F	G	H	I
1			High-Low Method				Month	Activity Level	Total Costs
2	Step 1						July	550	$110,543
3	ΔRise	=	$37,490	=			August	725	$131,480
4	ΔRun		229		$163.71		September	675	$127,005
5							October	580	$109,885
6	Step 2						November	603	$109,998
7							December	496	$93,990
8	Y	=	a	+	b	(x)			
9	$131,480	=	a	+	$164	725			
10	$131,480	-	$118,900	=	a				
11			$12,580	=	a				
12									
13									
14	Variable Costs		$164	per	unit				
15	Fixed Costs		$12,580						

FIGURE A.6 High-Low Method and Regression Analysis.

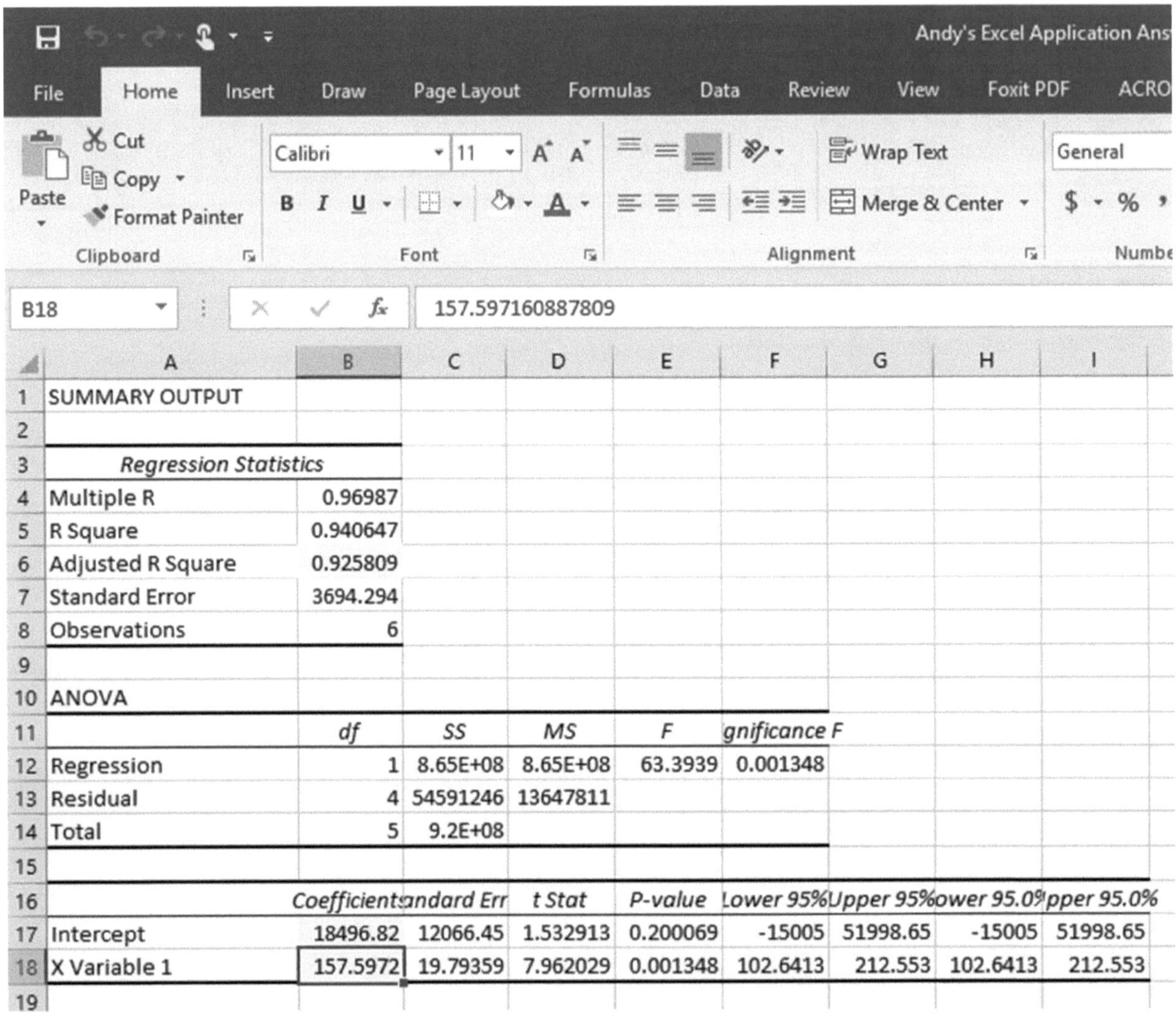

	A	B	C	D	E	F	G	H	I
1	SUMMARY OUTPUT								
2									
3	*Regression Statistics*								
4	Multiple R	0.96987							
5	R Square	0.940647							
6	Adjusted R Square	0.925809							
7	Standard Error	3694.294							
8	Observations	6							
9									
10	ANOVA								
11		*df*	*SS*	*MS*	*F*	*gnificance F*			
12	Regression	1	8.65E+08	8.65E+08	63.3939	0.001348			
13	Residual	4	54591246	13647811					
14	Total	5	9.2E+08						
15									
16		*Coefficients*	*andard Err*	*t Stat*	*P-value*	*Lower 95%*	*Upper 95%*	*ower 95.0%*	*pper 95.0%*
17	Intercept	18496.82	12066.45	1.532913	0.200069	-15005	51998.65	-15005	51998.65
18	X Variable 1	157.5972	19.79359	7.962029	0.001348	102.6413	212.553	102.6413	212.553
19									

FIGURE A.7 High-Low Method and Regression Analysis, continued.

CVP Analysis

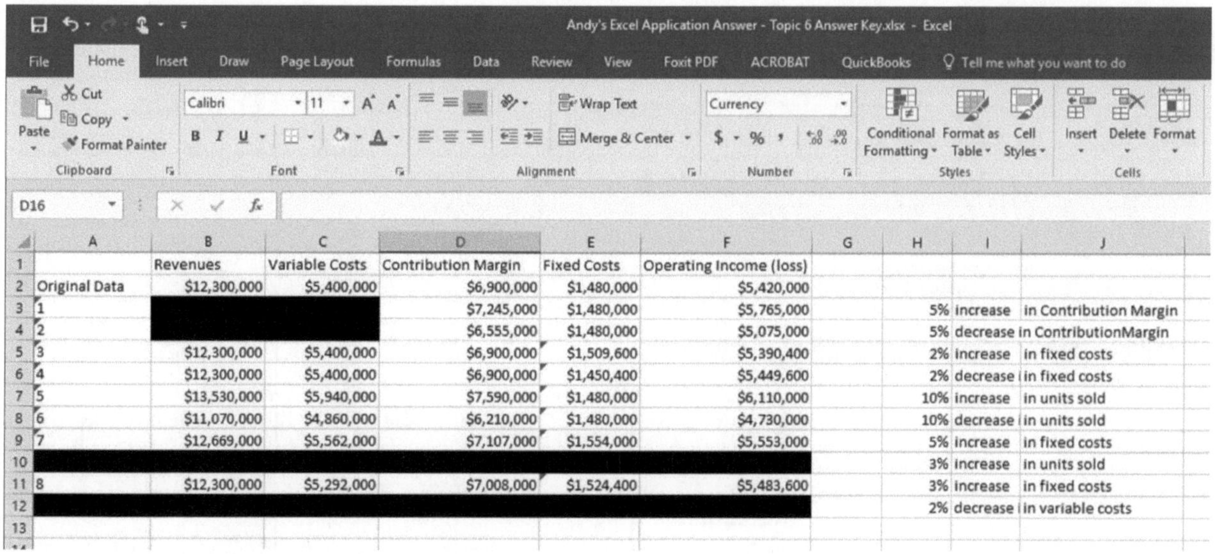

	A	B	C	D	E	F	G	H	I	J
1		Revenues	Variable Costs	Contribution Margin	Fixed Costs	Operating Income (loss)				
2	Original Data	$12,300,000	$5,400,000	$6,900,000	$1,480,000	$5,420,000				
3	1	[redacted]	[redacted]	$7,245,000	$1,480,000	$5,765,000		5%	increase	in Contribution Margin
4	2	[redacted]	[redacted]	$6,555,000	$1,480,000	$5,075,000		5%	decrease	in ContributionMargin
5	3	$12,300,000	$5,400,000	$6,900,000	$1,509,600	$5,390,400		2%	increase	in fixed costs
6	4	$12,300,000	$5,400,000	$6,900,000	$1,450,400	$5,449,600		2%	decrease	in fixed costs
7	5	$13,530,000	$5,940,000	$7,590,000	$1,480,000	$6,110,000		10%	increase	in units sold
8	6	$11,070,000	$4,860,000	$6,210,000	$1,480,000	$4,730,000		10%	decrease	in units sold
9	7	$12,669,000	$5,562,000	$7,107,000	$1,554,000	$5,553,000		5%	increase	in fixed costs
10	[redacted]							3%	increase	in units sold
11	8	$12,300,000	$5,292,000	$7,008,000	$1,524,400	$5,483,600		3%	increase	in fixed costs
12	[redacted]							2%	decrease	in variable costs
13										

FIGURE A.8 CVP Analysis.

Master Budgeting

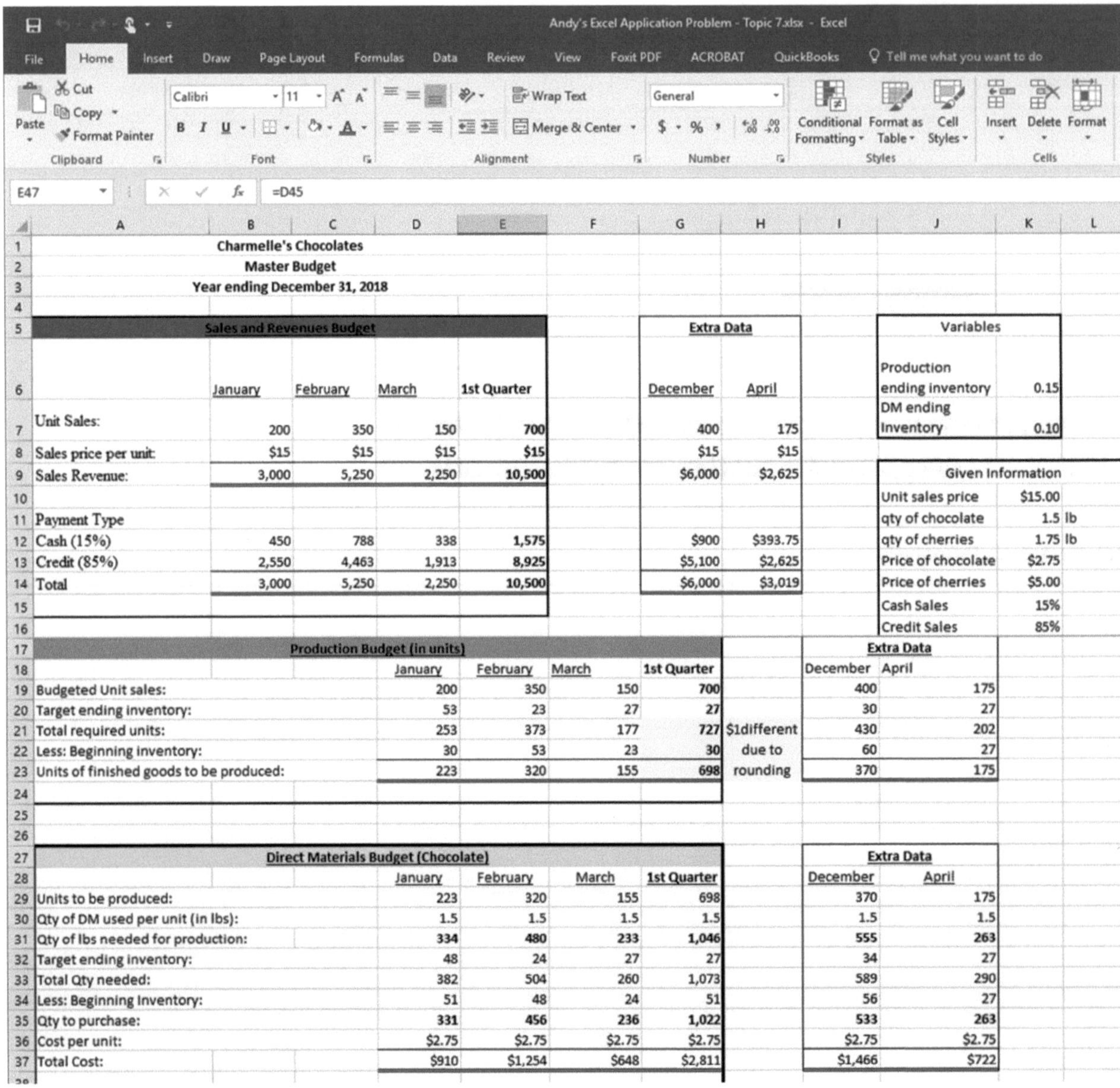

Charmelle's Chocolates
Master Budget
Year ending December 31, 2018

Sales and Revenues Budget	January	February	March	1st Quarter
Unit Sales:	200	350	150	700
Sales price per unit:	$15	$15	$15	$15
Sales Revenue:	3,000	5,250	2,250	10,500
Payment Type				
Cash (15%)	450	788	338	1,575
Credit (85%)	2,550	4,463	1,913	8,925
Total	3,000	5,250	2,250	10,500

Extra Data	December	April
Unit Sales	400	175
Sales price per unit	$15	$15
Sales Revenue	$6,000	$2,625
Cash (15%)	$900	$393.75
Credit (85%)	$5,100	$2,625
Total	$6,000	$3,019

Variables	
Production ending inventory	0.15
DM ending Inventory	0.10

Given Information		
Unit sales price	$15.00	
qty of chocolate	1.5	lb
qty of cherries	1.75	lb
Price of chocolate	$2.75	
Price of cherries	$5.00	
Cash Sales	15%	
Credit Sales	85%	

Production Budget (in units)	January	February	March	1st Quarter	
Budgeted Unit sales:	200	350	150	700	
Target ending inventory:	53	23	27	27	
Total required units:	253	373	177	727	$1different
Less: Beginning inventory:	30	53	23	30	due to
Units of finished goods to be produced:	223	320	155	698	rounding

Extra Data	December	April
Budgeted Unit sales	400	175
Target ending inventory	30	27
Total required units	430	202
Less: Beginning inventory	60	27
Units of finished goods to be produced	370	175

Direct Materials Budget (Chocolate)	January	February	March	1st Quarter
Units to be produced:	223	320	155	698
Qty of DM used per unit (in lbs):	1.5	1.5	1.5	1.5
Qty of lbs needed for production:	334	480	233	1,046
Target ending inventory:	48	24	27	27
Total Qty needed:	382	504	260	1,073
Less: Beginning Inventory:	51	48	24	51
Qty to purchase:	331	456	236	1,022
Cost per unit:	$2.75	$2.75	$2.75	$2.75
Total Cost:	$910	$1,254	$648	$2,811

Extra Data	December	April
Units to be produced	370	175
Qty of DM used per unit	1.5	1.5
Qty of lbs needed for production	555	263
Target ending inventory	34	27
Total Qty needed	589	290
Less: Beginning Inventory	56	27
Qty to purchase	533	263
Cost per unit	$2.75	$2.75
Total Cost	$1,466	$722

FIGURE A.9 Master Budgeting.

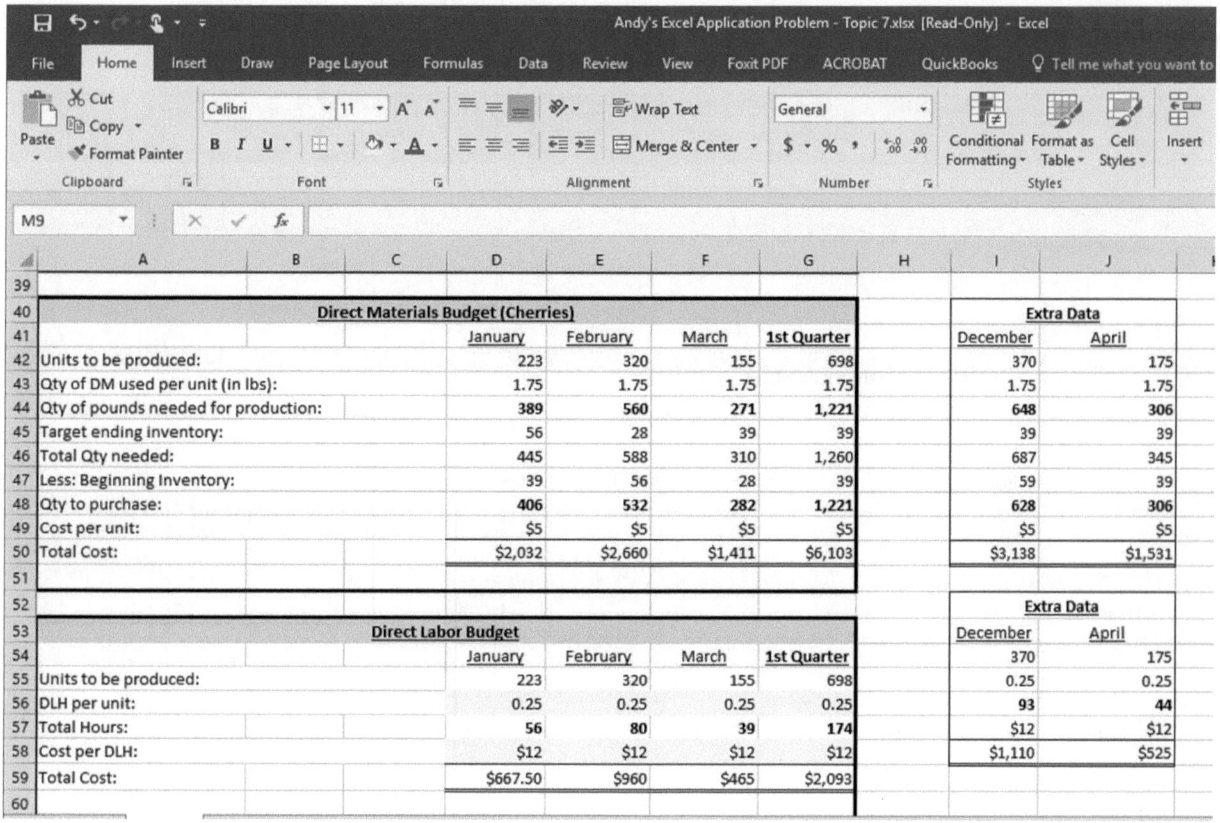

Direct Materials Budget (Cherries)	January	February	March	1st Quarter
Units to be produced:	223	320	155	698
Qty of DM used per unit (in lbs):	1.75	1.75	1.75	1.75
Qty of pounds needed for production:	**389**	**560**	**271**	**1,221**
Target ending inventory:	56	28	39	39
Total Qty needed:	445	588	310	1,260
Less: Beginning Inventory:	39	56	28	39
Qty to purchase:	**406**	**532**	**282**	**1,221**
Cost per unit:	$5	$5	$5	$5
Total Cost:	$2,032	$2,660	$1,411	$6,103

Extra Data	December	April
	370	175
	1.75	1.75
	648	**306**
	39	39
	687	345
	59	39
	628	**306**
	$5	$5
	$3,138	$1,531

Direct Labor Budget	January	February	March	1st Quarter
Units to be produced:	223	320	155	698
DLH per unit:	0.25	0.25	0.25	0.25
Total Hours:	**56**	**80**	**39**	**174**
Cost per DLH:	$12	$12	$12	$12
Total Cost:	$667.50	$960	$465	$2,093

Extra Data	December	April
	370	175
	0.25	0.25
	93	**44**
	$12	$12
	$1,110	$525

FIGURE A.10 Master Budgeting, continued.

Standard Costs

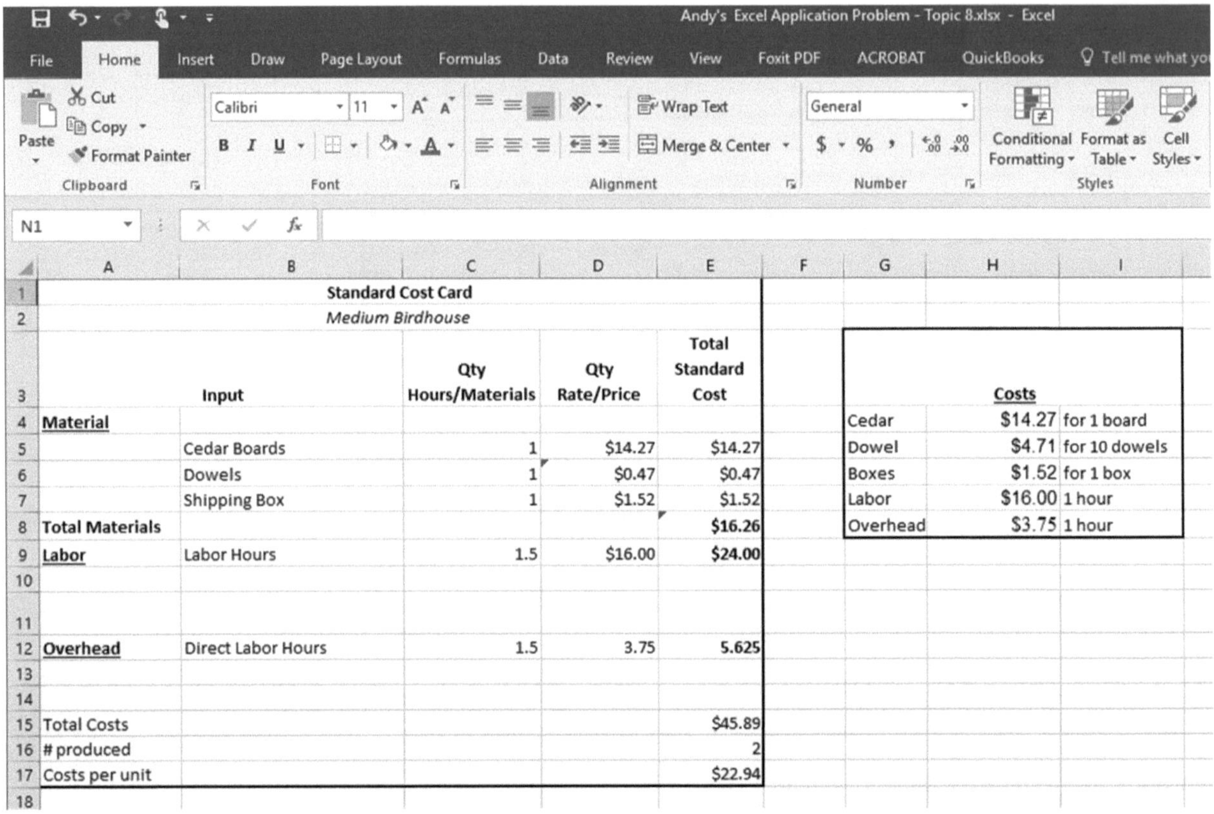

Standard Cost Card				
Medium Birdhouse				
	Input	**Qty Hours/Materials**	**Qty Rate/Price**	**Total Standard Cost**
Material				
	Cedar Boards	1	$14.27	$14.27
	Dowels	1	$0.47	$0.47
	Shipping Box	1	$1.52	$1.52
Total Materials				**$16.26**
Labor	Labor Hours	1.5	$16.00	**$24.00**
Overhead	Direct Labor Hours	1.5	3.75	**5.625**
Total Costs				$45.89
# produced				2
Costs per unit				$22.94

	Costs	
Cedar	$14.27	for 1 board
Dowel	$4.71	for 10 dowels
Boxes	$1.52	for 1 box
Labor	$16.00	1 hour
Overhead	$3.75	1 hour

FIGURE A.11 Standard Costs.

Capital Budgeting

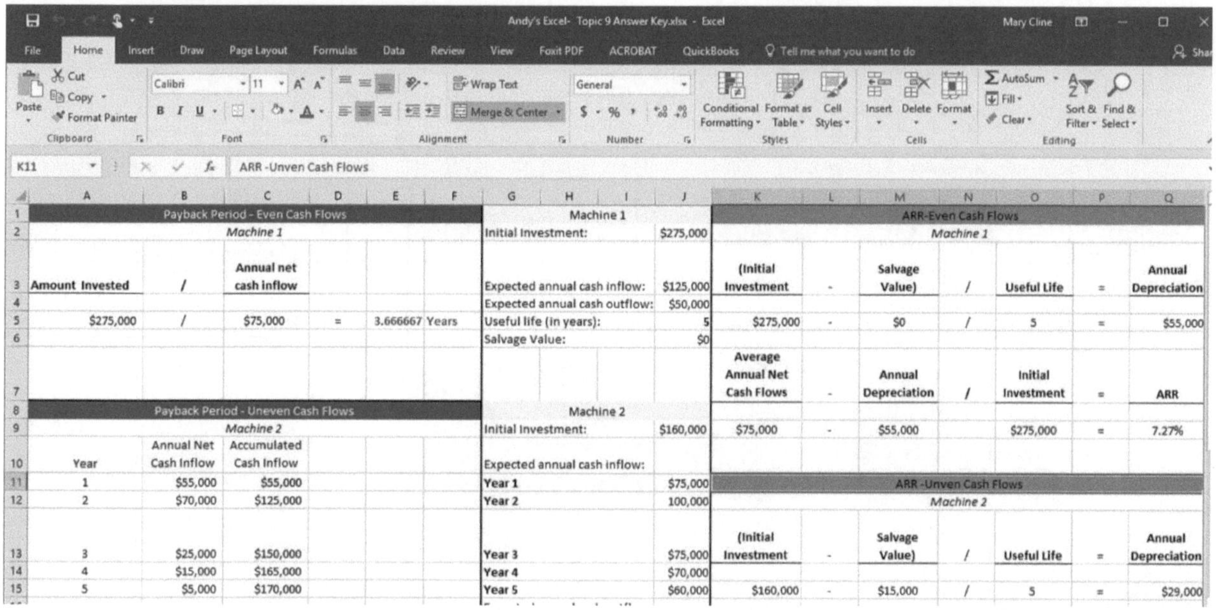

FIGURE A.12A Capital Budgeting.

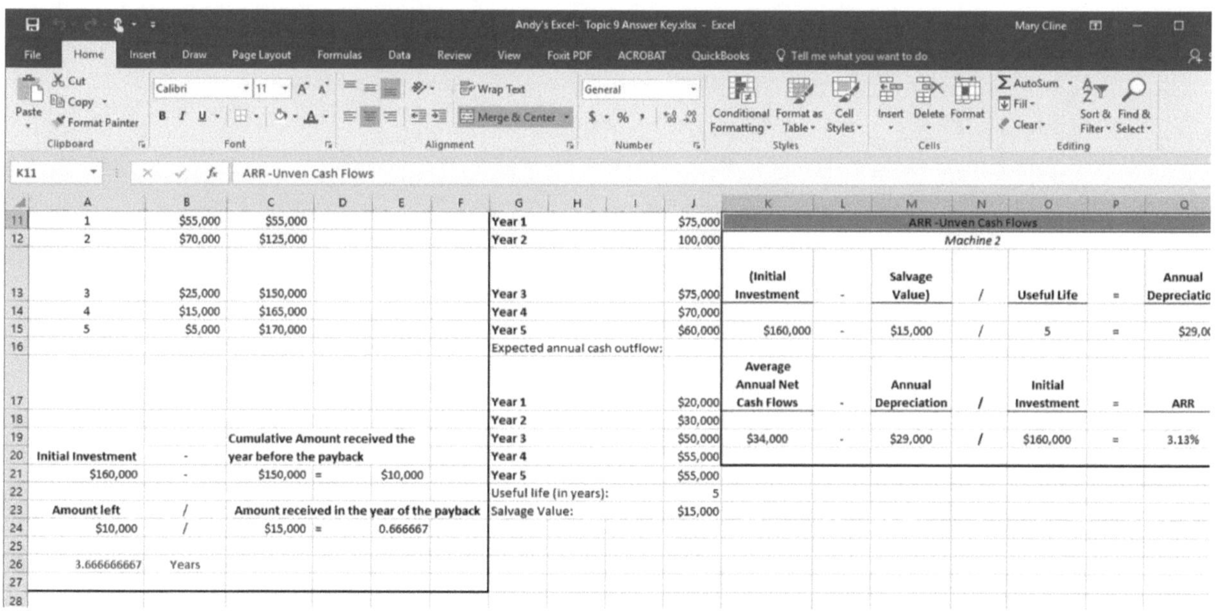

FIGURE A.12B Capital Budgeting.

Job Costing

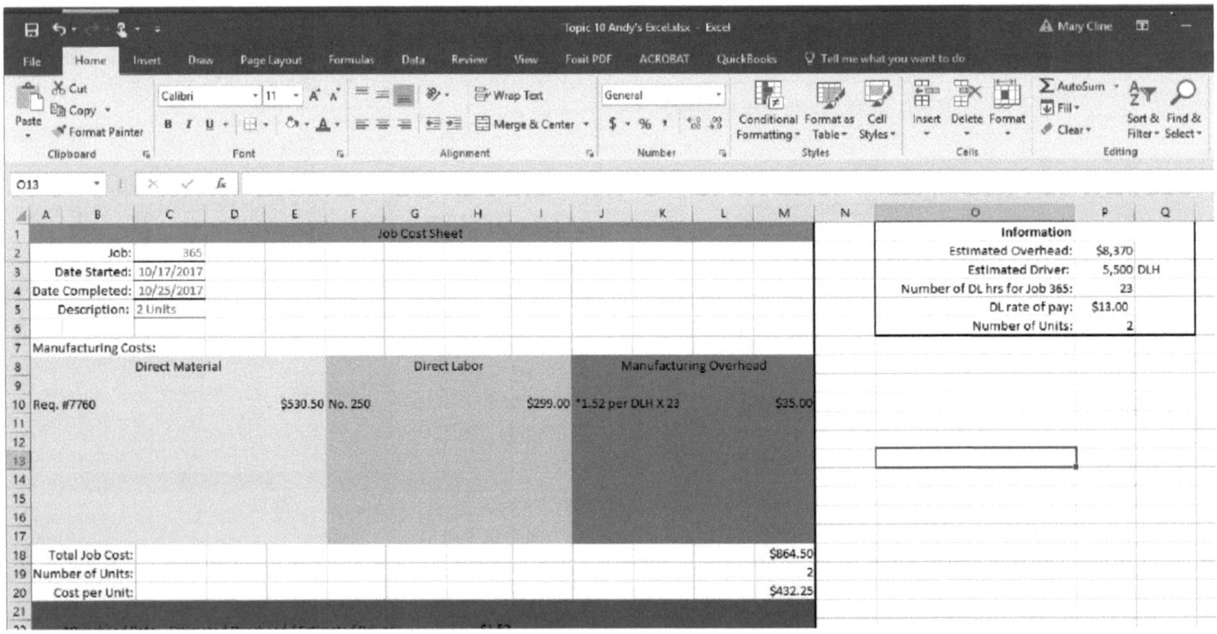

FIGURE A.13 Job Costing.

Process Costing

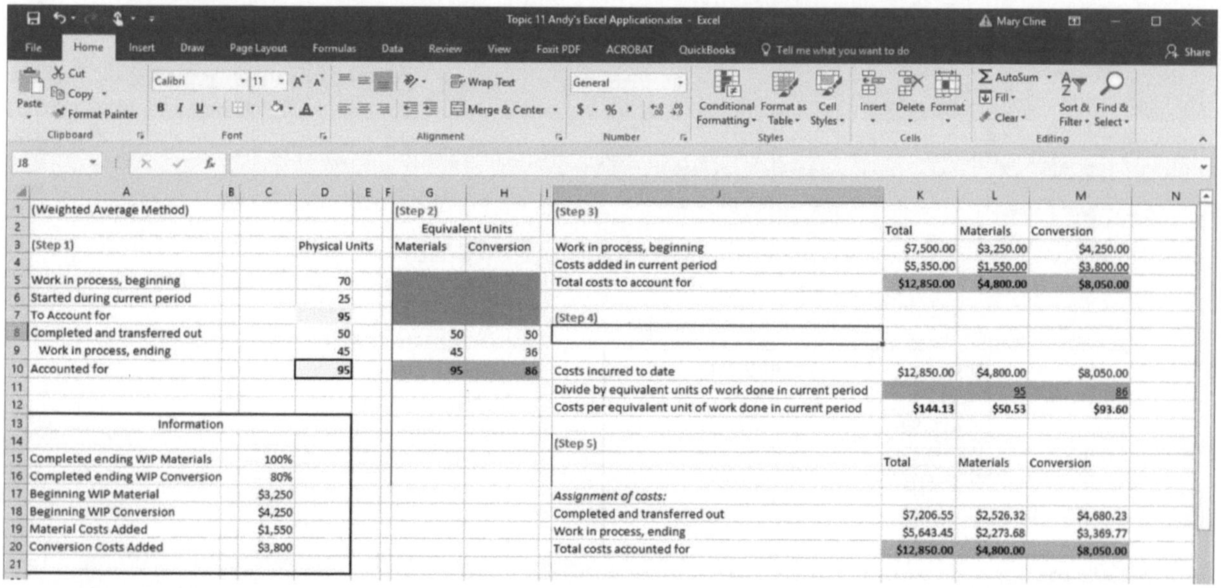

	A	C	D	G	H	J	K	L	M
1	(Weighted Average Method)			(Step 2)		(Step 3)			
2				Equivalent Units			Total	Materials	Conversion
3	(Step 1)		Physical Units	Materials	Conversion	Work in process, beginning	$7,500.00	$3,250.00	$4,250.00
4						Costs added in current period	$5,350.00	$1,550.00	$3,800.00
5	Work in process, beginning		70			Total costs to account for	$12,850.00	$4,800.00	$8,050.00
6	Started during current period		25						
7	To Account for		95			(Step 4)			
8	Completed and transferred out		50	50	50				
9	Work in process, ending		45	45	36				
10	Accounted for		95	95	86	Costs incurred to date	$12,850.00	$4,800.00	$8,050.00
11						Divide by equivalent units of work done in current period		95	86
12						Costs per equivalent unit of work done in current period	$144.13	$50.53	$93.60
13	Information								
14						(Step 5)			
15	Completed ending WIP Materials	100%					Total	Materials	Conversion
16	Completed ending WIP Conversion	80%							
17	Beginning WIP Material	$3,250				*Assignment of costs:*			
18	Beginning WIP Conversion	$4,250				Completed and transferred out	$7,206.55	$2,526.32	$4,680.23
19	Material Costs Added	$1,550				Work in process, ending	$5,643.45	$2,273.68	$3,369.77
20	Conversion Costs Added	$3,800				Total costs accounted for	$12,850.00	$4,800.00	$8,050.00

FIGURE A.14 Process Costing.

Activity-Based Costing

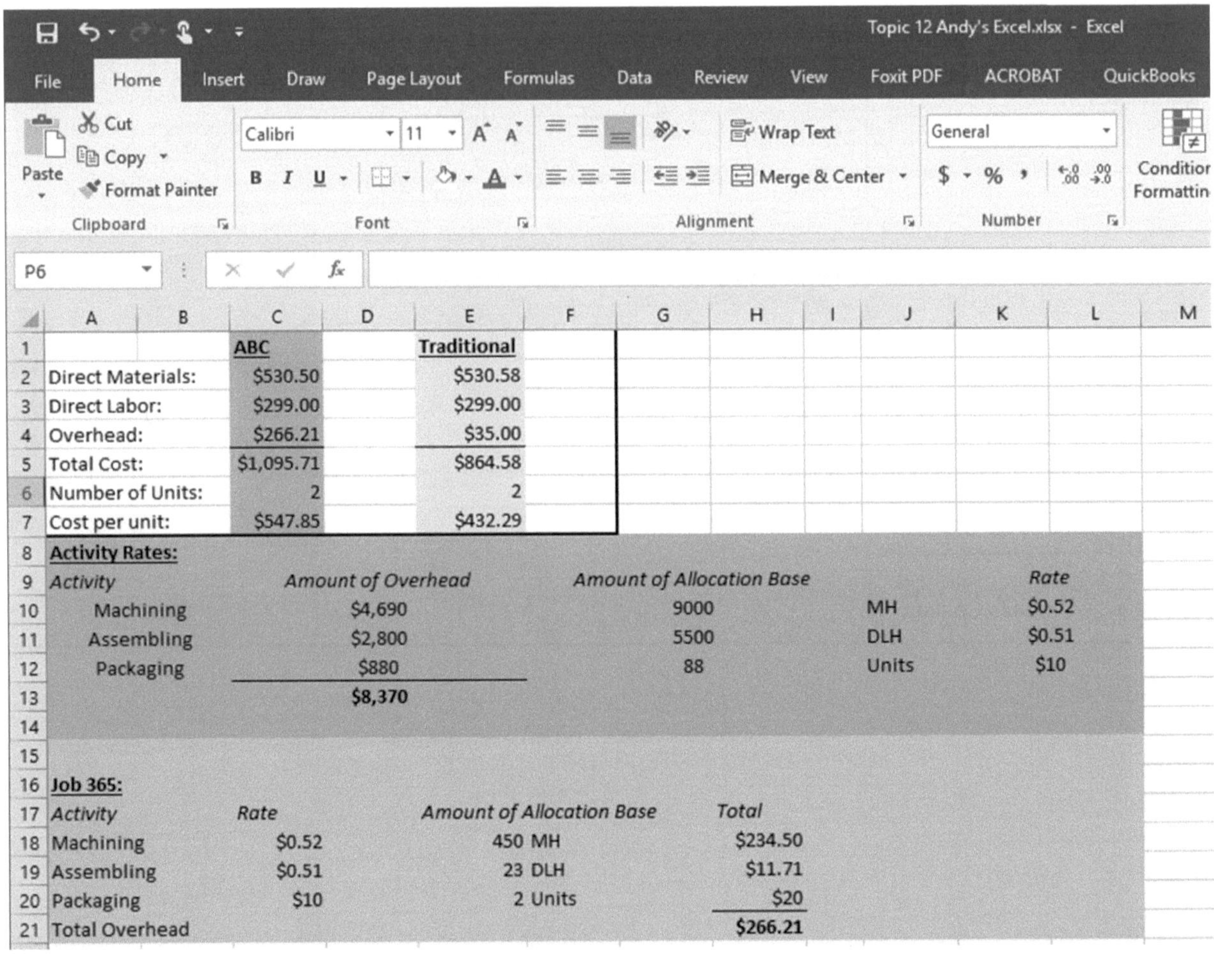

	ABC	Traditional
Direct Materials:	$530.50	$530.58
Direct Labor:	$299.00	$299.00
Overhead:	$266.21	$35.00
Total Cost:	$1,095.71	$864.58
Number of Units:	2	2
Cost per unit:	$547.85	$432.29

Activity Rates:

Activity	*Amount of Overhead*	*Amount of Allocation Base*		*Rate*
Machining	$4,690	9000	MH	$0.52
Assembling	$2,800	5500	DLH	$0.51
Packaging	$880	88	Units	$10
	$8,370			

Job 365:

Activity	*Rate*	*Amount of Allocation Base*	*Total*
Machining	$0.52	450 MH	$234.50
Assembling	$0.51	23 DLH	$11.71
Packaging	$10	2 Units	$20
Total Overhead			**$266.21**

FIGURE A.15 Activity-Based Costing.

Absorption vs. Variable Costing

Row	A–C	D	E
1	**Per Unit Data**		
2	Selling Price:	$75	
3	DM:	$32	
4	DL:	$12	
5	VOH:	$2	
6	Variable Operating Expense:	$3	
7	**Annual Data**		
8	Fixed MOH:	$142,000	
9	Fixed Operating Costs:	$79,000	
10			
11		Yr 1	Yr 2
12	Units Sold:	15,000	25,000
13	Units Produced:	20,000	20,000
14	Fixed MOH Reflected per Unit:	$7.10	$7.10

Row	F–G	H
1	**Yr 1 Traditional Format Income Statement**	
2	Sales Revenue:	$1,125,000
3	Less: COGS:	$796,500
4	**Gross Profit:**	$328,500
5	Less: Operating Expenses	
6	Fixed:	$79,000
7	Variable:	$45,000
8	Operating Income:	$204,500
12	**Yr 2 Traditional Format Income Statement**	
13	Sales Revenue:	$1,875,000
14	Less: COGS:	$1,327,500
15	**Gross Profit:**	$547,500
16	Less: Operating Expenses	
17	Fixed:	$79,000
18	Variable:	$75,000
19	Operating Income:	$393,500

Row	K–L	M
1	**Yr 1 Contribution Format Income Statement**	
2	Sales Revenue:	$1,125,000
3	*Less Variable Expenses*	
4	Variable COGS:	$690,000
5	Variable Operating Expenses:	$45,000
6	**Contribution Margin**	$390,000
7	*Less Fixed Expense*	
8	Fixed MOH:	$142,000
9	Fixed Operating Expenses:	$79,000
10	**Operating Income:**	$169,000
12	**Yr 2 Contribution Format Income Statement**	
13	Sales Revenue:	$1,875,000
14	*Less Variable Expenses*	
15	Variable COGS:	$1,150,000
16	Variable Operating Expenses:	$75,000
17	**Contribution Margin**	$650,000
18	*Less Fixed Expense*	
19	Fixed MOH:	$142,000
20	Fixed Operating Expenses:	$79,000
21	**Operating Income:**	$429,000

Row	P	Q
1	**Yr 1 Difference**	
3	Traditional Operating Income	$204,500
4	Contribution Margin Operating Income	$169,000
5		$35,500
6	Divided by number of units in ending Inventory	5,000
7		$7.10
12	**Yr 2 Difference**	
14	Traditional Operating Income	$393,500
15	Contribution Margin Operating Income	$429,000
16		($35,500)
17	Divided by number of units used from Inventory	5,000
18		($7.10)

FIGURE A.16 Absorption vs. Variable Costing.

Pricing Decisions

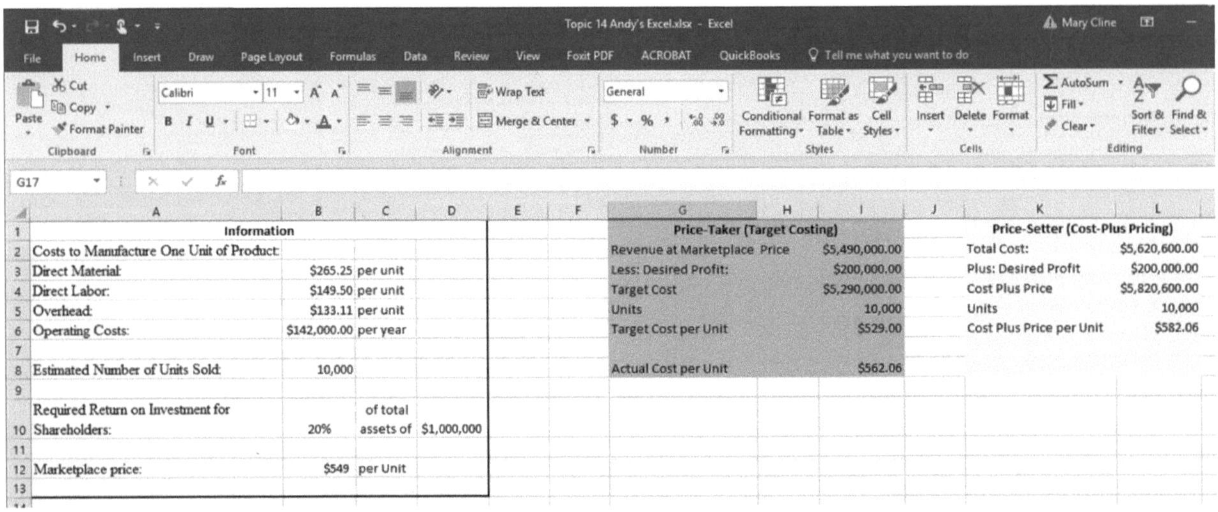

	A	B	C	D	G	I	K	L
1	Information				Price-Taker (Target Costing)		Price-Setter (Cost-Plus Pricing)	
2	Costs to Manufacture One Unit of Product:				Revenue at Marketplace Price	$5,490,000.00	Total Cost:	$5,620,600.00
3	Direct Material:	$265.25	per unit		Less: Desired Profit:	$200,000.00	Plus: Desired Profit	$200,000.00
4	Direct Labor:	$149.50	per unit		Target Cost	$5,290,000.00	Cost Plus Price	$5,820,600.00
5	Overhead:	$133.11	per unit		Units	10,000	Units	10,000
6	Operating Costs:	$142,000.00	per year		Target Cost per Unit	$529.00	Cost Plus Price per Unit	$582.06
7								
8	Estimated Number of Units Sold:	10,000			Actual Cost per Unit	$562.06		
9								
10	Required Return on Investment for Shareholders:	20%	of total assets of	$1,000,000				
11								
12	Marketplace price:	$549	per Unit					
13								

FIGURE A.17 Pricing Decisions.

Flexible Budgeting

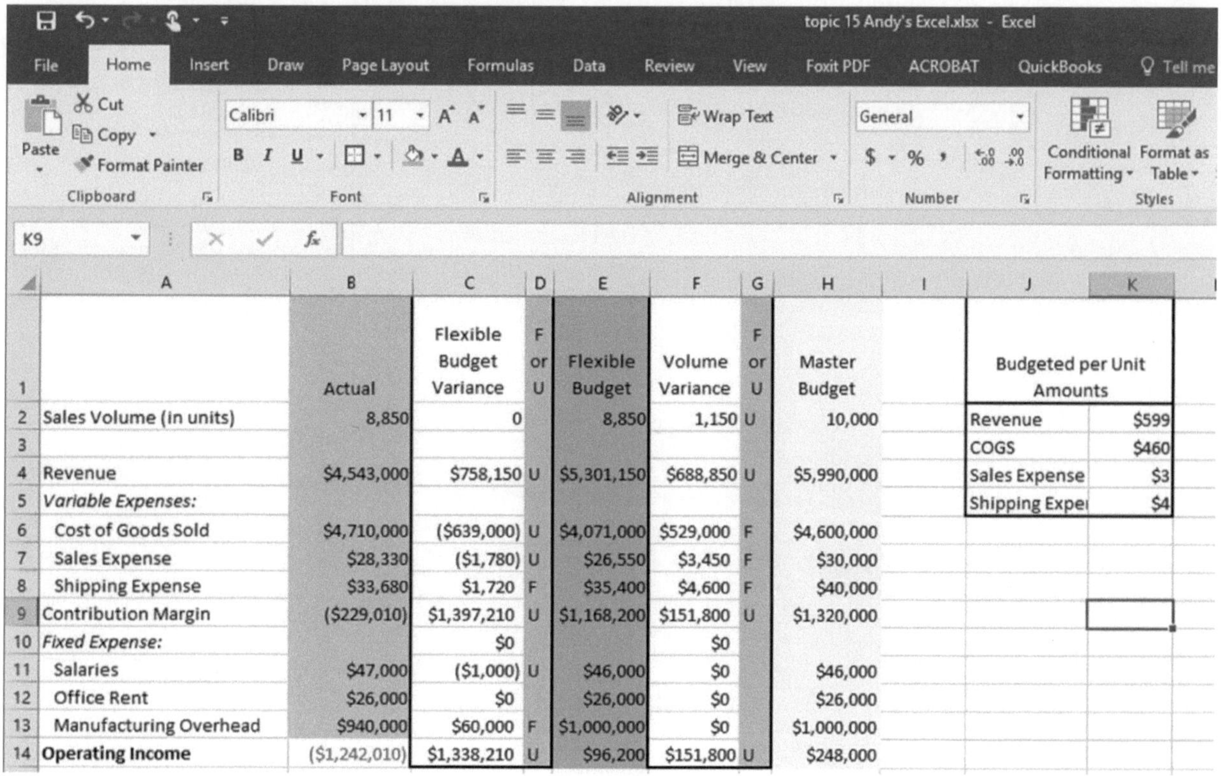

	A	B	C	D	E	F	G	H	I	J	K
1		Actual	Flexible Budget Variance	F or U	Flexible Budget	Volume Variance	F or U	Master Budget		Budgeted per Unit Amounts	
2	Sales Volume (in units)	8,850	0		8,850	1,150	U	10,000		Revenue	$599
3										COGS	$460
4	Revenue	$4,543,000	$758,150	U	$5,301,150	$688,850	U	$5,990,000		Sales Expense	$3
5	*Variable Expenses:*									Shipping Expe	$4
6	Cost of Goods Sold	$4,710,000	($639,000)	U	$4,071,000	$529,000	F	$4,600,000			
7	Sales Expense	$28,330	($1,780)	U	$26,550	$3,450	F	$30,000			
8	Shipping Expense	$33,680	$1,720	F	$35,400	$4,600	F	$40,000			
9	Contribution Margin	($229,010)	$1,397,210	U	$1,168,200	$151,800	U	$1,320,000			
10	*Fixed Expense:*		$0			$0					
11	Salaries	$47,000	($1,000)	U	$46,000	$0		$46,000			
12	Office Rent	$26,000	$0		$26,000	$0		$26,000			
13	Manufacturing Overhead	$940,000	$60,000	F	$1,000,000	$0		$1,000,000			
14	**Operating Income**	($1,242,010)	$1,338,210	U	$96,200	$151,800	U	$248,000			

FIGURE A.18 Flexible Budgeting.

Printed by Libri Plureos GmbH in Hamburg,
Germany